Clear and Effective
Legal Writing

ASPEN PUBLISHERS

Clear and

Effective

Legal Writing

FOURTH EDITION

Veda R. Charrow, Ph.D.

Myra K. Erhardt, Esq.

Robert P. Charrow, Esq.

Wolters Kluwer
Law & Business

AUSTIN   BOSTON   CHICAGO   NEW YORK   THE NETHERLANDS

© 2007 by Veda R. Charrow, Myra K. Erhardt, and Robert P. Charrow
Published by Aspen Publishers. All Rights Reserved.

No part of this publication may be reproduced or transmitted in any form or by any means, electronic or mechanical, including photocopy, recording, or any information storage and retrieval system, without permission in writing from the publisher. Requests for permission to make copies of any part of this publication should be mailed to:

Aspen Publishers
Attn: Permissions Department
76 Ninth Avenue, 7th Floor
New York, NY   10011-5201

To contact Customer Care, e-mail customer.care@aspenpublishers.com, call 1-800-234-1660, fax 1-800-901-9075, or mail correspondence to:

Aspen Publishers
Attn: Order Department
PO Box 990
Frederick, MD 21705

Printed in the United States of America.

1 2 3 4 5 6 7 8 9 0

ISBN 978-0-7355-5229-6

Library of Congress Cataloging-in-Publication Data

Charrow, Veda.
    Clear and effective legal writing / Veda R. Charrow, Myra K. Erhardt, Robert P. Charrow. — 4th ed.
        p. cm.
    Includes index.
    ISBN-13: 978-0-7355-5229-6
    1. Legal composition. I. Erhardt, Myra K. II. Charrow. Robert. III. Title.
KF250.C45 2007
808'.06634 — dc22
                                                                        2007015615

About Wolters Kluwer Law & Business

Wolters Kluwer Law & Business is a leading provider of research information and workflow solutions in key specialty areas. The strengths of the individual brands of Aspen Publishers, CCH, Kluwer Law International and Loislaw are aligned within Wolters Kluwer Law & Business to provide comprehensive, in-depth solutions and expert-authored content for the legal, professional and education markets.

CCH was founded in 1913 and has served more than four generations of business professionals and their clients. The CCH products in the Wolters Kluwer Law & Business group are highly regarded electronic and print resources for legal, securities, antitrust and trade regulation, government contracting, banking, pension, payroll, employment and labor, and healthcare reimbursement and compliance professionals.

Aspen Publishers is a leading information provider for attorneys, business professionals and law students. Written by preeminent authorities, Aspen products offer analytical and practical information in a range of specialty practice areas from securities law and intellectual property to mergers and acquisitions and pension/benefits. Aspen's trusted legal education resources provide professors and students with high-quality, up-to-date and effective resources for successful instruction and study in all areas of the law.

Kluwer Law International supplies the global business community with comprehensive English-language international legal information. Legal practitioners, corporate counsel and business executives around the world rely on the Kluwer Law International journals, loose-leafs, books and electronic products for authoritative information in many areas of international legal practice.

Loislaw is a premier provider of digitized legal content to small law firm practitioners of various specializations. Loislaw provides attorneys with the ability to quickly and efficiently find the necessary legal information they need, when and where they need it, by facilitating access to primary law as well as state-specific law, records, forms and treatises.

Wolters Kluwer Law & Business, a unit of Wolters Kluwer, is headquartered in New York and Riverwoods, Illinois. Wolters Kluwer is a leading multinational publisher and information services company.

To our children, Elizabeth and Alexandra Charrow, and Michael and Alexander Erhardt.

Summary of Contents

Contents

Preface

The first edition of this book, published in 1986, sought to provide students with a conceptually sound model for writing and analyzing legal documents. It was the first legal writing text to have been developed as a result of empirical studies of the way in which lawyers communicate and write. It was designed to take into account the most common difficulties that law students encounter and the special constraints that the law and legal situations impose on writing.

In the second edition, we reorganized the book to better incorporate the writing process into the legal process. We added material on sources of the law and our system of courts and the litigation process. We also added materials on analyzing and synthesizing the law from a set of cases. We provided examples of how the law can change over time to reflect changes in social values. In the third edition, we updated the material to take into account changes in the law. We also greatly expanded the chapter on writing appellate briefs by providing examples of various types of briefs, e.g., petition for certiorari, *amicus curiae*. The second and third editions, like the first, contained numerous examples of good and poor writing and provided many exercises to hone students' analytic and writing skills.

In this new edition, we have updated the just about everything, added new problems to exercises, and provided new examples of appellate briefs. In addition, we have added a new appendix to explain how to get the most out of word processing and electronic publishing capabilities that did not exist at the time our first edition came out.

Veda Charrow
Myra Erhardt
Robert Charrow

May 2007
Chevy Chase, Maryland

Acknowledgments

We would like to thank and acknowledge the following people who contributed to this edition of *Clear & Effective Legal Writing*:

Mary Lodge for creating the graphic designs of the charts and exhibits in the first edition, which we have continued to use.

Jeffrey W. Leppo for his motion in *Louisiana-Pacific Corp. v. ASARCO, Inc.* Hon. William K. Suter (MG, USA, Ret.), Clerk of the Supreme Court of the United States.

Thanks also to John Devins and Kaesmene Harrison Banks of Aspen Publishers, for shepherding the fourth edition and making sure we met our editorial deadlines.

INTRODUCTION

A   The Importance of Legal Writing

As you have undoubtedly been told, one of the primary goals of legal education is to help you learn how to "think like a lawyer." Thinking like a lawyer, however, is only one aspect of the practice of law. To be successful in the legal profession, you must not only approach and analyze a problem in a lawyer-like way, you must also communicate those analyses in an effective manner.

Many believe that in law, effective communication is synonymous with effective oral advocacy. Thus, many students are likely to believe that legal communication is primarily oral. The primacy of oral communication may be further emphasized during your first few months in law school, where your professors will expect you to present and defend your analyses of a given case, orally, before the entire class. Modern lawyering, however, relies heavily on written communication. In private practice, a disproportionate amount of your time will be spent writing. Brilliant legal insights, even when coupled with superb oratorical skills, are rarely enough, for a variety of reasons.

First, relatively few cases ever go to trial. The vast majority are either settled before trial or are resolved short of trial through written motions. Second, even when a case goes to trial, the bulk of an attorney's time is spent on drafting trial documents—motions, interrogatories, trial briefs, jury instructions, and post-trial papers. These documents are every bit as important as cross-examination. Third, many attorneys do not litigate cases. Instead, they draft opinion letters, wills, trusts, contracts, regulations, and numerous other types of documents. In short, lawyering places a premium on fast and effective writing. In fact, the way in which you will be evaluated, especially during your first year in law school, aptly reflects the importance of writing. Your grades will depend largely on your ability not only to thoroughly analyze an examination question, but also to write up your analyses in a cogent manner. Your classroom work, even if consistently excellent, will normally have little impact on your final grade.

B   Some Comments on the Way This Book Is Organized and Written

The primary purpose of this book is to help you learn good legal writing skills. The rules of good expository writing and good legal writing are identical. Both require clarity, logical organization, precision, and conciseness. However, as in any other technical or professional area, you cannot apply these rules unless you understand your subject matter. To understand the subject matter of the law, you will have to learn how to read and analyze legal cases and materials. Part I of this book, Learning to Read Legal Materials, is designed to help you begin to do this. This part is divided into six chapters. In Chapter 1, we present a short history of legal language. This is important because, when you first begin reading legal materials, you may feel as though you are reading another language. This chapter attempts to explain what legal language is and how it got to be that way. Once you know this, you will be more able to judge the quality of what you read. Chapter 2 provides a brief description of categories of legal documents. Chapters 3 through 6 constitute an overview of the legal process, which will help you understand the content and significance of what you read. Since all legal documents are created within the framework of the legal system, you need to understand the legal system in order to fully understand those documents. To understand the judicial opinions that you read, you need to know how the court system works and how cases work their way through that system. Chapter 3, Sources of Law and Our System of Courts, provides background information about our legal system, including the various sources of law and the relationship between the federal and state court systems. Chapter 4, The Litigation Process, focuses on the discrete stages in litigation from drafting a complaint through the actual trial. Chapter 5, Reading, Analyzing, and Briefing a Case, is designed to help you learn how to dissect and summarize a judicial opinion. Chapter 6, Synthesizing the Law from a Series of Cases, presents a set of judicial opinions dealing with the same legal principle. This chapter provides you with an opportunity to observe how that principle has evolved over time. In the final part of the chapter, we present a sample memorandum of law that ties these cases together.

Once you have begun to understand the style and content of legal materials, you will be ready to learn the process of legal writing. In Part II, Learning to Write Legal Documents, we teach you how to write clearly and effectively in a legal context. We demonstrate that good writing is not subjective or the result of luck; it is the result of following rules of planning, organization, and sentence structure. In short, good writing is a process, involving thinking, drafting, and reviewing. Chapter 7, A Systematic Approach to Legal Writing, provides the framework for what is to follow; in it, we present a writing plan for creating any document. Chapters 8 through 10 discuss how to implement the writing plan. Chapter 8, Understanding Your Context, discusses the importance of understanding and taking into account your audience, purpose, and constraints as the initial step in any writing process. In Chapter 9, Getting Organized, we explain how to organize your document before you write it, and Chapter 10, Writing Clearly, presents guidelines for clear writing. Chapter 11, Writing Effectively, explains how to construct a logical argument and presents techniques for writing persuasively and effectively. Chapter 12 provides guidelines for reviewing and editing.

Part III ties together the first two parts by taking you through the process of writing an intraoffice memorandum, a memorandum of points and authorities, and an appellate court brief.

Appendix A contains a guide to English sentence structure. Appendix B explains the importance of proper formatting for legal documents and illustrates the various components of good format.

Throughout this book, we have chosen to use a writing style that is intentionally direct and conversational because we believe that this style is best for communicating our ideas and techniques. This does not mean that the ideas and techniques themselves are simple. You will find that many of the exercises are challenging, and you may find yourself rereading portions of the book in order to complete them.

Clear and Effective
Legal Writing

PART I
Learning to Read Legal Materials

1

A Short History of
Legal Language

A Characteristics of Traditional Legal Writing

Traditional legal writing has many unique characteristics. Some of them have value and reflect the complexity of legal concepts and the nuances of the legal process. Other characteristics, however, are not necessary and survive only through habit. These include overly long, complicated sentences, intrusive phrases and clauses, redundant phrases, poorly organized sentences and paragraphs, and a host of similar problems that we will discuss in Chapter 10. Legal language also contains unusual and archaic words, phrases, and sentence structures that became part of legal language as the law evolved over the centuries. Often these constructions are so rigid and overused that neither lawyers nor lay people understand them.

1. Poor Writing

Some legal writing is simply poor writing. Examples of poor writing can be found in all types of legal writing, even in the opinions of judges. For instance, read the following passage from a court opinion that is often excerpted in contracts casebooks:

> If, on the other hand, the evidence shall disclose that springs such as defendant contracted for were not purchasable in the open market, or were of designs specially adapted for defendant's vehicles and obtainable only by special order to some manufacturer, so that they were not obtainable by such diligence as above defined, and that, by plaintiff's failure to deliver at the time agreed, defendant was prevented from producing from its factory the number of vehicles which, but for the plaintiff's delay in delivering, that factory would, with reasonable certainty, have produced, and that defendant, with reasonable certainty, would have been able to sell all of such output during the then current season, in such case it is clear the defendant would have lost the difference between the cost of manufacture and the net selling price of the vehicles it was so prevented from manufacturing and selling.

Kelley, Maus & Co. v. LaCrosse Carriage Co., 120 Wis. 84, 91, 97 N.W. 674, 676 (1903).

There is nothing legally complex in this passage—it is just poorly written. When you come across passages such as this in your casebooks, you will probably find yourself mentally "translating" them by untangling the parts of the passage, sorting out all of the information in a sentence, and rearranging the parts into a simpler and more familiar order. You may have some trouble doing this on occasion, because it will be hard to tell which clauses relate to which and how all of the information fits together.

2. Archaic Constructions

Archaic and obsolete constructions also appear in all types of legal documents. For example, you may come across the kind of language that appears in this short excerpt from a form release:

> Greetings:
> Know ye that I, John Smith of Columbus Ohio, for and in consideration of $3,000 dollars, to me in hand paid by Jane Jones, do by these presents for myself, my heirs and assigns, remise, release, and forever discharge Jane Jones . . .

These constructions may give you pause, until you become accustomed to them. You should not, however, become so accustomed to seeing them that *you* use them, unless they are absolutely necessary.

B Why Legal Writing Is the Way It Is

Legal writing does not have to have the characteristics shown in the examples above in order to have legal effect. It retains those characteristics because certain aspects of legal language have evolved separately from the rest of the English language and because, through the centuries, lawyers have continued to use archaic and poorly written documents as models.

Legal language, like the rest of the English language, has various functions—to explain, elicit information, and persuade, among other things. There are various ways of using different features of language—ways of organizing text, various sentence structures, and vocabulary—that fulfill those functions. Thus, there are a number of typical ways of organizing legal documents to make them more or less persuasive. A variety of sentence structures can be used to make legal documents more or less explanatory. Vocabulary can be used to impress or simply to communicate. But, to many people, the term "legal language" conjures up only jargon, terms of art, and "boilerplate"—the words, phrases, or larger structures whose meanings have been "stabilized" through legal interpretation and that appear to embody the power of the law. This aspect of legal language is what makes it exotic and special and different from other professional jargons, as well as from ordinary English. It is also the aspect that is most often criticized by lawyers and nonlawyers alike. This part of legal language is quite distinct from standard English: Its development, which has spanned centuries, has differed in several important ways from the development of ordinary English.[1] These differences stem from historical, sociological, political, and jurisprudential processes; each has helped make legal language a unique variety of English.

C Foundations of Legal Writing

1. Historical Factors

During the period that English common law was evolving, the English language was going through a number of linguistic changes. Those changes were not always reflected in legal language. Legal language had its own processes of change and growth, so that its development paralleled but did not always mirror that of the rest of the English language.

Ordinarily, languages change over time through ordinary use — words develop new meanings and old meanings are lost; terms that become archaic drop out of the language; grammatical constructions shift to reflect changes in the status of competing dialects (*ain't* versus *isn't* and *aren't*, for example). Legal terms also change through use. But legal language has developed a number of its forms and meanings through a different process — a legal-historical process. An example of this is the legal meaning of *fresh,* as in *fresh fish.* The lay person will probably understand fresh fish to mean fish that was recently caught. But the legal definition of fresh fish, which has been set by regulations, is fish that has never been frozen, no matter when it was caught. It is the courts, legislatures, and government agencies that decide the meaning of many legal terms, rather than ordinary usage and historical change.

The meaning of the legal term *negligence* developed through litigation. The term has been refined through a history of appellate court decisions, so that it now has a very specialized meaning in the law. In ordinary usage, *negligence* is synonymous with *carelessness,* but the legal meaning, honed by more than a century of litigation, is much narrower. In California, negligence is

the doing of something which a reasonably prudent person would not do, or the failure to do something which a reasonably prudent person would do, under a given set of circumstances.

Most legal meanings, like meanings of words in ordinary usage, do have a certain flexibility; a given word can have a range of meanings. But in legal usage, a word's

---

1. There is an excellent discussion of the evolution of legal language in D. Mellinkoff, The Language of the Law (1978).

range of meaning is narrower—the result of judicial, statutory, or regulatory interpretations or formal negotiations, not of ordinary linguistic processes.

Our legal system is derived from the legal system of England. Legal proceedings and legal writing in England were first done entirely in Latin, then in a mixture of French, Latin, and English, and finally in English alone. This complicated evolution has left us with some unusual clause and phrase structures and a good deal of terminology that combines Latin, French, and archaic English. These archaic constructions and words have survived for a number of reasons. When ordinary English changes, older words are replaced with newer ones, and either the meanings of the older words change or the words drop out of use. In legal language, on the other hand, older words are not always replaced; rather, new words are simply added to the previously used terms. This creates strings of synonymous words that are used as a single term.

As the use of French and Latin was giving way to English in the courts, the English word was often added to the French or Latin word to create a phrase. The lawyers of the time probably feared that in translating French or Latin into English some of the highly specialized meanings of the legal vocabulary would be lost. To avoid this, French or Latin terms were often retained and used *with* the English term to represent a concept. Even though the original problem of dealing with the multiple languages of the law no longer exists, the following multiple terms are still in active use:

> cease and desist
> null and void
> remise, release, and forever discharge
> good and sufficient
> rest, residue, and remainder
> false and untrue
> acknowledge and confess
> give, devise, and bequeath

A number of legal concepts were never translated into English, but have remained in Latin:

> prima facie
> res judicata
> mens rea
> nolo contendere
> habeas corpus

or French:

> in lieu of
> lien
> easement

tort

oyez

Also, some archaic English has never been updated:

witnesseth

wherein

aforesaid

heretofore

writ

Perhaps the most recognizable example of the use of archaic forms in legal language is the retention of *such*, *said*, and *which* as demonstrative adjectives (e.g., *this*, *that*) or determiners (e.g., *the*), and *absent* as a preposition. For example, "*said* contract will continue to be in force, *absent* proof that the defendant defrauded the plaintiff."

The differences between legal language and the rest of the English language are not just at the level of words. Whole phrases and clauses exist that have no counterpart in everyday language:

have you then and there this writ

malice aforethought

revoking all wills and codicils by me made

fee simple (here, the adjective *follows* the noun)

These phrases and clauses, frozen in legal language, come from grammatical constructions that are no longer in general use.

The effect of the independent development of legal language is nicely summed up in the discussion of the word *may* in Black's Law Dictionary. Unlike its use in ordinary language, in legal language *may* can carry mandatory meaning. Black's Law Dictionary explains that courts frequently "construe 'may' as 'shall' or 'must' to the end that justice may not be the slave of grammar."[2] Unfortunately, when grammar becomes the slave of justice, the result is often incomprehensible, poorly written documents, which may, in turn, affect the rendering of justice.

2. Sociological Factors

Legal language is the primary tool of the legal professional. Unlike physicians who have instruments and procedures, engineers who have blueprints and computers, and scientists who have microscopes, test tubes, balances, and oscilloscopes, lawyers rely mainly on legal language. True, all professions have a body

---

2. Black's Law Dictionary 883 (5th ed. 1979).

of thought and theory that is embodied in language, but for lawyers there is only one way of accessing and using this knowledge — through legal language.

In addition, one very important function of legal language is a *performative* function, where the words constitute the act.[3] Legal language carries the force of the law. A person who has been pronounced guilty by a court *is* guilty (whether he or she really is). When a divorce is granted, two people who were previously married become un-married, by a set of written and spoken words. And, interestingly, in most jurisdictions, if a person has been missing for seven years, a court, on petition, can declare that person dead, even though he or she may (without the court's knowledge) be alive and well.

Naturally, legal language by itself does not have all this power. Society has granted to certain persons the authority to make decisions over life and property. But these decisions are effected by means of language, and only in law does language carry so much power.

This power of legal language and the fact that the law can only be communicated through it have helped create the ritualistic quality of some legal discourse. The ritualistic quality, in turn, helps to enhance the power of the court. When you hear a uniformed bailiff crying "Oyez, oyez, oyez," demanding that "All rise," and requiring witnesses to state "the truth, the whole truth, and nothing but the truth, so help you God," you are meant to be impressed by the power of the law. This ritualistic quality is not necessarily harmful. A society needs laws, and legal incantation may help persuade people to follow them. According to Professor David Mellinkoff,

> This was the early history of the language of the law — made rememberable by repetition, rhythm, rhyme, alliteration and an awestruck respect for the magic potency of certain words. Planned for that effect or willy-nilly, these features fastened upon the language of the law in a time of illiteracy when the very survival of law depended on mnemonic devices, and where the memory of man did not run — there was no law.[4]

But as Mellinkoff also states, "the necessity for repetition and the tricks of verse to insure the law's survival passed long ago."[5]

This view of language as carrying the power of the law appears to be one reason that lawyers resist even minor changes. For example, many lawyers would hesitate to substitute *stop* for *cease and desist* because they would worry that tampering with a time-honored term might somehow bring about the wrong legal result. There may be legal reasons (because of either precedent or statute) for retaining many terms, but there are few valid legal reasons for clinging to Latinisms (prima facie, supra); strings of synonyms (null and void; any and all; rest, residue and remainder); or archaic words and phrases (witnesseth, thereinabove, hereinbefore).

---

3. J. Austin, How to Do Things with Words (1962).
4. D. Mellinkoff, The Language of the Law 33 (1978).
5. Id. at 284.

3. Political Factors

Some of the vagueness and ambiguity in legal documents is intentional. Laws are usually enacted as a result of discussion and compromise. The lawmaking process is not always a process of reconciling divergent views; often it is a process of carefully choosing language that everyone—even those with contradictory positions—can agree upon. Furthermore, many of the problems addressed in legislation are so complex that the legislature can provide only a vague framework, which must then be filled in by administrative agencies through the drafting of regulations.

Unfortunately, many of the political forces that cause a legislature to create a vague statute are still present when the regulation writers begin their job. In addition, many regulations are subject to comment by the public and lobbying by special interest groups. The result is often a compromise regulation, which may be intentionally vague or ambiguous. Government agencies may actually want to perpetuate vagueness. In order to maintain control over industries, institutions, and individual programs, federal agencies often prefer to decide questions on a case-by-case basis. The result, not surprisingly, can be regulations that are as vague as the statutes.

When a government agency wishes to extend its authority—perhaps beyond the explicit limits provided by the statute—it derives a certain degree of security by using language from the statute either in writing the regulation or in justifying it. For example, in 1996 the Food and Drug Administration (FDA) sought to regulate cigarettes and smokeless tobacco (i.e, chewing tobacco). The FDA had never regulated tobacco products. The FDA has authority to regulate, among other things, drugs, medical devices, and products that combine the attributes of both a drug and a device (i.e., combination drugs and devices). The Federal Food, Drug, and Cosmetic Act of 1938 (FD&C Act), as amended, 21 U.S.C. § 321 et seq., defines "drugs" as "articles (other than food) intended to affect the structure or any function of the body." 21 U.S.C. § 321(g)(1)(C). It defines a medical "device," in part, as "an instrument, apparatus, implement, machine, contrivance, . . . or other similar or related article, including any component, part, or accessory, which is . . . . intended to affect the structure or any function of the body." 21 U.S.C. § 321(h).

The FD&C Act does not explicitly authorize the FDA to regulate the sale of cigarettes or smokeless tobacco. Nonetheless, on August 28, 1996, the FDA issued a rule regulating tobacco sales. *See* 61 Fed. Reg. 44,396 (Aug. 28, 1996). The agency justified the extension of its traditional jurisdiction by noting

(i) that tobacco contains nicotine;

(ii) that nicotine is a drug because it is addictive and has other effects on the "function of the body"; and

(iii) that cigarettes, by delivering a dose of nicotine, affect the function of the body.

The FDA reasoned that since a cigarette delivers a dose of nicotine to the body, it is a drug delivery system, i.e., a combination of a device and drug; therefore, it is subject to regulation by the FDA. *See* 21 U.S.C. § 353(g)(1). The regulation and its justification used the words of the statute (including function of body, intended, drug, and device). A "cigarette" was therefore defined as "any product that consists of loose tobacco that contains or delivers nicotine." 21 C.F.R. § 897.3 (1999). By characterizing cigarettes in terms of the same statutory language that governs ordinary drugs and devices, the FDA believed that it could strengthen its case if the matter were litigated.

Soon after the regulation was published, various tobacco companies challenged it in court, arguing, among other things, that Congress never intended the FDA to regulate tobacco. In *FDA v. Brown & Williamson Tobacco Corp.*, 529 U.S. 120 (2000), the Supreme Court agreed and struck down the regulation. While language is powerful, it cannot save an otherwise invalid regulation.

Detailed regulations usually possess the grammatical and semantic earmarks of legal language (often further complicated by the presence of vocabulary from other technical jargons). These regulations, by the use of legal language and legal discourse style, and by the excessive use of detail, can serve political purposes: The detail lessens the scope of an industry's power to make decisions, and the legal language serves formal notice that it is the agency that possesses the authority to make the decisions. Here are two examples from a proposed regulation of the U.S. Environmental Protection Agency:

Example 1

(a) Any person who produces and disposes of no more than 100 kilograms (approximately 220 pounds) of hazardous waste in any one month period, or any retailer disposing of hazardous waste (other than waste oil), is not a generator provided that the hazardous waste:

(1) Is disposed of in an on-site or off-site solid waste disposal facility in a State with an approved State plan under Subtitle D of the Solid Waste Disposal Act, as amended, which facility has been permitted or otherwise certified by the State as meeting the criteria adopted pursuant to Section 4004 of the Act; or (2) Is shipped to and treated, stored, or disposed of in a facility permitted by the Administrator pursuant to the requirements of Subpart E of this part or permitted by an authorized State program pursuant to Subpart F of this Part.

Example 2

(1) Generators must send hazardous waste to a treatment, storage, or disposal facility permitted by the Administrator pursuant to the requirements of Subpart E and shall comply with the requirements of this Subpart as follows:

(i) If the generator sends the hazardous waste to an off-site treatment, storage or disposal facility which the generator does not own or the generator owns but which is not located in the State where the generation occurred, the generator shall comply with all requirements of this Subpart except §§ 250.23 (d), (e), (f), (g), and (h) and 250.28.

Note the long sentences and complex sentence structure; the statement of exceptions within the rule; the overuse of the passive voice; the noun string "off-site solid waste disposal facility"; the use of "which" instead of "and this"; the legal preposition "pursuant to"; the legal terms "shall," "amended," "certified," "authorized"; and the peculiar way of describing a person who is *not* a member of a class and for referring the reader elsewhere (in the last paragraph of the second example). All of these language characteristics help to mark this as a regulation with the force of authority, and the use of legal language ostensibly reinforces the power and authority of the agency that created the regulation.

4. Jurisprudential Factors

Common law is built on precedent. In the law, terms, phrases, even whole chunks of discourse mean what courts have decided they mean. While the common meaning of a word or phrase may still be the basis of a court's decision,[6] Chief Justice Hughes's statement that "a federal statute finally means what the Court says it means"[7] is probably more accurate, as the legal system actually operates. (This smacks of the absurd, like Humpty Dumpty's assertion in Lewis Carroll's *Through the Looking Glass*, "When I use a word, it means just what I choose it to mean — neither more nor less.")

Most nonlawyers would recognize the dictionary definition of the term *heir*:

1. *Law.* A person who inherits or is entitled by law or by the terms of a will to inherit the estate of another. 2. A person who succeeds or is in line to succeed to a hereditary rank, title or office. 3. One who receives or is expected to receive a heritage, as of ideas, from a predecessor.[8]

However, the strict legal definition of *heir* differs in a number of ways from the common dictionary definition. An heir is a person entitled by statute to the land of someone who dies *intestate*, that is, *without a will*. This means that a person who receives land under a will is not technically an heir according to the law. Furthermore, a person who receives personal property, even under the laws of intestate succession, is not technically an heir. Such a person is a *distributee* or *next-of-kin*.

There are numerous other instances where a definition decided either by the courts or by statute differs substantially from the common meaning of the term,

---

6. *See* R. Dickerson, Materials on Legal Drafting (1981).
7. C. Hughes, The Supreme Court of the United States 230 (1928). *See also,* Carroll, Lewis, *Alice in Wonderland*, and *Through the Looking Glass*.
8. American Heritage Dictionary of the English Language 611 (1973).

for example, *income, purchase,* and *domicile.* Another term with a strict legal definition built on precedent is *assault.* The dictionary definition accurately reflects common usage, describing assault as a violent attack that can be either physical or verbal. However, the legal definition, as set forth in the Restatement (Second) of Torts § 21, is as follows:

> An actor is subject to liability to another for assault if
>   (a) he acts intending to cause a harmful or offensive contact with the person of
>   the other or a third person, or an imminent apprehension of such a contact, and
>   (b) the other is thereby put in such imminent apprehension.

In other words, *legal* assault is an act coupled with an intention on the part of one person that produces a fear or expectation in another. It does not require physical contact but cannot be solely verbal.

The interaction between jurisprudence and legal language is nicely illustrated in the often contradictory rules that courts use to interpret the meaning of statutory language. Among them is the *plain meaning rule*, which states that a statute means what it says on its face. However, this rule can often be countered with the *purpose of the statute rule*, which states that a statute should be interpreted to fulfill its underlying purpose. In addition to these two broad rules, the courts have created a host of maxims to take care of specific situations. One well-known maxim is *ejusdem generis*, which says that if a list of two or more items is followed by a more general term that includes the prior items, then the more general term is limited by the nature of the prior items (thus, "dogs, cats, and other animals" would probably not include amoebas because amoebas have so little in common with dogs and cats). Some other maxims are *expressio unius est exclusio alterius*, meaning "a statement of one is an exclusion of another"; and *in pari materia*, which says, essentially, that two statutes on the same general subject ought to be construed in harmony with one another.

While the purpose of these rules is supposedly to provide "objective criteria" for resolving statutory ambiguity, courts often use these rules to support a particular interpretation *after* they have reached a decision. Consequently, different courts have, according to their various judicial philosophies, applied the various rules and maxims to the same term and have come up with a variety of contradictory meanings. For example, notwithstanding ordinary usage, courts have managed to totally confuse the meanings of *shall, may, must,* and *will,* so that *may,* as noted above, has been interpreted to have mandatory meaning (*must*). *Must* has been interpreted as *may,* and *shall* has been interpreted as *may, must,* or *will.* In *Kansas City v. J. I. Case Threshing Machine Co.,* the court decided that *may, must,* and *shall* are interchangeable in statutes, without regard to their literal meaning.[9]

---

9. 337 Mo. 913, 87 S.W.2d 195, 205 (1935). *See also* State ex rel. Hanlon v. City of Maplewood, 231 Mo. App. 739, 99 S.W.2d 138 (1936); In re Vrooman's Estate, 206 Okl. 8, 240 P.2d 754, 756 (1952); and Ballou v. Kemp, 68 App. D.C. 7, 92 F.2d 556, 559 (1937).

D Attitudes Toward Traditional Legal Writing

Obviously you cannot escape existing legal documents even if they are filled with grammatical and stylistic features that obscure meaning with confusing constructions. You must use the information in existing documents as the foundation for your own legal analyses. The important thing is not to write that way yourself if you can help it.

We have based this book on what some attorneys consider a revolutionary premise — that legal writing can be clear as well as effective. You may feel, either now or later in your law-school career, that the principles presented in this book are not important in law school or in the real world and that your ability to use traditional legal language is a marketable skill. In some ways this is true. There will be situations in which you may be discouraged from using clear, straightforward language. You may find yourself in that type of situation when writing for a conservative audience or creating documents from forms or models. But even if you must sometimes use the less clear, traditional legal language, you will ultimately benefit from learning the principles of clear writing. You will have learned to think more analytically, to avoid unintended ambiguity, and to communicate with a variety of audiences.

1. Conservative Audiences

You may find that some of your law school professors are reluctant to accept any attempts to alter traditional legal language. If you work for a law firm, you may find that a senior attorney will not allow you to change "remise, release, and forever discharge" to just "release," and he or she may send you to a form book or to the firm's files so that you can see how the firm expects a release to be written. In fact, some clients will not be satisfied with a document unless it contains the traditional *whereases* and *heretofores*.

You may run into similar problems in the courtroom. If you fail to use the appropriate boilerplate or terms of art, some courts may not be receptive to your document. If you have doubts about your writing, check with someone who has more experience before you submit a document.

The problems posed by conservative audiences do not invalidate the principles presented in this book. More and more law firms are becoming interested in improving the writing produced by their attorneys, and many courts prefer clear writing to boilerplate.

2. Forms and Model Documents

The amount of control you will have over your writing will also depend on the kind of document you are creating. For example, some documents are used time and again with little variation. The audience comes to expect a certain format and certain language, and the writer will use well-established, previously litigated language so that he or she can be fairly sure of how the courts will interpret the language. This includes such documents as very simple contracts, deeds, leases, and wills. Even though you might be able to draft your own, clearer version of these documents, your firm may want you to fill in the blanks in a form or to piece together portions of other documents to create a new one.

Thus, you may have little opportunity in your early years of practice to change the forms or models that your firm uses, even though they may contain poor writing, boilerplate, and unnecessarily difficult legal terms. There may come a time, however, when you will be able to change some of these forms. Professor David Mellinkoff describes how a new attorney might influence established legal language:

> One day you will be working on a contract, not writing a contract, but trying to find out what went wrong with a contract written by other lawyers, in other firms. Your client signed it, and now the contract is in court, the *Jones* case. In your memo, you point out that the contract is so wound up in long, long sentences, and three words for one, that it is impossible to find a single meaning. You say that they botched the job of writing the contract. It's ambiguous, and the road is wide open to testimony about what the parties meant. Your memo convinces the powers. Your client wins. You move up a notch in the pecking order. The next time around, the old man tells an associate, "Show it to what's-his-name, the young lawyer who wrote the memo in the *Jones* case."
>
> One day, you will be calling the shots. You will be in a position to insist that the writing the firm turns out be simpler, clearer, shorter, better.[10]

3. Memos and Briefs

If you are writing documents whose primary purpose is to inform, explain, or persuade, you will have a good deal more leeway. Memos and briefs are examples of these kinds of documents. You may be required to follow a certain format and use a formal tone and certain terms of art, but the writing itself is up to you. Because the audience for a memo or brief expects to have things explained, they are unlikely to be jarred or bothered if you deviate from the traditional way of saying things. Hence, you will generally be able to determine the style, vocabulary, and sentence structure of your document.

This book is designed to make you aware of *whom* you are writing for and *why* you might choose one or another way of expressing an idea or constructing an argument. It also provides guidelines to help you assess the quality of the writing in documents written by others. Your ability to judge the quality of communication will, in turn, make you a more discerning and effective legal advocate.

---

10. D. Mellinkoff, in Syllabus, A.B.A. Section of Legal Education & Admission to the Bar, vol. XIV, #2, June 1983, pp. 1, 8.

2

Categories of Legal Writing

The legal documents that law students and lawyers encounter most often can be divided into categories. We have listed some typical kinds of legal documents here. As you read through the list, note that most of the documents fall into one of two broad areas: They are intended either to inform or to persuade. There are exceptions, of course. Briefs, for instance, attempt to both inform and persuade. Interrogatories really do neither. And documents such as wills and contracts serve a recordkeeping function as well as an informative one.

Client letters are sent to clients for a number of purposes. One major purpose is to *inform* clients about the status of their legal affairs. An attorney might write a letter to a client to keep the client apprised of what the attorney is doing or plans to do regarding the client's case. A specific kind of letter to a client is the *opinion letter*. This letter is sent to the client to explain the lawyer's understanding of the law as it applies to the facts of the client's case.

Private documents such as contracts and wills are documents that *establish a record* or *memorialize an act or a status*. They describe a client's wishes, rights, or obligations. They can be used as a reference by the client, third parties, or a court.

Pleadings are documents that the parties to an action file with the court to explain their controversy to the court and to each other. They serve different purposes. For example, a pleading may *inform* the court about the sort of case that is involved; *inform* the opponent and other interested parties that suit has been filed; *petition* the court to dismiss a case before litigation; or *narrow and define* the legal issues in a given case. The following are three common types of pleadings:

1. A *complaint* is used to initiate suit and to disclose to the court and to the defendant the facts upon which the plaintiff is basing the claim.
2. An *answer* is the defendant's response to the complaint, denying or agreeing with some or all of the allegations in the complaint.
3. A *demurrer* (a type of motion to dismiss) is used to challenge the legal sufficiency of an opponent's pleading.

Interrogatories are written questions used by an attorney, usually in a civil case. They are designed to *elicit* certain kinds of information from an adversary.

The attorney serves these questions on the adversary, and the adversary is required to respond within a specific period of time.

A *memorandum* or *memo* is an informative document written after researching the points of law or the facts for a particular case. Its major purpose is to *inform* the reader, rather than to persuade, and to give the reader a decision-making tool. The reader may use this information to construct a brief or a pleading, to inform a client about the status of the case, or to decide whether to take a client's case. A memo is usually requested by, and addressed to, another lawyer — often, a colleague or supervisor — but the writer may also compose it for his or her own use. In writing a memo, you would compile all the relevant information you can find on each point and then sort out key cases in order to convey the present status of the law. Next, you would discuss the different ways to apply the law to the facts of the case and ways to interpret the law. You might also speculate on how your opponent or the court would interpret the facts and law and make some recommendations for future action.

An *appellate brief* is presented to an appellate court as a formal document that states the facts of the case, identifies the relevant issues, and presents an argument that is supported by statutes and previously decided cases. Its function is to *persuade* the court that legal principles and precedents support your client's position. Thus, a good brief integrates the facts with the relevant law. A brief also provides judges with reference materials: a list of relevant cases and statutes and a documented, well-reasoned analysis of the facts and the law.

A *memorandum of points and authorities,* also known as a *memorandum of law,* is a short adversarial document much like a brief. It usually accompanies a motion and is designed to *persuade* the court (usually a trial court) that the motion should be granted. For example, a defendant in a civil case who files a motion to dismiss under Fed. R. Civ. P. 12(b)(6) will usually attach a memorandum of points and authorities to that motion. Similarly, a party against whom a motion has been filed may wish to submit to the court a memorandum of points and authorities in opposition.

The traditional legal documents mentioned above have long histories. A more recent form of document — but one with which you are likely quite familiar — is electronic mail. E-mails can be written to colleagues, to clients, to adversaries, and even to courts. They tend to be informal, but they can have the same legal ramifications as a typed, signed document. Because many people consider e-mail to be similar to a telephone conversation, they may say things in an e-mail that they would not ordinarily say in a letter. They may also neglect to proofread e-mail communications. Careless, poorly written, or misdirected e-mails can be extremely embarrassing, as many politicians have found out the hard way. Similarly, many companies — and even government agencies — have discovered that employees, and worse, officials, can say things in e-mails that come back to haunt them when their messages are scrutinized by a judge or jury. The e-mail written by an in-house attorney at Arthur Andersen, LLP, literally made it to the Supreme Court. Andersen had been Enron's accounting firm. As Enron's accounting difficulties slowly became public, Nancy Temple, a lawyer for

Andersen, sent an e-mail reminding employees to "[m]ake sure to follow the [document retention] policy." *Arthur Andersen LLP v. United States*, 544 U.S. 696, 701 (2005). Most companies, as well as state and federal governments, have document retention policies which mandate that certain documents be destroyed after a set period. Partly because of Temple's e-mail, Andersen employees shredded thousands of documents, and due in part to this shredding, Andersen was indicted for and convicted of obstruction of justice. The Supreme Court overturned the conviction, but it was too late for Andersen, which was forced out of business as a result of the conviction.

3

Sources of Law and Our System of Courts

The United States Constitution divides responsibility for governing between the federal government and the states. It also provides a framework for the federal government by establishing three co-equal branches of government: the executive, legislative, and judicial branches. In school we are taught that the legislative branch enacts statutes, the executive branch enforces those statutes, and the judicial branch interprets them. In reality, though, all three branches have, to varying degrees, the authority to make law.

Each year Congress enacts nearly 200 new laws, many of which deal with highly complex issues. Congress frequently lacks the time or expertise to give those laws the detail that may be necessary to make them work effectively. In those cases, Congress expects, and usually requires, the executive branch to provide the needed detail by issuing regulations. It is by issuing regulations that the executive branch makes law. New regulations are published every weekday in the *Federal Register*. You may wish to go to the law library (or go online at www.gpoaccess.gov) and look at a few issues of the *Federal Register* just to get some idea of how pervasive executive branch rulemaking is. In the late 1980s, for example, Congress heard testimony from consumer advocates and officials of the Food and Drug Administration (FDA) that food labels were misleading or difficult to understand. Some witnesses testified that some food manufacturers were making scientifically unjustified claims that their foods would help prevent cancer or retard heart disease. Other manufacturers affixed misleading labels to their foods. In one case, a food label claimed that the product was "new, improved and lite" because it contained 25 percent fewer calories. The label did not mention that the manufacturer reduced the calories by reducing the amount of food in the package by 25 percent. All of this led Congress to enact the Nutrition Labeling and Education Act of 1990, Pub. L. 101-535. The law was 14 pages long and spoke in broad terms. In the end, the new law left it to the FDA to figure out what nutrition claims were scientifically justified. Two years after the law went into effect, the FDA issued a set of regulations that was over 2,000 typewritten pages long. These regulations are an example of the type of law that the executive branch creates.

Our courts also make laws. However, unlike the legislative branch, which passes a statute to address a specific problem, or the executive branch, which issues a regulation under the authority of a statute, the courts "make law" indirectly in the process of resolving concrete disputes between parties. This is referred to as the common law or case law. It is based on the proposition that in resolving a legal issue courts will look to see how other courts have resolved similar or related issues. In this way, a case can act as a precedent for future cases. In your torts class you are likely to read *Canterbury v. Spence*, 464 F.2d 772 (D.C. Cir. 1972), a District of Columbia medical malpractice case in which the plaintiff became paralyzed following back surgery. There was no evidence that the surgeon had done anything wrong during the operation. Instead, the plaintiff argued that the physician had failed to warn him about the risks associated with back surgery and that, had he known that there was a risk of paralysis, he would not have agreed to have the surgery. The physician argued that the risk of paralysis was only about 1 percent and that it was the custom in the medical community not to apprise patients of these small risks because they might be dissuaded from having needed surgery. The issue then before the court was whether a physician was obligated to tell a patient about these risks. The United States Court of Appeals for the District of Columbia Circuit ultimately concluded that a physician had a duty to fully apprise a patient of the risks associated with a proposed treatment.

In theory, the appellate court's ruling in *Canterbury* only affected the parties to that lawsuit. However, the decision in *Canterbury* set a precedent for trial courts in the District of Columbia: Those courts would be obligated by custom to follow the higher court's ruling. This is called *binding precedent* and means that a lower court is required to follow the law as set out by a higher court in the same jurisdiction. In addition, courts in other jurisdictions might choose to follow the holding in *Canterbury v. Spence*. This is called *persuasive precedent*. It is in these ways that the impact of a court's ruling in a single case may be magnified and may become as influential as a statute. As it happens, the court's holding in *Canterbury* — physicians have a duty to fully advise their patients of known risks — was subsequently adopted by most other courts in the United States.

Each United States Court of Appeals has circuit rules that dictate what is and what is not binding precedent. Thus, for example, the rule in most circuits is that a published decision by a single three-judge panel is binding on every federal court in that circuit, that is, district courts and other three-judge panels of the Court of Appeals, and may only be reversed by the full court, sitting en banc, or by the Supreme Court. Interestingly, under the rules of some circuits, an unpublished opinion of a three-judge panel is not binding precedent, but it is still persuasive precedent.[1] *See* Eleventh Circuit Rule 36-2; *Kelley v. Apfel*, 173 F.3d 814, 816 n.3 (11th Cir. 1999).

---

1. There has been significant debate over the status of unpublished opinions and whether a court may constitutionally preclude a party from citing to unpublished opinions. Recently, Chief Judge William Young in Islam v. Option One Mortgage Corp., No. 05-12175-WGY (D. Mass. May 5, 2006) aptly summarized the controversy: "Compare Anastasoff v. United States, 223 F.3d 898, 899-905 (8th Cir. 2000) (holding that local rule stating that unpublished opinions are not precedent was unconstitutional), vacated as moot 235 F.3d 1054 (8th Cir. 2000) (en banc), with Hart v. Massanari, 266 F.3d 1155 (9th Cir. 2001) (Kozinski, J.) (holding similar rule constitutional); Symbol Techs., Inc. v. Lemelson Med., 277 F.3d 1361, 1366-68 (Fed. Cir. 2002) (same); see also Richard S. Arnold, Unpublished Opinions: A Comment, 1 J. App. Prac. & Process 219 (1999); Stephen R. Barnett, In Support of Proposed Federal Rule 32.1: A Reply to Judge Alex Kozinski, Fed. Law. Nov./Dec. 2004, at 32; Anne Coyle, Note, A Modest Reform: The New Rule 32.1 Permitting Citation to Unpublished

Courts can also "make law" by interpreting statutes or regulations. One interesting case, *Bedroc Limited, LLC v. United States*, 541 U.S. 176 (2004), involved a controversy having its roots in the early Homestead Acts that provided incentives to settle the western states. One of those acts, the Pittman Act of 1919, was aimed at Nevada and authorized the government to grant lands to individuals who promised to prospect for water, which was essential if agriculture was to flourish in the desert. Under the Pittman Act, any settler who could successfully irrigate at least 20 acres of crops was eligible for a land grant of up to 640 acres (one square mile). The United States, however, retained the right to "coal and other valuable minerals in the lands." The Pittman Act was not terribly successful, although a number of individuals, including Newton and Mabel Butler, managed to obtain land by successfully irrigating the requisite acreage. Common sand and gravel were plentiful and visible on the surface of the Butlers' land, but there was no commercial market for them because of Nevada's sparse population and the land's remote location.

The Butlers' property was sold in 1993 to Earl Williams, who in turn sold it to Bedroc Limited. By that time, the expansion of Las Vegas had created a commercial market for the sand and gravel on the land. Williams and then Bedroc sought to take advantage of this new market and began extracting the sand and gravel. The government, however, objected, arguing that the sand and gravel were "valuable minerals" and, as such, were owned by the government. The matter ultimately ended up in the Supreme Court. Chief Justice Rehnquist, writing for the Court, ruled that

> [b]ecause the Pittman Act applied only to Nevada, the ultimate question is whether the sand and gravel found in Nevada were commonly regarded as "valuable minerals" in 1919. Common sense tells us, and the Government does not contest, that the answer to that question is an emphatic "No." Sand and gravel were, and are, abundant throughout Nevada; they have no intrinsic value; and they were commercially worthless in 1919 due to Nevada's sparse population and lack of development. Thus, even if Nevada's sand and gravel were regarded as minerals, no one would have mistaken them for valuable minerals.

By interpreting the Pittman Act in the way it did, the Supreme Court resolved an apparent ambiguity in the law's wording and in that way participated in "making law."

There is one difference between *Canterbury* and *Bedroc* worth noting. *Canterbury* was handed down by a federal intermediate appellate court, while *Bedroc* came from the Supreme Court. All else being equal, the status of the court that issues an opinion will affect the influence (or precedential value) that the opinion will have on other courts.

Opinions in Federal Courts of Appeals, 72 Fordham L. Rev. 2471 (2004); Lawrence J. Fox, Note, Those Unpublished Opinions: An Appropriate Expedience or an Abdication of Responsibility, 32 Hofstra L. Rev. 1215 (2004); Hon. Alex Kozinski, Letter, Fed. Law., June 2004, at 37; Gary Young, Cite, Publish or Perish?, Nat'l L.J., May 3, 2004, at S1." Despite being vacated as moot, the Anastasoff court's discussion of the history of precedent is extremely lucid and worth reading.

In the United States there are two parallel court systems — a state system and a federal one — each with the ability to hear certain types of cases. We have included, on pages 25 and 26, a diagram of the federal system and a diagram of one state system, Maryland, respectively. The federal system has three levels of courts: (1) trial courts, called the United States District Courts, (2) intermediate appellate courts, called the United States Courts of Appeals, and (3) the Supreme Court. For most purposes, the district and appeals courts are arranged geographically. In all, there are 94 United States District Courts, at least one for every state. Some states may have only one district court assigned to them (for example, Utah, Oregon, Maryland, Delaware). States with larger populations tend to have more than one district court. For example, New York, Texas, and California are each divided geographically into four federal districts, each with one district court, each of which may have many judges. Congress decides by law how many districts a state will be divided into and further decides the number of judges allocated to each district.

Once a trial court has entered a judgment or has issued a final order, the losing party may choose to appeal that decision to the next higher court in the system. In the federal system, an appeal from a district court decision would be heard by the United States Court of Appeals with jurisdiction over that district court. For purposes of appellate review in the federal system, the country has been divided into 12 geographic circuits; each circuit has at least one district and most have many more. Thus, the United States Court of Appeals for the Ninth Circuit has jurisdiction to hear most appeals from the federal district courts located in the western states and some territories (Alaska, Arizona, California, Hawaii, Idaho, Montana, Oregon, Washington, Guam, and Northern Mariana Islands). There is, however, one court of appeals whose jurisdiction is determined not by geography but by subject matter, and that is the United States Court of Appeals for the Federal Circuit, which sits in Washington, D.C. The Federal Circuit has exclusive jurisdiction to entertain all appeals involving cases arising under the patent laws, irrespective of which district court tried the case. The Federal Circuit also hears appeals from the United States Court of Federal Claims, the United States Court of International Trade, the United States Court of Appeals for Veterans Claims and from a number of federal agencies (for example, Merit Systems Protection Board, International Trade Commission, Boards of Contract Appeals, Patent and Trademark Office).

At the top of the judicial pyramid is the Supreme Court. Although litigants can appeal a case as a matter of right to a United States Court of Appeals, review by the Supreme Court is discretionary. Each year the Supreme Court is asked to hear more than 5,000 cases, but accepts fewer than 100 cases for review.[2]

All states have court systems that are similar in structure to the federal system. But while some states have no intermediate appellate court, others use four levels as opposed to the three in the federal system. In Maryland, for instance, there are two types of trial courts: one, called the district court, hears small cases

---

2. During the Court's 2005 Term (October 2005 – June 29, 2006), it issued 87 opinions.

(that is, civil cases in which the amount in controversy does not exceed $25,000 and criminal misdemeanor cases);[3] the other, known as the circuit court, is the trial court of general jurisdiction. The circuit court has broad subject matter jurisdiction. *Subject matter jurisdiction* refers to the types of cases and subjects over which the court has jurisdiction. Thus, for example, the circuit court hears criminal felony cases and civil cases where the amount in controversy exceeds $5,000; probates wills; dissolves marriages; resolves disputes over ownership of real property; and issues injunctions and other writs. As you will note, the district and circuit courts have concurrent jurisdiction in most cases when the amount in controversy is greater than $5,000 but less than $25,000. In these instances, the plaintiff has the option of choosing the court. Maryland also has a special court, called the Orphans Court, which deals with most probate matters. The Orphans Court functions in all but two counties: Hanford and Montgomery. In those two counties, there is no separate Orphans Court; its jurisdiction is subsumed by the Circuit Court.

Maryland is divided into eight circuits, each having one circuit court, but each circuit court can have many judges and locations. The state is also divided into twelve districts, each of which has a district court, but again, each district court can have multiple locations and judges. In addition, Maryland has a single intermediate appeals court, known as the Court of Special Appeals. And finally, at the top of the heap, is the Maryland Court of Appeals. While an appeal from a circuit court judgment to the Court of Special Appeals is a matter of right, appeals to the Court of Appeals are discretionary.

Because the United States has a dual system of courts, it is important to understand how the federal and state systems relate to one another. First, structurally, the two systems only intersect at the Supreme Court of the United States. The Supreme Court can hear appeals from the intermediate federal appeals courts and from the highest state court that considered the case. For example, if the Maryland Court of Special Appeals rules against Smith and the Maryland Court of Appeals declines to hear Smith's further appeal, Smith's only option is to seek review in the United States Supreme Court. Smith cannot seek review in the United States Court of Appeals for the Fourth Circuit. The "Rooker-Feldman" doctrine prevents the lower federal courts from exercising jurisdiction over cases brought by "state-court losers." *Exxon Mobil Corp. v. Saudi Basic Industries Corp.*, 544 U.S. 280, 284 (2005).

Second, the courts in the two systems have different subject matter jurisdictions. As a general rule, state courts resolve disputes that arise under state law, while federal courts hear cases arising under federal law.[4] There is one important exception. A United States district court has subject matter jurisdiction not only

---

3. The District Court's jurisdiction is somewhat more complex than indicated above. *See* Maryland Courts & Judicial Procedure § 4-40.
4. Usually, state courts can also hear cases that arise under federal law. However, when a plaintiff's cause of action arises under federal law, the defendant has the option of removing the case to federal court. Also, state courts are not permitted to entertain some types of cases. For example, state courts lack jurisdiction over claims that arise under the Employee Retirement Income Security Act of 1974 and under the Labor Management Relations Act of 1947.

over most suits arising under federal law but also over suits arising under state law between citizens of different states when the amount in controversy exceeds $75,000.[5] This latter jurisdiction is called *diversity jurisdiction* and is authorized by the Constitution.[6] Diversity jurisdiction reflects our Founding Fathers' apprehension that a nonresident involved in litigation with a resident of a state would run the risk of not being impartially treated by that state's tribunal. It was thought that a federal court would be better able than a state court to protect nonresidents from local favoritism.

Diversity jurisdiction works in two ways. It provides the plaintiff with the initial choice of court systems, but it provides the defendant with the ability to veto that choice if the plaintiff decides to sue in a state court.[7] For example, suppose that a citizen of California is injured when an oxygen tank manufactured by an Illinois corporation explodes in the plaintiff's hospital room. The injured person could sue either in a California superior court or in a federal district court if he is claiming damages in excess of $75,000. If the plaintiff opts to sue in state court (for example, Superior Court for the County of Los Angeles), then the defendant can, if it wishes, have the case removed to the federal court for the district in which the state court is located, in this case the United States District Court for the Central District of California.

The relationship between courts affects the precedential value of a given decision. For example, a decision issued by the Supreme Court of California would be binding on all California state courts. The Montana Supreme Court would be under no obligation to follow the California Supreme Court. Correspondingly, the decision in *Canterbury v. Spence*, which was issued by the United States Court of Appeals for the District of Columbia Circuit, would be binding precedent on the United States District Court for the District of Columbia. However, federal courts in other circuits, both district and appeals courts, would not be obligated to follow the decision in *Canterbury*. For those courts, *Canterbury* might be persuasive but not binding. Interestingly, cases that have been decided by a state supreme court and that raise issues under the United States Constitution or other federal law can be reviewed by the United States Supreme Court. The decision of the United States Supreme Court would then be binding on all courts in the land.

---

5. Deciding whether the amount in controversy exceeds $75,000 can be more complicated than it might appear. For example, if a plaintiff is seeking punitive damages, does that amount count toward the $75,000 threshold? Do attorneys' fees and court costs count toward the threshold?

6. Recently, Congress expanded diversity jurisdiction by permitting class actions to be removed to federal court, under certain circumstances, even though the damages suffered by each class member does not exceed $75,000. See Class Action Fairness Act of 2005, Pub. L. No. 109-2, 119 Stat. 4 (2005) (amending 28 U.S.C. § 1332).

7. Normally, a defendant seeking to remove a case to a federal court must do so within 30 days. Until recently, there was some confusion about whether the 30-day period started to run when the defendant was formally served with the complaint or when the defendant first received a copy of the complaint, irrespective of how the copy was acquired. In Murphy Brothers, Inc. v. Michetti Pipe Stringing, Inc., 526 U.S. 344 (1999), plaintiff argued that the 30-day period was triggered when it faxed a "courtesy copy" of the complaint to the defendant; the defendant was not formally served until two weeks later. The Supreme Court disagreed, holding that the 30-day period starts running from the day that the defendant is formally served.

FIGURE 3-1
The United States Court System

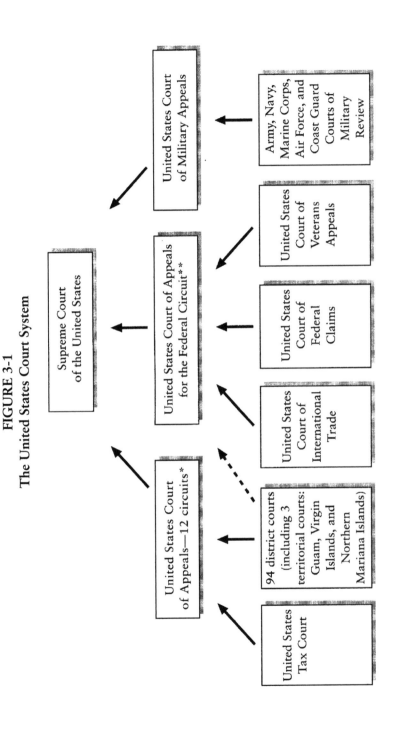

* The 12 regional courts of appeals also review cases from a number of federal agencies.
** The Court of Appeals for the Federal Circuit also reviews cases from the International Trade Commision, the Merit Systems Protection Board, the Patent and Trademark Office, and the Boards of Contract Appeals.

Courtesy of United States Administrative Office of Courts.

FIGURE 3-2
Maryland Court System

COURT STRUCTURE

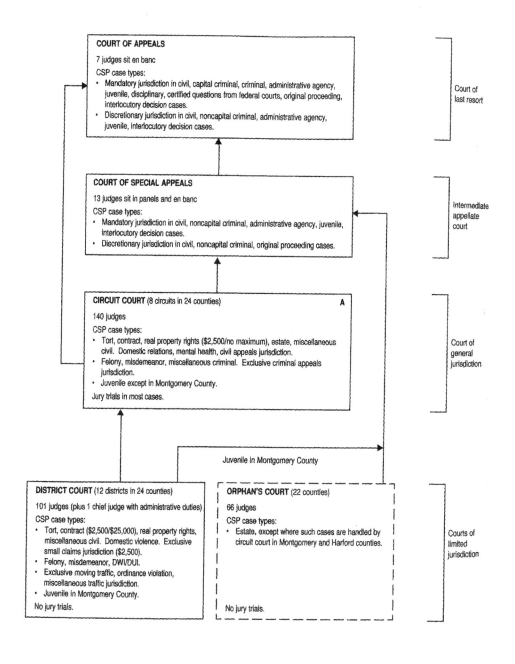

COURT OF APPEALS

7 judges sit en banc

CSP case types:
- Mandatory jurisdiction in civil, capital criminal, criminal, administrative agency, juvenile, disciplinary, certified questions from federal courts, original proceeding, interlocutory decision cases.
- Discretionary jurisdiction in civil, noncapital criminal, administrative agency, juvenile, interlocutory decision cases.

Court of last resort

COURT OF SPECIAL APPEALS

13 judges sit in panels and en banc

CSP case types:
- Mandatory jurisdiction in civil, noncapital criminal, administrative agency, juvenile, interlocutory decision cases.
- Discretionary jurisdiction in civil, noncapital criminal, original proceeding cases.

Intermediate appellate court

CIRCUIT COURT (8 circuits in 24 counties)   A

140 judges

CSP case types:
- Tort, contract, real property rights ($2,500/no maximum), estate, miscellaneous civil. Domestic relations, mental health, civil appeals jurisdiction.
- Felony, misdemeanor, miscellaneous criminal. Exclusive criminal appeals jurisdiction.
- Juvenile except in Montgomery County.

Jury trials in most cases.

Court of general jurisdiction

Juvenile in Montgomery County

DISTRICT COURT (12 districts in 24 counties)

101 judges (plus 1 chief judge with administrative duties)

CSP case types:
- Tort, contract ($2,500/$25,000), real property rights, miscellaneous civil. Domestic violence. Exclusive small claims jurisdiction ($2,500).
- Felony, misdemeanor, DWI/DUI.
- Exclusive moving traffic, ordinance violation, miscellaneous traffic jurisdiction.
- Juvenile in Montgomery County.

No jury trials.

ORPHAN'S COURT (22 counties)

66 judges

CSP case types:
- Estate, except where such cases are handled by circuit court in Montgomery and Harford counties.

No jury trials.

Courts of limited jurisdiction

4

The Litigation Process

A Preparing and Serving the Complaint

Litigation is a formal method for resolving a dispute in a socially acceptable manner. When we think of litigation, we are likely to think of a courtroom trial, usually followed by some sort of appeal to a higher court. A lawsuit commences when a plaintiff files a complaint with a court. A *complaint* is a legal document that, among other things, names the parties to the controversy, sets out the facts giving rise to the controversy, identifies the legal bases of the plaintiff's claims (for example, breach of contract, negligence, violations of a civil rights act), and specifies the types of remedies he or she wants the court to grant (for example, payment for lost wages, for medical expenses, or for pain and suffering). In essence, a well-drafted complaint tells a story and links that story to some recognized *cause of action*. Below is a sample complaint that might be used in a case in which the plaintiff is attempting to recover money for personal injuries.[1]

After filing the complaint with the court, the plaintiff must then serve the defendant with a copy of that complaint together with a *summons* (a document that requires the defendant to answer the complaint within a specified number of days). Sometimes it is difficult to complete service, especially if defendants go out of their way to avoid being served. In one case, for example, a North Carolina company instituted suit against a woman who owed the company over $300,000. For months, the plaintiff unsuccessfully tried to locate the woman so that she could be served with the complaint. Finally, the plaintiff hired a private detective. He discovered that the woman lived with a man who had been named as a defendant in other unrelated lawsuits and that he too was evading being served. The investigator also learned that neither the man nor the

---

1. It would be a mistake to view litigation as synonymous with courtroom trials. Most litigation does not take place in a courtroom. A growing percentage of litigation is now being conducted privately through binding arbitration. The Federal Arbitration Act permits parties to contract away their normal right to sue in court and to replace that right with private arbitration. The Supreme Court, in a series of recent cases, has affirmed that an arbitration clause in a contract can oust a trial court of jurisdiction to hear the case. See Circuit City Stores, Inc. v. Adams, 532 U.S. 105 (2001). Also, a significant percentage of litigation is before state and federal administrative agencies. See, e.g., 5 U.S.C. § 554 et seq. Depending on the agency, administrative adjudication can involve relatively simple disputes, such as whether an individual is entitled to receive Social Security Disability, or complex disputes such as determining the rates that interstate pipelines can charge their commercial customers. Arbitrations and administrative adjudications, although tending to be less formal than traditional courtroom litigation, can be every bit as intense and acrimonious as traditional litigation.

woman ever answered their door. Instead, their child would answer and find out whom the caller wanted to see. If the caller was looking for the man, the woman would then come to the door and tell the caller that he did not live there and that she had never heard of him. Similarly, if someone came around looking for the woman, the man would come to the door and state that the woman did not live there. After discovering this, the investigator knocked at the door and told the child that he was looking for the man. When the woman came to the door, she was served with the summons and complaint.

SAMPLE COMPLAINT

IN THE UNITED STATES DISTRICT COURT FOR THE CENTRAL DISTRICT OF CALIFORNIA

Alan Booth,	)	Civil Action No. 92-1456
	)	
Plaintiff,	)	Complaint
	)	
v.	)	
	)	
LifeAir, Inc., an Illinois Corporation	)	
	)	
Defendant.	)	

This is a diversity action to recover money damages for serious bodily injury caused when the defendant's oxygen system exploded in a hospital room where plaintiff was a patient. Plaintiff demands a trial by jury.

Jurisdiction

1. This court has jurisdiction on the basis of diversity of citizenship pursuant to 28 U.S.C. §1332. Venue is appropriate in this court under 28 U.S.C. §1391.

DISCUSSION

CAPTION — This is called the "caption" of the lawsuit and indicates the court, the parties, the Docket Number (Civil Action No.), and the type of pleading (e.g., Complaint). When the complaint is filed with the court, the clerk gives it a civil action number. All subsequent papers filed with the court will contain the identical caption and civil action number, except of course for the name of the document.

INTRODUCTION — Short statement summarizing the case. The plaintiff also indicates that he wants the case tried by a jury as opposed to a judge.

JURISDICTIONAL STATEMENT — Informs the court that it has jurisdiction to hear this case because it is one between citizens of different states (i.e., diversity jurisdiction).

Parties

2. The defendant LifeAir, Inc., is a corporation organized under the laws of Illinois with its principal place of business in that state.

3. The plaintiff Alan Booth is a citizen of the State of California. Plaintiff resides at 8230 Aorta Street, Los Angeles, California.

PARTIES — Identifies the parties to the lawsuit. Notice how the plaintiff indicates that each party is a citizen of a different state. This is necessary because this is a "diversity" action in federal court.

Background

4. At all times relevant to this case, defendant LifeAir, Inc. manufactured and distributed oxygen systems to hospitals and other health care providers in at least 25 states, including California. An oxygen system of the type manufactured by defendant consists of a metal tank which contains gaseous oxygen under extreme pressure. The pressure in the tank is regulated by a series of valves and gauges.

5. On or about June 26, 1990, defendant entered into a two-year contract with Mercy Hospital, Los Angeles, California. Under the terms of that contract, defendant agreed to supply Mercy with 100 tanks of oxygen each month. At the end of each month, defendant would pick up the empty tanks and replace them with full tanks of oxygen.

6. The oxygen tanks supplied to Mercy by defendant were manufactured by defendant at its Illinois manufacturing facility. The tanks were refilled by defendant at its Los Angeles facility and were to be used by Mercy without further inspection.

7. On or about May 15, 1991, defendant sent a letter to all of its customers, including Mercy, advising them that it was introducing a new, highly innovative oxygen tank, known as the OX-A100. According to the announcement, the new tank was extraordinarily light and furthermore, incorporated a "state-of-

BACKGROUND — Lays out the facts that give rise to the complaint by telling the court and the defendant how the plaintiff was injured. Notice that the section is organized chronologically, like a story. This complaint contains details that could only have been gathered with a fair amount of investigation or significant help from the hospital. Indeed, the detail should alert defense counsel to the likelihood that the hospital and plaintiff may be working together.

The facts contained in this section will be used to support recognized "causes of action" or "claims."

the-art" computerized valve system. On or about June 1, 1991, defendant supplied to Mercy 100 OX-A100 tanks.

8. On June 2, 1991, Alan Booth underwent delicate surgery at Mercy Hospital. Following surgery, an OX-A100 oxygen tank was placed in Booth's hospital room and the oxygen from the tank was supposed to assist him in breathing following the surgery. The tank was located no more than 5 feet from Booth.

9. Shortly thereafter, on June 2, 1991, defendant's OX-A100 oxygen tank exploded, seriously injuring Booth.

Claim I
Strict Liability

10. Plaintiff incorporates by reference the allegations set forth in ¶¶1-9, above.

11. Defendant's OX-A100 oxygen tank contained a defect in design or manufacture, or both, which made the tank unreasonably dangerous.

12. As a proximate cause of the defect noted above, the tank exploded, seriously and permanently injuring the plaintiff.

13. As a result, the plaintiff has incurred and will continue to incur medical expenses, lost wages, and pain and suffering, all in excess of $75,000.

Claim II
Negligence

14. Plaintiff incorporates by reference the allegations set forth in ¶¶1-9, above.

15. Defendant negligently designed or manufactured, or both, the OX-A100 oxygen tank.

16. As a proximate cause of the defendant's negligence, the tank exploded, seriously and permanently injuring the plaintiff.

CLAIM I — Strict Liability: Plaintiff uses the facts in the background section to satisfy each element of a strict liability claim.

To support a strict liability claim, plaintiff must allege that the product was defective and that as a result of the defect the plaintiff was injured and incurred damages. This causal link is called "proximate causation." Notice that the plaintiff alleges that the amount of his damages exceeds $75,000. This allegation is presented to satisfy the minimum amount of damages necessary for diversity jurisdiction.

CLAIM II — Negligence: Plaintiff uses the facts in the background section to satisfy each element of a negligence claim.

To support a negligence claim, plaintiff must allege that the product was negligently designed or manufactured or both and that as a result of the negligence the plaintiff was injured and incurred damages.

17. As a result, the plaintiff has incurred and will continue to incur medical expenses, lost wages, and pain and suffering, all in excess of $50,000.

THEREFORE, plaintiff requests that the court enter judgment in his favor and against the defendant

RELIEF — Plaintiff sets forth the remedies that he is asking the court to grant.

    a. For damages in such amounts as to compensate the plaintiff for injuries sustained as a result of the defendant's conduct as described above;

    b. For court costs and post-judgment interest; and

    c. For such other relief as the court deems appropriate.

Ames, Fisher & Chun
Albert Ames (Bar #4350045)
113 Main Street
Smallville, California 91607
(818) 555-1234
Attorney for Plaintiff

SIGNATURE — Complaint must be signed by an attorney or by the plaintiff. Many jurisdictions require the attorney to note his or her bar number.

B   Pretrial Proceedings and Procedures

Drafting and filing the complaint and perfecting service on the defendant represent only the initial phase of litigation. The subsequent steps are designed to ready the case for trial by narrowing down the factual differences, resolving legal issues, and providing the parties with opportunities to settle the matter short of trial. For purposes of simplicity, it may be helpful to view the pretrial happenings as falling into three categories: (1) responsive pleadings; (2) discovery; and (3) pretrial statements.

1. Responsive Pleadings: Responding to the Complaint

a. *The Answer*

Once a defendant has been served with the complaint, he or she is required to file some sort of response. In the federal system, the response usually must be filed within 20 days of the date that service is perfected.[2] The initial response can take a variety of forms. One common response is called an answer. One purpose of an answer is to flesh out those factual aspects of the case where the plaintiff and defendant agree and to highlight those where they disagree. A typical answer consists of two parts. In the first part, the defendant responds to each of the factual allegations in the complaint by either admitting that a given allegation is true or denying that allegation. In the second part of the answer, the defendant can set forth certain affirmative defenses. For example, a defendant might allege as an affirmative defense that the statute of limitations has run (that is, the plaintiff waited too long to file suit). Below is a sample answer that defendant might use to respond to the sample complaint in *Booth v. LifeAir*.

SAMPLE ANSWER

IN THE UNITED STATES DISTRICT COURT
FOR THE CENTRAL DISTRICT OF CALIFORNIA

Alan Booth,	)	Civil Action No. 92-1456
	)	
	)	
Plaintiff,	)	Answer
	)	
	)	
v.	)	
	)	
LifeAir, Inc., an Illinois	)	
Corporation	)	
	)	
Defendant.	)	

The defendant, LifeAir, Inc., answers the plaintiff's Complaint in the above-captioned matter as follows:

1. Defendant lacks sufficient information to respond to the allegations contained in ¶1 of the Complaint and, therefore, denies each allegation in that paragraph.
2. Defendant admits the allegations set forth in ¶2 of the Complaint.

---

2. The federal government is normally given 60 days in which to file an answer to a complaint. This time period may vary, though, depending on the type of action involved. For instance, in suits arising under the Freedom of Information Act, the federal government must respond within 20 days, and in suits arising under the National Childhood Vaccine Compensation Act, the government is required to respond within 45 days.

3. Defendant lacks sufficient information to respond to the allegations contained in ¶3 of the Complaint and, therefore, denies each allegation in that paragraph.

4. Defendant admits the allegations contained in the first sentence of ¶4, and denies the allegations set forth in the remainder of that paragraph.

5. Defendant admits the allegations contained in the first sentence of ¶5, and denies the allegations set forth in the remainder of that paragraph.

6. Defendant denies the allegations in ¶6 to the extent that those allegations imply that all of the oxygen tanks supplied to Mercy by the defendant were manufactured at its Illinois facility and refilled at its Los Angeles facility. Defendant further denies the allegation that the oxygen systems supplied to Mercy by defendant were to be used by Mercy without further inspection.

7. Defendant admits the allegations contained in ¶7 of the Complaint.

8. Defendant lacks sufficient information to respond to the allegations contained in ¶¶8 and 9 of the Complaint and, therefore, denies each allegation in those paragraphs.

9. Defendant responds to the allegations in ¶10 by incorporating ¶¶1-8 of its Answer.

10. Defendant denies the allegations in ¶¶11-13.

11. Defendant responds to the allegations in ¶14 by incorporating ¶¶1-8 of its Answer.

12. Defendant denies the allegations in ¶¶14-17.

13. Defendant further denies that it is liable to the plaintiff in any sum and asks that judgment be entered in favor of the defendant and against the plaintiff.

Affirmative Defenses

FIRST DEFENSE

The Complaint fails to state a claim upon which relief may be granted, because plaintiff's action is preempted by the provisions of the Federal Food, Drug, and Cosmetic Act.

SECOND DEFENSE

Plaintiff's injuries, if any, were caused by a third party and not by the defendant.

THIRD DEFENSE

The product in question was used by a third party not in accordance with the manufacturer's instructions and that use was the sole cause of the injuries the plaintiff allegedly sustained.

Claire Winston, Esq. (Bar 44603)
Johnson & Winston
16144 Gold Coast Avenue
Los Angeles, CA 96387
(213) 555-1212
Attorneys for defendant LifeAir, Inc.

b. *Motion to Dismiss*

Rather than immediately filing an answer, a defendant may choose to file a motion to dismiss, which if granted by the trial court would terminate the suit immediately. A *motion to dismiss* is a direct challenge to the legal sufficiency of the complaint. For example, suppose that the suit in *Booth v. LifeAir* was filed on July 2, 1992, 13 months after the oxygen tank exploded. In California, suits to recover for personal injury must be filed within one year of the date of the injury — that is, the statute of limitations is one year. Thus, LifeAir could move to dismiss because the statute of limitations had run before the suit was filed. As you will learn in your civil procedure class, there are a variety of grounds on which a defendant can move to dismiss a complaint. A motion to dismiss, though, has one important limitation: When a court passes on the validity of the motion, it can only consider what has been presented in the complaint and, furthermore, the court must assume that all of the allegations in that complaint are true. For instance, if Booth did not state in the complaint the date on which the oxygen tank exploded, LifeAir could not file a motion to dismiss because it would not be apparent from the face of the complaint that the statute of limitations had run.

c. *Motion for Summary Judgment*

A motion to dismiss does not provide a terribly efficient means of disposing of meritless lawsuits because a court must assume, when ruling on that motion, that all the allegations in the complaint are true. As long as the plaintiff's allegations are legally sufficient, a court is duty bound to deny a motion to dismiss even though the court may know that the plaintiff will never be able to prove the allegations in his or her complaint. A motion for summary judgment (*see* Fed. R. Civ. P. 56(b)) is designed to fill this gap; it provides the courts with a way of "weeding out" meritless cases. It is designed to permit an early resolution to a case.

Summary judgment means a judgment without a trial; it can be entered in favor of either party. Summary judgment, however, is only appropriate if the evidence before the court indicates that there are no disputed issues of material fact and that the party making the motion is entitled to prevail on the undisputed facts. If there is a dispute over a material fact, then the court must deny the motion for summary judgment and permit the case to go to trial. The party against whom a summary judgment motion is filed does not have to prove his or her case in order to defeat the motion. All that party has to do is present *some* evidence that a material fact is in dispute. It is then up to the jury (if the case is tried before a jury) to figure out whose version is correct.

For example, in the sample complaint, *Booth v. LifeAir* (pages 28–31) the plaintiff alleged that the oxygen tank that exploded in his hospital room had been manufactured and distributed to the hospital by the defendant, LifeAir. LifeAir, in its answer, denied that the tank that exploded was one of its products. Suppose that during the course of discovery LifeAir learns that Mercy Hospital also purchased some of its oxygen tanks from another company, one of LifeAir's competitors. LifeAir, after reviewing Mercy's inventory records, discovers that after the explosion there were still 100 LifeAir tanks in the hospital. If the explosion had involved a LifeAir tank, there should only have been 99 tanks. LifeAir also learns that the hospital is unable to account for one of its competitor's tanks. To get to the bottom of the matter, LifeAir is provided with a piece of metal from the exploded tank. A metallurgical analysis reveals that the metal is not the type used by LifeAir but rather is identical to the metal used by its competitor.

Given all of this information, LifeAir is now in a position to file a motion for summary judgment. It attaches to its motion the hospital's inventory records and an affidavit from its expert metallurgist. In its motion, LifeAir argues that the plaintiff named the wrong defendant because the tank that exploded was not a LifeAir product. If the plaintiff, Booth, cannot produce some evidence rebutting LifeAir's evidence, then there is no genuine dispute over a material fact — that the tank that exploded was not a LifeAir product — and the court should enter a summary judgment.

However, suppose that Booth also has the metal tested by an expert retained by his attorney. That expert disagrees with LifeAir's expert and she concludes that the metal came from a LifeAir tank and not from a tank manufactured by LifeAir's competitor. Even though LifeAir's evidence is stronger (metallurgist plus inventory records) than Booth's evidence (metallurgist only), the court should deny LifeAir's summary judgment motion because there is now a genuine dispute over which company manufactured the tank. The jury will be left to decide which party is correct.

2. Discovery: Discovering What Happened

In the federal system and in all of the state systems, there are elaborate rules that permit the parties in civil actions to get a better idea of what really happened and what evidence the other side plans to introduce at trial. The discovery process, as it is known, is designed to minimize unpleasant surprises during the trial. As a result of discovery, each party should know, well before the trial ever starts, the identities of the witnesses whom the other party will call to testify, the nature of their testimony, and the documents that the other side will attempt to introduce into evidence. Aside from helping to shape trial strategy, discovery serves other critical purposes. First, it provides each party with sufficient information to objectively judge the merits of its case. Consequently, discovery ought to help the parties settle their dispute, thereby eliminating the need for an expensive and time-consuming trial. Second, discovery, if conducted in good faith, should also help the parties narrow the questions of fact that need to be resolved at trial, thereby shortening the trial.

All too frequently, though, discovery itself is extraordinarily expensive and time-consuming. In many cases, the parties spend more time fighting over the scope of discovery than actually trying the case.

There are a variety of different types of discovery, each with its own set of rules and procedures. Since this section is intended to provide you with an overview of the litigation process, we will describe only briefly some of the more common types of discovery. You will learn the limitations, intricacies, and nuances of the various discovery techniques in your civil procedure course.

a. *Interrogatories*

Interrogatories are written questions drafted by one party and intended to be answered by the other party. Normally, only parties to a lawsuit can be compelled to answer written interrogatories. While a party has wide latitude in developing interrogatories, some courts restrict the number of questions that can be asked.

Another type of discovery that is closely related to interrogatories is known as *requests for admissions*. Requests for admissions consist of a set of factual statements prepared by one party and sent to an opposing party. The party that receives the document is required to either admit or deny the validity of each assertion.

b. *Document Production*

Each side in a dispute normally asks the other to produce documents in its possession that meet certain critieria. In federal courts, document production is governed by Fed. R. Civ. P. 34, and most states have comparable rules. Under Rule 34, "[a]ny party may serve on any other party a request . . . to produce and permit the party making the request . . . to inspect and copy, any designated documents." Fed. R. Civ. P. 34(a). "The request shall set forth, either by individual item or by category, the items to be inspected and describe each with reasonable particularity." In practice, each side usually copies or scans its own documents and forwards them to the other side either in hard copy or on a CD or DVD.

Before a party produces its documents, it normally goes through each page of each document to make certain that the document does not contain material protected either by the attorney-client privilege or the attorney work-product privilege. *See Hickman v. Taylor*, 329 U.S. 495 (1947) (establishing the attorney work-product privilege). Materials protected by either privilege and that consequently will not be provided to the other side must be listed on a "privilege log," which is provided to the opposing side along with the documents produced. *See* Fed.R.Civ.P. 26(b)(5). The privilege log allows the receiving party to see which documents the other side has declined to produce and the reason why. The log must be detailed enough to allow the other side to evaluate the merit of the claimed privilege.

Because so much of discovery is now done using computers (for example, through the production of CDs and DVDs) and because more and more communication is being done through electronic mail, the Federal Rules of Civil Procedure have recently been modified to take into account electronic communications, both for filing documents and providing notices and for purposes of discovery. *See* Letter from Chief Justice Roberts to the Speaker of the House of Representatives and Vice President of the United States transmitting amendments to the Federal Rules of Civil Procedure (April 12, 2006).

c. *Depositions*

A *deposition* is an oral examination of a person under oath conducted by an attorney representing one of the parties. A party can depose any person who has evidence relevant to the case. The person being deposed does not have to be a party to the case. After the party that has initiated the deposition has completed his or her questioning, the other parties are permitted to question the witness.

Depositions are normally conducted in the office of one of the attorneys. The questions and answers are transcribed by a court reporter and can be used not only for certain purposes during the trial but to flesh out the facts in the event that a party wishes to file a motion for summary judgment.

C The Trial Brief

Once discovery has been completed, most courts require the parties in civil cases to submit trial briefs. A *trial brief* is a detailed outline of a party's case. The typical trial brief includes, among other things, a listing of each element of each claim that the party intends to prove at trial, along with the names of the witnesses and the documentary evidence that will be used to prove that element. The court may also require the parties to review the documentary evidence and other tangible exhibits that will be offered into evidence at trial and to stipulate beforehand, wherever possible, to the authenticity of a given piece of evidence. These stipulations are designed to streamline the actual trial by eliminating the need for a witness to authenticate a given exhibit.

Frequently, well before trial, a party may become aware of certain types of evidence which the opposing party may seek to introduce, but which the party believes to be legally objectionable. As part of the trial brief, a party may seek an advance ruling from the court concerning the admissibility of such evidence. This is often done through a "motion *in limine*."

In cases that will be tried before a jury, the trial brief will contain a party's proposed jury instructions. *Jury instructions* are the rules of law that the court will read to the jury immediately before the jury begins its deliberations. Each party is responsible for assembling a complete packet of proposed jury instructions, together with the relevant statutory and case law supporting each proposed instruction. The instructions that the judge actually reads to the jury will usually be drawn from the proposed instructions submitted by the parties.

D The Trial

Finally, after conducting innumerable depositions, drafting and arguing countless motions, reviewing and summarizing hundreds of documents, interviewing scores of witnesses, and engaging in many agonizing settlement conferences, your case is called for trial. All of your thorough pretrial preparation will give way to intense pretrial anxiety: Your stomach may knot up, you may wonder whether you are really prepared, and you may even conjure up the specter of your star witness being demolished during cross-examination. These are natural emotions and ones that you are likely to experience no matter how many cases you have tried. Indeed, some experienced trial attorneys have likened the opening morning of a trial to the opening night of a Broadway play — only without a script.

If you are about to start your first trial, these anxieties are likely to be amplified by fear of the unknown. You will be surprised by the number of seemingly trivial questions that will race through your mind when you enter the courtroom. Where should I sit? Should I look at the jury? How much latitude will the judge give me in questioning prospective jurors? These are a few of the questions that are not addressed in most law schools because the answers are best learned through experience.

In the following pages, we will outline the various stages of the typical civil trial and will emphasize those phases that normally receive scant attention in law school. However, we are doing so only to provide you with a context in which to better understand and appreciate the case materials that you will be reading in your other courses. This section is not intended to be a primer on trial practice.

1. Selecting the Jury

If a case is being tried before a jury, the first phase involves the selection of that jury. In civil actions, the size of the jury will vary from jurisdiction to jurisdiction. Typically, civil juries range in size from six to twelve jurors. Since the rules governing jury selection vary greatly from court to court and even from judge to judge, we will present only one of a number of possible methods.

Before the trial begins, court personnel will escort a large number of prospective jurors into the courtroom. Counsel for both parties will be provided with a list of the names, addresses, and perhaps professions of these individuals. The judge will then introduce the parties and their attorneys and will briefly tell the prospective jurors the type of case that will be tried. The judge will then ask the prospective jurors, usually en masse, a number of basic questions designed to determine if any members of the panel would be unable to judge the case without bias. For example, the judge might ask whether any prospective juror knows the parties, their attorneys, or any of the witnesses. Thereafter, the clerk of the court will randomly draw the names of a number of prospective jurors equal to the size of the jury. Thus, if the jury is to consist of six jurors, the clerk will draw six names. Those individuals will then be seated in the jury box, and the judge might then ask each of those individuals a series of more detailed questions. Many of these questions will have been submitted by the attorneys in advance in the trial briefs. In some courts, the attorneys may be given an opportunity to question each of these individuals. After the questioning has been completed, the court will ask each attorney if he or she wishes to challenge any juror for cause — that is, to ask the court to remove a prospective juror because the attorney believes that that juror will be unable to discharge his or her responsibilities in an unbiased manner. If a juror is removed for cause, the clerk will draw another name and that juror will be seated in place of the one who was stricken for cause. This new juror will then be asked a series of questions by the judge and perhaps by the attorneys. This process will continue until all parties have "passed for cause." Thereafter, each side will be given the opportunity to exercise a limited number of peremptory challenges, which means they may ask to strike any juror as a matter of right and without reason. Jurors who have been peremptorily challenged are replaced, and the process continues until both parties pass or exhaust their peremptory challenges, whichever occurs first.

2. Opening Statements

After the jury has been empaneled, counsel for each party is given the opportunity to make an opening statement to the jury, with plaintiff's counsel going first. In the opening statement, the attorney will outline her case and detail what she intends to prove at trial. An opening statement, unlike a closing argument, should not be argumentative.

3. The Cases-in-Chief

Following the opening statements, each party will be given an opportunity to present its case-in-chief, with the plaintiff again going first. The plaintiff will then call her first witness. Each witness who is called will be subjected to a direct examination by the party that called him or her, followed by cross-examination. After the cross-examination, the witness may be subjected to a redirect examination and a recross-examination. After the plaintiff has presented all of her witnesses, the plaintiff's case-in-chief is concluded and the plaintiff will "rest."

After the plaintiff has rested, the defendant presents his case-in-chief. The evidence introduced by the defendant should not only undercut the plaintiff's case, it should also support whatever affirmative defenses the defendant may have raised (for example, contributory negligence). Normally, a defendant will have both the burden of producing evidence (that is, introducing the first evidence) and the burden of proof (that is, proving the point by a preponderance of the evidence) with respect to each affirmative defense.

4. Motions after the Cases-in-Chief

At the conclusion of each party's case-in-chief, the opposing party, out of the jury's presence, may move for a directed verdict. For example, a defendant's motion for a directed verdict is a challenge to the sufficiency of the plaintiff's case-in-chief. The defendant is asking the court to take the case away from the jury and end the trial immediately because either the plaintiff has failed to present evidence supporting an essential element of the claim or the evidence presented was so weak that no rational jury could find for the plaintiff. In short, a motion for a directed verdict tests whether the party against whom the motion has been filed has discharged its burden of producing evidence.

5. Rebuttal

After the parties have presented their cases-in-chief—and assuming that the court denies the various motions for a directed verdict—the plaintiff will be given a limited opportunity to introduce evidence rebutting the evidence presented during the defendant's case-in-chief. The defendant is then given an opportunity to present evidence rebutting evidence presented during the plaintiff's rebuttal. It is important to recognize, though, that the scope of a rebuttal is limited to challenging evidence presented by the opposing party. Thus, a plaintiff may not use the rebuttal to cure defects in his or her case-in-chief.

6. Closing the Trial

After the evidentiary phase of the trial has ended, the parties make their closing arguments to the jury. A closing argument should be designed to convince the jury of the merits of a party's case. An effective closing argument will link the evidence presented to the law that the judge will read to the jury. Thus, if a given claim has four elements, the plaintiff's closing argument should highlight the evidence that has been presented to support each of these four elements and should aim to convince the jury that such evidence is more reliable and credible than the contrary evidence presented by the defendant.

Following closing arguments, the judge will *charge* the jury; that is to say, the judge will read to the jury the instructions of law that the jury must use in resolving the case. The jury will then retire to deliberate its verdict.

7. Motions Following the Verdict

The case does not end with a jury verdict. Rather, following the jury verdict, the parties may make a number of motions designed to overturn or modify that verdict.

a. *Motion for a Judgment Notwithstanding the Verdict*

One common post-trial motion filed by the party against whom the jury verdict was rendered is called a *motion for a judgment notwithstanding the verdict* or, simply, a motion for a judgment n.o.v. In federal courts, a judgment n.o.v. is now called a "judgment as a matter of law." Fed. R. Civ. P. 50. As its name implies, this motion is designed to nullify and take the place of the jury verdict. A motion for a judgment n.o.v. is similar to a motion for a directed verdict and the same criteria apply.

b. *Motion for a New Trial*

Another device designed to overturn a jury verdict is a *motion for a new trial*. In a motion for a new trial, a party seeks only to abrogate the jury verdict and not to have the court substitute its verdict for that of the jury. If a court were to grant a motion for a judgment n.o.v., it would enter a judgment in favor of the moving party. In contrast, if a court were to grant a motion for a new trial, it would set aside the jury verdict and order the case tried for a second time.

5

Reading, Analyzing, and Briefing a Case

A How to Approach a Case: A Primer

For more than a century, American law schools have been teaching students how to "think like a lawyer" through the so-called case method of study. In the *case method*, a student is asked to read, analyze, and critique a judicial opinion, usually an appellate court decision, and then to compare that case to other related cases. Each case should provide some insight into the law on a given legal issue. By piecing the various cases together, the student should be able to ascertain or synthesize the law on that issue. By studying cases, you will not only sharpen your analytical skills and learn the substantive law in a variety of areas, but you will also learn how to spot legal issues. The following material is intended to give you an overview of the case method of instruction and the basics of legal thinking and analysis.

During law school, you will read hundreds of judicial opinions or cases. You may wish to think of these judicial opinions as structured stories about legal disputes. Like any well-told story, a well-written opinion should flow logically. In the typical opinion, for instance, the judge will (1) set the scene by recounting the facts giving rise to the dispute, (2) put the dispute in a legal context by describing the case's procedural history and posture (for example, reviewing a motion to dismiss, a motion for summary judgment, a motion for a judgment n.o.v.), (3) formulate the legal issue or issues that must be resolved, (4) set out the legal rule that the court believes should apply to the case, (5) apply that rule to the facts of the case, thereby resolving the legal issue, and (6) present the rationale supporting the resolution.

Although there are similarities between a story and a case, for many reasons we recommend that you do not read an opinion as if it were merely a piece of fiction. First, if you do, you may be disappointed. Court decisions are usually written to inform and not to entertain.[1] Judges are more concerned with creating

---

1. Some judges do have a flair for the zany, and they occasionally interject this into their writings. Take *United States v. Syufy*, 903 F.2d 659 (9th Cir. 1990), an antitrust case involving movie theaters. Judge Alex Kozinski wove into his 8,500-word opinion the names of 200 movies and challenged movie critics and other aficionados of the cinema to find the concealed titles. For weeks the opinion was the hottest item on the desks of movie critics across the nation. One critic threw in the towel after having spent over a week going over the opinion word-by-word and finding only 70 titles.

a well reasoned opinion that will withstand the test of time (and review by a higher court) than they are with turning a phrase that will impress a literary critic. In fact, some opinions may be poorly written. Second, if you read an opinion as if it were a novel or newspaper, you are apt to miss many important nuances. As you will find, judicial opinions can be densely packed with subtle arguments and disclaimers. Third, a court's opinion is just that, an opinion, and as with any opinion, it is susceptible to criticism. Remember, the losing party's lawyer believed that his or her position was correct, and his or her client spent money to have that position forcefully argued. In short, there are at least two sides to every dispute. If you read an opinion too quickly or without a touch of skepticism, you may be ill-prepared either to evaluate it critically or to compare it to other cases dealing with related issues. And finally, court opinions should give you a glimpse into the future by indicating, sometimes quite obliquely, how a court might resolve similar disputes when and if they arise. Only by reading a case carefully and thoughtfully will you be in a position to appreciate its import and limitations. Accordingly, we suggest that you read each case as many times as possible. You may be surprised to find that on the third reading you are seeing things that you totally missed on the first or second reading. We also strongly recommend that after you have fully digested the case, you write a case brief.

Reading a case carefully will also provide you with clues about how judges, who are experienced writers, structure legal arguments. On page 48 is the case of *Lyons v. Lyons*, 2 Ohio St. 2d 243, 208 N.E.2d 533 (1965), from the Ohio Supreme Court. Read the case before proceeding further. The opinion in *Lyons* represents one type of case, namely, one where the court is reconsidering whether a well-established doctrine should continue to be the law in that jurisdiction. The plaintiff/husband is arguing that the doctrine of interspousal immunity (which bars one spouse from suing the other) should be curtailed. The opinion is organized around two themes. First, the court explains the reasons why the doctrine of interspousal immunity makes sense. And second, the court explains why its earlier opinions, cited by the husband, do not apply to the current dispute. The court is distinguishing the *Lyons* case from those other cases based on the facts of each.

There are other types of opinions. For example, courts are frequently asked to decide whether a well-established legal principle should apply to the facts of a given case. Sellers or manufacturers of products, for instance, can be held liable for injuries caused by their products even if they were not careless in making or designing the product. This is called *strict liability*. In contrast, individuals who provide a service (for example, physicians and lawyers) can only be held liable if they acted negligently. Suppose a newly constructed building collapses. A court might be asked to decide whether the building should be treated as a product, in which case the architect can be held strictly liable for designing a defective building, or whether designing a building should be treated as a service, in which case the architect can only be held liable if he or she acted negligently.

B Case Briefs

1. What Is a Case Brief?

A law school *case brief* (or *case abstract,* as it is sometimes called) is a formulaic condensation of a reported case, and it usually contains the following parts: (1) procedural posture or history of the case — discussion of how the case ended up before the appellate court (for example, defendant's motion to dismiss was granted and plaintiff appeals); (2) statement of the facts — a brief outline of those facts that appear to be significant to the court; (3) statement of the issue — a description of the legal issue addressed by the court; (4) holding of the case — a summary of how the court resolved the legal issue; (5) rationale — the reasoning used by the court in reaching its holding; and (6) comments and criticisms — your own observations about the court's holding and rationale. We will discuss each of these parts of a case brief in greater detail below.

2. Why Brief a Case?

Case briefing serves a number of valuable purposes. First, case briefing is a learning tool. It helps you focus on the structure of the opinion and on the thought processes used by the judge (or judges). Thus, case briefing will prevent you from reading an opinion as if it were a textbook and will get you into the habit of reading with a careful and critical eye. Second, case briefing serves as a valuable study aid. During your first year, your professors will call on you to discuss cases in class. A quick glance at your case brief will jog your memory and help you recall the salient aspects of the case. At the end of the semester, your case briefs, coupled with your class notes and outside reading, will enable you to assemble a course outline. And third, case briefing gives you an opportunity to practice legal writing.

3. Sample Case and Case Brief

To give you a better idea of what a case brief typically looks like, we have briefed the *Lyons* case and then discussed the brief.

Lyons, Appellee,
v.
Lyons, Appellant
No. 38915

2 Ohio St. 2d 243
Supreme Court of Ohio
June 16, 1965

Plaintiff . . . instituted this suit in the Common Pleas Court of Hancock County, seeking damages for personal injuries allegedly sustained as a result of the negligent operation of a motor vehicle by the defendant, plaintiff's wife, in Hancock County. . . .

It is agreed that at all times pertinent to this action the parties were married and living together as husband and wife.

A motion by the defendant for judgment on the pleadings was sustained by the Court of Common Pleas. Judgment was entered for the defendant.

The Court of Appeals reversed the judgment of the Court of Common Pleas. . . .

[The Supreme Court then agreed to hear the case.]

The question presented is whether one spouse may maintain an action for personal injuries resulting from the negligence of the other spouse, where the parties were married and living together as husband and wife at the time of the alleged injury.

At common law, a married woman lacks capacity to sue or be sued in her own name. This rule has been changed by statute in Ohio. Sections 2307.09 and 2323.09, Revised Code; *Damm v. Elyria Lodge No. 465, Benevolent Protective Order of Elks*, 158 Ohio St. 107, 107 N.E.2d 337. These statutes, however, do not remove *all* common-law immunities and disabilities as between spouses.

The public policy of this state is to promote marital harmony. Encouraging litigious spouses tends to foster marital disharmony. If a husband and wife are free to sue each other for real or fancied wrongs, this will place an additional burden upon the marriage relationship, and the home may well be split apart by the adversary roles which the spouses will be required to assume. *Thompson v. Thompson* (1910), 218 U.S. 611, 31 S. Ct. 111, 54 L. Ed. 1180; *Rubalcava v. Gisseman* (1963), 14 Utah 2d 344, 384 P.2d 389; *Goode v. Martinis* (1961), 58 Wash. 2d 229, 361 P.2d 941; *Campbell v. Campbell* (1960), 145 W. Va. 245, 114 S.E.2d 406.

Likewise, it is the public policy of this state to prevent fraud and collusion.

There is the real danger of fraud or collusion between the spouses in such suits against each other, where insurance is involved. Such suits encourage raids upon insurance companies. *See* dissenting opinion of Chief Justice Sims in *Brown v. Gosser* (Ky. 1953), 262 S.W.2d 480, 485, 43 A.L.R.2d 626.

It is argued that the task of weeding out fraudulent or collusive suits is properly within the sphere of courts and juries.

In truly adversary [sic] cases, fraud is likely to be uncovered because of the desire of the defendant to avoid the loss. Where insurance is involved, the risk of loss is removed, and both spouses stand to gain from a decision adverse to the defendant. This creates a strong inducement to trump up claims and conceal possible defenses. Smith v. Smith (1955), 205 Or. 286, 287 P.2d 572.

This court is aware that a number of jurisdictions allow such a suit as is before this court. *See, e.g., Penton v. Penton* (1931), 223 Ala. 282, 135 So. 481; *Klein v. Klein* (1962), 58 Cal. 2d 692, 26 Cal. Rptr. 102, 376 P.2d 70; *Overlock v. Ruedemann* (1960), 147 Conn. 649, 165 A.2d 335; *Lorang v. Hays* (1949), 69 Idaho 440, 209 P.2d 733; *Brown v. Gosser, supra.*

The Court of Appeals and appellee herein rely upon the case of *Damm v. Elyria Lodge, supra.* The question here presented was not before the court in that case. There the question was: "'May the wife of a deceased member of a voluntary unincorporated association maintain an action in tort against the association for a tort committed against her during her husband's lifetime?'" In the *Damm* case, there was not the danger of marital disharmony which this case presents, since the member spouse had died, and since the lodge was an impersonal organization. There was not the danger of collusion, since the member spouse had no opportunity to control the defense of the suit, and there was ample assurance, from the nature of the parties involved, that the suit would be conducted in an adversary [sic] manner. Further, there was authority for allowing suit in tort by a member of the immediate family against an unincorporated association with which another member of the family, who would ordinarily be immune from suit, was associated. *Signs v. Signs,* 156 Ohio St. 566, 103 N.E.2d 743. *See also Poepping v. Lindemann* (1964), 268 Minn. 30, 127 N.W.2d 512.

The focus of the *Damm* case was not whether a wife could sue her husband in tort, although that was discussed at great length. The focus of the case was upon allowing suit against an unincorporated association by one who, but for the concepts of personal immunity from a suit between spouses and the disability of a member to sue the organization, would have been prevented from recovering for an injury which was not in any logical sense committed by her husband. *See Koogler et al., Trustees v. Koogler,* 127 Ohio St. 57, 186 N.E. 725.

A distinction may be drawn between suits against unincorporated associations to which members of the family belong and suits by members of a family against other members of the family. A husband and wife have reciprocal duties of support under Section 3103.01, Revised Code, and parents have the duty to maintain and support their children under Section 3109.05, Revised Code. An organization has no such obligation and stands in a different relationship to those whom it injures from a member of a family who is charged with continued support and maintenance. The duty of support replaces the duty of compensation for injuries sustained by one because of the negligence of the other. . . .

This court is not convinced that a useful purpose would be served in overthrowing the rule of interspousal immunity from suit so well established in a majority of jurisdictions in this country. If there is to be a change in the public policy of the state in this regard, it should come from the General Assembly.

Saunders, Admr., v. Hill, Admr. (Del. 1964), 202 A.2d 807; *Ensminger v. Ensminger* (1955), 222 Miss. 799, 77 So. 2d 308; *Brawner v. Brawner* (Mo. 1959), 327 S.W.2d 808, 813, *certiorari denied* (1960), 361 U.S. 964, 80 S. Ct. 595, 4 L. Ed.2d 546; *Smith v. Smith, supra*; *Castellucci v. Castellucci* (R.I. 1963), 188 A.2d 467.

For the foregoing reasons, the judgment of the Court of Appeals is reversed. Judgment reversed.

TAFT, C.J., and ZIMMERMAN, MATTHIAS, HERBERT, SCHNEIDER and PAUL W. BROWN, JJ., concur.

<u>*SAMPLE CASE BRIEF*</u>

P/appellee   <u>D/appellant</u>
Lyons v. Lyons
Supreme Court of Ohio
2 Ohio St. 2d 243, 208 N.E.2d 533 (1965)

Procedural Posture

Trial court sustained D's motion for judgment on pleadings. Court of Appeals reversed. Supreme Court granted D's petition to review.

Facts

H

P injured in automobile accident as a result of his wife's allegedly negligent driving. P instituted negligence suit against his wife. At the time of the accident, P and D were living together as husband and wife.

Issues

Where spouses are living together at the time of the accident as husband and wife, does the doctrine of interspousal immunity bar one from suing the other for negligence?

Holding

Doctrine of interspousal immunity still pertains in Ohio and one spouse is barred from suing other spouse for negligence, if they are living together as husband and wife at the time of the accident.

Rationale

Doctrine of interspousal immunity promotes family harmony which would be undermined if spouses are placed in adversary roles. Doctrine also minimizes likelihood of collusive lawsuits, which may occur when insurance is available to pay the judgment. The doctrine is so well established in a majority of jurisdictions that if there is to be a change it should come from the legislature and not the courts.

Comments/Criticism

The doctrine of interspousal immunity appears to be a court-made doctrine. Therefore, there is no reason why a court should feel compelled to look to the legislative branch to change the doctrine. The court states that the doctrine promotes family harmony, but it provides no evidence to support that conclusion. Is the divorce rate, for example, higher in those states that permit spouses to sue one another? Similarly, are there more fraudulent and collusive lawsuits in those states that do not adhere to the interspousal immunity doctrine?

4. Discussion of Sample Brief

a. *The Names of the Parties and the Court*

Figuring out the cast of characters and their roles is generally a simple matter. In the majority of instances, the party filing the suit is called the *plaintiff* and the party being sued is called the *defendant.* The plaintiff's name appears first. In *Lyons,* for instance, the husband is the plaintiff, and the wife is the defendant. As you will learn, in certain situations the names of the parties may be different. For example, the party instituting the suit may be referred to as the *petitioner,* instead of the plaintiff, and the party defending the suit may be called the *respondent.*[2] The terms petitioner and respondent are usually used when a party is not seeking money, but instead is asking the court to force the other party to do something or not to do something.

When a case moves through the appellate system, the titles of the parties will be modified to reflect their status in the appellate process. In most jurisdictions, the party bringing the appeal before an intermediate appellate court is referred to as the *appellant,* and the party against whom the appeal is being brought is known as the *appellee.* Thus, a defendant in the lower court may be the appellant at the appeals court, if the defendant is the one appealing the case. In some state systems, the appellant may be referred to variously as the *plaintiff in error* or *petitioner* and the appellee as the *defendant in error* or *respondent.*

---

2. In admiralty law cases, the party instituting suit is sometimes called the *libelant,* and the person being sued is the *libelee.* In some of your courses, you may come across cases with the following type of odd caption: United States ex rel. Toth v. Quarles. Here the United States is the plaintiff, but the suit was not actually instituted by the government. Instead, the claims of the government were actually prosecuted by a private citizen called a relator. Thus, "United States ex rel. Toth" really means the "United States by the relator Toth." The relator is acting as a private attorney general, and if the relator wins, he or she can get a substantial reward, amounting to as much as 30 percent of what is collected. *See* False Claims Act, as amended, 31 U.S.C. § 3729 et seq.

As you may have noticed, we have put letters ("P" and "D") above the names of the parties to indicate who is who. You may find this convention useful because in some state systems (and in the Supreme Court of the United States) the order in which the parties appear in the case name may change on appeal. As a general rule, the order remains the same through the first level of appeal. For convenience, you may want to underline the party that prevailed in the case you are briefing.

b. *The Procedural Posture of the Case*

Each case that you have read has a procedural history. For example, in *Lyons* the plaintiff (husband) instituted suit against the defendant (wife) to recover for injuries sustained in an automobile accident. However, the case never went to trial. Instead, the defendant filed a motion for *judgment on the pleadings*, which is a type of motion to dismiss.[3] In this motion, the defendant is telling the court that even if everything that the plaintiff said in the complaint was true (for example, the defendant drove negligently and as a result the plaintiff sustained bodily injuries), the plaintiff still cannot maintain the suit. The trial court agreed with the defendant, granted the motion, and dismissed the case (that is, entered a judgment in favor of the defendant). The plaintiff then appealed to the intermediate appellate court, which reversed the trial court's judgment. The defendant then asked the state supreme court to review the intermediate appellate court decision. The state supreme court granted the defendant's request (that is, petition) to review.

c. *Statement of Facts*

In this section of your case brief, you should set out those facts that you believe were important to the court. A fact is worth mentioning in your case brief if you believe that a change in that fact could have changed the court's holding or reasoning. For example, notice how little the court tells us about how the accident occurred. We are not told how the wife drove negligently (did she speed, run a stop sign, fail to yield?), nor are we even told whether the husband was a passenger in the car. The court's statement of the facts neglects to mention how the accident arose because the manner in which the accident occurred is not really relevant to the way in which the court resolved the case. Nothing in the court's opinion depends on whether the wife was speeding or whether she ran a red light. Do you think it is relevant that the husband was injured in an automobile accident as opposed to some other form of accident? Although the court's

---

3. The primary difference between a motion to dismiss and a motion for judgment on the pleadings is timing: A motion to dismiss must be made before the defendant files her answer, and a motion for judgment on the pleadings can only be filed after the answer has been filed. *See* Fed. R. Civ. P. 12(b)-12(c).

reasoning does not depend on the nature of the accident, the fact that it involved an automobile accident, where insurance is usually available to pay any judgment, may have influenced the court. Do you think it is relevant that this was a negligence action as opposed to one in which one spouse is suing the other for battery, for example, wife or husband beating? This fact is probably relevant. Where spouse beating is involved, there may not be much "family harmony" to disrupt, and further, it is less likely that insurance would be available to cover the damages. Do you think that it is relevant that the spouses were living together as husband and wife at the time of the accident? If the accident occurred before marriage and they still decided to marry notwithstanding any lawsuit, it seems unlikely that the lawsuit would disrupt family harmony. If the parties got divorced or after the accident were living apart, do you believe that the doctrine should still apply?

d. *Statement of the Issue*

A well-written opinion should state up front the issue to be resolved. Sometimes, though, judges assume that the issue is so obvious that it need not be stated explicitly. In other cases, courts may state the issue and then actually proceed to resolve a whole set of other issues. Notice how we stated the issue in our case brief of *Lyons*:

> Where spouses are living together at the time of the accident as husband and wife, does the doctrine of interspousal immunity bar one from suing the other for negligence?

The issue could have been formulated in a number of other ways:

1. Where spouses are living together at the time of the accident as husband and wife, does the doctrine of interspousal immunity bar one from suing the other in negligence for injuries that arose in an automobile accident?
2. Where spouses are living together at the time of the accident as husband and wife, does the doctrine of interspousal immunity bar one from suing the other in negligence for injuries that arose in an automobile accident in Hancock County?
3. Does the doctrine of interspousal immunity bar one spouse from suing the other in tort?

Compare the issue as it appears in the case brief with restatements 1 and 2 above; they are progressively narrower. The first relates to cases involving the negligent operation of an automobile and the second to the negligent operation of an automobile in Hancock County. The more facts from a case that are included in the issue, the narrower the issue becomes. Conversely, the fewer the number of facts, the broader the issue. Thus, the third restatement does not include any limitation on whether the spouses were living together as husband and wife either at the time of the accident or at the time suit was filed, nor is it limited to negligence cases. Since the holding is nothing more than the resolution of the issue, the broader the issue, the broader the holding; conversely, the narrower the issue, the narrower the holding.

e. *Holding of the Case*

The holding section of your brief should summarize the court's resolution of the issue. The holding of the case is a measure of its precedent-setting value. An extremely narrow holding may limit the precedential value of the case. For example, suppose the court in *Lyons* had said: "Thus, we hold that the doctrine of interspousal immunity applies when (1) the spouses were living together as husband and wife at the time of the accident and suit, (2) the action is one for negligence, and (3) the negligent conduct involved the operation of an automobile." Arguably, such a holding would not directly apply to a case involving any accident other than one involving an automobile. It would not cover a case involving a household accident or one in which the accident occurred before the couple was married; it covers only suits instituted after marriage. There may be reasons why the interspousal immunity doctrine should be narrow. Can you think of some of them?

A court may make statements that go beyond the facts of the case and that are unnecessary to support its holding. Statements in a court's opinion that are not part of its holding and that are broader than justified by the facts of the case are called "dicta" (or in the singular, "dictum"). Although dicta can provide valuable clues about how the court would decide future cases involving different facts, dicta have only limited precedential value. For example, suppose that in *Lyons*, the court had stated the following: "While our holding in this case is limited to instances in which the spouses were living together at the time of the accident, there may be other situations, including cases when the accident occurred before marriage, in which the doctrine of interspousal immunity should be applied." This statement, had it been made by the court, could be classified as dictum: It is not necessary to support the holding, and it goes beyond the facts of the case. Even though it is dictum and therefore not a binding precedent, lower courts in Ohio could still view it as highly persuasive because it was issued by the highest court in that state.

f. *Rationale*

The most important part of any decision is the thought process used by the judges in reaching their holding. The rationale of the court gives you a glimpse into how that court or other courts might in the future decide a related case. Before you write up the court's rationale, you should try to dissect the reasoning to see precisely how the court's argument is constructed. The decision in *Lyons* is relatively straightforward and actually consists of two parts. In the first part, the court sets out the public policy supporting the doctrine of interspousal immunity: (1) the doctrine promotes family harmony, (2) the doctrine minimizes the likelihood of collusive (or fraudulent) lawsuits, and (3) the doctrine is so well established that any change should come from the legislature.

In the second part, the court explains why the case cited by the intermediate appellate court and by the husband, *Damm v. Elyria Lodge No. 465, Benevolent Order of Elks*, 158 Ohio St. 107, 107 N.E.2d 337 (1952), is not applicable. Notice how the supreme court distinguishes that case from *Lyons*. The court states that *Damm* did not address the same issue that is before the court in *Lyons*, and therefore, by implication, its holding does not apply. The court goes on to note that the facts of *Damm* and *Lyons* are different. We are told that in *Damm* the wife was not suing her husband directly but rather was suing an association that he happened to be a member of; also we are told that the husband was dead. Accordingly, in *Damm* there was no danger that family harmony would be disrupted nor that the suit was collusive.

Are there facts in *Damm* that the court fails to tell us about? Did the association commit the tort or did the husband, acting as an officer of the association, commit the tort? You may wish to go to the library and read *Damm*.

g. *Comments and Criticisms*

This is the place in your case brief where you can summarize your observations about the court's decision. You may also want to raise hypotheticals that test the outer limits of the opinion. For example, suppose that the automobile accident had occurred before the plaintiff and defendant were married. Would this affect the outcome of the case? Suppose that the husband had beaten his wife: Would the rationale of *Lyons* make sense?

Suppose that you represented a man who was injured when the car he was driving was rear-ended by a car driven by a woman. The man institutes suit against the woman, alleging that she drove negligently and ran a stop sign, with the result that he sustained a whiplash. The woman is insured, and she is defended by attorneys hired by the insurance company. During discovery in the case, the man and woman fall madly in love and want to get married. The man is worried, though, that if they get married the lawyers representing the woman will move to dismiss the lawsuit on the basis of *Lyons*. Should the two wait until after the suit is decided before getting married?

Immunizing certain groups or classes from normal civil suit has always been troubling for courts. Some courts have been able to grapple logically with issues of immunity, and other courts have not. Troubling doctrines can highlight a simple fact: Judges are only human, and sometimes their decisions are less than models of rational thought. You may wish to read *Roller v. Roller*, 37 Wn. 242, 79 P. 788 (1905), in which the Washington State Supreme Court held that a minor, unemancipated daughter could not maintain a civil action against her father for rape, even though her father had been convicted criminally of raping her and had served time in the state penitentiary for the crime. In reaching this conclusion, the court stated that common law prohibits a minor child from suing a parent for damages arising in tort. The *Roller* Court went on to note that this rule was based on society's interest in preserving family harmony. Should the *Roller* Court have applied the common-law rule where family harmony, if it ever existed, had been irreparably destroyed? *See Borst v. Borst*, 41 Wn.2d 642, 251 P.2d 149 (1952) (overruling *Roller v. Roller*). You may also wish to read *Abramson v. Reiss*, 334 Md. 193, 638 A.2d 743 (1994), where the Maryland Court of Appeals reaffirmed its century old rule of "charitable immunity," effectively barring suit against charitable organizations, other than hospitals. *Abramson* involved a basketball game at a Jewish Community Center that devolved into a punching match. Maryland remains one of the few states that still adheres to the rule.

While most courts have been able to develop logical and sound approaches to resolving issues of intrafamily immunity, many courts have had great difficulty applying similar techniques to the Foreign Sovereign Immunities Act, 28 U.S.C. § 1602 *et seq.*, which insulates most foreign governments from suit in the United States unless certain specific conditions exist. For the modern equivalent of *Roller v. Roller*, you may wish to read *Af-Cap Inc. v. Republic of Congo*, 462 F.3d 417 (5th Cir. 2006).

6

Synthesizing the Law from a Series of Cases

One of the most interesting aspects of the law is seeing how it responds to changing conditions and political winds. The law of torts is particularly interesting in this respect. During the nineteenth and early twentieth centuries, many courts imposed rules that made it difficult for a plaintiff to recover for injuries even when the defendant acted negligently. Responding in part to changing economic conditions, courts gradually began to adopt rules that made it somewhat easier for a plaintiff to prevail. In the opinion of many scholars, however, during the 1960s and 1970s the pendulum swung too far in the plaintiff's favor. Some courts responded by constricting the plaintiff's ability to maintain certain causes of action. The cases that follow document this evolution in the State of California in one small area of tort law: instances where a plaintiff witnesses an accident and suffers a severe emotional reaction as a result. After you read each case, try to figure out how that case modified the law, if at all. Read the cases carefully and critically. You should also brief each case. After each case is a series of questions that you should try to answer. Your instructor may discuss these questions during class.

As background, since early times courts had little difficulty dealing with cases a person suffered a physical injury, a broken arm, or paralysis, for example, as a result of an accident. Physical injuries were easy to see, easy to diagnose, and in most instances, hard to fake. Courts, however, had difficulty dealing with emotional distress caused by an accident. Most courts would not permit a plaintiff to recover for emotional distress unless the plaintiff first suffered a direct physical injury that in turn led to the emotional distress. This was called the *impact rule*. A few courts in limited instances, however, permitted a plaintiff to maintain a cause of action when there was no physical impact, as long as the emotional distress caused some discernible physical injury.

For example, in *Amaya v. Home Ice, Fuel & Supply Co.*, 59 Cal. 2d 295, 379 P.2d 513, 29 Cal. Rptr. 33 (1963), the plaintiff, after witnessing a truck negligently run over her 17-month-old child, suffered a severe nervous shock and subsequent bodily illness. She instituted suit against the company that owned the truck, seeking to recover for the emotional shock and illness. The California Supreme Court rejected the impact rule and held that a person could recover for mental anguish caused by witnessing a relative being injured, but only if the

55

person at risk of being physically injured, standing in the path of the truck, for instance. This became known as the *zone of danger rule*. The court in *Amaya* went on to hold that since the plaintiff was not in the zone of danger (she was not in the path of the truck), she could not maintain a cause of action against the truck company.

The first case presented below, *Dillon v. Legg*, 68 Cal. 2d 728, 441 P.2d 912, 69 Cal. Rptr. 72 (1968), expands the rule in *Amaya* by doing away with the zone of danger rule and replacing it with a more flexible standard. The next case, *Krouse v. Graham*, 19 Cal. 3d 59, 562 P.2d 1022, 137 Cal. Rptr. 863 (1977), further expands the rule. In the third case, *Thing v. La Chusa*, 484 Cal. 3d 64, 771 P. 814, 257 Cal. Rptr. 865 (1989), the California Supreme Court attempts to curtail the flexible standard and replace it with a more rigid standard designed to create greater certainty. The final three cases (*Fife v. Astenius, Wilks v. Hom,* and *Bird v. Saenz*) apply this new, more rigid standard. In reading these cases, always bear in mind the problems that could arise if courts were to treat emotional distress the same way they have treated physical injuries. For example, should a vegan be permitted to sue a vaccine manufacturer upon learning that the vaccine he had just received was manufactured with animal products? *See Friedman v. Merck & Co., Inc.* 107 Cal.App. 4th 454, 131 Cal.Rptr.2d 885 (2003).

Dillon v. Legg

Supreme Court of California
68 Cal. 2d 728, 441 P.2d 912, 69 Cal. Rptr. 72 (1968)

TOBRINER, Justice.

. . . In the instant case plaintiff's[1] first cause of action alleged that on or about September 27, 1964, defendant drove his automobile in a southerly direction on Bluegrass Road near its intersection with Clover Lane in the County of Sacramento, and at that time plaintiff's infant daughter, Erin Lee Dillon, lawfully crossed Bluegrass Road. The complaint further alleged that defendant's negligent operation of his vehicle caused it to "collide with the deceased Erin Lee Dillon resulting in injuries to decedent which proximately resulted in her death." (Complaint, p.3.) Plaintiff, as the mother of the decedent, brought an action for compensation for the loss.

Plaintiff's second cause of action alleged that she, Margery M. Dillon, "was in close proximity to the . . . collision and personally witnessed said collision." She further alleged that "because of the negligence of defendants . . . and as a proximate cause [*sic*] thereof plaintiff . . . sustained great emotional disturbance and shock and injury to her nervous system" which caused her great physical and mental pain and suffering.

---

1. For convenience, plaintiff will be used in the singular to denote the mother, although a minor sister is joined as plaintiff.

Plaintiff's third cause of action alleged that Cheryl Dillon, another infant daughter, was "in close proximity to the . . . collision and personally witnessed said collision." Because of the negligence, Cheryl Dillon "sustained great emotional disturbance and shock and injury to her nervous system," which caused her great physical and mental pain and suffering.

On December 22, 1965, defendant, after he had filed his answer, moved for judgment on the pleadings, contending that "No cause of action is stated in that allegation that plaintiff sustained emotional distress, fright or shock induced by apprehension of negligently caused danger or injury or the witnessing of negligently caused injury to a third person. *Amaya v. Home Ice, Fuel & Supply Co.*, 59 Cal. 2d 295, 29 Cal. Rptr. 33, 379 P.2d 513 (1963). Even where a child, sister or spouse is the object of the plaintiff's apprehension no cause of action is stated, *supra*, p.303, 29 Cal. Rptr. 33, 379 P.2d 513, *unless the complaint alleges that the plaintiff suffered emotional distress, fright or shock as a result of fear for his own safety. Reed v. Moore*, 156 Cal. App. 2d 43 (1957) at page 45 [319 P.2d 80]." (Italics added.) The court granted a judgment on the pleadings against the mother's count, the second cause of action, and denied it as to the sister's count, the third cause of action. The court, further, dismissed the second cause of action. Margery M. Dillon, the mother appealed from that judgment.

Thereafter, on January 26, further proceedings took place as to the third cause of action, Cheryl Dillon's claim for emotional trauma from witnessing her sister's death while "watching her sister lawfully cross Bluegrass Road."

Defendant moved for summary judgment on this count. In opposition, plaintiff contended that the declaration of one McKinley disclosed that Mrs. Dillon testified at her deposition that when she saw the car rolling over Erin she noted that Cheryl was on the curb, but that the deposition of Cheryl Dillon contradicts such statements. Plaintiff therefore submitted that "Since the declarations filed by defendant are contradictory and the testimony contained in the testimony of Mrs. Dillon does not establish as a matter of law that Cheryl Dillon was not in the zone of danger or had fear for her own safety, plaintiff respectfully submits that the motion must be denied."

The court denied the motion for summary judgment on the third cause as to Cheryl on the ground that the pretrial order precluded it. The trial court apparently sustained the motion for judgment on the pleadings on the second cause as to the mother because she was not within the zone of danger and denied that motion as to the third cause involving Cheryl because of the possibility that she was within such zone of danger or feared for her own safety. Thus we have before us a case that dramatically illustrates the difference in result flowing from the alleged requirement that a plaintiff cannot recover for emotional trauma in witnessing the death of a child or sister unless she also feared for her own safety because she was actually within the zone of physical impact.

The posture of this case differs from that of *Amaya v. Home Ice, Fuel & Supply Co.*, (1963) 59 Cal. 2d 295, 298, 29 Cal. Rptr. 33, 35, 379 P.2d 513, 515, which involved "fright or nervous shock (with consequent bodily illness) induced solely by . . . apprehension of negligently caused danger or injury to a third person" because the complaint here presents the claim of the emotionally traumatized mother, who admittedly was *not* within the zone of danger, as contrasted with that of the sister, who *may have been* within it. The case thus illustrates the fallacy of the rule that would deny recovery in the one situation and grant it in the other. In the first place, we can hardly justify relief to the sister for trauma which she suffered upon apprehension of the child's death and yet deny it to the mother merely because of a happenstance that the sister was some few yards closer to the accident. The instant case exposes the hopeless artificiality of the zone-of-danger rule. In the second place, to rest upon the zone-of-danger rule when we have rejected the impact rule becomes even less defensible. We have, indeed, held that impact is not necessary for recovery (*Cook v. Maier* (1939) 33 Cal. App. 2d 581, 584, 92 P.2d 434). The zone-of-danger concept must, then, inevitably collapse because the only reason for the requirement of presence in that zone lies in the fact that one within it will fear the danger of *impact*. At the threshold, then, we point to the incongruity of the rules upon which any rejection of plaintiff's recovery must rest. . . .

The possibility that some fraud will escape detection does not justify an abdication of the judicial responsibility to award damages for sound claims: if it is "to be conceded that our procedural system for the ascertainment of truth is inadequate to defeat fraudulent claims . . . , the result is a virtual acknowledgment that the courts are unable to render justice in respect to them." (*Chiuchiolo v. New England Wholesale Tailors* (1930) 84 N.H. 329, 335, 150 A. 540, 543.)

Indubitably juries and trial courts, constantly called upon to distinguish the frivolous from the substantial and the fraudulent from the meritorious, reach some erroneous results. But such fallibility, inherent in the judicial process, offers no reason for substituting for the case-by-case resolution of causes an artificial and indefensible barrier. Courts not only compromise their basic responsibility to decide the merits of each case individually but destroy the public's confidence in them by using the broad broom of "administrative convenience" to sweep away a class of claims a number of which are admittedly meritorious. The mere assertion that fraud is possible, "a possibility [that] exists to some degree in all cases" (*Klein v. Klein, supra*, 58 Cal. 2d 692, 695, 26 Cal. Rptr. 102, 104, 376 P.2d 70, 72), does not prove a present necessity to abandon the neutral principles of foreseeability, proximate cause and consequential injury that generally govern tort law.

Indeed, we doubt that the problem of the fraudulent claim is substantially more pronounced in the case of a mother claiming physical injury resulting from seeing her child killed than in other areas of tort law in which the right to recover damages is well established in California. For example, a plaintiff claiming that fear for his own safety resulted in physical injury makes out a well recognized case for recovery. (*Lindley v. Knowlton* (1918) 179 Cal. 298, 176 P. 440; *Webb v. Francis J. Lewald Coal Co.* (1931) 214 Cal. 182, 4 P.2d 532; *Vanoni v. Western Airlines* (1967) 247 Cal. App. 2d 793, 56 Cal. Rptr. 115.) Moreover, damages are allowed for "mental suffering," a type of injury, on the whole, less amenable to objective proof than the physical injury involved here; the mental injury can be in aggravation of, or "parisitic [sic] to," an established tort. (*Sloane v. Southern California Ry. Co.*, *supra*, 111 Cal. 668, 44 P. 320; *Acadia, California, Ltd. v. Herbert* (1960) 54 Cal. 2d. 328, 5 Cal. Rptr. 686, 353 P.2d 294; *Easton v. United Trade School Contracting Co.* (1916) 173 Cal. 199, 159 P. 597.) In fact, fear for another, even in the absence of resulting physical injury, can be part of these parisitic [sic] damages. (*Acadia, California, Ltd. v. Herbert*, *supra*, 54 Cal. 2d 328, 337, 5 Cal. Rptr. 686, 353 P.2d 294; *Easton v. United Trade School Contracting Co.*, *supra*, 173 Cal. 199, 202, 159 P. 597.) And emotional distress, if inflicted intentionally, constitutes an independent tort. (*State Rubbish Collectors Assn. v. Siliznoff* (1952) 38 Cal. 2d 330, 338, 240 P.2d 282.) The danger of plaintiffs' fraudulent collection of damages for nonexistent injury is at least as great in these examples as in the instant case. . . .

We note, first, that we deal here with a case in which plaintiff suffered a shock which resulted in physical injury and we confine our ruling to that case. In determining, in such a case, whether defendant should reasonably foresee the injury to plaintiff, or, in other terminology, whether defendant owes plaintiff a duty of due care, the courts will take into account such factors as the following: (1) Whether plaintiff was located near the scene of the accident as contrasted with one who was a distance away from it. (2) Whether the shock resulted from a direct emotional impact upon plaintiff from the sensory and contemporaneous observance of the accident, as contrasted with learning of the accident from others after its occurrence. (3) Whether plaintiff and the victim were closely related, as contrasted with an absence of any relationship or the presence of only a distant relationship.

The evaluation of these factors will indicate the *degree* of the defendant's foreseeability: obviously defendant is more likely to foresee that a mother who observes an accident affecting her child will suffer harm than to foretell that a stranger witness will do so. Similarly, the degree of foreseeability of the third person's injury is far greater in the case of his contemporaneous observance of the accident than that in which he subsequently learns of it. The defendant is more likely to foresee that shock to the nearby, witnessing mother will cause physical harm than to anticipate that someone distant from the accident will suffer more than a temporary emotional reaction. All these elements, of course, shade into each other; the fixing of obligation, intimately tied into the facts, depends upon each case.

In light of these factors the court will determine whether the accident and harm was *reasonably* foreseeable. Such reasonable foreseeability does not turn on whether the particular defendant as an individual would have in actuality foreseen the exact accident and loss; it contemplates that courts, on a case-to-case basis, analyzing all the circumstances, will decide what the ordinary man under such circumstances should reasonably have foreseen. The courts thus mark out the areas of liability, excluding the remote and unexpected.

In the instant case, the presence of all the above factors indicates that plaintiff has alleged a sufficient prima facie case. Surely the negligent driver who causes the death of a young child may reasonably expect that the mother will not be far distant and will upon witnessing the accident suffer emotional trauma. As Dean

Prosser has stated: "when a child is endangered, it is not beyond contemplation that its mother will be somewhere in the vicinity, and will suffer serious shock." (Prosser, The Law of Torts, *supra*, at p.353. *See also* 2 Harper & James, The Law of Torts, *supra,* at p.1039.)

We are not now called upon to decide whether, in the absence or reduced weight of some of the above factors, we would conclude that the accident and injury were not reasonably foreseeable and that therefore defendant owed no duty of due care to plaintiff. In future cases the courts will draw lines of demarcation upon facts more subtle than the compelling ones alleged in the complaint before us. . . .

The judgment is reversed.

OBSERVATIONS AND QUESTIONS

1. The procedural history of this case is interesting and illustrates the difference between a motion to dismiss and a motion for summary judgment. The defendant, after answering the complaint, filed a motion for a judgment on the pleadings. A judgment on the pleadings is identical to a motion to dismiss except that it is filed *after* an answer has been filed. A motion to dismiss is filed *before* the answer is filed. In resolving a motion for judgment on the pleadings, the court must assume that everything in the plaintiffs' complaint is true. Here, the sister, Cheryl, alleged that she witnessed her sister's death while "watching her sister lawfully cross Bluegrass Road." Apparently, the trial court liberally construed this statement as an allegation that Cheryl was in the zone of danger. Therefore, the trial court denied the defendant's motion. However, the mother's cause of action did not contain this statement, and therefore, the trial court concluded that the mother had not alleged that she was in the zone of danger. The trial court granted the defendant's motion and dismissed the mother's cause of action for the negligent infliction of emotional distress.

   Later the defendant filed a motion for summary judgment against the sister's claim for the negligent infliction of emotional distress. The court denied the motion because there was conflicting evidence regarding precisely where Cheryl was when she witnessed her sister being struck by the defendant's car. Where there is conflicting evidence on a material issue of fact, courts will let the jury decide.

2. The structure and logical flow of the California Supreme Court's opinion is worth noting. The court begins by showing that the zone of danger test is unnecessarily rigid and makes little sense. The court then discusses and rejects the notion that a rigid test is needed where emotional injuries are involved because emotional distress is too easily faked. Finally, the court presents its own more flexible test.

3. Under *Dillon*, what must a plaintiff prove to successfully maintain an action for the negligent infliction of emotional distress? The court sets

out three factors that a trial court can use in deciding whether the defendant can reasonably foresee injury to the plaintiff. Look at how the court applies these factors to resolve the issue in *Dillon*. Note that the three "factors" used to decide "foreseeability" were not intended to be hard-and-fast requirements. Thus, in *Archibald v. Braverman*, 275 Cal. App. 2d 253, 79 Cal. Rptr. 723 (1969), the court permitted a mother to recover for the negligent infliction of emotional distress even though she did not witness the accident but arrived at the scene moments after it had occurred. The *Archibald* court believed that the emotional distress to the mother was reasonably foreseeable.

4. Under the court's opinion, does the judge or jury decide whether a plaintiff has satisfied *Dillon*'s foreseeability test? Actually, both the judge and the jury get an opportunity to apply the test. The judge first must decide whether the plaintiff has introduced some evidence to prove foreseeability. If the plaintiff has introduced some evidence of foreseeability, the case then goes to the jury, which decides whether the plaintiff has actually proven his or her case.

5. How important do you believe the particular facts of this case were to the court's decision? Notice how the court uses the facts to argue that the zone of danger test leads to illogical results. Specifically, the court argues that under the zone of danger test the sister (Cheryl) could recover, but the mother, who witnessed the very same events, could not recover because she was a few yards farther away from the accident and thus outside the zone of danger.

6. Do you believe that the court recognized the possibility that its new test might be too flexible? Read the final sentence of the edited case.

7. Justice Tobriner, while on the California Court of Appeal, also wrote the opinion in *Amaya,* which was later reversed by the California Supreme Court.

Krouse v. Graham

Supreme Court of California
19 Cal. 3d 59, 562 P.2d 1022, 137 Cal. Rptr. 863 (1977)

RICHARDSON, Justice.

. . . Multiple plaintiffs—Benjamin Krouse, the five Krouse children and Vinka Mladinov—brought this action for personal injuries, emotional suffering, and wrongful death against defendant, the driver of an automobile which was being operated in the City of Burbank and struck the Krouses' parked car, killing Elizabeth Krouse and injuring her husband, Benjamin, and Mladinov, their neighbor. Immediately prior to the collision, the Krouse automobile had been parked at the curb in front of Mladinov's house. While Benjamin remained in the driver's seat, his wife, Elizabeth, and Mladinov removed groceries from the back seat of the car. When Elizabeth and Mladinov returned to the curb and commenced to shut the car door, defendant's vehicle approached the rear of the Krouse vehicle, straddled the curb, and struck both women before colliding with the rear of the parked car. The force of the impact propelled the Krouse vehicle 70 feet forward, threw Mladinov approximately 20 feet into an embankment, and hurled Elizabeth under defendant's vehicle.

Defendant admitted liability, and the trial of the case was limited to the issue of damages. The evidence and instructions to the jury concerned various theories of recovery for the respective plaintiffs, including (1) wrongful death damages for Benjamin Krouse and the five Krouse children, (2) damages for the physical and emotional injuries sustained by Benjamin, and (3) damages for the physical injuries suffered by Mladinov.

The jury returned three separate verdicts for plaintiffs in the aggregate sum of $442,000. Benjamin and the Krouse children were awarded $300,000 in a lump sum for Elizabeth's wrongful death, to be divided by the trial court between these plaintiffs. Benjamin was also awarded $52,000 for his personal injuries and emotional suffering. Mladinov was awarded $90,000 for her personal injuries. The court denied defendant's motion for new trial, which motion was supported by jurors' declarations regarding certain alleged jury misconduct.

Defendant appeals, asserting that the trial court erred in (1) instructing the jury that Benjamin could recover wrongful death damages for loss of his wife's "love, companionship, comfort, affection, society, solace or moral support [and] any loss of enjoyment of sexual relations . . .," (2) instructing the jury that the Krouse plaintiffs could recover wrongful death damages for "mental and emotional distress," (3) instructing the jury that Benjamin could recover for his physical and emotional injuries incurred by reason of his mere presence at the accident scene, (4) admitting assertedly inflammatory photographs and testimony regarding the accident scene, and (5) denying defendant's motion for new trial.

We examine defendant's claims, combining in one section his first two contentions, both pertaining to the wrongful death instructions. . . .

2. The Verdict for Emotional Distress Inflicted upon Benjamin Krouse

In addition to his participation in the wrongful death action, Benjamin asserted a separate cause of action for himself both for his physical injuries and emotional distress resulting from his presence at the accident scene, and his perception of Elizabeth's death. His physical injuries included a broken shoulder bone and scalp laceration which required sutures. These injuries evidently were not severe for Benjamin was discharged from the hospital on the day following the accident, and his shoulder was substantially healed within a month thereafter.

He also sought recovery for the emotional trauma incident to his witnessing of his wife's death. (*See Dillon v. Legg, supra*, 68 Cal. 2d 728, 69 Cal. Rptr. 72, 441 P.2d 912.) The evidence on this issue was extensive. It included Benjamin's own description of the event, the Krouse children's testimony as to Benjamin's emotional suffering after the accident, psychiatric testimony explaining the psychological therapy necessary to treat Benjamin's severely depressed state of mind, and medical testimony detailing the physical effects of the emotional trauma sustained by Benjamin during this extended period of depression. Cross-examination of the psychiatrist who treated Benjamin disclosed that Benjamin's anger and feelings of retribution toward defendant contributed in part to his condition, although other testimony indicated that the depression due to the loss of his wife weighed more heavily as a cause of his psychological injury.

The following instruction was requested by Benjamin and, over defendant's objection, was read to the jury with respect to Benjamin's claim for emotional distress: "In the event you find that Benjamin Clifford Krouse suffered emotional distress or mental depression as a result of *being present* at the time his wife Elizabeth Krouse was injured on January 20, 1972, you are instructed to award reasonable compensation to Benjamin Clifford Krouse for emotional distress, fright, shock, mental depression, psychological upset, and physical harm associated with the elements of mental distress." (Italics added.) As previously noted, the jury returned a separate verdict in Benjamin's favor for $52,000, presumably representing damages for both his personal injuries and his emotional distress.

Defendant criticizes the foregoing instruction on two grounds. First, he contends that the instruction was inappropriate because Benjamin admitted that he did not actually see his wife being struck by defendant's car nor immediately observe the effect of the impact upon her. Second, defendant argues that the instruction was an improper statement of the legal principle announced in *Dillon v. Legg, supra,* 68 Cal. 2d 728, 69 Cal. Rptr. 72, 441 P.2d 912, because it permitted recovery on the basis of Benjamin merely being "present" at the accident scene without proof, additionally, that he suffered physical injury as a result of having viewed the accident. We disagree with the first contention and agree with the second.

In *Dillon v. Legg, supra,* we held that, "a mother who suffers emotional trauma and physical injury from witnessing the infliction of death or injury to her child" (p.730, 69 Cal. Rptr. p.74, 441 P.2d p.914) should be permitted to recover damages therefor. In *Dillon,* the plaintiff alleged that she " 'was in close proximity to the . . . collision and personally witnessed said collision,' " (p.731, 69 Cal. Rptr. p.74, 441 P.2d p.914) and that, as a proximate result she " 'sustained great emotional disturbance and shock and injury to her nervous system' which caused her great physical and mental pain and suffering.' " (Ibid.) In considering whether the foregoing allegations stated a tortious cause of action, we emphasized the primary nature of the element of foreseeability in establishing the essential ingredient of a duty of care, using the following language: "We note, first, that we deal here with a case in which plaintiff suffered a shock which resulted in physical injury and we confine our ruling to that case. In determining, in such a case, whether defendant should reasonably foresee the injury to plaintiff, or, in other terminology, whether defendant owes plaintiff a duty of due care, the courts will take into account such factors as the following: (1) Whether plaintiff was located near the scene of the accident as contrasted with one who was a distance away from it. (2) Whether the shock resulted from a *direct emotional impact upon plaintiff from the sensory and contemporaneous observance of the accident,* as contrasted with learning of the accident from others after its occurrence. (3) Whether plaintiff and the victim were closely related, as contrasted with an absence of any relationship or the presence of only a distant relationship." (Id., at pp.740-741, 69 Cal. Rptr. at p.80, 441 P.2d at p.920, italics added.)

We have, subsequently, reemphasized the requirement that the traumatic shock which plaintiff suffers must result in some form of physical injury. In *Capelouto v. Kaiser Foundation Hospitals* (1972) 7 Cal. 3d 889, 892, footnote 1, 103 Cal. Rptr. 856, 858, 500 P.2d 880, 882, we upheld the rejection of an instruction to the effect that " '. . . a witness to injuries to his child may recover damages for any physical effects upon himself as well as for any mental or emotional distress which he may suffer,' " stating "[t]he refused instruction would permit recovery on an additional ground: injuries caused to the parents by the mere *witnessing* of the child's suffering. The trial judge properly rejected this latter instruction, which was based upon our holding in *Dillon v. Legg* (1968) 68 Cal. 2d 728 [69 Cal. Rptr. 72, 441 P.2d 912, 29 A.L.R.3d 1316]. *Dillon* makes clear that a parent may recover for witnessing a child's distress only if the parent suffers actual physical injury. (68 Cal. 2d at p.740, 69 Cal. Rptr. 72, 441 P.2d 912.) The record in the present case, while demonstrating that Kim's parents suffered the emotional distress and mental anguish that is normal for parents of a seriously ill or injured child, does *not* reveal that the parents suffered the actual physical injury necessary for recovery under *Dillon*." (Ibid.; *see also Hair v. County of Monterey* (1975) 45 Cal. App. 3d 538, 542, 119 Cal. Rptr. 639.)

Decisional law has also imposed on the remedy temporal limitations which flow from *Dillon's* requirement that the injury result "from the sensory and contemporaneous observance of the accident. . . ." (*Dillon, supra,* at p.740, 69 Cal. Rptr. at p.80, 441 P.2d at p.920.) The appellate court in *Archibald v. Braverman* (1969) 275 Cal. App. 2d 253, 79 Cal. Rptr. 723, for example, extended recovery to the mother of an injured child who "did not actually witness the tort *but viewed the child's injuries within moments* after the occurrence of the injury-producing event." (*Id.,* at p.255, 79 Cal. Rptr. at p.724, italics added.) Conversely, however, in *Deboe v. Horn* (1971) 16 Cal. App. 3d 221, 94 Cal. Rptr. 77, the court denied recovery to a wife who was not present at the scene of the accident and was unaware of her husband's injury until summoned to the hospital emergency room. Recovery was also refused in *Powers v. Sissoev* (1974) 39 Cal. App. 3d 865, 114 Cal. Rptr. 868, to a parent who first learned of the child's injury 30 to 60 minutes after the accident.

We confirm the propriety of the expression in *Archibald, supra,* that the *Dillon* requirement of "sensory and contemporaneous observance of the accident" does not require a *visual* perception of the impact causing the death or injury. In the matter before us, although Benjamin did not see Elizabeth struck by defendant's automobile, he fully perceived the fact that she had been so struck, for he knew her position an instant before the impact, observed defendant's vehicle approach her at a high speed on a collision course, and realized that defendant's car must have struck her. Clearly, under such circumstances Benjamin must be deemed a percipient witness to the impact causing Elizabeth's catastrophic injuries.

In evaluating defendant's second contention, we note that there was substantial evidence from which the jury could find that Benjamin suffered serious shock to his nervous system causing a gastric disturbance for which he was subsequently treated. This gastric problem constituted a sufficient "physical injury" to qualify under *Dillon* if it can be said fairly that it was caused by Benjamin's shock occasioned by his perception of the collision.

The jury had before it, however, conflicting evidence with respect to the precise cause of the gastric condition. Doctor Dasher, an internist, surmised that the gastrointestinal symptoms were most likely aggravated by Benjamin's "involvement in an accident with his wife." Similarly, Doctor Schmidt, a psychiatrist, testified that Benjamin's severe depression "was brought about by Mr. Krouse's witnessing his wife's death and suffering the loss of his wife." On the other hand, Doctor Schmidt also testified that Benjamin's feelings of anger and retribution were a contributing factor to the latter's state of mind. This latter testimony, together with the fact that apparently there was a remission of Benjamin's symptoms upon his remarriage, could have supported a contrary finding. Doctor Schmidt opined that Benjamin's depression "due to the loss of his wife" contributed more heavily to defendant's [sic] condition than such factors as anger or retribution. Doctor Schmidt, however, never established that Benjamin's depression resulted primarily from *witnessing the accident* (as opposed to his sustaining of grief and sorrow incident to her death). Therefore, there remained a substantial question for jury resolution—was Benjamin's physical injury caused by (1) witnessing his wife's death, (2) his understandable feelings of anger and retribution, or (3) his feelings of grief and sorrow over the loss of his wife?

The instruction at issue did not correctly and accurately assist the jury in its critical inquiry, for it permitted Benjamin to recover damages for emotional distress because of his mere presence at the accident scene, without regard to whether or not such distress was caused by the direct emotional impact of his sensory and contemporaneous observance of the accident. (In passing, we note that a correct formulation of the relevant principles is contained in newly adopted BAJI instructions (Cal. Jury Instructions, Civil, Supp. Service, Pamphlet No. 2 (1976) 12.83, 12.84, pp.58-60).

Furthermore, the giving of the foregoing instruction, permitting recovery because of Benjamin's merely "being present," coupled with the substantial conflict regarding the precise cause of Benjamin's emotional distress and resulting injuries, was clearly prejudicial. It is reasonable to assume that a significant portion of the $52,000 award in Benjamin's favor may have been intended by the jury to compensate him for such improper elements as grief, sorrow, anger and retribution. We conclude that the improper instruction probably misled the jury and affected its verdict. (*See Henderson v. Harnischfeger Corp., supra*, 12 Cal. 3d 663, 670, 117 Cal. Rptr. 1, 527 P.2d 353.) It follows, accordingly, that the verdict in Benjamin's favor must be set aside.

OBSERVATIONS AND QUESTIONS

1. What is the procedural posture of this case? Notice that the defendant lost in the trial court and is now arguing that the judge improperly instructed the jury on the issue of emotional trauma. What is it about the jury instruction that the defendant argues was incorrect? The defendant argues that the instruction on the negligent infliction of emotional distress was incorrect in two ways. Thus, the jury instruction gives rise to two distinct issues. What are those two issues?

2. What are the holdings in *Krouse*?

3. How do you believe the *Amaya* court would have resolved the issue of whether it is necessary to visually perceive the accident? Was Krouse in the zone of danger? How would Krouse have fared under the impact rule?

4. The court in *Krouse* reversed the judgment in favor of the plaintiff because the jury instruction did not require the jury to find that the plaintiff's emotional distress caused a physical injury. Three years later, in *Molien v. Kaiser Foundation Hospitals, Inc.*, 27 Cal. 3d 916, 616 P.2d 813, 167 Cal. Rptr. 831 (1980), the court eliminated this requirement and permitted a plaintiff to recover even though the emotional distress did not lead to any physical illness.

Thing v. La Chusa

Supreme Court of California
48 Cal. 3d 644, 771 P.2d 814, 257 Cal. Rptr. 865 (1989)

EAGLESON, Justice.

The narrow issue presented by the parties in this case is whether the Court of Appeal correctly held that a mother who did not witness an accident in which an automobile struck and injured her child may recover damages from the negligent driver for the emotional distress she suffered when she arrived at the accident scene. The more important question this issue poses for the court, however, is whether the "guidelines" enunciated by this court in *Dillon v. Legg* (1968) 68 Cal. 2d 728, 69 Cal. Rptr. 72, 441 P.2d 912, are adequate, or if they should be refined to create greater certainty in this area of the law. . . .

I

On December 8, 1980, John Thing, a minor, was injured when struck by an automobile operated by defendant James V. La Chusa. His mother, plaintiff Maria Thing, was nearby, but neither saw nor heard the accident. She became aware of the injury to her son when told by a daughter that John had been struck by a car. She rushed to the scene where she saw her bloody and unconscious child, whom she believed was dead, lying in the roadway. Maria sued defendants, alleging that she suffered great emotional disturbance, shock, and injury to her nervous system as a result of these events, and that the injury to John and emotional distress she suffered were proximately caused by defendants' negligence.

The trial court granted defendants' motion for summary judgment, ruling that, as a matter of law, Maria could not establish a claim for negligent infliction of emotional distress because she did not contemporaneously and sensorily perceive the accident. Although prior decisions applying the guidelines suggested by this court in *Dillon v. Legg, supra*, 68 Cal. 2d 728, 69 Cal. Rptr. 72, 441 P.2d 912, compelled the ruling of the trial court, the Court of Appeal reversed the judgment dismissing Maria's claim after considering the decision of this court in *Ochoa v. Superior Court* (1985) 39 Cal. 3d 159, 216 Cal. Rptr. 661, 703 P.2d 1. The Court of Appeal reasoned that while Maria's argument, premised on *Molien v. Kaiser Foundation Hospitals* (1980) 27 Cal. 3d 916, 167 Cal. Rptr. 831, 616 P.2d 813, that she was a direct victim of La Chusa's negligence, did not afford a basis for recovery, contemporaneous awareness of a sudden occurrence causing injury to her child was not a prerequisite to recovery under *Dillon*.

We granted review to consider whether *Ochoa* supports the holding of the Court of Appeal. We here also further define and circumscribe the circumstances in which the right to such recovery exists. To do so it is once again necessary to return to basic principles of tort law. . . .

IV

Post-Dillon *Extension*

The expectation of the *Dillon* majority that the parameters of the tort would be further defined in future cases has not been fulfilled. Instead, subsequent decisions of the Courts of Appeal and this court, have created more uncertainty. And, just as the "zone of danger" limitation was abandoned in *Dillon* as an arbitrary restriction on recovery, the *Dillon* guidelines have been relaxed on grounds that they, too, created arbitrary limitations on recovery. Little consideration has been given in post-*Dillon* decisions to the importance of avoiding the limitless exposure to liability that the pure foreseeability test of "duty" would create and towards which these decisions have moved.

Several post-*Dillon* decisions of this court are particularly noteworthy in this expansive progression. In the first, *Krouse v. Graham* (1977) 19 Cal. 3d 59, 137 Cal. Rptr. 863, 562 P.2d 1022, this court held that the NIED [negligent infliction of emotional distress] plaintiff need not "visually" perceive the third party injury to satisfy the *Dillon* guideline suggesting that the plaintiff suffer shock from "'the sensory and contemporaneous observance of the accident, . . .'" It was sufficient that the plaintiff knew the position of his wife just outside the automobile in which he was seated the instant before she was struck by defendant's automobile which he had seen and realized was going to strike her. He was, therefore, a "percipient witness to the impact causing [her] injuries." (19 Cal. 3d 59, 76, 137 Cal. Rptr. 863, 562 P.2d 1022.)

We also find in *Krouse, supra,* 19 Cal. 3d 59, 137 Cal. Rptr. 863, 562 P.2d 1022, the roots of the uncertainty reflected by the instant case over whether the plaintiff must perceive the injury causing incident at all or may recover for emotional distress suffered on viewing its "immediate consequences" even though not present at the scene when it occurred. *Krouse* created uncertainty as to the meaning and importance of the plaintiff's status as a "percipient witness" by approving the conclusion of the Court of Appeal in *Archibald v. Braverman* (1969) 275 Cal. App. 2d 253, 79 Cal. Rptr. 723, that visual perception of the accident was not required without commenting on the context in which the *Archibald* court made its ruling. That decision had allowed recovery by a mother who "did not actually witness the tort but viewed the child's injuries within moments after the occurrence of the injury-producing event." (275 Cal. App. 2d 253, 255, 79 Cal. Rptr. 723.) Thus, it appeared that this court agreed that persons who were not present at the accident scene could recover damages for the emotional distress they later suffered when told by others of the injury to their loved one or when they later came to the scene. . . .

Ochoa v. Superior Court, supra, 39 Cal. 3d 159, 172, 216 Cal. Rptr. 661, 703 P.2d 1, partially explained and limited "direct victim" recovery under *Molien, supra,* 27 Cal. 3d 916, 167 Cal. Rptr. 831, 616 P.2d 813, to situations in which the defendant's negligence is "by its very nature directed at" the plaintiff. However, *Ochoa* also indicated that the dimensions of the NIED tort might be expanded further for "bystander" plaintiffs. *Ochoa* confirmed that recovery was permitted even though the injury producing event was not sudden or accidental, and even though its negligent cause was not immediately apparent. The court observed that the factors set forth in *Dillon* had been offered only as guidelines, and suggested that none was essential to recovery for NIED. Foreseeability that the injury would cause emotional distress was the proper inquiry. (*Ochoa,* 39 Cal. 3d at p.170, 216 Cal. Rptr. 661, 703 P.2d 1.)

That dictum in *Ochoa* was broader than the issue presented in *Ochoa,* however. The plaintiff mother had observed the effects of the defendants' negligent failure to diagnose and properly treat the illness of her teenage son. Her observation of his pain and suffering, and his deteriorating condition, as the defendants failed to either properly care for him or accede to her entreaty that she be permitted to obtain care for him, was the cause of the emotional distress for which she sought to recover. The allegations of the complaint satisfied only two of the *Dillon* factors — she was at the scene of the negligent injury producing conduct and was closely related to the person whose physical injury caused her distress. Defendants' negligence in failing to give proper medical treatment, however, was not a sudden accidental occurrence and thus the second *Dillon* factor was not met: "Whether the shock resulted from a direct emotional impact upon plaintiff from the sensory and contemporaneous observance of the accident. . . ." (*Dillon v. Legg, supra,* 68 Cal. 2d 728, 740-741, 69 Cal. Rptr. 72, 441 P.2d 912.)

This court, after reviewing several decisions of the Courts of Appeal which had limited recovery for NIED to percipient witnesses of a "sudden occurrence," held that this requirement was an unwarranted restriction on the cause of action authorized in *Dillon.* "Such a restriction arbitrarily limits liability when there is a high degree of foreseeability of shock to the plaintiff and the shock flows from an abnormal event, and, as such, unduly frustrates the goal of compensation—the very purpose which the cause of action was meant to further." (*Ochoa v. Superior Court, supra,* 39 Cal. 3d 159, 168, 216 Cal. Rptr. 661, 703 P.2d 1.)

Ochoa also held that the NIED plaintiff need not be aware that the conduct was "tortious." Reasoning that such a requirement leads to anomalous results, the court held that "when there is observation of the defendant's conduct and the child's injury and contemporaneous awareness the defendant's conduct or lack thereof is causing harm to the child, recovery is permitted." (*Ochoa v. Superior Court, supra,* 39 Cal. 3d 159, 170, 216 Cal. Rptr. 661, 703 P.2d 1.) Thus, the plaintiff in that case did not have to know that the defendants had negligently misdiagnosed her son. It was enough that she knew that they were refusing or neglecting to give him additional treatment and this was the cause of the additional injury he was suffering.

In sum, however, as to "bystander" NIED actions, *Ochoa* held only that recovery would be permitted if the plaintiff observes both the defendant's conduct and the resultant injury, and is aware at that time that the conduct is causing the injury. The Court of Appeal erred in concluding that *Ochoa, supra,* 39 Cal. 3d 159, 216 Cal. Rptr. 661, 703 P.2d 1, held that these NIED plaintiffs need not witness the defendant's conduct. . . . http://www.loislaw.com/snp/fpopwind.htm

Ochoa v. Superior Court, supra, 39 Cal. 3d 159, 165, footnote 6,[9] 216 Cal. Rptr. 661, 703 P.2d 1, offers additional guidance, justifying what we acknowledge must be arbitrary lines to similarly limit the class of potential plaintiffs if emotional injury absent physical harm is to continue to be a recoverable item of damages in a negligence action. The impact of personally observing the injury-producing event in most, although concededly not all, cases distinguishes the plaintiff's resultant emotional distress from the emotion felt when one learns of the injury or death of a loved one from another, or observes pain and suffering but not the traumatic cause of the injury. Greater certainty and a more reasonable limit on the exposure to liability for negligent conduct is possible by limiting the right to recover for negligently caused emotional distress to plaintiffs who

---

9. "[A] distinction between distress caused by personal observation of the injury and by hearing of the tragedy from another is justified because compensation should be limited to abnormal life experiences which cause emotional distress. While receiving news that a loved one has been injured or has died may cause emotional distress, it is the type of experience for which in a general way one is prepared, an experience which is common. By contrast few persons are forced to witness the death or injury of a loved one or to suddenly come upon the scene without warning in situations where tortious conduct is involved. In the present case, for example, while it is common to visit a loved one in a hospital and to be distressed by the loved one's pain and suffering, it is highly uncommon to witness the apparent neglect of the patient's immediate medical needs by medical personnel." (Ochoa v. Superior Court, *supra,* 39 Cal. 3d 159, 165, fn.6, 216 Cal. Rptr. 661, 703 P.2d 1.)

personally and contemporaneously perceive the injury-producing event and its traumatic consequences. . . .

We conclude, therefore, that a plaintiff may recover damages for emotional distress caused by observing the negligently inflicted injury of a third person if, but only if, said plaintiff: (1) is closely related to the injury victim; (2) is present at the scene of the injury producing event at the time it occurs and is then aware that it is causing injury to the victim; and (3) as a result suffers serious emotional distress — a reaction beyond that which would be anticipated in a disinterested witness and which is not an abnormal response to the circumstances. These factors were present in *Ochoa* and each of this court's prior decisions upholding recovery for NIED.

The dictum in *Ochoa* suggesting that the factors noted in the *Dillon* guidelines are not essential in determining whether a plaintiff is a foreseeable victim of defendant's negligence should not be relied on. The merely negligent actor does not owe a duty the law will recognize to make monetary amends to all persons who may have suffered emotional distress on viewing or learning about the injurious consequences of his conduct. To the extent they are inconsistent with this conclusion, *Nazaroff v. Superior Court, supra*, 80 Cal. App. 3d 553, 145 Cal. Rptr. 657, and *Archibald v. Braverman, supra*, 275 Cal. App. 2d 253, 79 Cal. Rptr. 723, are disapproved. Experience has shown that, contrary to the expectation of the *Dillon* majority, and with apology to Bernard Witkin, there are clear judicial days on which a court can foresee forever and thus determine liability but none on which that foresight alone provides a socially and judicially acceptable limit on recovery of damages for that injury.

VI

Disposition

The undisputed facts establish that plaintiff was not present at the scene of the accident in which her son was injured. She did not observe defendant's conduct and was not aware that her son was being injured. She could not, therefore, establish a right to recover for the emotional distress she suffered when she subsequently learned of the accident and observed its consequences. The order granting summary judgment was proper.

The judgment of the Court of Appeal is reversed.

Each party shall bear its own costs on appeal.

Lucas, C.J., and Panelli and Arguelles, JJ., concur.

QUESTIONS

1. How would you characterize the court's primary concern with *Dillon*?
2. What is the holding in *Thing*? Are the court's concerns with *Dillon* reflected in its holding in *Thing*? Note that the court's holding does two

things. First, it modifies somewhat the second *Dillon* factor, and second, it transforms those factors into hard-and-fast requirements.

3. Are the differences between *Thing* and *Dillon* that significant? Would *Krouse* have been decided differently under *Thing*? Would *Braverman* have been decided differently under *Thing*? How do you believe the *Dillon* court would have resolved the controversy in *Thing*? Do you believe that the court in *Thing* was really concerned with how *Dillon* was being applied in real accident cases? Probably not. It appears that the court was concerned with how *Dillon* was being expanded to permit recovery in cases not involving accidents at all. For example, in *Ochoa*, which is discussed in the opinion, the court hinted that it might further expand NIED to even more remote bystanders. The opinion in *Thing* was intended to curtail future expansion.

4. Do you believe that *Thing* eliminates the uncertainty in the law?

Fife v. Astenius

California Court of Appeal, 4th District
232 Cal. App. 3d 1090, 284 Cal. Rptr. 16 (1991)

OPINION

SONENSHINE, Acting Presiding Justice.

The parents and brothers of Meghan K. Fife appeal a summary judgment granted to Jennifer Astenius. The Fifes are seeking recovery for the alleged negligent infliction of emotional distress (hereafter NIED) caused when they heard a car crash and went to the street to discover Meghan had been injured. The Supreme Court's guidelines for recovery in *Thing v. La Chusa* (1989) 48 Cal. 3d 644, 257 Cal. Rptr. 865, 771 P.2d 814 require a plaintiff's presence at the accident scene and an awareness that a relative is then being injured. The Fifes allege their perceptions of the accident and Meghan's injuries were contemporaneous, within the *La Chusa* guidelines. We conclude they cannot recover for NIED because they did not know at the time the accident occurred that Meghan was being injured.

I

Meghan was injured when the truck in which she was a passenger collided with another car. The accident occurred on the street directly behind Meghan's house. Her parents and three brothers, who were in the house at the time, heard the crash and saw debris fly above a wall which separated their yard from the street. Although none of the family members saw the accident, Meghan's father and brothers immediately went outside and, after climbing the wall, found

Meghan still inside the truck. Meghan's mother remained in the house until one of her sons informed her that Meghan had been hurt.

Meghan's parents and brothers filed the underlying lawsuit alleging the negligence of the truck's driver, Jennifer Astenius, was a proximate and contributing cause of their emotional distress. They maintained she should have provided a seatbelt for Meghan and insisted that she use it.[1] The trial court granted Astenius' motion for summary judgment.

II

The court in *Thing v. La Chusa, supra,* 48 Cal. 3d 644, 257 Cal. Rptr. 865, 771 P.2d 814, refined the factors enunciated in *Dillon v. Legg* (1968) 68 Cal. 2d 728, 69 Cal. Rptr. 72, 441 P.2d 912, concluding that "the societal benefits of certainty in the law, as well as traditional concepts of tort law, dictate limitation of bystander recovery of damages for emotional distress. In the absence of physical injury or impact to the plaintiff himself [or herself], damages for emotional distress should be recoverable only if the plaintiff: (1) is closely related to the injury victim, (2) is present at the scene of the injury-producing event at the time it occurs and is then aware that it is causing injury to the victim and, (3) as a result suffers emotional distress beyond that which would be anticipated in a disinterested witness." (*Thing v. La Chusa, supra,* 48 Cal. 3d 644, 647, 257 Cal. Rptr. 865, 771 P.2d 814.)

A plaintiff must "contemporaneously perceive the injury-producing event and its traumatic consequences." (Id. at p.666, 257 Cal. Rptr. 865, 771 P.2d 814.) The Fifes argue their observance of Meghan's injuries was contemporaneous with their perception of the accident because the father and brothers rushed to the street and saw Meghan within seconds of hearing the impact.[2] They contend "contemporaneously" does not mean simultaneously, but rather within a short period of time.

If we were to accept the Fifes' definition of "contemporaneous observance," we would be regressing to the "ever widening circles of liability" *La Chusa* was trying to avoid. (*Thing v. La Chusa, supra,* 48 Cal. 3d 644, 653, 257 Cal. Rptr. 865, 771 P.2d 814.) *La Chusa* makes clear that recovery for NIED is possible

---

1. Because we affirm, we need not address Astenius' argument that she did not owe such a duty.
2. The Fifes allege they were present at the scene of the accident because they heard the collision. In Krouse v. Graham (1977) 19 Cal. 3d 59, 137 Cal. Rptr. 863, 562 P.2d 1022, the Supreme Court held sensory perception of an accident could be sufficient to establish a plaintiff's presence at the scene; "visual" perception was not required. The facts of *Krouse*, however, show why the word "visual" appears in quotation marks. "It was sufficient that the [*Krouse*] plaintiff knew the position of his wife just outside the automobile in which he was seated the instant before she was struck by defendant's automobile which he had seen and realized was going to strike her. He was, therefore, a 'percipient witness to the impact causing [her] injuries.' [Citation.]" (Thing v. La Chusa, supra, 48 Cal. 3d 644, 656, 257 Cal. Rptr. 865, 771 P.2d 814.) That is not our situation.

   Krouse further relied on Archibald v. Braverman (1969) 275 Cal. App. 2d 253, 79 Cal. Rptr. 723, which allowed recovery without any perception of the actual injury-producing event. However, *Archibald* was disapproved in *La Chusa* because without any perception of an accident, the contemporaneous observance requirement cannot be met. (Thing v. La Chusa, supra, 48 Cal. 3d 644, 668, 257 Cal. Rptr. 865, 771 P.2d 814.).

only if a plaintiff is present at the scene of an accident and *is then aware* a family member is being injured. Recovery is precluded when a plaintiff perceives an accident but is unaware of injury to a family member until minutes or even seconds later.[3] Therefore, the Fifes, even if considered present at the scene, cannot recover because they did not know Meghan was involved in the accident at the time they heard the collision.[4]

Judgment affirmed. Respondent to receive costs on appeal.

CROSBY and WALLIN, JJ., concur.

QUESTIONS

1. What argument do the plaintiffs make to try to bring themselves within the holding in *Thing*? Notice that they alleged in their complaint that they were "present" at the scene of the accident because they heard the collision.

2. Do you believe that this case would have been decided differently under *Dillon*? Suppose that *Dillon* were still the law in California. What arguments would you make if you represented Meghan's family? The plaintiffs would have likely argued that they were "near" the scene of the accident and that it was therefore foreseeable that they would suffer injury. What arguments would the defendant make?

Wilks v. Hom

California Court of Appeal, 4th District
2 Cal. App. 4th 1264, 3 Cal. Rptr. 2d 803 (1992)

FROEHLICH, Associate Justice.

After a tragic explosion and fire in which one young girl was killed and another severely burned, a suit was brought alleging wrongful death and personal injury against the landlords of the residence where the explosion occurred. In this appeal we confirm that the mother of the injured child may receive damages for emotional distress occasioned by the negligently caused injuries to her daughter. We determine such damages are appropriate because the mother was contemporaneously aware that the explosion was causing the injuries although she did not actually see or hear her daughter being injured. . . .

---

3. Justice Broussard notes in his dissenting opinion that "[u]nder the majority's strict requirement, a mother who arrives moments after an accident caused by another's negligence will not be permitted recovery." (Id. at p.684, 257 Cal. Rptr. 865, 771 P.2d 814.)
4. As a matter of law, the Fifes' alternative "zone of danger" argument is meritless.

FACTUAL AND PROCEDURAL BACKGROUND

Kimberly Wilks (Wilks) and her three daughters lived in a residence they rented from George Hom, Tom Hom, Herbert Hom and Campo Lake Properties (appellants). On October 12, 1987, after the family had lived at the residence for about six months, Wilks's boyfriend, Arthur Ayres (Ayres) hooked up the house's existing propane system, which had not previously been in use, to a propane stove. Ayres then left the house to do an errand. At about that time Wilks and her three-year-old daughter, Janelle, were in the living room, where Wilks was using a vacuum cleaner. Wilks's other two daughters, nine-year-old Jessica and seven-year-old Virginia, were in their respective bedrooms. When Wilks finished vacuuming, she called to Virginia to pull the plug out of the socket in Virginia's room. As Virginia pulled the plug, there was an immediate explosion. Wilks and Janelle were blown out of the house. Wilks tried to return to the living room but was repelled by the heat. She went around the side of the house, broke down a door to Jessica's room and pulled Jessica out. She then went into Virginia's room and brought Virginia out of the house. Virginia died of her injuries several hours later. Jessica survived but was severely burned.

Wilks, as an individual and as guardian ad litem for Janelle and Jessica, and Steven Donnelly, Virginia's father, brought a cause of action against appellants for the wrongful death of Virginia and for damages for personal injuries to Janelle, Jessica and Wilks. A jury found that appellants Ayres and Wilks had been negligent, that Wilks's negligence was not a legal cause of damage to the plaintiffs, that Ayres's negligence was 15 percent responsible, and that appellants' negligence was 85 percent responsible. The judgment allocated to appellants 85 percent of the non-economic damages and awarded damages to plaintiffs in the following amounts: Virginia's heirs, $307,964.80; Wilks, $876,755.93; Jessica, $1,778,608.40; and Janelle, $4,172.32.

Appellants contend the court erred in instructing the jury regarding recovery for emotional distress damages by a bystander[.] . . .

DISCUSSION

I. The Trial Court Properly Instructed the Jury on Awarding Damages for Emotional Distress to a Bystander

Appellants contend the trial court erred in instructing the jury on liability to a bystander who observes a negligently caused injury to a loved one.[5] The

5. The trial court instructed that the rules governing entitlement by a bystander to recovery of damages were as follows:

Kimberly Wilks is entitled to recover damages for serious emotional distress caused by witnessing an event producing injury to her daughter, Jessica Faulkner, from a defendant whose negligence caused injury to Jessica Faulkner.

   In order to recover, plaintiff must establish (1) the defendant was negligent; (2) defendant's negligence was a legal cause of injury to Jessica Faulkner; (3) plaintiff was present at the scene of the

bystander theory of recovery for emotional distress caused by witnessing an injury was definitively established in *Dillon v. Legg* (1968) 68 Cal. 2d 728, 69 Cal. Rptr. 72, 441 P.2d 912. In *Dillon*, a mother and her daughter sought damages for the emotional distress they experienced when watching a car hit and roll over another daughter/sister as she crossed the street. The Supreme Court determined that in deciding whether such damage could be deemed the proximate result of a defendant's negligence, courts should take into account such factors as:

> (1) Whether plaintiff was located near the scene of the accident as contrasted with one who was a distance away from it. (2) Whether the shock resulted from a direct emotional impact upon plaintiff from the sensory and contemporaneous observance of the accident, as contrasted with learning of the accident from others after its occurrence. (3) Whether plaintiff and the victim were closely related, as contrasted with an absence of any relationship or the presence of only a distant relationship. (Id. at pp.740-741, 69 Cal. Rptr. 72, 441 P.2d 912.)

The court predicted that more definitive boundaries of liability would be drawn in subsequent cases. (Id. at p.741, 69 Cal. Rptr. 72, 441 P.2d 912.)

Courts after *Dillon* did attempt further definition of the limits of liability. Evolution of the law under their several rulings, however, was neither uniform nor predictable. The Supreme Court in *Thing v. La Chusa* (1989) 48 Cal. 3d 644, 257 Cal. Rptr. 865, 771 P.2d 814 observed that the trend of court of appeal decisions had resulted in relaxed guidelines and produced inconsistent rulings and critical comment. The factual setting of *Thing* was that of a mother whose emotional distress resulted from being informed her son had been struck by a car, then rushing to the scene and witnessing the damage minutes after the accident happened. The trial court had found this scenario inadequate to permit the mother's claim, ruling against her on summary judgment. The Court of Appeal disagreed, concluding the elements of negligent infliction of emotional distress were sufficiently established. The Supreme Court reversed the appellate court ruling and then set out "to create a clear rule under which liability may be determined." (Id. at p.664, 257 Cal. Rptr. 865, 771 P.2d 814.) The court opined:

> In order to avoid limitless liability out of all proportion to the degree of a defendant's negligence, and against which it is impossible to insure without imposing unacceptable costs on those among whom the risk is spread, the right to recover for negligently caused emotional distress must be limited. (Ibid.)

---

accident at the time it occurred; (4) plaintiff was then aware that such accident caused the injury to Jessica Faulkner; and (5) as a result plaintiff suffered serious emotional distress.

"Serious emotional distress" is an emotional reaction beyond that which should be, which would be anticipated in a witness not related to the injured person, and which is not an abnormal response to the circumstances; it is found when a reasonable person would be unable to cope with the mental distress caused by the circumstances of the accident and injury to the near relative.

To illustrate how the *Dillon* guidelines had been relaxed, the *Thing* court reviewed prior cases, first pointing to *Krouse v. Graham* (1977) 19 Cal. 3d 59, 137 Cal. Rptr. 863, 562 P.2d 1022. There, the court had held that the plaintiff need not visually perceive the third party injury in order to satisfy the *Dillon* guideline, suggesting only that he must suffer shock from " ' " the sensory and contemporaneous observance of the accident. . . ." ' " (*Thing v. La Chusa, supra*, 48 Cal. 3d at p.656, 257 Cal. Rptr. 865, 771 P.2d 814, quoting *Krouse v. Graham, supra*, 19 Cal. 3d at p.76, 137 Cal. Rptr. 863, 562 P.2d 1022.) In *Krouse*, the plaintiff sat in the driver's seat of his car and knew that his wife was at the curb closing the door to the backseat when a car negligently driven by the defendant approached the rear of the plaintiff's car, straddled the curb and hit and killed the plaintiff's wife. The *Krouse* court ruled it was sufficient that the plaintiff knew his wife's position an instant before she was struck, saw the defendant's car coming toward her at high speed, and knew it must have hit his wife. (*Krouse v. Graham, supra*, 19 Cal. 3d at p.76, 137 Cal. Rptr. 863, 562 P.2d 1022.)

The *Thing* court noted:

> We also find in *Krouse, supra*, 19 Cal. 3d 59 [137 Cal. Rptr. 863, 562 P.2d 1022], the roots of the uncertainty reflected by the instant case over whether the plaintiff must perceive the injury causing incident at all or may recover for emotional distress suffered on viewing its "immediate consequences" even though not present at the scene when it occurred. (*Thing v. La Chusa, supra*, 48 Cal. 3d at p.656, 257 Cal. Rptr. 865, 771 P.2d 814.)

The court observed that the uncertainty it noted derived from the *Krouse* court's approval of *Archibald v. Braverman* (1969) 275 Cal. App. 2d 253, 79 Cal. Rptr. 723. *Archibald* had extended the potential scope of the bystander claim for negligent infliction of emotional distress by permitting recovery by a mother who did not witness the accident but arrived on the scene very shortly thereafter to see her son's injuries. The court in *Thing* distinguished the facts of *Dillon* and presumably *Krouse* by noting:

> Thus, it appeared that this court agreed that persons who were not present at the accident scene could recover damages for the emotional distress they later suffered when told by others of the injury to their loved one or when they later came to the scene. (*Thing v. La Chusa, supra*, 48 Cal. 3d at p.656, 257 Cal. Rptr. 865, 771 P.2d 814.)

The *Thing* court then went on to illustrate how the *Dillon* guidelines had been relaxed in other areas by discussing cases which followed *Krouse*. (Id., 48 Cal. 3d at pp.657-661, 257 Cal. Rptr. 865, 771 P.2d 814.)[6] Then, reiterating the

---

6. The court's analysis included consideration of Justus v. Atchison (1977) 19 Cal. 3d 564, 139 Cal. Rptr. 97, 565 P.2d 122, which denied recovery for fathers who were told their children had been stillborn, but led later courts to infer the injury-producing event need not be a sudden occurrence or accident; Molien v. Kaiser Foundation Hospitals (1980) 27 Cal. 3d 916, 167 Cal. Rptr. 831, 616 P.2d 813, which led to the assumption by courts that physical injury was not required for direct victims or

necessity of limiting liability (Id. at p.664, 257 Cal. Rptr. 865, 771 P.2d 814), the court determined recovery must be limited "to plaintiffs who personally and contemporaneously perceive the injury-producing event and its traumatic consequences." (Id. at p.666, 257 Cal. Rptr. 865, 771 P.2d 814.)[7]

The court thus set forth the rule as follows:

> [A] plaintiff may recover damages for emotional distress caused by observing the negligently inflicted injury of a third person if, but only if, said plaintiff: "(1) is closely related to the injury victim; (2) is present at the scene of the injury-producing event at the time it occurs and is then aware that it is causing injury to the victim; and (3) as a result suffers serious emotional distress — a reaction beyond that which would be anticipated in a disinterested witness and which is not an abnormal response to the circumstances." (*Thing v. La Chusa, supra,* at pp.667-668, 257 Cal. Rptr. 865, 771 P.2d 814.)

The court noted: "These factors were present in *Ochoa* and each of this court's prior decisions upholding recovery for NIED [negligent infliction of emotional distress]."[8] (*Thing v. La Chusa, supra,* at p.668, 257 Cal. Rptr. 865, 771 P.2d 814.)

Thus, the *Thing* court affirmed that bystander damages may be recovered only by a plaintiff who is present at the injury-producing event at the time it occurs and is then aware that it is causing injury to the victim. The court's analysis did not indicate disapproval, however, of the holding in *Krouse* that the plaintiff need not visually perceive the injury while it is being inflicted.

The instruction in this case closely tracked the teaching of *Thing* and was also tailored to the facts of the case. It required that the plaintiff be "present at the scene of the accident at the time it occurred" and be "aware that such accident caused the injury to Jessica." Notable is the omission of a requirement that the plaintiff actually "witness" the injury to Jessica as and when it occurred. We find this instruction to be entirely in accord with the *Dillon* principle as refined in *Thing*. Following *Krouse*, we conclude it is not necessary that a plaintiff bystander actually have witnessed the infliction of injury to her child, provided that the plaintiff was at the scene of the accident and was sensorially aware, in some important way, of the accident and the necessarily inflicted injury to her child. Here, although Wilks could not visually witness the infliction of injuries to Jessica, she was most evidently present at the scene of the accident, was

---

bystanders in actions for negligent infliction of emotional distress; and Ochoa v. Superior Court (1985) 39 Cal. 3d 159, 216 Cal. Rptr. 661, 703 P.2d 1, which held the injury-producing event need not be sudden or accidental and the negligent cause need not be immediately apparent. (Thing v. La Chusa, *supra,* 48 Cal. 3d at pp.657-661, 257 Cal. Rptr. 865, 771 P.2d 814.)

7. The court specifically disapproved the holdings of Archibald v. Braverman, *supra,* 275 Cal. App. 2d 253, 79 Cal. Rptr. 723 and Nazaroff v. Superior Court (1978) 80 Cal. App. 3d 553, 145 Cal. Rptr. 657 that contemporaneous awareness of the accident as it occurred was not necessary to state a cause of action. (Thing v. La Chusa, *supra,* 48 Cal. 3d at p.668, 257 Cal. Rptr. 865, 771 P.2d 814.)

8. In *Ochoa,* a mother had witnessed her son's suffering, because defendants refused to treat his illness properly or allow her to take him from juvenile hall to the family doctor. (Ochoa v. Superior Court, *supra,* 39 Cal. 3d 159, 216 Cal. Rptr. 661, 703 P.2d 1.)

personally impressed by the explosion at the same instant damage was done to her child, and instantly knew of the likely severe damage to the child. . . .

DISPOSITION

The judgment is affirmed.

QUESTIONS

1. A case of colossal chutzpah: Suppose that a cement truck collides with a car at an intersection. The truck had the right-of-way. The 16-year-old driver of the car is killed instantly. The uninjured truck driver gets out of his truck soon after the crash, approaches the mangled car, and views the teenage driver's body in the wreckage from close range. As a result of viewing the body, the truck driver allegedly suffers severe emotional distress and institutes suit against the teenage driver's estate. He suffered no physical injury. Applying California law, would a complaint based on these facts survive a demurrer (i.e., motion to dismiss)? *See Camper v. Minor*, 915 S.W.2d 437 (Tenn. Sup. Ct. 1996).

2. Suppose that an airplane crashes near a house that is occupied by a husband and three children. The spouse is on her way home at the time of the impact. She hears the crash and sees its effects but is unaware that her family is being injured until she nears her house, which is engulfed in flames. Her family perishes. Based on the cases that you have read, including *Wilks*, how do you believe a court would resolve the issue?

3. Suppose that plaintiff's sister was killed in an automobile accident because the head restraint system in the vehicle failed to provide appropriate protection. The plaintiff was not a passenger in the vehicle and did not witness the accident. Would such a suit be permitted under California law? *See Gu v. BMW of North America, LLC*, 132 Cal.App.4th 195, 33 Cal. Rptr.3d 617 (2005).

4. From the cases that you have read in this chapter, how would you approach a case in which a wife sues her husband for negligently transmitting the Human Immunodeficiency Virus to her? *See John B. v. Superior Court*, 38 Cal.4th 1177, 45 Cal.Rptr.3d 316, 137 P.3d 153 (2006).

5. Courts still have difficulty dealing with emotional distress. Should a plaintiff be permitted to recover damages if he receives a pacemaker that he later learns may be defective? Should a person be able sue even though the medical device has not failed, because the risk of failure is greater than he was led to believe?

Bird v. Saenz

Supreme Court of California
28 Cal.4th 910, 123 Cal.Rptr.2d 465, 51 P.3d 324 (2002)

WERDEGAR, Justice.

We granted review to consider whether plaintiffs have viable claims as bystanders for negligent infliction of emotional distress arising out of alleged medical malpractice directed to their close relative. We conclude they do not.

FACTS AND PROCEDURAL BACKGROUND

This is an action for wrongful death and negligent infliction of emotional distress (NIED) based on medical malpractice. Plaintiffs are the adult daughters of decedent Nita Bird. Nita succumbed to cancer on January 15, 1996. Defendants are the physicians who treated Nita. The superior court granted summary judgment for defendants on both claims, but the Court of Appeal reversed. In granting review, we limited briefing and argument to the question "whether defendants' motion for summary judgment was properly granted on plaintiffs' claim for negligent infliction of emotional distress."

* * *

On [November 30, 1994], plaintiff Janice Bird brought her mother Nita to the hospital to undergo an outpatient surgical procedure. The goal of the procedure was to insert a Port-A-Cath—a venous catheter surgically implanted to facilitate the delivery of chemotherapeutic agents. . . . Nita was taken into the operating room about 1:45 or 2:00 p.m. Janice expected the procedure to take about 20 minutes. After an hour had elapsed, . . . Janice heard the announcement [over the loudspeaker], "[t]horacic surgeon needed in surgery, stat." Janice assumed the call related to Nita because she believed all other surgeries had been completed. An hour to an hour and a half later, defendant Dr. Eisenkop [told Janice] "that they had more trouble inserting the Port-A-Cath than they had anticipated, that when they went to insert it, they thought that they got a bubble in her vein, and they think that she might have had a mild stroke." Janice telephoned her sister, plaintiff Dayle Edgmon, with this news and returned to the waiting room. About 4:30 p.m., someone told Janice that Nita was "sleeping right now" and "should be going up to the fifth floor in about an hour." Soon thereafter, Janice saw Nita "being rushed down the hallway to the CCU—I presume she was going to the CCU [critical care unit]. She was bright blue. The angle of the bed was like this (indicating). Her feet were way up in the air, her head was almost touching the ground, there was all these doctors and nurses around there and they're running down the hallway, down to that end of the hospital. . . ." The medical personnel rushed Nita into a room and closed the door behind them. Janice, who was in the hallway, asked Dr. Dowds what was happening. Dr. Dowds went to check and returned with this news: "From what I can see," Janice remembers him saying, "I think they nicked an artery or a vein, and it looks like all the blood went into her chest. They're going to have to insert a drainage tube into her chest to drain out the fluid, and they're pumping — they're trying to pump as much fluids and blood into her to keep her alive until the vascular surgeon gets there." Ten or 15 minutes later, Janice saw Dr. Dowds running down the hall with multiple units of blood.

At this point Dayle arrived. Janice told her briefly what was happening. Dr. Dowds then told Dayle what he had already told Janice, namely, that an artery or vein had been nicked and that major surgery would be necessary. Shortly thereafter, Janice and Dayle saw Nita being rushed down the hallway to surgery. In Dayle's words, "All of a sudden I saw, I would say, approximately at least 10 doctors and nurses running down the hall with my mother and I remember her head was towards the floor, her feet were up in the air and she was blue." Janice's description is essentially identical, with the addition that she understood her mother's angle as intended "to keep the blood moving to the heart."

Those are the events on which plaintiffs base their claim for NIED. Soon thereafter, emergency surgery stopped Nita's internal bleeding. But plaintiffs do not claim that this subsequent procedure caused them to suffer actionable emotional distress. Nita was discharged from the hospital 33 days later, on January 2, 1995, and resumed chemotherapy the next month.

In pleading their NIED claim, plaintiffs allege they "were all present at the scene of the injury-producing events at issue herein at the time when they occurred" and that they "were all aware that Defendants, and each of them, were causing injury to their mother, Nita Bird." Defendants moved for summary judgment on the ground that the undisputed evidence showed plaintiffs had not been present in the operating room at the time Nita's artery was transected, had not observed the transection, and had learned about it from others only after it had occurred. Plaintiff Kim Moran, moreover, had been out of the state. In support of their motion, defendants cited *Thing v. La Chusa* (1989) 48 Cal.3d 644, in which we held "that a plaintiff may recover damages for emotional distress caused by observing the negligently inflicted injury of a third person if, but only if," the plaintiff satisfies three requirements, including the requirement that the plaintiff be "present at the scene of the injury-producing event at the time it occurs and [be] then aware that it is causing injury to the victim." (Id. at pp. 667-668.)

* * *

The superior court, as already noted, granted defendants' motion for summary judgment. The Court of Appeal reversed. "To the extent that the injury-producing event includes the alleged negligent care and treatment of [Nita] outside the operating room," the court reasoned, "it remains a triable issue of fact as to whether appellants meet the test under *Thing*." We granted review.

II.

DISCUSSION

This case requires us to consider once again the circumstances under which bystanders to an event injuring a third party may sue the allegedly negligent actor for emotional distress. In *Amaya v. Home Ice, Fuel & Supply Co.* (1963) 59 Cal.2d 295, we declined to recognize such claims, foreseeing if we did a "fantastic realm of infinite liability." (Id. at p. 315.) Five years later, in *Dillon v. Legg* (1968) 68 Cal.2d 728 (Dillon), we reversed course. Equating the duty to avoid causing emotional harm to bystanders with the foreseeability they might suffer such harm, we articulated a set of nonexclusive guidelines for assessing foreseeability, and thus duty, on a case-by-case basis. Over the ensuing two decades we, and the lower courts, attempted to apply those guidelines. Looking at that effort in retrospect, however, in *Thing v. La Chusa, supra,* 48 Cal.3d 644 (*Thing*), we discerned that *Dillon* had produced arbitrary and conflicting results and "ever widening circles of liability." (*Thing, supra,* at pp. 653, 662.) Recognizing this, we did not reverse course yet again, but we did make an important course correction. In place of *Dillon's* nonexclusive guidelines, we set out three mandatory requirements that claims for NIED must satisfy to be accepted as valid. Specifically, we held "that a plaintiff may recover damages for emotional distress caused by observing the negligently inflicted injury of a third person if, but only if, said plaintiff: (1) is closely related to the injury victim; (2) is present at the scene of the injury-producing event at the time it occurs and is then aware that it is causing injury to the victim; and (3) as a result suffers serious emotional distress — a reaction beyond that which would be anticipated in a disinterested witness and which is not an abnormal response to the circumstances." (*Thing,* supra, at pp. 667-668, fns. omitted, italics added.) We emphasized the mandatory, exclusive nature of the new requirements by expressly rejecting the suggestion that liability for NIED should be determined under the more general approach set out in *Rowland v. Christian* (1968) 69 Cal.2d 108, 112-113, for identifying duties of care. (*See Thing,* supra, at p. 668, fn. 11.)

Applying these requirements to the facts before us in *Thing, supra,* 48 Cal.3d 644, we held that the plaintiff as a matter of law could not state a claim for NIED. The plaintiff mother had been nearby when the defendant's automobile struck and injured her minor child, but the plaintiff had not seen or heard the accident; instead, she became aware of it only when someone told her it had occurred and she rushed to the scene and saw her child lying injured and unconscious on the road. Under these facts, the plaintiff could not satisfy the requirement of having been present at the scene of the injury-producing event at the time it occurred and of having then been aware that it was causing injury to the victim. We reinforced our conclusion by disapproving the suggestion in prior cases that a negligent actor is liable to all those persons "who may have suffered emotional distress on viewing or learning about the injurious consequences of his conduct" rather than on viewing the injury-producing event, itself. (Id. at p. 668, italics added, disapproving *Nazaroff v. Superior Court* (1978) 80 Cal.App.3d 553, and *Archibald v. Braverman* (1969) 275 Cal.App.2d 253, to the extent inconsistent with *Thing*.)

Here, only the second *Thing* requirement is at issue. Defendants argue that plaintiffs, who admittedly did not perceive the transection of their mother's artery, were not present at the scene of the injury-producing event at the time it occurred and were not then aware that it was causing injury to the victim.

Certainly defendants are correct that plaintiffs cannot prevail on a claim for NIED based solely on the transection of Nita's artery. The undisputed facts establish that no plaintiff was present in the operating room at the time that event occurred. Indeed, plaintiffs assert that even the defendant physicians, who were present and actively involved in Nita's care, failed to diagnose the transection for some time. Plaintiffs first learned an accident had taken place when they heard that news from a physician and saw some of the injurious consequences. The earlier call for a thoracic surgeon over the hospital's loud-speaker system may seem full of portent in retrospect, but it carried no clear information to a bystander in a waiting room about the progress of a particular surgical procedure. To be sure, *Thing*'s requirement that the plaintiff be con-temporaneously aware of the injury-producing event has not been interpreted as requiring visual perception of an impact on the victim. A plaintiff may recover based on an event perceived by other senses so long as the event is contemporaneously understood as causing injury to a close relative. (*Wilks v. Hom* (1992) 2 Cal.App.4th 1264, 1272-1273 [3 Cal.Rptr.2d 803] [plaintiff was in the living room speaking to her children in their bedrooms when she saw, heard and felt one bedroom explode from a gas leak].) But this slight degree of flexibility in the second *Thing* requirement does not aid plaintiffs here because they had no sensory perception whatsoever of the transection at the time it occurred. Thus, defining the injury-producing event as the transection, plaintiffs' claim falls squarely within the category of cases the second *Thing* requirement was intended to bar.

* * *

The problem with defining the injury-producing event as defendants' failure to diagnose and treat the damaged artery is that plaintiffs could not meaningfully have perceived any such failure. Except in the most obvious cases, a misdiagnosis is beyond the awareness of lay bystanders. Here, what plaintiffs actually saw and heard was a call for a thoracic surgeon, a report of Nita suffering a possible stroke, Nita in distress being rushed by numerous medical personnel to another room, a report of Nita possibly having suffered a nicked artery or vein, a physician carrying units of blood and, finally, Nita still in distress being rushed to surgery. Even if plaintiffs believed, as they stated in their declarations, that their mother was bleeding to death, they had no reason to know that the care she was receiving to diagnose and correct the cause of the problem was inadequate. While they eventually became aware that one injury-producing event — the transected artery—had occurred, they had no basis for believing that another, subtler event was occurring in its wake.

*   *   *

Plaintiffs in the case before us rely almost entirely on *Ochoa v. Superior Court* (1985) 39 Cal.3d 159 (*Ochoa*), a case predating *Thing*, supra, 48 Cal.3d 644. But *Ochoa* does not support their position. In that case, a boy confined in a juvenile detention facility died of pneumonia after authorities ignored his obviously serious symptoms, which included vomiting, coughing up blood, and excruciating pain. We permitted the mother, who observed the neglect and recognized it as harming her son, to sue as a bystander for NIED. Anticipating the formula we would later adopt in *Thing*, we explained that "when there is observation of the defendant's conduct and the child's injury and contemporaneous awareness the defendant's conduct or lack thereof is causing harm to the child, recovery is permitted." (Ochoa, supra, at p. 170, italics added.) The injury-producing event was the failure of custodial authorities to respond significantly to symptoms obviously requiring immediate medical attention. Such a failure to provide medical assistance, as opposed to a misdiagnosis, unsuccessful treatment, or treatment that turns out to have been inappropriate only in retrospect, is not necessarily hidden from the understanding awareness of a layperson. Even before *Thing*, supra, 48 Cal.3d 644, decisions applying the looser guidelines of *Dillon*, *supra*, 68 Cal.2d 728, denied recovery to bystanders for emotional distress suffered while observing medical procedures. (*See Justus v. Atchison* (1977) 19 Cal.3d 564, 584-585 [fathers of stillborn children who had been present in the delivery rooms and observed the obstetrical procedures could not recover for NIED because they were not aware until told by physicians that their children had not survived]; *Jansen v. Children's Hospital Medical Center* (1973) 31 Cal.App.3d 22 [mother watched her child sicken and die in the hospital of an undiagnosed ulcer].)

*   *   *

The Court of Appeal in the case before us rejected that reasoning. "We do not believe," the court wrote, "that the bystander theory of recovery requires the plaintiff to have more medical acumen than the defendant doctor so as to be able to 'perceive' and understand that a misdiagnosis is being made; rather, all that *Thing* requires is that the plaintiff be present at the scene of the victim's treatment and be aware that the course of treatment is causing injury to the victim." The Court of Appeal did not explain how a bystander without medical acumen, except in the most extreme case (see ante, at p. 9), could meaningfully be aware that a course of treatment is causing injury. In any event, a rule permitting bystanders to sue for NIED on account of unperceived medical errors hidden in a course of treatment cannot be reconciled with *Thing*'s requirement that the plaintiff be aware of the connection between the injury-producing event and the injury. The Court of Appeal's rule would, moreover, impose nearly strict liability on health care providers for NIED to bystanders who observe emotionally stressful procedures that turn out in retrospect to have involved negligence. We may reject such a rule as inconsistent with *Thing* even without accepting defendants' more radical suggestion that as a matter of policy we categorically bar bystanders' NIED claims based on medical malpractice.

In summary, plaintiffs have not shown they were aware of the transection of Nita's artery at the time it occurred. Nor have they shown they were contemporaneously aware of any error in the subsequent diagnosis and treatment of that injury in the moments they saw their mother rolled through the hall by medical personnel. In view of these undisputed facts, plaintiffs cannot show they were "present at the scene of the injury-producing event at the time it occur[ed] and [were] then aware that it [was] causing injury to the victim." (*Thing*, supra, 48 Cal.3d 644, 668.) Accordingly, the superior court properly granted defendants' motion for summary judgment on plaintiffs' claim for NIED.

III. DISPOSITION

The decision of the Court of Appeal is reversed in part and remanded for further proceedings consistent with this opinion.

QUESTIONS

1. Suppose that a factory worker is hit by a flying piece of metal and the entire incident is witnessed by his son, who is present in the factory at the time of the accident? Would *Bird v. Saenz* bar recovery? Suppose the same set of facts, but that instead of being hit by metal, the worker is accidentally irradiated by an industrial x-ray machine? Does the form of projectile matter? Suppose the same set of facts, but rather than occurring in a factory, the lethal overdose of radiation occurs while a child is undergoing radiation therapy as part of cancer treatment and the treatment is witnessed by his parents. Does the outcome depend on whether the parents were aware, at the time that they were witnessing the treatment, that their child was receiving a lethal overdose?

2. Is *Bird* primarily aimed at precluding non-patients from suing for medical malpractice? If so, why do you think it was necessary for the California Supreme Court to take up such a highly specific type of NIED case?

3. Does *Bird* effectively limit recovery in bystander malpractice cases to a "knowledgeable observer"?

Presented below is a memorandum that, in the course of discussing these issues, ties together the cases that you have read.

SAMPLE MEMORANDUM

MEMORANDUM

TO: LAWRENCE FIELD
FROM: JACOB MEYER
SUBJECT: Martha Goodman's Action for the Negligent Infliction of
            Emotional Distress
DATE: May 7, 2005

Our client, Martha Goodman, suffered severe emotional distress upon witnessing her home, with her entire family inside, burn to the ground after an airplane crashed into the Goodmans' neighborhood. This memorandum briefly examines whether Martha can recover for the negligent infliction of emotional distress even though she did not actually see her family perish.

Facts

On the morning of June 1, 2004, Martha Goodman left her home to buy breakfast food at a nearby grocery store. When she left for the store, her husband was in his pajamas at the breakfast table reading the newspaper; her three children were asleep in their bedrooms. Twenty minutes later, on her way home from the store, Martha saw, heard, and felt a giant explosion. Although she did not know it at the time, a passenger airliner had just crashed near her house. Within minutes, Martha had maneuvered her way through the debris and arrived at her home to find it engulfed in flames. Upon seeing her home in flames and knowing that her family was still inside, she went into shock and collapsed from the emotional distress. When she awoke in the hospital, Martha learned that her entire family had perished in the disaster. The medical examiner determined that the family had died as a result of the fire.

The National Transportation Safety Board, which investigated the crash, determined that it was caused by pilot error. Actions have already been instituted against the airline for the wrongful deaths of Mr. Goodman and the three children. Martha is considering instituting a separate action to recover damages for the negligent infliction of emotional distress caused when she witnessed the flames engulfing her home with her family inside.

Issue

Can a plaintiff recover damages for the negligent infliction of emotional distress caused when she witnessed her home in flames and knew that her family was inside, but did not actually see the original impact that caused the fire and did not actually see her family perish?

Short Answer

It appears that Martha will be able to maintain an action for the negligent infliction of emotional distress. Under California law, a plaintiff who is present at an injury-producing event and is aware that a close relative is being injured can maintain an action for the negligent infliction of emotional distress. The plaintiff must be able to prove that the emotional distress arose as a result of witnessing the injury-producing event. Inasmuch as Martha actually witnessed her house in flames and knew that her family was inside, she satisfies the "awareness" requirement. The fact that she did not know that the airliner had crashed or exploded near her house is irrelevant. The injury-producing event was the resulting fire, and it was that fire that she witnessed and that caused the deaths of husband and children.

Analysis

In *Thing v. La Chusa,* 48 Cal. 3d 644, 257 Cal. Rptr. 865, 771 P.2d 814 (1989), the California Supreme Court modified the law regarding the negligent infliction of emotional distress and held that

> [a] plaintiff may recover damages for emotional distress caused by observing the negligently inflicted injury of a third person if, but only if, said plaintiff: (1) is closely related to the injury victim; (2) is present at the scene of the injury-producing event at the time it occurs and is then aware that it is causing injury to the victim; and (3) as a result suffers serious emotional distress. . . .

Thing v. La Chusa, 257 Cal. Rptr. at 880-881, 771 P.2d at 829-830 (footnotes omitted).

Martha Goodman satisfies the first and third requirements. At issue here is whether she satisfies the second requirement.

In *Thing,* the plaintiff's son was injured when he was struck by a negligently driven automobile. The plaintiff's mother, although nearby, neither saw nor heard the accident. She only became aware that her son was injured when she was told by her daughter. She then rushed to the scene where she saw her unconscious child. Based on the facts of that case, the court held that the second requirement had not been satisfied because the plaintiff was not present at the accident scene, did not observe the defendant's conduct, and "was not aware that her son was being injured." *Thing v. La Chusa,* 257 Cal. Rptr. at 881, 771 P.2d at 830. She learned of her son's injuries only after the fact.

Correspondingly, in *Fife v. Astenius,* 232 Cal. App. 3d 1090, 284 Cal. Rptr. 16, 18 (1991), the court, relying on *Thing,* emphasized that "[r]ecovery is precluded when a plaintiff perceives an accident, but is unaware of injury to a family member until minutes or even seconds later." In *Fife,* plaintiffs were the parents and brothers of Meghan, who was injured when the truck in which she was riding collided with a car. The accident occurred directly behind the plaintiffs' house and as a result the plaintiffs heard the crash and saw debris flying. However, no family member saw the accident and none had reason to believe that Meghan was involved in the accident. Meghan's father and brothers learned that she was involved in the accident only after they rushed outside to see what was happening. They then told Meghan's mother that Meghan had been injured. In denying recovery to the plaintiffs, the *Fife* court concluded that even if one member of the family were considered to be "present" at the accident, none of them knew that Meghan was being injured until later. Finally, in *Bird v. Saenz*, 28 Cal.4th 910, 123 Cal.Rptr.2d 465, 51 P.3d 324 (2002), a patient's relatives claimed to have been present during an alleged medical malpractice. As a result, they claimed to have suffered emotional distress. In *Bird*, however, the court emphasized that while one or more of the relatives may have been physically present in the hospital when the alleged malpractice occurred, none of them was aware that it was occurring until well after the fact. Indeed, part of the alleged malpractice in *Bird* stemmed from the allegation that not even the physicians were aware that they had injured the patient by nicking a blood vessel.

Here, Martha heard the explosion and saw her house in flames. Unlike the plaintiffs in *Fife*, *Thing*, and *Bird*, she was aware that her family was being injured at the time they were being injured even though she did not actually see them suffer injury. She saw her house engulfed in flames, and she knew that they must have been inside. There was no reason for her to believe otherwise. Indeed, she left the house for the express purpose of purchasing breakfast food to serve to her family. When she left, her children were asleep and her husband was in his pajamas. She had every reason to believe they were still inside when she returned to the house 20 minutes later. Thus, she must have been aware that her family was in the house at the time of calamity.

This case is analogous to *Wilks v. Hom,* 2 Cal. App. 4th 1264, 3 Cal. Rptr. 2d 803, 807 (1992), where the court confirmed that even under *Thing* "it is not necessary that a plaintiff bystander actually have witnessed the infliction of injury to her child, provided that the plaintiff was at the scene of the accident and was sensorially aware, in some important way, of the accident and the necessarily inflicted injury to her child." It was this contemporaneous sensory awareness that was missing in *Bird*.

In *Wilks,* the plaintiff mother, Wilks, did not see or hear her daughter being injured. Wilks had just finished vacuuming when she called to her daughter, Virginia, to pull the cord out of the socket in Virginia's room. A second daughter was also in the house at the time. When Virginia pulled the plug, there was an immediate explosion. Wilks was blown out of the house and she saw the explosion come from Virginia's room. The court, in sustaining a judgment against the landlord of the house in which she lived for the negligent infliction of emotional distress, concluded that Wilks must have known at the time of the explosion that Virginia and the other daughter were being injured.

The defendant is likely to argue that Martha Goodman was not aware that her family was being injured at the time of the "injury-producing event." Specifically, the airline might argue that the injury-producing event was the plane crashing and exploding near the Goodman house. At the time of the actual impact, Martha was not aware that the explosion, which she had heard and felt, involved her house, and was therefore not aware that her family was being injured. Such an argument ignores the fact that the accident in this case, unlike the automobile accidents in *Thing* and *Fife*, was a continuous event. Moreover, this case, unlike *Bird*, does not involve a subtle injury that only those with requisite knowledge could comprehend. This case involves an airplane crash, an event that is difficult to ignore. The crash caused an explosion, which in turn caused a fire. The injury-producing event, according to the medical examiner, was neither the crash nor the explosion, but rather the resulting fire. In *Fife*, the plaintiffs learned that their family member had been injured only after the injury-producing event, that is, the automobile accident, had ended. Here, in contrast, Martha was present and actually witnessed her house going up in flames and was aware that her family was being injured.

In short, the injury-producing event was still in progress when witnessed by Martha. Therefore, Martha can maintain an action for the negligent infliction of emotional distress.

PART II
Learning to Write Legal Documents

7

A Systematic Approach to Legal Writing

Part I of this book was designed to help you learn to read and analyze legal writing. Part II is designed to help you develop your own writing style in a careful and systematic way. It presents legal writing as a step-by-step process that can help you build effective writing skills and avoid the pitfalls that can destroy clarity and credibility.

It is valuable to begin any writing task by articulating the steps you plan to take. Carefully thinking through each step will help you to construct a complete, well-formed document. It is also worthwhile to place the steps in a workable order, even though you may have to be flexible in the way you carry out various parts of the writing process. As you write, you may end up moving the steps around, adding one or two, or even omitting some of them.

A suggested writing plan, based on the chapters of Part II of this book, appears on page 92. Whether you use this plan, modify it, or create your own, it is important that you have a writing plan and that you are comfortable with it.

A | Pre-writing Stage

Before you begin to write any legal document, you need to go through three essential steps. You should clearly *identify your purpose or purposes* in writing the document and keep them in mind as you write. You must *understand your audience:* What does it know? What does it want to know? How might it react to what you have to say? Finally, you must *be aware of any constraints* that circumstances, rules, or customs place on the form or content of your document. Only when you have taken these three steps do you begin to apply your writing skills—writing and rewriting to create a document that does what you want it to do.

Begin by asking yourself what the purpose of the document is: What is it supposed to accomplish? How much material should you include to accomplish your purpose? Is there a risk of conflicting messages in the document because you have several purposes and you have not yet thoroughly thought out how to balance them? Are you confused about whether you are trying to persuade or

FIGURE 7-1

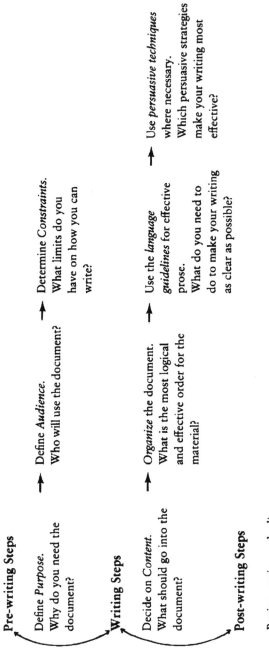

Pre-writing Steps

Define *Purpose.*
Why do you need the
document?

→ Define *Audience.*
Who will use the document?

→ Determine *Constraints.*
What limits do you
have on how you can
write?

Writing Steps

→ Decide on *Content.*
What should go into the
document?

→ *Organize* the document.
What is the most logical
and effective order for the
material?

→ Use the *language
guidelines* for effective
prose.
What do you need to
do to make your writing
as clear as possible?

→ Use *persuasive techniques*
where necessary.
Which persuasive strategies
make your writing most
effective?

Post-writing Steps

Review, revise, and *edit.*
How can you improve each
draft of a document?

merely to inform? The more you work out these conflicts *before* you write, the easier and faster the writing task will be.

Next, ask yourself who will use the document. A single document may have more than one *audience*: judges, other attorneys, your client, other private citizens. These diverse audiences may have varying degrees of sophistication and varying needs. Finding the proper amount of information and the right level of sophistication to serve these different audiences is not a simple task. Documents should not be so difficult that they seem obscure to some readers nor so simple that they seem patronizing to others. But keep in mind that even highly sophisticated audiences will appreciate a well-organized, clearly written document.

There are usually *constraints* on what you can do when you write a legal document; you should understand your constraints before you begin to write. Time is a major limitation that attorneys must consider, no matter what legal task they are performing. Practicing attorneys must juggle the affairs of many clients and still meet court and filing deadlines. In law school, too, you will have deadlines, and you must tailor your writing plans to meet them.

There are often other constraints to deal with, such as format, paper size, mailing requirements, and reproduction needs. Many times these are dictated by courts or by a law firm or agency.

B Writing Stage

Next you must *organize* your material — arrange what you want to express in a logical sequence. Ask yourself what kind of document you are writing. Is it a basic expository document or something more complex that will require you to present the pros and cons of a particular subject or issue? Once you identify the kind of document you will be producing, you can set up an outline that will help you accomplish your ultimate purpose with the document.

Once you have organized the document and worked out an outline, it is time to begin the actual writing. As you write, you will use sentence structure and style techniques that produce clear and readable prose. Thus, if the purpose of the document is to persuade, there are specific strategies you can use that will make your document more effective. These include using a logical framework to present your reasoning and carefully choosing appropriate vocabulary, grammatical constructions, and forms of discourse that will make your arguments more forceful. In addition, recognizing and avoiding organizational, grammatical, and lexical pitfalls will keep you from inadvertently weakening your arguments.

C Post-writing Stage

At the post-writing stage, you will have a full draft of a document in your hands. This does not mean your job is finished, however. One draft of a document is rarely enough, especially in legal writing. After you finish a first draft, read through the document critically. This is the time to edit and revise: Check both content and form to make sure that your document is complete, correct, and presented in the best possible way. Also check your citations to make sure they are correct and complete and in the proper form. In the final draft, you will also want to check for typographical errors.

8

Understanding
Your Context

A Determining the Purpose

Writing before you have identified your purposes is like trying to plot a route on a road map without knowing your destination. Only if you know where you are going can you hope to construct the shortest, most expedient route. Good writers identify and articulate their purposes — what they want to accomplish — when they are first planning a document. This allows them to make calculated decisions about content, organization, tone, vocabulary, and sentence structure. Thus, the experienced writer is able to construct a document that is likely to achieve precisely what he or she wants it to.

Legal documents serve a variety of purposes. Various legal documents are written:

to inform	to satisfy court rules, federal, state, or local law
to elicit information	to threaten
to persuade	to make someone act or not act
to record	to give notice
to describe	

A legal document can serve more than one purpose. For example, the purpose of a deed to real property is to convey title to that property from one person to another. However, when the deed is recorded, it also serves to place others on notice that a particular piece of land is owned by a particular person.

A letter written by an attorney to a client may inform the client about the merits of the client's case. It may also serve other purposes. For example, if the attorney feels that it is not in the client's best interests to pursue the matter further, he or she may try to persuade the client to drop the case. Thus, the letter would serve both to inform and to persuade the client.

A written contract serves a number of purposes. One purpose is to memorialize the contract so that the parties can refer to it to find out about their rights and obligations. Another purpose is to serve as a record of the agreement should a dispute arise. A final purpose for putting a contract into writing is to ensure that it will be enforceable. In many states certain types of contracts can be enforced only if they are in writing.

_____

1. Specifying Your Purposes

One of the first steps in planning any document is to list every purpose you have for writing that document. Next, sort these purposes into categories so that you can decide how much value to assign to each one and how to relate each purpose to the others. There are no rigid formulas for sorting out your purposes, but we suggest using the following guidelines, which are discussed in more detail in the next few pages.

1. Look at your ultimate or long-range purposes for writing the document. What do you want to gain in the end?
2. Examine your immediate or short-term purposes for writing. What are you trying to accomplish right away?
3. Sort through all of your purposes, both long-and short-term, and rank them according to their importance to you.

Start by thinking about your ultimate purposes for the document. For example, you write trial documents (e.g., briefs, memos, interrogatories, pleadings) with the ultimate goal of winning a client's case. The goal of contracts, wills, trust agreements, warranties, leases, and similar documents, on the other hand, is to create a permanent record of an agreement or a client's request and to establish and define certain legal relationships or legal statuses. Your ultimate goal is to ensure that your client's wishes are carried out and that your client is protected if there is a dispute.

Each document you write will probably also have an immediate purpose or purposes. You write client letters and memos to inform, briefs to persuade, interrogatories to elicit information, and so on.

How do your ultimate and immediate purposes relate to each other? Knowing your ultimate goals will help you decide how to accomplish your immediate purposes. If you lose sight of your ultimate goal when you design a document, you risk sacrificing your long-range effectiveness for the sake of an immediate result. For example, your ultimate goal in writing interrogatories is to help win your client's case, but the more immediate goal is to elicit useful information. Thus, you may design a set of interrogatories in the early stages of your client's case with the immediate purpose of obtaining as much information as you can. In your enthusiasm to do so, you design questions that elicit a wealth of information but are framed in such a way that they give the opposition insight into how much you already know and what kind of trial strategy you are planning. In other words, you may have damaged your chances of accomplishing the ultimate goal of winning your client's case by creating particularly "successful" interrogatories.

Weighing your immediate purposes against your ultimate goals may sound simplistic, but it can be difficult to do in a field such as law, where strategy is crucial, the time span between events in a case can be very great, and an enormous number of documents interrelate to accomplish a final goal or goals. Thus, you may write your interrogatories *years* before your client's case finally comes to trial and culminates in a judgment. You should have that judgment in mind from the beginning, and it should influence everything you write.

2. Ranking Your Purposes

Once you are aware of all of your purposes — both ultimate and immediate — establish a hierarchy, so that you will know which purposes deserve the most emphasis.

Establishing a hierarchy is a subjective activity: There are no rules to tell you how to do it. Your decisions will be based on the specific circumstances of each case. Following is an example of how an attorney might determine and articulate a hierarchy for a particular document.

Imagine an attorney who is representing the husband in a divorce case. The attorney is charging this client a flat fee. He has met with the client several times. Every time the attorney tries to discuss the details of a separation agreement and property settlement with him, the client becomes angry. He protests over and over again that his wife has refused to have relations with him for the last two years, verbally abuses him, and regularly commits adultery. However, he has admitted that he has committed adultery himself on several occasions. The client frequently telephones his attorney to tell him each new offense that the wife has committed.

The client has said that he does not want his wife to get any support payments or any personal or real property. He also wants custody of their two children. He says that if he does not get custody, he does not want to pay child support. In fact, he does not care if his wife and children lose the family home and car, since he feels that his wife will somehow find alternatives. He acknowledges that his wife makes a good deal less money than he does, but he feels that she deserves to struggle to make ends meet. So far, the client has been unyielding about accepting a more balanced proposal to present to his wife's attorney.

The husband's attorney must now draft a preliminary separation and property settlement agreement. The attorney's first step is to identify the ultimate goal of the agreement. In this case the attorney feels that this goal is to produce the best possible settlement for the client — one that is workable and unlikely to lead to repeated litigation and renegotiation.

Next, the attorney will probably think about other, more immediate purposes for the agreement, purposes that will contribute to achieving the ultimate goal. Here are some that the attorney has identified.

1. Informing the court why the husband and wife have separated, and what they have agreed to.
2. Informing the client of his rights.
3. Persuading the client that he has to give up some of what he wants in order to negotiate with his wife and that concessions are reasonable and necessary.
4. Persuading the wife and her attorney that the client is being reasonable.
5. Persuading the court that the agreement is reasonable.

6. Settling property rights, alimony, attorney's fees, child custody, child support payments, and other issues arising from the dissolution of the marriage.
7. Describing the couple's possessions and other property with precision.
8. Recording the agreement for future reference.
9. Formalizing the separation and property agreement to effect a legal act.

Having identified major purposes for writing the separation and settlement agreement, the attorney creates the following hierarchy.

1. It is of the utmost importance to persuade the client that he must make concessions, because the case cannot go any further until the two parties come to some agreement.
2. It is also important to settle rights and describe the property accurately so that the husband and wife will have something concrete to refer to and will better understand exactly what they are agreeing to.
3. It would be useful to formalize the separation quickly, because once the husband and wife are legally separated some of the tension between them will likely abate.
4. Persuading the court that the agreement is reasonable is somewhat less of a concern. (The attorney knows from past experience that the court will accept the agreement if it is within certain reasonable bounds — and he knows how to draft within those bounds.)

Once an attorney creates a hierarchy, he or she can use it, along with information about the audience for the document (see Section B) to determine how best to use the following elements:

content
organization
sentence structure and style
vocabulary
tone

Skillful use of these elements can ensure that a document accomplishes what the attorney wants it to and does not create any problems along the way.

3. Accomplishing Your Purposes

Different purposes lead to different strategies for writing. Thus, if your purpose is to *inform*, you will have to

- Find out what your audience does and does not know.
- Gather the relevant information, anticipating questions.
- Know the relative importance of each piece of information.

- Put the information in a logical sequence, either chronologically or so that the sequence emphasizes (or obscures) certain information.
- Highlight the information you want the reader to be most aware of.
- Guide the reader through the document.

If your purpose is to *elicit information*, you will have to

- Decide what information you need.
- Find out what information your audience is likely to have.
- Ask relevant questions.
- Order your questions to fit your needs.

If your purpose is to *persuade*, you will have to

- Review all available information and decide what will be most favorable to your case.
- Organize to stress the major points of your argument.
- Anticipate counterarguments.
- Develop a strategy to deal with counterarguments.
- Create a logical progression to lead readers to the conclusions you want them to reach.
- Present the available information in a way that is most favorable to your case.
- Choose words carefully for maximum connotative effect.

If your purpose is to *draft a document as a record*, you will have to

- Find out your client's desires.
- Translate the client's desires into legally accurate language.
- Define legal relationships.
- Anticipate possible contingencies.
- Eliminate undesired or irrelevant provisions.
- Comply with correct procedures and legal requirements.

These are general guidelines for creating documents with different purposes. In later chapters, we will present specific strategies for writing different types of documents.

4. Dealing with Conflicting Purposes

Sometimes the multiple purposes of a document will conflict, and it will be necessary to judge which ones should take precedence. If you do not make clear distinctions and choices, you risk including conflicting messages in your writing or hopelessly obscuring your meaning and intentions.

In the example of the attorney representing the husband in a divorce case, the attorney must accommodate multiple, conflicting purposes to accomplish the primary goal of persuading the husband to reach an agreement with his wife. The attorney must try to satisfy a client who is angry and unreasonable and at the same time try to convince the wife's attorney that the husband is willing to make a reasonable settlement. If the husband's attorney does not acknowledge this conflict and attempt to resolve it or to carefully balance these purposes, then the document may be weakened.

Conflicting purposes can influence all kinds of documents, under all kinds of circumstances. A doctor, for example, must inform a patient about the details of a medical procedure before performing that procedure. To avoid a future claim of malpractice, the doctor must make sure that the patient has not only consented to undergo the procedure but also understands the procedure well enough to know what he or she has consented to.

Doctors frequently provide their patients with pamphlets or booklets that explain the details of a particular medical procedure. One purpose of these documents is to inform. The doctor wants the patient to understand what will occur and to be aware of the possible risks and side effects. Another purpose is to reassure the patient and, indirectly, to persuade a patient who really needs a procedure to submit to it, in spite of the risks.

The two purposes of these documents may conflict. The informative aspects may frighten the patient, so that he or she decides not to submit to the procedure or becomes so distressed that his or her physical and emotional health are affected. Unless it is written with care, the document may have an undesirable effect: The patient may know exactly what a necessary procedure will involve but may refuse to consent to it out of fear. Only a writer who recognizes these conflicting purposes will be able to achieve the necessary balance.

A related issue in writing legal documents is the need that they be both legally sufficient and comprehensible. A legal document may sometimes require technical legal terms established by precedent or statute, but it should still be comprehensible to everyone who has to deal with it. Some lawyers believe that these purposes cannot be reconciled and that they must sacrifice comprehensibility for legal sufficiency. A major purpose of this book is to demonstrate that it is possible to achieve both.

5. Writing for Multiple Purposes: An Example

Jury instructions provide a good example of multiple purposes. Jury instructions, as we noted earlier, are directions given orally by the judge to the jurors before they deliberate. The judge uses the instructions to inform the jury of the law that applies to the facts of the case. This major purpose includes two subpurposes: to provide the jury with instructions that are legally sufficient and to provide the jurors with instructions that they can understand.

Typically, jury instructions achieve the goal of legal sufficiency but not the goal of comprehensibility. Legal sufficiency is crucial: An appellate court can reverse a judgment if the appellant shows that the jury instructions were incorrect or imprecise. As a consequence, trial courts tend to use, verbatim, language that has been previously approved by appellate courts, even though the jurors may not be able to understand that language. However, research has shown that jury instructions can be both legally sufficient and comprehensible, provided some changes are made in the way the instructions are written.[1]

Here is a typical jury instruction. It may be legally sufficient, but it is certainly difficult to understand.

> One test that is helpful in determining whether or not a person was negligent is to ask and answer whether or not, if a person of ordinary prudence had been in the same situation and possessed of the same knowledge, he would have foreseen or anticipated that someone might have been injured by or as a result of his action or inaction. If such a result from certain conduct would be foreseeable by a person of ordinary prudence with like knowledge and in like situation, and if the conduct reasonably could be avoided, then not to avoid it would be negligence.[2]

The first sentence contains 62 words and 9 subordinate clauses. Not only is the entire instruction difficult to read, it is even more difficult to follow if you are sitting in the jury box *listening* to it. Only in recent years have the courts come to recognize that many legally sound jury instructions are difficult for people to understand. The hypertechnical language may satisfy an appellate court, but it can lead to confused jury deliberations or an unjust verdict. The same results would probably be achieved without any instructions, since jurors tend to fall back on their own notions of the law when they cannot understand the court's instructions.

The same jury instruction can be written to ensure it will be both legally sufficient and understandable. Keep in mind that these jury instructions are normally read orally to the jury, so that they are written in a different style than they would be if they were meant only to appear on paper.

> In order to decide whether or not the defendant was negligent, there is a test you can use. Consider how a reasonably careful person would have acted in the same situation. Specifically, in order to find the defendant negligent, you would have to answer "yes" to the following two questions:
>
> 1. Would a reasonably careful person have realized in advance that someone might be injured as a result of the defendant's conduct?
> And
> 2. Could a reasonably careful person have avoided behaving as the defendant did?

---

1. Charrow & Charrow, Making Legal Language Understandable: A Psycholinguistic Study of Jury Instructions, 79 Col. L. Rev. 1306 (1979).
2. California Jury Instructions — Civil — Book of Approved Jury Instructions, §3.11 (5th ed. 1969).

> If your answer to both of these questions is "yes," then the defendant was negligent. You can use the same test in deciding whether the plaintiff was negligent.

In an empirical study, jurors who heard this modified instruction understood the law significantly better than those who heard the original version.[3] To see how it is possible to be both understandable and legally accurate, let's look in detail at what the writers did in producing the modified jury instruction.

Context. The original instruction lacks context. It begins by talking about "one test," which is totally new information for the jurors. They have never heard of any test before and have no idea what it is for until well into the instruction. People understand better if familiar information is used to introduce new information. If *all* information is unfamiliar, comprehension suffers severely. Since the jurors are familiar with the terms "defendant" and "negligence" by the time they hear this instruction, the rewritten instruction uses those terms to introduce the new idea of a test to determine negligence. Thus, the drafters have provided a context for the unfamiliar information.

Style. The style of the original instruction is impersonal; the message is not directed *to* anyone. It states, for example, that "one test that is helpful [to whom?] . . . is [for whom?] to ask and answer. . . ." People understand information that is directed to them personally better than information that is directed to no one in particular. Furthermore, the impersonal phraseology is vague and could lead to an imprecise interpretation: The listener can't always tell to whom the information is addressed or who is being discussed. The modified version has a precise and personal style; it addresses the jurors directly as "you": "There is a test *you* can use." "*You* would have to answer 'yes.'"

Organization. The original instruction is not organized logically. Not only does it begin with unfamiliar information, it tells the listener to apply a test without first explaining it. The instruction first tells the listener to "ask and answer whether or not . . . a person of ordinary prudence" would have foreseen the possibility of injury. Only at the very end does the instruction explain that the defendant was negligent if the answer is "yes." There are no signals to alert the listeners to what is expected of them; people need to know that in order to carry out instructions properly.

---

3. Charrow & Charrow, Making Legal Language Understandable: A Psycholinguistic Study of Jury Instructions, 79 Col. L. Rev. 1306 (1979). In Mitchell v. Gonzales, 54 Cal. 3d, 1041, 819 P.2d 872, 1 Cal. Rptr. 2d 913 (1991), the California Supreme Court invalidated that state's standard jury instruction on proximate cause because the instruction was incomprehensible. The instruction, which contained only 27 words, read as follows: "A proximate cause of an injury is a cause which, in natural and continuous sequence, produces the injury, and without which the injury would not have occurred."

The modified version provides a logical progression of ideas. It describes the purpose of the listeners' task before describing the task itself: *"In order to find the defendant negligent*, you would have to answer 'yes' to the following two questions." The modified instruction contains signals to guide listeners through the instruction. They know from the outset that they have to answer "yes" to two questions in order to find the defendant negligent; the two questions are separated and numbered; and, finally, the listeners are told again that if the answer to the two questions is "yes," the defendant was negligent.

Sentence structure.   The original instruction consists of two long sentences, each containing many subordinate clauses in unusual order. The human mind can process only a few pieces of information at a time, and long, complex sentences like these put an undue burden upon the listener. The information in the modified instruction is divided into several shorter sentences, with fewer subordinate clauses. The words in the new sentences are arranged in a more normal order than the original. (*See* Chapter 10 for a discussion of word order.)

Vocabulary.   The original instruction contains "terms of art" as well as unfamiliar and archaic phrases. It also contains legalistic "doublets." None of the legalistic terms or phrases are necessary for the legal accuracy of the instruction. Therefore, the drafters of the modified instruction replaced the term of art *person of ordinary prudence* with the semantically equivalent phrase *reasonably careful person*. They eliminated the archaism *possessed of* and changed *like situation* to *the same situation*. They replaced the first doublet *foreseen or anticipated* with the phrase *realized in advance*; eliminated one term in the second doublet so that *by or as a result of* became *as a result of*; and changed *action or inaction* to the single word *conduct*.

The modified jury instruction was created systematically, following the principles that we present in this book. The drafters identified their purposes before they began to write and let those purposes shape their decisions about the organization, sentence structure, and vocabulary of the modified instruction. They did not ignore legal accuracy, but they did not sacrifice comprehensibility in order to preserve archaic boilerplate. Rather, the drafters chose to emphasize the informative purpose of the instruction, while carefully choosing words that would still accurately reflect the intent of the law.

EXERCISES

1. Read the MECO warranty below and the RDL warranty on page 99. Then do the following:
   a. List the purposes of these documents.
   b. Compare the documents. Is one more effective? If so, can you tell why?

MECO Black and White Television

LIMITED WARRANTY

Who Is Covered?

This warranty covers the original buyer of this MECO TV set.

What Is Covered?

This warranty covers your new MECO TV set for any defects in materials or workmanship.

What Is NOT Covered?

This warranty does not cover:

- the antenna
- the power cord
- any accessories used with the TV
- a broken cabinet
- parts damaged by misuse.

This warranty will not apply if the TV set was dropped, abused, or damaged when altered or repaired by anyone except an authorized MECO service center.

What MECO Will Do and For How Long

For the first 90 days, MECO will supply parts and labor free to repair or replace any defects in materials or workmanship.

After 90 days and up to 1 year, MECO will supply the part free but you will pay a $9.00 service charge. The $9.00 service charge must be paid when you bring or send in the TV.

After the warranty period (one year), you will pay for labor and parts.

At all times, you are responsible for bringing or sending your MECO TV in for repairs.

What You Must Do

The set must have been installed and used normally during the warranty period.

If you bring or send the TV in to an authorized MECO service center, it must be in its original packing case.

You must present an original sales receipt, showing the original date of purchase.

How To Get Warranty Service

Look in the Yellow Pages of your telephone book for the authorized MECO service center nearest you.

This warranty gives you specific legal rights, and you may also have other rights which vary from state to state.

The warranty that this product will work normally is limited to one year. No one has the right to change or add to this warranty.

Five Year Limited Warranty

These units have been properly designed, tested and inspected before they are shipped. Each speaker system is warranted free from defects (workmanship and material) for five years from date of delivery to the original purchaser. The warranty includes parts and labor for the first year. After the first year, and continuing through the fifth year of the warranty, the warranty extends to parts only and a nominal charge will be made for labor. The speaker system is to be delivered or shipped to us, or an authorized warranty station, for warranty repair, freight charges prepaid. The duration of all warranties other than this written warranty, whether express, implied or created by operations of law, trade usage or course of dealing is five years from date of delivery to the original purchasers. The Company shall not be liable for any loss or damage, direct, incidental or consequential arising out of the use of, or the inability to use the product, and The Company's obligation in any event is expressly limited to the repair of the product as provided herein above. The warranty is not extended to the cabinet or grill. This warranty does not apply to units which have been subject to misuse, abuse, neglect, accident or improper installation; nor does it apply to repairs or alteration by unauthorized personnel. We retain the right to make such determination on the basis of factory inspection. Any claims under this limited warranty must be asserted prior to the expiration date of this written warranty.

2. Read the version of the "Holder in Due Course Notice" below, from a consumer credit contract. What do you think the purposes of this notice are? Does it achieve those purposes? Try to rewrite the notice so that it better achieves its purposes.

> Any Holder of this Consumer Credit Contract is subject to all claims and defenses which the Debtor could assert against the Seller of goods or services obtained pursuant hereto or with the proceeds hereof. Recovery hereunder by the Debtor shall be limited to amounts paid by the Debtor hereunder.

3. Skim the airline ticket below. What are the purposes of this document? What can be done to help the document better achieve its purposes?

ADVICE TO INTERNATIONAL PASSENGERS ON LIMITATION OF LIABILITY

Passengers on a journey involving an ultimate destination or a stop in a country other than the country of origin are advised that the provisions of a treaty known as the Warsaw Convention may be applicable to the entire journey, including any portion entirely within the country of origin or destination. For such passengers on a journey to, from, or with an agreed stopping place in the United States of America, the Convention and special contracts of carriage embodied in applicable tariffs provide that the liability of certain carriers, parties to such special contracts, for death of or personal injury to passengers is limited in most cases to proven damages not to exceed U.S. $75,000 per passenger, and that this liability up to such limit shall not depend on negligence on the part of the carrier. The limit of liability of U.S. $75,000 above is inclusive of legal fees and costs except that in case of a claim brought in a state where provision is made for separate award of legal fees and costs, the limit shall be the sum of U.S. $58,000 exclusive of legal fees and costs. For such passengers traveling by a carrier not a party to such special contracts or on a journey not to, from, or having an agreed stopping place in the United States of America, liability of the carrier for death or personal injury to passengers is limited in most cases to approximately U.S. $10,000 or U.S. $20,000.

The names of carriers, parties to such special contracts, are available at all ticket offices of such carriers and may be examined on request. Additional protection can usually be obtained by purchasing insurance from a private company. Such insurance is not affected by any limitation of the carrier's liability under the Warsaw Convention or such special contracts of carriage. For further information please consult your airline or insurance company representative.

NOTICE OF BAGGAGE LIABILITY LIMITATIONS

Liability for loss, delay, or damage to baggage is limited as follows unless a higher value is declared in advance and additional charges are paid: (1) For most international travel (including domestic portions of international journeys) to approximately $9.07 per pound ($20.00 per kilo) for checked baggage, and $400 per passenger, for unchecked baggage; (2) For travel wholly between U.S. points, to $750 per passenger on most carriers (a few have lower limits). Excess valuation may not be declared on certain types of valuable articles. Carriers assume no liability for fragile or perishable articles. Further information may be obtained from the carrier.

---

4. One of the purposes of a complaint is to disclose to the court and to the defendant the facts upon which the plaintiff is basing the complaint. The complaint should contain a concise, clear statement of the facts. *See* sample complaint on pages 00-00 Read through the statement of facts below. Identify any features that obscure its meaning and explain why each feature has this effect. Finally, rewrite the passage so that it is legally sufficient, but more comprehensible.

> On or about September 3, 1980, at or about 6:20 p.m., plaintiff Jack Marshall was operating his 1979 Chevrolet Citation automobile, license number 676 ABC, at, near, or about Springfield Boulevard northbound and near Royal Oaks Drive, in the County of Los Angeles, State of California, and at the said time and place, the defendant, Lawrence Cutler, so negligently, carelessly, and recklessly owned, manufactured, controlled, maintained, repaired, leased, used, rented, operated, permitted, entrusted, supervised, managed, and drove his said property on, about, or near said streets and highways, so as to cause the same to violently collide with the right rear side of the vehicle of the plaintiff, and to violently collide a second time with the right door of

the vehicle of the plaintiff, and to violently collide a third time with the right front portion of the vehicle of the plaintiff, causing plaintiff to lose control of his vehicle and thereby damaging the vehicle and property of plaintiff and injuring plaintiff as hereinafter set forth.

That immediately thereafter and as soon as plaintiff was able to regain control of his vehicle, plaintiff pulled over to the right-hand side of Springfield Boulevard, in an effort to comply with the statutory requirements of the laws of the state of California to exchange information with the driver of the other vehicle, and plaintiff attempted to motion the defendant, Lawrence Cutler, to pull over his vehicle for said exchange of information, and the defendant, Lawrence Cutler, proceeded northbound on Springfield Boulevard, without stopping, and defendant Lawrence Cutler, as he passed the plaintiff herein, made a gesture to the plaintiff herein with the middle finger of his right hand, and proceeded to flee the scene at a high rate of speed.

B Identifying the Audience

Most courtroom lawyers develop some remarkable language abilities. They learn to change their verbal style so that they argue differently before an appellate court than before a trial court; they address a jury very differently from the way they address a judge. In addition, research by sociologist Brenda Danet of the Hebrew University in Jerusalem and by anthropologist William O'Barr of Duke University has shown that trial lawyers change their questioning style considerably from direct examination to cross-examination.[4] They use different grammatical structures and different vocabulary — as well as a different tone of voice. Consciously or unconsciously, courtroom lawyers change their style and language to suit the purpose and the audience.

Many lawyers — even those with excellent courtroom skills — are not able to transfer verbal skills into writing. Because they cannot adjust their writing styles to fit the audience and the purpose, their writing often fails to communicate. Those lawyers who can adapt their presentations to appeal to specific audiences have an edge over other attorneys: They are better able to inform, instruct, or elicit information and, most important, they are better able to persuade. You can fine-tune your writing in the same way that skilled courtroom lawyers fine-tune their oral presentations. To do this, however, you must learn to identify your audience and its needs even before setting pen to paper.

1. Lawyers' Audiences

Lawyers write many documents for other members of the legal community. However, they do not communicate just with one another or with the courts.

---

4. Danet, Language in the Legal Process, 14 Law and Society Review 445 (1980); O'Barr & Conley, When a Juror Watches a Lawyer, 3 Barrister 8 (1976).

They produce numerous documents that are directed toward nonlawyers. For example, lawyers regularly write to or for the following audiences.

1. *Individual clients:* Lawyers write letters to clients and create documents for clients to use, such as wills, leases, deeds, contracts, etc.
2. *Business clients* (such as insurance companies, private investigators, corporations, banking institutions): Lawyers write letters, articles of incorporation, by-laws, contracts, release agreements, etc.
3. *Government agencies:* Lawyers outside government agencies write, among other things, letters of inquiry and comments on regulations. Lawyers within agencies write regulations, guidelines, preambles, position papers, etc.
4. *Lay people who are not clients:* Lawyers write letters to nonlawyers on behalf of their clients. Lawyers also write documents such as journal articles, books, and speeches for the general public.

Lawyers rarely write a document that is meant for only a single audience. Even when they write for other members of the legal profession, they are often writing for various people with different backgrounds and different roles. Thus, a brief will be read by both the judge and opposing counsel, and each of these audiences will use the document for different purposes.

Attorneys sometimes misperceive the expectations of the courts or other lawyers when they write, assuming that all lawyers speak the same language and are familiar with the same subject matter. Modern law is complex, and a lawyer who specializes in one area of the law may not be familiar with the nuances of other areas. And no matter how well versed attorneys are in the law, it will not help them decipher writing that is ambiguous, unclear, or badly written. The attorney who assumes that his or her peers will understand a document risks having it misunderstood by the court, misinterpreted to the client's disadvantage, or made the subject of a malpractice suit.

Even documents that one might suppose are written primarily for other members of the legal profession often have important nonlegal audiences. Thus, although some attorneys would argue that a will is written primarily for the probate court, it is important that the client, beneficiaries, executor, trustees, guardians, and other fiduciaries be able to understand it without continually turning to a lawyer for translation.

Picture the following situations.

1. An attorney drafts a will in typical legal language for an elderly client. She explains to the client that she has incorporated all the client's wishes in the will. Three months later, the client, pondering his decisions about his estate, decides to check his will and finds that he cannot understand it. He calls the attorney several times a day for the next week, asking questions about his will. The attorney realizes that although she had discussed all these matters with the client before drafting the will and before the client signed the will, the will is useless as a reference document for the client.

Calling the attorney is time-consuming and costly for both the client and the attorney.

2. A woman in her thirties has a will drafted in traditional legal language. Both she and her husband read it, but they do not really understand it and do not realize that it doesn't reflect what they want. Years later, the woman dies, and, much to the husband's dismay, the probate court follows the provisions of the will, refusing to accept the husband's arguments that these were not his wife's original intentions. The attorney who drafted the will has been dead for twenty years, and so the husband has no recourse.

These situations could have been avoided if the attorneys had written the wills so that they were comprehensible to their clients.[5]

a. *Writing for Multiple Audiences*

Because attorneys sometimes assume that the primary purpose of most legal documents is to communicate with the courts, they concentrate on using the language that is necessary to make a document legally sufficient. They may regard clear writing as a desirable, but secondary, goal. Some attorneys even believe that writing clearly and comprehensibly for nonlawyers is unnecessary. They consider it an attorney's function to serve as translator for the lay person and to act as a go-between for the lay person and the legal system.

As the will examples demonstrate, an attorney cannot always take the place of a legal document as a source of information. These situations are not farfetched. They demonstrate the kinds of unforeseen or poorly handled circumstances that often lead to lawsuits. There are other instances of poorly drafted language resulting in problems because an attorney is not always available to serve as a translator. An attorney cannot serve as an "interpreter" during jury deliberations, and judges will rarely do more than merely repeat an instruction. Many tenants have little or no idea of the terms of their leases, even though by signing them they have consented to those terms. Similarly, consumers often do not know exactly what a product warranty covers. Consumers and tenants would not normally think of consulting an attorney before encountering a problem, even if they could afford to do so. Readable documents would help avoid many of the disputes and complications that clog the court system unnecessarily.

---

5. Although it is not an easy task, it is possible to write a complex will that is understandable to the testator (the person making the will) and beneficiaries and still legally sufficient. A number of experienced probate lawyers have created complex wills that satisfy these conflicting audiences, and, in fact, in March 1983, the American College of Probate Council tackled just this problem in a course it presented on "Drafting with Clarity." *See also* Squires & Mucklestone, Drafting a Truly Simple Will that Can Effectively Communicate to Both Client and Court, Estate Planning, March 1983, at 80.

b. *Writing for Conflicting Audiences*

The problem of conflicting audiences is similar to the problem of conflicting purposes. Even though you may realize that a document should be addressed to more than one audience, you may feel that the needs of each are mutually exclusive. The solution is similar to the solution for dealing with conflicting purposes: You can frequently accommodate the needs of many audiences at once by knowing *how* to present the information.

If complex legal language does not really serve most of your audiences, then what changes should you make? It is a good idea to start with the premise that you should design your document for the *audience that is least likely to understand it*; that way you will encompass *all* of your audiences. This is a sound strategy as long as it won't damage your credibility or render the document useless for some audiences. Usually, there will be no such threat: The modifications we suggest will not result in a simplistic or condescending tone, nor will they damage legal sufficiency. If properly used, they will merely clarify your message.

What if you feel that you absolutely cannot afford to gear your document to the audience that is least likely to understand it, because it will damage your credibility with a more sophisticated audience or because it will mean that you cannot include all of the material necessary for other audiences? If that is the case, you should ask yourself the following questions.

1. Can I rearrange the document? You might divide the document into sections addressed to different audiences. Alternatively, you might include a glossary of major terms and concepts for some audiences.
2. Do I really want just one document? Perhaps you should create several versions.

If you cannot write more than one document and your document cannot be broken into sections, you will have to do some weighing and balancing. Carefully review all of your audiences. Who is your most important audience? Whom do you have to be sure to address? Be careful not to make hasty assumptions about who does or does not matter.

2. Classifying the Audience

a. *Identifying Your Audience*

How do you decide who your audience is? First, list all possible audiences. Don't stop at the obvious ones or those that appear to be primary; you may be neglecting other, equally important, audiences. For example, if you were an attorney working for a federal or state regulatory agency and you were corresponding with regulated industries, you would be aware that industries are the major audience. It might not immediately occur to you, however, that it might be an engineer and not an attorney who will read your letter.

You will have other audiences as well—your superiors within the agency, for example. If you are writing a document for a case, the document may be discoverable, and your opponent may read it. You will surely want to choose your content and modify your style on the basis of this information.

Sometimes you may have trouble determining who your audience is, and you will need to do some research. For example, you may have to find out how the review system works in your agency to learn who will review your letters, or you may have to research the law to find out if a particular document is discoverable.

b. Analyzing Your Audience

Once you have identified all possible audiences, consider their different characteristics, needs, and expectations. If you are addressing a letter to your client, ask yourself about that client. Is the client a physician? Is the client another attorney who has hired you as counsel? An insurance agent? A criminal defendant? A retired farmer? A plumber? How would your writing differ for members of these groups?

There are other things you might want to consider when writing letters or other documents.

1. *Age.* Will the age of your audience affect how you write the document? If your reader is a child who is being asked to sign an assent form in an adoption case, is the form written in language a child can understand? If your client is elderly and has expectations about formality and respect, is the document written in a suitable style?

2. *Native language.* Does your audience have any problems with the English language? An attorney for the Immigration and Naturalization Service who writes forms and instructions for aliens or a practicing attorney who has a foreign client must keep in mind that his or her readers may not be native speakers of English.

3. *Education and reading level.* Does your audience have any significant education or reading level characteristics for which you should tailor your vocabulary and style? For example, is your client a person who can barely read, or is your client a corporation with a highly sophisticated board of directors?

4. *Familiarity with subject matter.* Is your audience familiar with the subject of the document? If you are handling a medical malpractice case, is your client the defendant physician or the plaintiff?

5. *Familiarity with legal language.* Is your client familiar with legal language? Is your client a judge or another attorney, or an airline pilot or school teacher who may never have had any dealings with the court system?

6. *Attitude.* What kind of attitude does your client have about documents such as the one you are creating? Is your audience composed of members of a regulated industry who resent the paperwork and complicated regulations that your agency produces? Are the members of your audience lay people who may be annoyed or intimidated by legal documents that they can't understand?

7. *Physical or other problems.* Do the members of your audience have any physical, mental, or emotional problems that might affect the way you should write for them? For example, does your client have vision problems that might make small print difficult to read? Does your client have a short attention span? Is your client sensitive about certain kinds of subject matter?

8. *Individual concerns.* Does your audience have other individual concerns, unique characteristics, or obvious biases? Does your audience have a particular desire to be involved in what you are doing? Are there considerations associated with the audience's profession, gender, or marital status?

Sexist writing can be particularly offensive to many members of your audience. There are a number of ways to avoid sexist writing.

1. Rewrite the sentence so that you do not have to use the gender pronouns *he* or *she*. You can do this by repeating the noun instead.

> An attorney will often write a letter to the client in order to keep *him* informed.

> An attorney will often write a letter to the client in order to keep *the client* informed.

2. If possible, rewrite the statement in the plural.

> The student should bring *her* torts book to class.

> Students should bring *their* torts books to class.

> However, you should try to avoid overusing the plural, especially in cases in which it can lead to ambiguity. For example, the statement "students must all submit reports" obscures information about whether students must submit one or several reports.

3. If you are talking about or directly to your readers, address them in the second person.

> A *lawyer* must pass the state bar exam if *he* wants to practice law.

> *You* must pass the state bar exam if *you* want to practice law.

4. You can often replace third person singular possessives (*his* or *her*) with articles.

> A judge must wear *her* black robe while in court.

> A judge must wear *a* (or *the*) black robe while in court.

5. Avoid gender-specific titles such as *chairman, policeman,* or *stewardess.* You can often replace these terms with neutral terms such as *chair, police officer,* or *flight attendant.* Similarly, you can replace generic terms such as *mankind* with *the human race.* Avoid awkward constructions such as *chairperson* or *police-person.* Use them only if you cannot find a better alternative.

6. You can sometimes use the passive voice to avoid a sexist construction. However, the passive voice can cause more problems than it solves (see Chapter 10).

7. You may sometimes use *he or she* and *his or hers.* However, *s/he* and *he/she* are awkward, and you should avoid them.

8. In certain types of documents and especially in presenting examples, you can use *she* and *he* in alternate sentences, paragraphs, or sections, as we have done in c, below. However, you should carefully reread what you have written to make certain the result makes sense.

9. Don't try to cure a sexist statement by using a third person plural pronoun to refer to a third person singular antecedent. For example:

> A *student* can work in a law firm or for a judge, depending on what *they* want to do when *they* graduate.

This construction is not grammatical and can make you appear illiterate.

c. *The Unfamiliar Audience*

If you know who your audience is, but don't know enough about it to list its relevant characteristics, then do some research. You might protest that you are not a researcher, and that you don't have time to perform such an analysis. However, audience analysis is really an extension of what most good attorneys do when they practice law — they evaluate people. Attorneys make judgments and draw conclusions about others in order to make sound business decisions and construct successful strategies. When an attorney talks to a client, the attorney probes for nonlegal information about that client: How intelligent is the client — will he make a good witness? Is she telling the truth? Is he emotionally stable? Will she pay me my fee? Should I take this case, or will it be more aggravation than it is worth? Lawyers systematically (sometimes unconsciously) use this information to make decisions about how to handle a case. The same information is also valuable for making decisions about how to write.

A conscious audience analysis is not reserved just for clients. If you become a litigator, you will learn a great deal by observing judges and juries, and over time you will learn to gauge their reactions. What does a certain judge expect from an attorney? How will this jury respond to a certain strategy or approach? Will emotion or logic be more effective?

If you cannot observe your audience directly, you may be able to find out about it by asking others or by reading. You might ask another attorney for an assessment of a particular judge. However, if you are unable to assess your audience at firsthand or through another's experience, be wary of books or articles, especially on trial advocacy, that make generalizations that are not based on empirical research.

3. Writing for a Specific Audience: Some Examples

Here are examples of two documents that deal with essentially the same subject matter but are directed at different audiences. The first document is a portion of a medical consent form, which has been used by the National Institutes of Health for adults who volunteer to participate in medical research projects. When the patient signs the form, he or she gives legal consent to being treated as an experimental subject by NIH.

The second document is part of a child's assent form from NIH, which has been used when the subjects chosen for the study are below the age of consent (that is, their parents must consent for them). When the child signs the form, he or she is indicating willingness to participate as an experimental subject.

CONSENT FOR ADULTS

We invite you to participate in a research study conducted by the National Institutes of Health. It is important that you read and understand the following general principles, which apply to all participants in our studies: 1) participation is entirely voluntary; 2) it is possible that you may not personally benefit from participating in the study, although we may gain knowledge that will benefit others; and 3) you may withdraw from the study at any time without any consequences.

We will explain what the study is about, its risks, inconveniences, discomforts, and other relevant information. If you have any questions, please feel free to ask us.

What this study is about: This study attempts to discover the causes of neurological (nervous system) damage, which may be related to infections in pregnant women, children, and adults. It involves a physical examination and routine laboratory tests, including drawing 1-4 tablespoons of blood at the time of your first visit and at later times if necessary. We may also do cultures of sputum and of any lesions (sores) in the throat, eye, skin, or the urinary or genital tract.

We may find that it is necessary to do a lumbar (spinal) puncture in order to define the extent or possible cause of the illness. If we find it necessary to do a lumbar puncture, you will have to lie on your side, and we will insert a needle into the space between the bones in your lower back to collect spinal fluid. We will use a local anesthetic so that you won't feel very much pain.

Even though this is an outpatient study, we will ask you to stay in the hospital for one to three days if we do a lumbar puncture.

ASSENT FROM CHILD

How You Can Help Us

We are asking you to help us because we want to find out why some children have your illness. One way we can find out is to do some tests on children like you. These tests may not help you, but the things we learn may help other children.

This paper explains what we want to do to you. Read this paper and ask us questions about anything that you do not understand. Then you decide if you want to be in the test. You can stop being in the test any time you want. When you come to the Clinical Center, we will talk to you and your parents. We will examine you and we will explain more about the different tests we will do.

What We Will Do

The first thing we will do is stick a small needle in a vein in your arm to take 4 spoonfuls of your blood. The needle will hurt for a minute, but the pain will go away quickly. We may also take swabs from your throat, eyes, or skin. This means that we will use a tool like a big Q-tip to scrape off a few cells from your throat, eyes, or skin. You may feel a little uncomfortable when we do this, but it will not really hurt. You will go home as soon as we finish these tests.

You may have to stay in the hospital for a while if we decide to take some liquid from in between the bones of your spine (the bones that go down the middle of your back). The liquid is called spinal fluid. Before we get the spinal fluid, we will give you some medicine so you won't feel any pain. Then we will put a small needle between the bones of your spine in the lower part of your back. After we take out the fluid, we will ask you to lie down flat on your back for a few hours. If you feel any pain in your back or head, you should tell us.

You will notice that the two documents differ in the following major ways.

1. The adult form assumes that the adult will have some idea of why research studies are conducted and what it means to be in a research study. But the child's assent form begins by telling the child *why* he or she is being asked to participate in the study and what this means to the child. The child's form immediately connects the study to the child's own illness because it is easier to understand new information if it is tied to the reader's own experience.

2. The internal organization of the adult form reflects an adult way of thinking: The form first presents general principles regarding all NIH studies, then the rationale for this study, and then the procedures involved. In the description of procedures, there is little discussion of immediate consequences, such as pain. These are explained in a separate section, which we have not reproduced.

The child's form has a different internal organization. It starts by relating the rationale for the study directly to the child's experience. It then talks about specific procedures, beginning with participation in the study and going on to the steps involved in the tests.

Because children are generally less adept than adults at making causal connections, the child's form fills in the gaps between procedures and results. The child is told right after each step whether he or she will experience discomfort. Because a child's experience is more limited, the form explicitly states information that would be self-evident to an adult.

3. The adult form contains a number of technical terms and concepts, such as "neurological damage," "lesions," and "lumbar puncture." These are terms that adults might understand or that they can figure out from the context provided by the rest of the document. Even so, the terms are clarified in the text. The child's form, on the other hand, contains none of these technical terms. Furthermore, because children tend to think about things in very concrete ways, the assent form gives a step-by-step description of each activity or process.

4. Neither of these forms contains long, complex sentences. The use of short, relatively simple sentences is particularly important in the child's form, because children are still learning to read and to decipher basic sentence structures, and complicated sentences are more difficult to follow. These forms were written with the help of writing experts and use many of the techniques we describe in this book in order to accomplish their purpose: communication with a specific audience.

Here is another example of a document written by an attorney for a very specific and familiar audience.

Mr. Leppo, the attorney who wrote the following motion, must have been absolutely certain that his audience (the judge to whom he was making his motion) would be receptive to his humorous treatment. (The judge's order, which follows the motion, is proof that Mr. Leppo's estimate of his audience was accurate.)

If you are not absolutely certain that you can use a humorous tone in addressing a traditionally serious audience—such as a judge—do *not* try it. You risk offending your audience.

UNITED STATES DISTRICT COURT
WESTERN DISTRICT OF WASHINGTON, AT TACOMA

LOUISIANA-PACIFIC CORPORATION, a Delaware corporation,	)))	
Plaintiff,	))	Consolidated NO. C88-217TB
vs.	))))	
ASARCO INCORPORATED, a New Jersey corporation, et al.,	)))	MOTION FOR RECONSIDERATION OF SECOND AMENDED
Defendants.	)	TRIAL DATE
PORT OF TACOMA, a Washington municipal corporation,	)))	
Plaintiff,	)))	
vs.	)))	
ASARCO INCORPORATED, a New Jersey Corporation; PORTAC, INC., a Delaware corporation; MURRAY PACIFIC CORPORATION, a Washington corporation; WASSER & WINTERS COMPANY, a Washington corporation; NICHIMEN AMERICA, INC., a New York corporation; and CASCADE TIMBER COMPANY, a Washington corporation,	))))))))))))))	
Defendants.	))	

I. Introduction

Counsel for plaintiff Port of Tacoma, Jeffrey W. Leppo ("Counsel"), respect-fully requests that this Court reconsider its decision to amend the trial date of this litigation to October 1, 1990. For personal, but not less important reasons, Counsel requests that the trial begin one week later on October 8, 1990.

II. Marital Facts

Counsel bases this motion upon the following uncontroverted facts:

1. It has taken Counsel over 34 years to find someone whom he loves and who loves him.
2. Counsel became engaged on January 31, 1990, at a time when this matter was set for trial beginning May 21, 1990.
3. Scheduling for a wedding, especially one involving the concurrence of two out-of-town families and the Roman Catholic Church, requires considerable advance planning.
4. Counsel's wedding was scheduled for September 8, 1990, at a time when this matter was set for trial beginning May 21, 1990.
5. Counsel's Honeymoon was scheduled for September 11 through September 30, 1990, at times when this matter was set for trial beginning either May 21, 1990, or June 26, 1990. As with all other aspects of the wedding, the Honeymoon has required extensive advance planning.
6. Counsel has been devoted to the practice of law for ten years. He has dutifully worked long hours, weekends, holidays, and birthdays, cancelled long-scheduled plans and irritated, ignored, offended, and otherwise pissed-off friends, family, and former girlfriends in pursuit of justice for his clients.
7. On very solid information and belief, Counsel believes his betrothed will feel very irritated, ignored, offended, and otherwise extremely pissed-off if the Honeymoon must be canceled, delayed, or cut short. Counsel further believes such feelings would be justified.
8. Counsel is loathe to begin what he very sincerely hopes and intends to be his one and only marriage by offending his bride-to-be, in-laws, associated friends, and the Roman Catholic Church.
9. Neither Counsel nor his client have sought or contributed to any undue delay of this litigation.
10. A one week difference in the start of this trial will prejudice no party.
11. This Court will enjoy the eternal gratitude of Counsel, his betrothed, family, friends, and the Roman Catholic Church should he find merit in this motion for reconsideration.

III. Prayer for Relief

The merits of this motion are founded upon common notions of respect, fairness, and compassion. Accordingly, they speak for themselves. Nevertheless, one point bears further brief discussion.

After enduring four months of marriage preparation classes insisted upon by the parish priest of Counsel's betrothed, Counsel has been informed that his proposed marriage is now blessed and sacred to the Roman Catholic Church. Counsel is not exactly sure what this means, but is convinced after experiencing the prescribed preparation, that the Roman Catholic Church has little sense of humor about such matters. Counsel seriously suspects that it would be a Mortal Sin (in secular terms, a "Big Mistake") to disappoint the Roman Catholic Church at this point in time. Counsel believes that the Roman Catholic Church will be heavily influenced in this matter by his betrothed, her family, friends, and parish priest.

Accordingly, as noted in paragraph II(11) above, Counsel respectfully offers the eternal gratitude of himself, his heirs, his assigns, and his issue (if any there be), in return for the Court's compassion. Counsel warrants that this eternal gratitude will be far more valuable a gift should he be so fortunate as to spend his days on Earth in the state of Marital Bliss and the Everlasting in a state of heavenly repose. Counsel further warrants that should the trial begin on October 1, 1990, he will be required to disappoint the Roman Catholic Church through the above-referenced representatives, thereby committing a Mortal Sin, and thereby ensuring that, after spending his days on Earth in the courts of the state of Washington, he will spend the Everlasting in a considerably lower and warmer jurisdiction. Counsel believes that the likelihood of eternal damnation constitutes undue prejudice.

For the foregoing reasons, and in the interest of truth, justice, the American Way, and all that is good and fair, and in the best sense of humor he can muster under circumstances that are truly not funny, the undersigned respectfully requests that this Court reconsider its second amended trial date and grant a one week extension to October 8, 1990.

DATED this 29th day of May, 1990

/s/ _____

Jeffrey W. Leppo
Counsel of Record for Plaintiff
Port of Tacoma

UNITED STATES DISTRICT COURT
WESTERN DISTRICT OF WASHINGTON
AT TACOMA

LOUISIANA-PACIFIC CORPORATION, a Delaware corporation,
 	
     Plaintiff,
 	
     v.
 	
ASARCO, INCORPORATED, a New Jersey corporation, et al.,
 	
    Defendants/Third
    Party Plaintiffs,
	NO. C88-217TB
	CONSOLIDATED
	
	ORDER GRANTING
	PORT OF TACOMA'S
	MOTION FOR
	RECONSIDERATION OF
	SECOND AMENDED
	TRIAL DATE

PORT OF TACOMA, a municipal corporation,
 	
     Plaintiff,
 	
     v.
 	
ASARCO INC., a New Jersey corporation, et al.,
 	
     Defendants.	

This Matter comes before the court on the Motion of Plaintiff Port of Tacoma for Reconsideration of Second Amended Trial Date. The court has reviewed the pleadings filed in support of this motion.

In this court's twenty years of judicial experience, counsel's motion for reconsideration is unprecedented in its creativity and urgency. In a spirit of cooperation with Mr. Leppo's efforts to avoid eternal damnation and to please (and appease) his intended, their families and friends, as well as the Roman Catholic Church, it is hereby

ORDERED that the Port of Tacoma's Motion for Reconsideration of Second Amended Trial Date is GRANTED and the trial date of this case is hereby continued to October 9, 1990.

The Clerk of the Court is instructed to send uncertified copies of this Order to all counsel of record.

DATED this __3rd__ day of _____ May _____ , 19 _90_ .

/s/ _____

Robert J. Bryan
United States District Judge

4. Writing for Multiple Audiences: An Example

On page 123 is a copy of a Massachusetts automobile insurance policy. Skim this document, then compare it with the modified version on pages 124 and 125. The modified version accommodates various audiences without sacrificing legal sufficiency or appropriateness for any individual audience.

Before comparing the policies, consider who the audiences for this type of insurance policy are. It has at least six readily identifiable audiences.

1. Consumers (insureds and potential insureds)
2. Insurance agents or employees who administer the policies
3. Members of the Massachusetts Insurance Commission (the Commission regulates insurance companies and approves plans and policies)
4. Banks and finance companies that require anyone who takes out an automobile loan to have insurance on that automobile
5. Other insurance companies (if the insured is covered by more than one company, companies often pay *pro rata* shares of the insured's liabilities)
6. Insurance company attorneys, private attorneys, and the courts, when questions or disputes arise

Notice that only one of these audiences consists of people who are likely to have legal backgrounds. Members of the lay audiences have different backgrounds and varying degrees of familiarity with a legalistic writing style and with insurance terms and concepts. They are probably the least well equipped to deal with this document, yet, because they use the document frequently, these are the people who most need the information in the policy. Attorneys and insurance company employees can also have trouble interpreting insurance policies. Insurance company employees do not always understand the language of the policies generated by their own companies; they frequently rely on verbal explanations or written translations provided by the people who write the policies. A private attorney who does not regularly handle insurance cases might also have trouble deciphering the provisions. Even an attorney who is well versed in insurance law would probably be relieved to see some of the needless complexity removed.

The person who revised the Massachusetts insurance policy chose to modify the original so that the lay audiences could understand it, but the modifications do not damage the document's usefulness for any audience. Let's examine the modifications and the differences they make.

Context. The original policy does not provide a context for the information in the policy. There is nothing that explains to the reader what the document is about. It begins with a statement about an agreement of some sort that the insurance company has with the insured. The statement is never discussed, nor is it labeled with an informative heading. There is no introduction to explain what the policy is for, what divisions or sections it contains, or what kinds of coverage it provides. Instead, the policy jumps from the agreement boilerplate into "Coverage A." The reader isn't told how many different kinds of coverage there are, why there are different kinds of coverage, or how each kind fits into the overall scheme.

In contrast, the modified policy clearly labels the agreement provision with a large title in boldface type and explains exactly what the insurer and insured are agreeing to. This section also provides the reader with a definition of what an insurance policy is (that is, a contract) and tells the reader exactly what this contract consists of.

The main body of the modified policy also has a boldface title and contains an introduction. This section defines compulsory insurance and provides a roadmap for what is ahead: It tells the reader how many parts the policy contains and where to find information on coverage and costs.

Tone. The tone of the original policy is impersonal: The information is not directed to anyone in particular. In addition, the sentences do not always tell *who* is being discussed. For example, Coverage A, Division 2, states that "The company will pay [to whom?] . . . subject to any applicable deductible [whose deductible?] all reasonable expenses incurred within two years [by whom?] from the date of the accident [whose accident?] for necessary medical, surgical, x-ray, and dental services."

The modified policy has a personal tone; it addresses the insured as "you" and refers to the insurer as "we." The sentences all contain subjects and objects, so that the reader can always tell who is being addressed and who is being discussed. For example, Part 1 opens with the following statement: "Under this Part, *we* will pay damages *to people injured* or killed by *your* auto in Massachusetts accidents. The damages *we* will pay are the amounts *the injured person* is entitled to collect."

Organization. The original policy presents information in an illogical order, without natural topic or section divisions. It is divided into broad sections that cover a hodgepodge of different subjects. Part 1, for example, has the following heading: LIABILITY, PERSONAL INJURY PROTECTION, MEDICAL PAYMENTS AND PHYSICAL DAMAGE INSURING AGREEMENTS. This vast area is then divided into different coverages that are in turn subdivided. There is no roadmap to clarify the logic or meaning of these divisions for the reader.

BLANK INSURANCE COMPANY

A . . . . insurance company herein called the company

In consideration of the payment of the premium, in reliance upon the statements in the declarations made a part hereof and subject to all of the terms of this policy, agrees with the insured named in the declarations as follows:

(For policy issued by two companies)

In consideration of the payment of the premium, in reliance upon the statements in the declarations made a part hereof and subject to all of the terms of this policy, severally agree with the insured named in the declarations as follows, provided the Blank Casualty Company shall be the insurer with respect to coverages . . . . and no other and the Blank Fire Insurance Company shall be the insurer with respect to coverages . . . .

PART I—LIABILITY, PERSONAL INJURY PROTECTION,

PROPERTY PROTECTION, MEDICAL PAYMENTS AND PHYSICAL DAMAGE

INSURING AGREEMENTS

1 Coverage A

Division 1—Bodily Injury Liability—Statutory—The Commonwealth of Massachusetts—(This Coverage is Compulsory)

The company will pay on behalf of the insured, in accordance with the "Massachusetts Compulsory Automobile Liability Security Act," Chapter 346 of the Acts of 1925 of the Commonwealth of Massachusetts and all Acts amendatory thereof or supplementary thereto, all sums which the insured shall become obligated to pay by reason of the liability imposed upon him by law for damages to others for bodily injury, including death at any time resulting therefrom, or for consequential damages consisting of expenses incurred by a husband, wife, parent or guardian for medical, nursing, hospital or surgical services in connection with or on account of such bodily injury or death, sustained by any person or persons during the policy period as defined in Item [3]² of the declarations and caused by the ownership, operation, maintenance, control or use of the insured motor vehicle upon the ways of the Commonwealth of Massachusetts or in any place therein to which the public has a right of access.

This division of coverage A is subject to the following provisions:

(1) No statement made by the insured or on his behalf, either in securing this policy or in securing registration of the insured motor vehicle, no violation of the terms of this policy and no act or default of the insured, either prior to or subsequent to the issuance of this policy, shall operate to defeat or avoid this coverage so as to bar recovery by a judgment creditor proceeding in accordance with the Laws of the Commonwealth of Massachusetts. The terms of this policy shall remain in full force and effect, however, as binding between the insured and the company, and the insured agrees to reimburse the company for any payment made by the company under this policy on account of any accident, claim or suit involving a breach of the terms of this policy.

(2) Notwithstanding the provisions of the Cancelation Condition of this policy, if this policy is canceled by the company and subsequently the effective date of cancelation is changed by an order of the Board of Appeal or by a decree of the Superior Court or Municipal Court of the City of Boston or a Justice of either, under the provisions of the Massachusetts Compulsory Automobile Liability Security Act, the insurance provided in this coverage shall be canceled as of the date of cancelation effective by such order or decree and premium adjustment shall be made accordingly; if after the issuance of notice of cancelation by the company, a finding that such cancelation is not proper and reasonable or is invalid is made under the provisions of said Act either by the Board of Appeal from which finding the company takes no appeal, or by a decree of the Superior Court or Municipal Court of the City of Boston or a Justice of either, the company will continue the insurance provided in this coverage in full force and effect if such order or decree is based upon a complaint made prior to the effective date of cancelation stated in the company's notice, and will reinstate the insurance provided in this coverage in full force and effect as of the date specified in such order or decree if such order or decree is based upon a complaint made within the ten days after the effective date of cancelation stated in the company's notice. If the company shall cease to be authorized to transact business in the Commonwealth of Massachusetts, this policy shall be canceled and premium adjustment shall be made on a pro rata basis as of the effective date of the new certificate of insurance filed by the named insured with the Registrar of Motor Vehicles in Massachusetts, or if no certificate is filed, then as of the effective date of the revocation of registration of the insured motor vehicle.

(3) This policy, the written application therefor, if any, and any endorsement, which shall not conflict with the provisions of said Massachusetts Compulsory Automobile Liability Security Act and all Acts amendatory thereof or supplementary thereto, shall constitute the entire contract between the parties.

(4) The Other Insurance Condition of this policy shall be applicable to this coverage only in the event that other insurance referred to therein is carried in a company authorized to transact insurance in the Commonwealth of Massachusetts.

(5) This agreement is made in accordance with Sections 112 and 113 of Chapter 175 of the General Laws of Massachusetts.

Division 2—Personal Injury Protection—Statutory—(This Coverage is Compulsory)

The company will pay, in accordance with Chapter 670 of the Acts of 1970 of the Commonwealth of Massachusetts and all Acts amendatory thereof or supplementary thereto, subject to any applicable deductible, all reasonable expenses incurred within two years from the date of accident for necessary medical, surgical, X-ray and dental services, including prosthetic devices, and necessary ambulance, hospital, professional nursing and funeral services, and, in the case of persons employed or self-employed at the time of an accident, any amounts actually lost by reason of inability to work and earn wages or salary or their equivalent, but not other income, that would otherwise have been earned in the normal course of an injured person's employment, and for payments in fact made to others, not members of the injured person's household, and reasonably incurred in obtaining from those others ordinary and necessary services in lieu of those that, had he not been injured, the injured person would have performed not for income but for the benefit of himself or members of his household, and, in the case of persons neither employed nor

2

Our Agreement

This policy is a legal contract under Massachusetts law. Because this is an auto policy, it only covers accidents and losses which result from the ownership, maintenance or use of autos. The exact protection is determined by the coverages you purchased.

We agree to provide the insurance protection you purchased for accidents which happen while this policy is in force.

You agree to pay premiums and any Merit Rating surcharges when due and to cooperate with us in case of accidents or claims.

Our contract consists of this policy, the Coverage Selections page, any endorsements agreed upon, and your application for insurance. Oral promises or statements made by you or our agent are not part of this policy.

There are many laws of Massachusetts relating to automobile insurance. We and you must and do agree that, when those laws apply, they are part of this policy.

Compulsory Insurance

3

There are four Parts to Compulsory Insurance. They are called Compulsory Insurance because Massachusetts law requires you to buy all of them before you can register your auto. No law requires you to buy more than this Compulsory Insurance. However, if you have financed your auto, the bank or finance company may legally insist that you have some Optional Insurance as a condition of your loan.

The amount of your coverage and the cost of each Part is shown on the Coverage Selections page.

Your Compulsory Insurance does not pay for any damage to your auto no matter what happens to it.

Part 1.
Bodily Injury
To Others

Under this Part, we will pay damages to people injured or killed by your auto in Massachusetts accidents. Damages are the amounts an injured person is legally entitled to collect for bodily injury through a court judgment or settlement. We will pay only if you or someone else using your auto with your consent is legally responsible for the accident. The most we will pay for injuries to any one person as a result of any one accident is $5,000. The most we will pay for injuries to two or more people as a result of any one accident is a total of $10,000. This is the most we will pay as the result of a single accident no matter how many autos or premiums are shown on the Coverage Selections page.

We will *not* pay:

1. For injuries to guest occupants of your auto.

2. For accidents outside of Massachusetts or in places in Massachusetts where the public has no right of access.

3. For injuries to any employees of the legally responsible person if they are entitled to Massachusetts workers' compensation benefits.

The law provides a special protection for anyone entitled to damages under this Part. We must pay their claims even if false statements were made when applying for this policy or your auto registration. We must also pay even if you or the legally responsible person fails to cooperate with us after the accident. We will, however, be entitled to reimbursement from the person who did not cooperate or who made any false statements.

If a claim is covered by us and also by another company authorized to sell auto insurance in Massachusetts, we will pay only our proportional share. If someone covered under this Part is using an auto he or she does not own at the time of the accident, the owner's auto insurance pays up to its limits before we pay. Then, we will pay up to the limits shown

Moreover, the information in each section of the original policy is rarely presented in an effective manner. Each division consists of tightly packed paragraphs that are not divided into useful parts. For instance, one key fact — that the accident must occur on property open to the public in Massachusetts — is almost lost at the bottom of the first paragraph in Coverage A, Division 1. It occurs at the end of a 162-word sentence.

The modified version, on the other hand, is divided into logical, manageable sections. The reader is told from the outset that the policy has four parts. Each part covers only one subject or a few closely related subjects. Part 1, for example, covers only "Bodily Injury to Others." The modified policy further sorts information into short sections that highlight important points and that are useful to the reader. Part 1 is divided into sections explaining what the policy covers and what it does not cover. The reader does not have to dig out this information; the policy clearly states, for example, that "We will not pay: For accidents outside of Massachusetts or in places in Massachusetts where the public has no right of access."

Sentence structure.   The original policy contains many long sentences. For instance, the second paragraph in Coverage A, Division 1 consists of one 251-word sentence. It contains many phrases and subordinate clauses and is extremely difficult to follow.

However, it is not length alone that makes the sentences hard to read. Inserted phrases add complexity. The sentence that constitutes paragraph three is somewhat shorter but has so much verbiage between the subject and verb and such an unusual ordering of ideas that it is painful to read.

> (3) *This policy*, the written application therefor, if any, and any endorsement which shall not conflict with the provisions of said Massachusetts Compulsory Automobile Liability Security Act and all Acts amendatory thereof or supplementary thereto, *shall constitute the entire contract* between the parties.

Readers have to get to the end of the sentence before they realize why all of this information is given: These documents make up the whole contract between insurer and insured.

The modified policy breaks all of its information into relatively short sentences and uses a standard word order. The sentences also have an internal logic; for example, the reader is told at the beginning of the following sentence that the topic is the content of the insurance contract.

> *Our contract consists* of this policy, the Coverage Selections page, any endorsements agreed upon, and your application for insurance. Oral promises or statements made by you or our agent are not part of this contract.

Vocabulary.   The original policy is full of technical legal terms and concepts. For example, the policy mentions "consequential damages," "compulsory coverage," and "default of the insured." None of these is explained or defined. In addition, this policy lists full citations for the Massachusetts laws that govern particular provisions. These citations disrupt the flow and are of little or no use to many of the audiences that use the policy.

The modified version has eliminated much of the technical language and has provided explanations for terms that could not be eliminated. The modified version also has eliminated the full citations of Massachusetts law. Instead, the policy retains its legal integrity by incorporating the applicable laws by general reference at the end of "Our Agreement." The audiences that need the citations can get them from another source.

Layout, type style, etc.   The layout of the original policy consists of large blocks of print, with little white space to break up the text and few visual cues to guide the reader through the document. The few headings do not contrast much with the rest of the text, so they don't really stand out.

The type size of the original is tolerable, but the type style is quite hard to read; the letters are tall and thin, giving words and sentences a "crowded" look.

The overall effect is of a mass of dense type that is hard on the eyes and that is certainly uninviting — and possibly intimidating — to the reader.

In contrast, the layout of the modified policy consists of smaller, discrete chunks separated by visible markers — lines and white space. Major headings, at the tops of the pages, are large and bold. Subheadings, in boldface type, are "hung" in the wide left margin, where they are easily visible and can provide signposts to guide the reader through the document.

The type size is larger than in the original policy, and the type style is far more readable; even elderly policyholders should have no difficulty reading the modified policy. The overall visual effect is pleasant, even inviting, to the reader.

EXERCISES

1. Describe the purposes of the following document, and then list the audiences for the document.

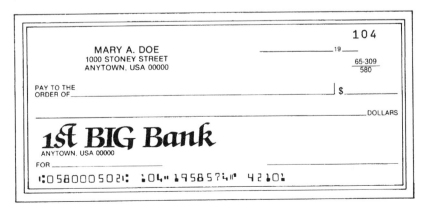

2. The document reproduced below is an agreement for legal services between a lawyer and a client. The rules of legal ethics encourage lawyers to put such agreements in writing in order to avoid disputes that otherwise might arise over the fee or the services that the attorney will render. Obviously, it is extremely important to *both* parties that a client fully understand what he or she is signing. Read through the agreement, then comment on how well you think this document addresses its major audience. What changes might make the agreement more effective?

RETAINER AGREEMENT

THIS AGREEMENT is made for the purpose of retaining the law firm of _____, to represent us in our claim for damages which were sustained as a result of injuries and property damage due to an accident which occurred at _____, at approximately _____ o'clock _____.m., on the _____ day of _____ 200_____.

    Said Law Firm is hereby retained on a contingent basis and is to receive an amount equal to Thirty-three and one-third Percent (331/3%) of any amount which is recovered for us, by settlement; an amount equal to Forty Percent (40%) of any amount which is recovered for us if this matter goes to trial and a favorable verdict is rendered; and an amount equal to Fifty Percent (50%) of any amount which is recovered for us if this matter goes to trial and then an appeal is taken. It is further understood and agreed that we will pay all reasonable and necessary costs arising out of the handling of this claim by our attorneys, including any expenses incurred during litigation of this matter. We agree that said Law Firm has made no promises or guarantees regarding the outcome of our claim. We understand that _____, will investigate our claim and if, after so investigating the claim does not appear to said Law Firm to have merit, then said Law Firm shall have the right to cancel this Agreement.

IN THE EVENT NO RECOVERY IS MADE, IT IS UNDERSTOOD THAT WE ARE NOT OBLIGATED TO PAY ANY FEE TO SAID LAW FIRM.

    IN WITNESS WHEREOF, we hereunto set our hands and seals this _____ day of _____, 200_____.

WITNESS:

_____   _____

_____   _____

Accepted: _____
        (name of firm)

By: _____

C Identifying Your Constraints

Obviously, we cannot discuss — or even imagine — *all* of the possible constraints that you might encounter when writing a legal document. However, there are some constraints that writers of legal documents encounter more often than others, and these are the ones to keep in mind and attempt to accommodate. We concentrate on the most common constraints, but the strategies described for dealing with them can also help you identify and prepare for unique constraints.

1. Constraints of Time and Space

In your first year of law school, you will learn firsthand about two of the most significant constraints affecting those who write in the legal profession: *time* and *space*. When your professor assigns the first memo or brief, he or she will probably give you a rigid deadline and possibly a rigid page limit. These limitations are established for practical reasons — most professors have neither the time nor the desire to grade voluminous memos — but primarily so that you will learn to think and write efficiently.

Most practicing attorneys, as well, will tell you that they conduct a running battle to keep up with deadlines and the obligations that come with each client, as well as balancing the needs of all their clients. Because of time and resource constraints, attorneys must write efficiently — to produce high quality work in a limited time. Furthermore, the readers of legal documents — judges, law clerks, senior partners, clients, and others — also have time constraints. A busy judge, for example, will not have the time or the inclination to wade through pages and pages of writing to find the relevant information. You will have more success with a document that is well organized, concise, and to the point.

Learn as much as you can about your time and space limits before you start writing. Budget your time early so you can allot enough to each major issue. Be sure to leave adequate time for revising, since legal documents tend to grow and change as you refine your research, and even while you are writing. And, of course, leave time for typing and editing.

You should also budget your writing space with care. If your memo can be only 15 pages long, keep this fact in mind from the moment you start planning the memo until you complete the final draft. Throughout the time you are researching and gathering materials, organizing the content, and drafting, you should continually question the relative value of each piece of information and the time and space you can devote to it. Be ready to shift and reallocate as you rethink your writing strategy or reevaluate your research materials. Expect to write more than one draft. And expect to be making changes until you complete your last draft.

2. Format Requirements

The constraints imposed by format requirements are also important. There are formal and informal rules for the format of legal documents; you should be aware of them before you write.

Formal rules.   Most courts and agencies have requirements for the format of specific documents and rules for how to write them. For example, courts and agencies specify a page limit for certain documents and prescribe the divisions and titles you must create, the size and kind of paper you must use, the size and style of type, and where certain provisions must appear in the document.

To get some idea of how precise and demanding format requirements can be, look at the following excerpt from the Rules of the Supreme Court of the United States. This passage is just a small part of Rule 33, which prescribes format requirements for the major documents that are submitted to the Court.

RULE 33

Document Preparation: Booklet Format; 8½-by 11-Inch Paper Format

1. *Booklet Format:* (a) Except for a document expressly permitted by these Rules to be submitted on 8½-by 11-inch paper, see, e.g., Rules 21, 22, and 39, every document filed with the Court shall be prepared in a 6⅛-by 9¼-inch booklet format using a standard typesetting process (e.g., hot metal, photocomposition, or computer typesetting) to produce text printed in typographic (as opposed to typewriter) characters. The process used must produce a clear, black image on white paper. The text must be reproduced with a clarity that equals or exceeds the output of the laser printer.

(b) The text of every booklet-format document, including any appendix thereto, shall be typeset in Roman 11-point or larger type with 2-point or more leading between lines. The typeface should be similar to that used in current volumes of the United States Reports. Increasing the amount of text by using condensed or thinner typefaces, or by reducing the space between letters, is strictly prohibited. Type size and face shall be consistent throughout. Quotations in excess of 50 words shall be indented. The typeface of footnotes shall be 9-point or larger with 2-point or more leading between lines. The text of the document must appear on both sides of the page.

(c) Every booklet-format document shall be produced on paper that is opaque, unglazed, and not less than 60 pounds in weight, and shall have margins of at least three-fourths of an inch on all sides. The text field, including footnotes, may not exceed 4⅛ by 7⅛ inches. The document shall be bound firmly in at least two places along the left margin (saddle stitch or perfect binding preferred) so as to permit easy opening, and no part of the text should be obscured by the binding. Spiral, plastic, metal, or string bindings may not be used. Copies of patent documents, except opinions, may be duplicated in such size as is necessary in a separate appendix.

(d) Every booklet-format document shall comply with the page limits shown on the chart in subparagraph 1(g) of this Rule. The page limits do not include the questions presented, the list of parties and the corporate disclosure statement, the table of contents, the table of cited authorities, or any appendix. Verbatim quotations required under Rule 14.1(f), if set out in the text of a brief rather than in the appendix, are also excluded. For good cause, the Court or a Justice may grant leave to file a document in excess of the page limits, but application for such leave is not favored. An application to exceed page limits shall comply with Rule 22 and must be received by the Clerk at least 15 days before the filing date of the document in question, except in the most extraordinary circumstances.

(e) Every booklet-format document shall have a suitable cover consisting of 65-pound weight paper in the color indicated on the chart in subparagraph 1(g) of this Rule. If a separate appendix to any document is filed, the color if its cover shall be the same as that of the cover of the document it supports. The Clerk will furnish a color chart upon request. Counsel shall ensure that there is adequate contrast between the printing and the color of the cover. A document filed by the United States, or by any other federal party represented by the Solicitor General, shall have a gray cover. A joint appendix, answer to a bill of complaint, motion for leave to intervene, and any other document not listed in subparagraph 1(g) of this Rule shall have a tan cover.

(f) Forty copies of a booklet-format document shall be filed.

If you violate formal rules of format for legal documents, you risk having your document rejected. This can mean that the document has been permanently rejected or that you have to redo and resubmit it. Resubmitting a document to a court or an agency can result in additional complications: You can end up missing a filing deadline before you are able to resubmit. Obviously, you must make it your business to find out what the formal rules for the format of a document are. Often you can find these by consulting volumes that contain court rules and other rules of procedure. If you are unable to find the information in the books, you can try telephoning the agency or talking to the court clerk.

In fact, many court clerks are remarkably helpful. There is nothing wrong or embarrassing about calling a clerk's office to find out how something ought to be done. In the end, calling can save time, money, and heartache.

William Suter (Maj. Gen., USA Ret.) is the Clerk of the Supreme Court of the United States and former Deputy Judge Advocate General of the United States Army. He urges attorneys to call with questions. He and his staff attorneys bend over backward to help lawyers deal with the ordinary and the extraordinary. He even offers attorneys who are scheduled to argue in the Court the next day the opportunity to stand at the podium (when the Court is not hearing cases) so that they can get a feel for what it will be like physically to argue in the Court's relatively small setting. The only thing General Suter cannot provide in advance is nine Justices peppering you with questions.

Informal rules: Rules of usage and tradition.   Some format rules are not strictly prescribed but have evolved over the years into accepted or expected standards. For example, many courts do not prescribe a rigid formula for briefs, but most attorneys follow a basic format, with minor variations. Informal guidelines can be as important as formal rules, because the reader often expects a particular type of document to follow certain patterns. At best, an unfamiliar arrangement may slow the reader down; at worst, the reader may feel that the document is insufficient or inappropriate.

Before writing, find out the informal format rules for your document. For briefs and memos, law professors can often provide you with outlines or sample documents, or you may be able to obtain a memo or brief from a practicing attorney. This book has a sample brief and two sample memos, and you may find other books that also have samples. However, you must choose your document models carefully. Not all "model" briefs are well organized, well written, or well formatted. The same is true of documents in form books: Many are full of antiquated provisions and archaic language. The goal of this book is to teach you how to create your own documents and to help you recognize and choose good models to follow.

3. Citation Constraints

Because our legal system is based primarily on case law and statutes, legal arguments and explanations are derived from or based on these sources. A writer must include complete, precise references or citations to supporting materials whenever they are used.

Citation form.   Citations can be placed either in the text or in footnotes, depending upon the type of document. For example, law review articles and legal treatises are footnoted, while most citations in briefs and memos are in the text itself. You will find most of the rules for citing legal sources in *The Bluebook: A Uniform System of Citation* by the Harvard Law Review Association.

There are rules that you can follow to keep your references from disrupting the flow of the text. One general rule for using footnotes is to write the textual part of the document so that it stands on its own — that is, the footnotes should elaborate on the text, but the reader should be able to follow the text without them. Otherwise, you force the reader to continually switch from text to footnotes in order to understand the document. Many law review articles contain good examples of text that stands on its own. This system allows the reader to cover the text fairly quickly for a superficial review of the article or to read footnotes together with the text for more thorough coverage.[6]

Avoid using long string citations within the text itself. String citations are lists of sources that are meant to substantiate a particular point or statement in the text. String cites are bad style; they can disrupt the flow of your text. Furthermore, they may cast doubt upon the credibility of your claims because they can give the impression that your case is so weak that you have to substantiate it with

---

6. However, footnotes should be used sparingly and only for certain purposes, e.g., citing sources, qualifying or providing context for statements made in the body of the text, or interjecting humorous bits that might be inappropriate in the body of the document. Footnotes should not be used to interject random thoughts or as a way to avoid organizing your thoughts. (Does this footnote qualify?) The overuse of footnotes has drawn significant criticism. *See* David Mellinkoff, Legal Writing: Sense & Nonsense 94-95 (1982). Recently, Justice Scalia chided Justice Souter for using dense footnotes: "In any case, the portion of [Justice Souter's opinion] that I consider irrelevant is quite extensive, comprising, in total, about one-tenth of the opinion's size and (since it is in footnote type) even more of the opinion's content." Crosby v. National Foreign Trade Council, 530 U.S. 363 (2000) (Scalia, J., concurring). For an excellent spoof on legal writing and footnoting, *see* Anthony D'Amato, *The Contribution of the Infield FlyRule to Western Civilization (And Vice Versa)*, 100 Nwu L. Rev. 189 (2006).

every source you can find. You can substantiate your claims far more effectively by using only one or two of your strongest sources.[7]

Referencing and cross-referencing. Legislation, regulations, codes, and other similar documents and texts often contain complex cross-referencing. If improperly used or overused, references to other parts of the text can disrupt the flow of the document.

Here is an example of what can happen when the text contains so many references that the reader must turn to them just to understand what is going on. Section 179 of the 1977 Internal Revenue Code reads as follows:

> *§179 Additional First-year Depreciation Allowance for Small Business*
>
> (a) General rule — In the case of section 179 property, the term "reasonable allowance" as used in section 167(a) may, at the election of the taxpayer, include an allowance, for the first taxable year for which a deduction is allowable under section 167 to the taxpayer with respect to such property, of 20 percent of the cost of such property.

The term "section 179 property" is not defined until part (d) of section 179 and, if you want to know what is in section 167, you must flip through many pages. In other words, you must read forward to section (d) and backward to section 167 before you can finish the first paragraph of section 179.

These kinds of reference problems can be avoided. If you have to refer to other sections of the document or to different documents in your discussion, try giving a short description of what is in the reference or refer to it by its title. That way, the reader can follow the flow and logic of your discussion without having to search for the actual reference. For example:

> General rule for section 179 property (tangible personal property, as specifically defined in (d)):
>
> > If the taxpayer chooses, the term "reasonable allowance," as used in section 167(a) (for figuring a reasonable depreciation deduction for exhaustion, or wear and tear of business property) may include an allowance of 20 percent of the cost of that property, for the first taxable year for which section 167 allows the taxpayer a deduction for that property.

4. Constraints on Content

Some constraints are imposed by the kinds of information that typically goes into legal documents. You will often find that you do not have access to all of the information you may think you need: The law may be vague, in flux, or ambiguous, so that you cannot find the legal "answers" you want. The facts of a case

---

7. *See* Laurel C. Oates, Anne Enquist & Kelly Kunsch, The Legal Writing Handbook 504 (1993).

may be incomplete or distorted, leaving you with no clear picture of what has happened.

Clients can seldom provide a complete picture of the circumstances surrounding an event. And even if a client knows all the details and is able to articulate them, he or she is naturally going to see the events from only one point of view. You can use discovery to get additional information from your adversary, but even that is unlikely to provide you with a full picture of the facts. There is also the chance that a client or witness will intentionally withhold information, unintentionally invent information to fill in gaps or to please the attorney, or simply lie.

Legal writers who ignore the constraints on content can fall into the trap of "filling in the gaps" in the facts or the law themselves. They may assume that certain things are true or that certain events occurred, or they may draw unfounded inferences from the information they do have.

Before you write a legal document, you need to know what information exists and what is missing, and you need to plan how best to present what you do know. One way to do this is to acknowledge a lack of information and then to argue the *likelihood* that something has occurred. You then build your case around "logical" inferences or "reasonable" assumptions. Here is an example of what we mean.

Attorney X represented the estate of Brian Smith in a wrongful death case with the following facts. Smith's car was moving through an intersection on the road perpendicular to the road the defendant was on. Smith's car was struck broadside by the defendant's car after the defendant allegedly ran a red light. The only witness to the accident was a police officer who saw the incident while sitting at the intersection. He was on the same road as Smith, coming from the opposite direction. The police officer was waiting for the light to change. Below is a map of the intersection. The **A** represents Smith's car, **B** is the defendant's car, and **C** is the police car. Just before the accident, the police officer noticed that his own light had turned green. He saw Smith move forward into the intersection. Before the police officer could move, the defendant sped across the intersection. The police officer is ready to testify that the defendant ran a red light.

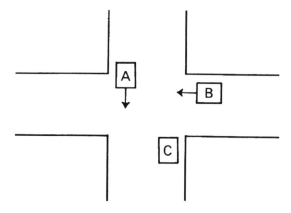

In his brief, Attorney X wrote that the defendant had violated a traffic law by running a red light. He used this information as a foundation for his theory that the defendant was driving with reckless disregard for the safety of others and was thus liable in tort for the plaintiff's death.

The defendant's brief, however, destroyed the very foundation of the plaintiff's argument: The only witness, the police officer, did not *see* the defendant's traffic light turn red. He only deduced that it had. The attorney for the defendant pointed out that the defendant's traffic light could have been malfunctioning and may never have turned red at all.

Attorney Y, representing the plaintiff in an identical case, wrote her brief with a different strategy. First, she realized that there were facts missing: No one had seen the traffic light change. Second, Attorney Y was careful not to draw conclusions about what had happened. Instead, she acknowledged the gap in information. She then proceeded to argue *around* the missing information by showing that all of the facts pointed to a high probability that the defendant had run a red light. She noted that it is extremely rare for lights on the perpendicular roads of an intersection to be green at the same time. She also made use of the occupation and experience of her witness, the police officer, stating that the police officer was familiar with the area and with road conditions and had learned a great deal about accidents in his work. She also emphasized his credibility and honesty. She built the rest of her case upon the "highly reasonable assumption" that the defendant ran a red light. She was thus able to overcome the constraints on content and win her case.

EXERCISES

1. Look at the pleading on page 136. As you may remember, a pleading is a legal document used to state the facts that make up a plaintiff's cause of action or a defendant's defense. In other words, pleadings give each party an opportunity to tell his or her story to the court, to articulate grievances or deny accusations.

   A pleading can be fairly complicated or quite simple, depending upon the particulars of the case or the kind of case. The pleading reproduced here is a simple, relatively informal complaint that can be filed in a trial court if the case involves uncomplicated facts or small damages, or is the kind of case that is routinely handled in that particular court. Because these cases are fairly small or routine, an attorney can create a pleading by merely filling in the blanks.

   To complete the sample, the plaintiff's attorney must supply the "particulars" or relevant facts of the case in concise form. The space on this form under the title "Statement of Claim" has room for approximately 200 words. As a practice exercise, write up a 200-word summary of the relevant facts contained in the following attorney-client interview. Keep in mind that the case is one involving *bailment*, a situation in which one person (the *bailee*) holds the property of another person (the *bailor*) for a particular purpose.

File original and one copy
for each defendant

FORM NO. 3

DISTRICT COURT OF MARYLAND FOR.................................
City/County

Located at.. Case No. ....
Court Address

(1) ....   (1) ....
Exact name of individual or corporation   Exact name of individual or corporation

....
Trade name of party suing   Address for service

....
Full mailing address   City/Town, State, Zip code   County

....
City/Town, State, Zip Code   County   **Sues**   Name, title & address of agent to be served

(2) ....   (2) ....
Full name of individual or corporation   Full name of individual or corporation

....
Trade name of party suing   Address for service

....
Full mailing address   City/Town, State, Zip Code   County

....
City/Town, State, Zip Code   County   Name, title & address of agent to be served

Plaintiff   **STATEMENT OF CLAIM**   **Defendant**

Clerk: Please docket this case in an action of ☐ contract ☐ tort ☐ replevin ☐ detinue
The particulars of this case are...
....
....
....
....
....
....
....
....
....
....

The Plaintiff claims:
☐ $............. with interest of $............. and attorney's fees of $............. plus court costs of $.............
☐ Return of the property and damages of $............................. for its detention in an action of replevin.
☐ Return of the property, or its value, plus damages of $..................... for its detention in an action of detinue.
☐ Other ....
....

....
Signature of Attorney   Address of Attorney

....
Signature of Plaintiff   Telephone No. of Plaintiff or Attorney

WRIT OF SUMMONS

TO THE DEFENDANT: You have been sued and you are hereby notified that the trial will be held in the
District Court.

IMPORTANT NOTICE:

If you intend to be present at the trial, at which time you may present a defense to the claim, you must notify the
court in writing within 21 days of receiving this notice. (You may use the form below.) If you fail to file such notice
judgment by default may be given against you for the amounts claimed above.

To addressee's postal agent If you signed the postal receipt for this   ....
summons and cannot deliver it or make its contents known to the   Date
defendant in time for the defendant to appear as directed, please
advise the Court at once in writing, giving reasons.   ....
                                                                             Clerk

NOTICE OF INTENTION TO DEFEND

Case No. ....   Trial Date ....

I intend to be present at the trial of this case and demand proof of the Plaintiff's claim.

....
Defendant   Attorney for defendant

....
Address   Telephone No.   Address   Telephone No.

CV-1 (Rev. 6/78)   (complete reverse side)

The elements of a bailment are

1. A delivery of the property by the bailor to the bailee; and
2. A contract, express or implied, that the bailee will keep the property for a given purpose and, after the purpose has been fulfilled, will return the property to the bailor, account for the property, or keep the property until the bailor claims it, depending upon the circumstances.

The bailee has certain obligations or duties to the bailor: If the bailment is for the mutual benefit of the bailor and the bailee, the bailee must exercise ordinary due care in keeping the property. In State X, this has been interpreted to mean that the bailee must treat the property with as much care as a person of ordinary prudence would use in taking care of his or her own property. If the bailee fails in this duty to the bailor, then the bailee is guilty of negligence.

Do not try to analyze the law and facts, but do try to use the elements of bailment as guidelines for selecting the facts to include in your summary. For example, the fact that the garage had signs of previous break-ins is relevant to whether the owner used ordinary care in the way he kept the plaintiff's car. On the other hand, the fact that the plaintiff never saw the place where the car was wrecked is not relevant.

ATTORNEY (A): Tell me about your problem.

CLIENT (C): My car was stolen and totalled.

A: When?

C: On March 3.

A: Have you reported this to the police?

C: Yes—actually, I didn't have to. They called me at 1:00 in the morning—Saturday morning—to tell me that they had found it wrecked on a back road—way out somewhere. Anyway, my mother and I later drove out to check to see where the road was, but we never could find it. It must be a small farm road or something.

A: Where did the police take the car after they found it?

C: To a towing place. That's where I went to get it after they called me. I never saw the place where it was smashed. It hit a tree.

A: And the police made a report?

C: Yes. But only after we towed the car again, back to Schmidt's.

A: Schmidt's?

C: Where the car was when it was stolen. It was being repaired there. It was stolen late Friday night. It was supposed to be picked up on Saturday. They had finally fixed it.

A: How long had it been at Schmidt's?

C: Well, I called them on that Monday and asked if they could fix the car and they said yes, bring it by.

A: Who told you this?

C: Jimmy, the mechanic. He said he was really busy, but to bring it over and he'd try to fit it in sometime during the week.

A: And he did, I take it. You say he worked on it Friday?

C: Yes, finally. He said to call every evening and he'd let me know if he got to it that day. I called all week, but he didn't work on it til Friday.

A: Where was the car all this time?

C: In their parking lot. It was on the very edge of the lot. You know, the thing that gets me is that nobody seemed to take this very seriously. When we got the car back to Schmidt's, all the mechanics were looking at it and going "wow," and they all took turns sitting in it.

A: What about the policeman?

C: He didn't care. Everybody was just joking around. I don't think anybody was taking it too seriously. I heard several guys saying that Schmidt's gets broken into all the time, that stuff happens a lot.

A: Guys?

C: The mechanics.

A: Have there been other car thefts?

C: Not that I know of. But one of the mechanics said that he came in one day in December and the door of the office part of the garage had been bashed in. And another guy said that another time someone got in and took an adding machine, and that tires are stolen all the time.

A: Do you know the names of these people or do you remember what they look like?

C: One's name is Bruce. He drove the tow truck. I don't know about the other one. Schmidt is Bruce's father-in-law.

A: Is there a fence or anything around the lot?

C: No. It's right off the street.

A: How did they start your car? Do you know how it was taken?

C: They got the key when they broke into the garage.

A: Wait a minute — you mean that someone broke into the garage first?

C: Yes.

A: How did they get in?

C: They just broke a pane of glass in the bay door of the garage and pulled a lever inside. Then you can just slide the door up. From the garage, you can walk right into the office. The keys are all on a keyboard up on the wall. I think that that kind of thing has happened before because one of the other panes of glass in the bay door was replaced by plexiglass.

A: Can you see the keys from outside?

C: Oh yes. The office is like in a gas station. It's mostly glass. The keys are right on the wall.

A: Did anyone else hear these comments that the mechanics were making?

C: My mother was with me.

A: Have you talked to the owner of the place?

C: Yes, and he said his insurance would pay for the car. But the insurance company called me and said that it wouldn't because Mr. Schmidt wasn't liable or responsible, that it wasn't his fault. Anyway, at least Schmidt paid for the towing.

A: Do they light their lot at night?

C: Well, the cop told me that Plunket Donuts, next door, used to be open all night and their lights used to light up the garage's lot too, but since Plunket started closing at ten, things get dark around the area. Schmidt doesn't have his own lights.

---

2. Using the interview in question number 1, come up with 10 interrogatories that you would like to ask Mr. Schmidt, the owner of the garage. Each interrogatory must ask for only one thing: You cannot disguise two questions as one. (For example, you cannot ask: "Are you married and how many children do you have?") Also, try to ask the most pertinent questions you can because you will want to use your limited number of interrogatories to find out all kinds of background and additional information, as well as to verify the information that your client gave you.

9

Getting

Organized

After going through the steps in Chapter 8, you will have answered the following questions.

1. What are you writing about? What is the *topic* (the main idea)? What is your *thesis* (the point you want to make)?
2. Who is your audience?
3. What is the purpose of the document? Are you presenting information, or trying to elicit it? Is the document a teaching device? Does it simply present pros and cons, or are you arguing for or against an idea?
4. What are your constraints?

The answers to these pre-writing questions will help to determine the way you organize your document.

A Why Organize?

You must always impose order on your writing. Legal documents, in particular, demand a tight, logical structure. In other documents poor organization may interfere with readers' comprehension, but in legal documents poor organization can cause even greater problems. In an adversarial document, for example, your opponents will be looking for any weak spots they can find. A gap in your logic caused by poor organization can give your opponents an opening for attack. In a nonadversarial document, poor organization can make the reader believe that either your knowledge and research are not thorough or that your thinking is not logical. While you are in law school, your professors will be judging the organization and logical progression of your writing assignments and examinations.

One of the best ways to organize a document is to create a written outline. This can be a simple list or something more elaborate, with many topics and subtopics. The complexity of the outline usually depends on the complexity of the document.

When you create an outline, you give yourself the opportunity to organize and reorganize your ideas to provide the most effective focus for the document.

If you are constructing a document intended to persuade, writing and rewriting an outline will help you build a more effective argument and will also help you spot any gaps or weaknesses in your logic. Outlining can in itself suggest new ideas and fresh perspectives.

When should you organize? You should start organizing material into an outline as soon as you have identified the main issues and decided what points you want to make. No doubt you will revise this outline as you continue to research and even after you have started writing. That is both normal and useful: The document will evolve in a thorough, systematic manner. Minutes invested in outlining will save you hours later. A well-developed outline will make your writing task easier and will keep you from going off on tangents in research or in writing.

B How to Organize an Expository Document

Let's start with a basic type of document—one that has the purpose of simply informing, not of persuading or eliciting information. Here is an example of an outline for an expository document.

1. Introduction providing a context
   - introduces the topic
   - amplifies the topic
   - gives some background
   - states the thesis
   - sets out a "roadmap" explaining what the document will cover and the order in which the material will be covered
2. First event or idea
   - information to amplify event or idea
3. Other events or ideas
   - information to amplify events or ideas
4. Closing or conclusion

1. Providing a Context

It is essential to provide a context at the beginning of every legal document for the information that is to follow. You can never assume that your readers will know beforehand what you are writing about. If they have to read far into the document before they discover the topic and the purpose of the document, then you have not done a good job. If the reader has to deduce the context or guess at it, then your document may be ineffective.

Sometimes an informative title can provide enough context. Other times a document may require several pages of introductory material. How much context you need depends on the purpose, audience, and length of the document.

The purpose of providing a context is to link new information to information that you know the reader has or is very likely to have. Thus, in general, you should begin by telling the reader, as specifically as possible, what you will be talking about. Then, depending on how complex the document is and how familiar the reader is with the topic, you can amplify the topic by providing more information about the ideas you will be covering in the body of the document.

If it is appropriate, you might then want to provide a small amount of background. This could consist of a sentence or two briefly outlining the history of the issue you are dealing with, describing the extent of the problem, or providing any other type of background information the reader might need. If this is a document in which you will be making a point, state your thesis, or what you are proposing, here. In a memo, especially, it is helpful for the reader to know what your position is from the beginning. And, in fact, experienced readers will expect a *short answer*—a condensed version of your conclusion—at this point. (*See* Chapter 13.)

Finally, if you are writing a fairly long document, you should set up a "roadmap" of what will follow: Tell your readers what you will cover and the order in which you will cover it. It is also helpful to refer to "signposts"—section headings or chapter headings—in which specific information is to be found. Following is a proposed rewrite of the introduction to a trade regulation rule for proprietary vocational and home-study schools. Notice how this introduction describes what is in each section of the rule.

WHAT THIS RULE IS ABOUT

The purpose of the Rule is to provide students with information that will enable them to make an informed decision on whether to buy a course, to discourage abusive sales practices by representatives of vocational schools, and to give the student the right to cancel at will without a heavy financial loss.

The Rule is organized in the following way: The first section lists a number of the unfair and deceptive acts and practices that schools have engaged in. The next section tells when and how this Rule becomes effective. The third section defines the schools, courses, and students covered by the Rule. All of the subsequent sections deal with the specific steps a school must follow to avoid violations: the kinds of records a school should keep to comply with the Rule; the rules a school must follow when it advertises a course and makes job or earnings claims; what a school must do when a student applies; the special rules a school must follow if it furnishes a student with course materials during the cooling-off period; and what the school must do if a student cancels an enrollment contract during or after the cooling-off period. The Rule is followed by appendices that contain forms which the school must use to comply with the Rule.

2. Presenting the Substance of the Document

The next part of a document contains the information or ideas you want to present — the substance of the document. If there is a thesis or main point to the document, the information you present here will explain the basis for it.

How do you decide what is a logical order for the events, ideas, or information you are presenting? First, write down all the ideas, events, or pieces of information that you think are relevant to your topic or thesis.[1] Next, decide on an "organizing principle" — the principle that will unify your material and govern its order. In choosing an organizing principle, look for a conceptual relationship among the ideas, events, or pieces of information you are dealing with. Analyze the material to see if the pieces of it are strongly related or ordered by any of the following.

1. *Cause and effect:* Totally different events *B, C,* and *D* all appear to have happened as a result of incident *A.*
2. *Time: A, B,* and *C* follow each other in a time sequence.
3. *Similarity of events or ideas:* Several events appear to have similar characteristics.
4. *Priority: A, B,* and *C* are all exceedingly important and must be considered together, before *D, E, F,* and *G.*

There are other possible ways of grouping material. The point is to have a reasonable plan for organizing information. Look for any unifying factors. For example, if Party *A* and Party *B* are both involved in an action, you can use "parties" as your overall organizing principle, discussing all of the information concerning Party *A* first, then dealing with the information that is relevant to Party *B.* You might also order your information by legal issue or by action, when there are more than one. Sometimes your organizing principle will be dictated or influenced by outside sources. For example, usually the most logical and efficient way to order a reply brief is to follow the order of the arguments in your opponent's brief. That way, you can answer the arguments point by point.

One way to make the process of organizing and grouping information easier is to put each piece of information on an index card. You can then try out different groupings and subgroupings of information by rearranging the cards. You will find that some groupings are more logical or more satisfying than others.

Once you have chosen an organizing principle for a document, do not depart from it in the overall structure of the document. In other words, if your organizing principle for a memo is *priority,* make sure that each major issue is presented in order of its importance. Don't suddenly start presenting events in the order in which they happened (unless that order coincides with priority).

---

1. *See* N. Brand & J. O. White, Legal Writing: The Strategy of Persuasion (3d ed. 1994), for information and exercises on how to "brainstorm" an idea or issue, that is, how to come up with all the arguments, points to consider, and supporting evidence.

The same general principles apply to grouping and organizing material within each subpart of your document. However, once your overall organizing principle has been set out clearly, you can then use different organizing principles *within* a given subpart or paragraph. For example, your overall organizing principle for a memo may be order of importance of issues, but the organizing principle within a discussion of one issue might be cause-and-effect.

3. Writing the Conclusion

Finally, provide a conclusion or closing statement for the document. The nature of your conclusion will depend upon the length and the complexity of the document. If the document is short and fairly straightforward, you might close by telling the reader what will happen next or by inviting the reader to ask questions. If the document is long or complex, it is a good idea to briefly summarize the information you have presented in the document and restate your main point or thesis and the reasons for it.

4. Organizing an Expository Document: An Example

Read the following letter written by an attorney to a client. After the letter, we discuss the way it is organized in terms of the outline we have presented.

Dear Mr. Williams:

I am writing to summarize the status of your discrimination suit against Wambush, Inc., and to tell you about what we have to do next. As I mentioned to you in our telephone conversation of July 29, Wambush filed two motions seeking to dismiss your lawsuit and we intended to vigorously oppose both motions. I am pleased to report that the court denied both of Wambush's motions to dismiss.

In its first motion, Wambush sought to have your lawsuit dismissed for improper venue. Wambush tried to convince the court that we should have filed this lawsuit in San Francisco rather than in Washington, D.C. In its motion Wambush argued that since its principal place of business was San Francisco, California, this lawsuit should have been brought in San Francisco. However, the law on that point is fairly clear. Under Title VII of the Civil Rights Act of 1964, you are entitled to file a lawsuit in any federal court located in the state where the act of racial discrimination occurred. Since you unsuccessfully applied for a job with Wambush's Washington, D.C., office, then the act of racial discrimination, if one is proven, occurred in the District of Columbia. The court agreed with our interpretation of the law and denied Wambush's motion to dismiss for improper venue.

In its second motion, Wambush claimed that it was not an "employer" within the meaning of Title VII of the Civil Rights Act of 1964. As I mentioned to you during our earlier telephone conversations, Title VII only applies to companies that have 15 or more employees. Wambush argued that since its Washington, D.C., office had only nine employees, it is not covered by Title VII. In response, we argued that for Title VII purposes you must count all of a company's employees, no matter where they are employed. Since Wambush's San Francisco office employs 275 people, we argued that Wambush was clearly an employer and was obligated to abide by the provisions of Title VII. Once again, the court agreed with our position and denied Wambush's motion.

Yesterday, I received a letter from Wambush's attorneys indicating that they would like to take your deposition. In a deposition a party like yourself is questioned under oath by the attorney for the other side. The attorney's questions and the witness's answers are recorded by a court stenographer and a typewritten record is then made. It is important that I spend at least a full day with you preparing you for the deposition. Please call my office as soon as possible so that we can arrange a seven-or eight-hour block of time during which I will fully prepare you for the deposition.

If you have any questions concerning any of the matters that I have discussed in this letter, please do not hesitate to contact me.

Sincerely yours,
Elizabeth A. Brown

The *context* for the letter is provided by the introductory paragraph. Sentence 1 tells the *purpose* of the letter and the *topics* to be discussed: to summarize the status of the suit and discuss plans. Sentence 2 provides *background*, which in this case is the lawyer's and client's shared understanding of the contents of a previous conversation. Sentence 3 presents the outcome (the court denied both motions) of the events mentioned in that conversation. This is also the *main point* of the major part of the letter.

The next three paragraphs present the *substance* of the letter, the important points that the lawyer wishes to tell the client. Paragraph 2 presents and elaborates on Event 1. Sentence 1 describes the event — that Wambush tried to have the lawsuit dismissed for improper venue — and sentences 2 to 7 amplify it. Sentence 2 explains what "improper venue" means in terms of the client's own case. Sentence 3 elaborates, explaining the content of the motion and summarizing Wambush's argument. Sentences 4 to 6 recount the lawyer's counterargument. All of the sentences lead up to the next one, sentence 7, which tells the outcome: The court agreed with the lawyer's argument and denied the motion. Paragraph 3 follows the same pattern as Paragraph 2.

Paragraph 4 elaborates on the second topic referred to in the introductory paragraph: the deposition that will take place. Sentence 1 informs the client about the coming deposition and sentences 2 and 3 give a brief explanation of what is involved. Sentences 4 and 5 present an important point: what the client and attorney must do before the deposition. Paragraph 5 *concludes* by giving the client an opportunity to ask questions.

The overall organizing principle for the letter is a time sequence: These two events have occurred, and this third event will occur. The organizing principles *within* the paragraphs are different: Paragraphs 1, 2, and 3 are based primarily on cause-and-effect sequences, while paragraph 4 is basically a time sequence.

C How to Organize a Complex Legal Document

For more complex legal documents, the basic outline for an expository document must be expanded. For persuasive documents, such as briefs and motions, and for documents that present pros and cons, such as memoranda and law examinations, the main section of the document requires a special type of structure. Instead of the events or ideas that make up the main section of an expository document, the main section of a complex legal document will consist of an analysis of issues or subissues. Thus, the outline for a complex legal document might look like this:

1. Introduction providing a context
2. First claim
   a. What is the *claim* you are making? How are you proposing to resolve the issue or subissue? This can be further subdivided into
      i. A statement of the particular *issue* or subissue you have identified. At this point you may also wish to state how you believe the issue should be resolved.[2]
      ii. The *rule* of law that is most pertinent to the situation.
      iii. Why and how the rule should be *applied* to the facts of your case.
      iv. A *conclusion* based upon your analysis and the application of the law to the facts.
      (IRAC is the mnemonic for this method of organizing a claim.)
   b. What are the *objections* and counterarguments to your claim?
   c. What is your *response* to the objections and counterarguments?
   d. What is your *conclusion*? This section summarizes your reasoning and restates your claim.
3. Second claim
4. Conclusion

2. This is especially important in persuasive writing, in which you want to make a forceful opening statement.

This model works well for any level of analysis, from the general analysis of a whole problem down to the analysis of specific subissues. When you have used this model to analyze all of the issues or subissues, you will then be able to come to a final conclusion.

1. Identifying and Presenting Issues

Your first step in setting up the structure of a complex legal document is to identify the important issues that you will be discussing in your document. Here is an example of a fact situation and the issues that should be analyzed in a brief.

> Jones worked as a salesman for the Southern Corporation. His job required him to provide his own car and deliver perishable supplies to customers on his route. Jones had been told a number of times by his supervisor at Southern that it was extremely important that he stay on a strict time schedule with his deliveries.
>
> On March 10, Jones made a delivery during normal working hours. He returned to the parking lot in which he had left his car and found that Warner's car was blocking his car. After waiting ten minutes for Warner to return, Jones finally decided that he had to leave. Jones tried to move his car, but put a large dent in Warner's bumper and broke one of Warner's headlights in the process. Warner returned just as Jones broke the headlight. Warner demanded payment for the damage to his car and refused to move his car so that Jones could leave. Jones angrily got out of his car and moved towards Warner, yelling that he was already late for his deliveries and that it was Warner's fault. Warner angrily shook his fist at Jones and again demanded payment for the damage to his car. Jones, in anger, hit Warner, knocking him to the ground. Warner had Jones arrested.
>
> After Jones's arrest, Southern Corporation learned from the local police that Jones had been convicted of aggravated assault three years before Southern had hired him. When Southern hired Jones, the corporation did not inquire into his background. Warner is suing Southern for the personal injuries he suffered as a result of Jones's attack.

ISSUE 1: Did the defendant commit an intentional tort when he knocked the plaintiff to the ground, or was the action privileged?

ISSUE 2: Is an employer liable for injuries that its employee intentionally inflicted upon the plaintiff while the employee was trying to make deliveries on behalf of the employer?

ISSUE 3: Can the defendant employer be held liable for negligence in hiring and retaining an employee who has a criminal record for assault if the employer did not investigate the employee's background and does not know of the record?

Once you have identified the main issues, you may find that you can deal with them more easily by breaking them down into smaller, more manageable subissues (or sub-subissues). For example, you might see the following subissues under Issue 1.

1. Did the act of the plaintiff in shaking his fist at the defendant place the defendant in imminent threat of physical injury?
   a. If the plaintiff's act placed the defendant in imminent threat of physical injury, did he have a duty to retreat?
   b. If the defendant did not have a duty to retreat, did he use excessive force in repelling the imminent threat?
2. Did the act of the plaintiff in refusing to move his vehicle constitute the tort of false imprisonment?
3. Did the act of the plaintiff in refusing to move his vehicle constitute the tort of trespass to chattel?

2. Presenting the Rule

The rule of law that you use in your analysis can come from case law or enacted laws. Once you have established the applicable rule in a particular case, you should present it in a way that will make it easy to apply the law to the facts. For example, if you are discussing a particular tort or crime, or the definition of a particular legal concept, describe it by breaking it up into its elements. Thus, if the issue is whether a defendant has committed a battery, a good way to present the rule would be to take the definition from section 13 of the Restatement (Second) of Torts.

§13 Battery: Harmful Contact

An actor is subject to liability for battery if
   (a) he *acts intending* to cause harmful or offensive contact with the person of the other or a third person, or an imminent apprehension of such a contact, and
   (b) a harmful contact with the person of the other directly or indirectly *results* (emphasis added).

If you have to synthesize the rule from case law, this will probably take more time and space. This is because you will often need to go through the steps that you took and the sources that you used in your distillation of the rule. See Chapter 6.

3. Application: Analyzing Facts and Law

The next step is to examine the facts and decide whether a rule is satisfied or the elements of an offense or tort are present. You should organize this section so that it follows the order of the elements of the rule. For example, you could discuss the facts in the Jones case by applying them to the elements of battery.

> First, the defendant, Jones, *acted* when he attempted to strike the plaintiff in the parking lot. Second, the defendant *intended* to harm the plaintiff, since he spoke angrily to the plaintiff, shook his fist at the plaintiff, and then struck him. Third, the defendant struck the plaintiff and knocked the plaintiff to the ground. Thus, the defendant's act *resulted in* the harmful contact to the plaintiff.

The application section of your document is the most crucial, for it is here that you have to convince your audience that your analysis is sound and that your conclusions follow logically. We have presented only the most basic application of facts to law in the example above. In Chapter 11 we will cover sophisticated and specialized techniques for applying the facts to the law so that you can guide your reader smoothly from your claims to your conclusions.

4. Anticipating Counterarguments

One of the best ways to ensure that you have treated an issue thoroughly is to try to anticipate all possible counterarguments and defenses. Put yourself in your opponent's position: List all of the ways that you can attack or weaken your own argument. Be ruthless. After you compile the list, develop responses or rebuttals for each area of attack.

There are a number of counterarguments that the defendant might raise in the battery case. The defendant might attack the way in which you applied the law to the facts; or the defendant might raise the defense that he was using reasonable force to prevent the plaintiff from committing a tort against his property (the plaintiff refused to let the defendant remove his car from the lot) or against his person (the plaintiff prevented the defendant from leaving by holding something of great value to the defendant).

5. Providing a Conclusion

The contents of your conclusion will depend upon the length and complexity of the information that you have presented in the other portions of your analysis. For example, if your application section is long and intricate, then you might want to refresh your reader's memory by briefly recounting the steps in your reasoning. If the application section is short, however, you would probably not want to reiterate your reasoning. In either case, you would finish with a statement of your position or your interpretation of the facts and the law. Here is an example of a simple way to conclude the battery issue:

> Because all three elements of battery are present in the defendant's conduct, the defendant is liable for the tort of battery.

6. Organizing a Complex Legal Document: An Example

Now that we have presented and explained the different parts of the model on page 146, look at the following fully developed issue analysis. This analysis follows the standard IRAC—issue, rule, application, conclusion—outline.

The issue presented in this case is whether one spouse can sue the other for injuries caused by the negligence of the other spouse.

Issue

In *Sink v. Sink*, 239 P.2d 933 (1952), this court held that neither spouse may maintain an action in tort for damages against the other. Although a number of states have recently enacted legislation that allows these suits, Kansas has not joined them. This can be seen in the fact that the Kansas legislature has just enacted, in 1981, a law authorizing any insurer to exclude coverage for any bodily injury to "any insured or any family member of an insured" in its insurance policies. Even though this law does not go into effect until January 1, 1982, it is clear that Kansas's position on interspousal tort immunity has not changed.

Rule

In the present case, the plaintiff, who is the defendant's wife, was injured when the car the defendant was driving crashed into a telephone pole. The plaintiff was sitting in the passenger seat at the time of the accident. She sustained a broken leg and cuts and bruises. Although the defendant may have been negligent, the accident obviously involved injuries inflicted by one spouse upon another.

Application

Therefore, this case clearly falls within the mandate of *Sink*, and the plaintiff's case should be dismissed on the basis of Kansas's very viable interspousal immunity.

Conclusion

The plaintiff has claimed that a decision upholding interspousal immunity violates logic and basic principles of justice. She notes that the new law has not yet gone into effect, so that it does not apply to the present case. She also contends that the foremost justification for immunity laws is illogical, since it is based on the premise that personal tort actions between husband and wife would disrupt the peace and harmony of the home. She cites the Restatement of the Law of Torts, which criticizes this justification by stating that it is based upon the faulty assumption that an uncompensated tort makes for peace in the family.

Counterargument

Response   However, it is no more logical to contend that family harmony will be better served if a husband and wife can drag each other into court and meet each other as legal adversaries. In addition, the plaintiff has overlooked a far more persuasive argument for interspousal tort immunity: Under Kansas law, any recovery that the plaintiff-wife would obtain if this action were allowed to proceed would inure to the benefit of the defendant-husband. All property acquired by either spouse during the marriage is "marital property" in which each spouse has a common ownership interest. If the injured spouse (plaintiff) should die, the surviving spouse could maintain an action for wrongful death and could share in any recovery of losses. This result would allow a negligent party to profit by his own actions. This is a result which would be truly offensive to anyone's sense of justice.

The doctrine of interspousal immunity is as viable today as it was when initially enunciated by this court. It not only fosters family harmony, but also prevents a spouse from profiting from his or her own negligence.

For some types of documents, you will want to abbreviate or rearrange the scheme presented above. For example, if you are answering an opponent's brief, you could begin by stating the opponent's objections and then follow with your own claims and conclusions. With this order, a separate "response" section may no longer be necessary, since the response may become part of your main argument. For example:

Issue   The issue presented in this case is whether one spouse can sue the other for injuries caused by the negligence of the other spouse.

Subissue   Does Kansas law presently require interspousal tort immunity?

The plaintiff in this case has claimed that a decision upholding interspousal immunity violates basic principles of justice and current Kansas law. She acknowledges that Kansas has enacted a law which authorizes any insurer to exclude coverage for any bodily injury to "any insured or any family member of an insured" in its insurance policies. However, she points out that this law does not establish blanket interspousal tort immunity. Also, because the law has not yet even gone into effect, it does not apply to the present case.

Rule   The plaintiff's reliance on the nature and effective date of the legislation is misplaced. The law to which the plaintiff alludes is one that the Kansas legislature has just enacted, in 1981. Even though this law does not go into effect until January 1, 1982, Kansas' position on interspousal tort immunity was established long ago and has not changed. In *Sink v. Sink*, 239 P.2d 933 (1952), this court held that neither spouse may maintain an action for tort for damages against the other. Although a number of States have recently enacted legislation which explicitly allows these suits, Kansas has not joined them. In fact, the legislation mentioned by the plaintiff makes it clear that Kansas is not attempting to establish a new policy on interspousal immunity, but is merely incorporating its current policy into the laws that govern insurers.

As the plaintiff has pointed out in her brief, she was injured when the car her husband was driving crashed into a telephone pole. Whether or not the defendant was negligent, the accident involved injuries inflicted by one spouse upon another. As such, Kansas' policy on interspousal tort immunity would apply.

Application

Is the rationale behind interspousal immunity illogical?

Subissue

The plaintiff further contends that the foremost justification for immunity laws is illogical, since it is based on the premise that personal tort actions between husband and wife would disrupt family harmony. She cites the Restatement of Torts, which criticizes this justification by stating that it is based upon the faulty assumption that an uncompensated tort makes for peace in the family.

The plaintiff and the Restatement have overlooked the even greater illogic behind a premise that family harmony can be better served if a husband and wife can drag each other into court and meet as legal adversaries. In addition, the plaintiff has overlooked a far more persuasive argument for interspousal immunity: under Kansas law, any recovery that the plaintiff-wife would obtain if this action were allowed to proceed would inure to the benefit of the defendant husband.

Rule

In the present case, the husband and wife could be forced to endure years as legal adversaries, waiting for an interspousal lawsuit to slowly wend its way through a complex legal system. In addition, the defendant could stand to profit by any recovery his wife receives from the couple's insurance.

Application

The doctrine of interspousal immunity is as viable today as it was when initially enunciated by this court. It not only fosters family harmony, but also prevents a spouse from profiting from his or her own negligence.

Some caveats. There are several caveats to consider when you use IRAC or any similar outline to analyze the issues in a law school problem. Students sometimes get the impression that they have done a complete, well-rounded analysis of a question once they have taken the obvious issues through the IRAC outline. IRAC can give you a false sense of security if you mistake the thorough analysis of an issue for the thorough analysis of a whole problem or question. Once you have completed analyzing the obvious issues, make sure that you reread the problem to search for subissues or elements of issues that you might have overlooked. These are important and can influence the outcome of your problem.

IRAC is merely a framework within which to build your analysis: It should not appear to your readers that you have merely plugged information into a rigid formula. Edit your writing to eliminate the mechanical effects of a series of statements that the issue is W, the rule is X, the analysis is Y, and therefore the conclusion is Z.

D The Importance of Headings

We have talked about providing a "roadmap" in your introduction to tell the reader what is going to be covered in your document. You can also use informative headings and a table of contents to show your organization to your readers. In fact, rules of court may require that you use headings and a table of contents in documents that you submit to the court.

Headings guide the reader through the text by describing what is included in each section of the document. For some documents the headings can then be collected and used as a table of contents. The table of contents tells the reader where things are located and gives the reader an overview of the contents of the whole document. Headings and tables of contents are particularly useful in reference documents such as memos, statutes, regulations, treatises, and any other document in which a reader might want to find specific information quickly. Even documents that are not usually used as references benefit from informative headings and a table of contents, especially if the documents are long. The example below is a table of contents from a very long will.

Table of Contents

Item 1:	Declarations	
	1.1	My will
	1.2	My family
Item 2:	Payment of Funeral and Administrative Expenses, Debts, and Taxes	
	2.1	Funeral and Administrative Expenses
	2.2	Debts
	2.3	Taxes

Item 3: Specific Gifts
    3.1   Personal property to my wife
    3.2   Personal property to children if my wife does not survive
    3.3   Discretion of executor
    3.4   Resolution of disputes
Item 4: Disposition of My Residuary Estate
    4.1   Beneficiaries
    4.2   Use of the residuary trust income and principal
    4.3   Invasion of principal for the benefit of my wife
    4.4   Limitation on a trustee-beneficiary
    4.5   Time limit of the residuary trust

Headings should mark logical divisions in a text. If you have outlined your document well and have chosen a good organizing principle, it will be fairly easy to decide where the headings belong and what the levels of these headings should be (full heading, subheading, run-in heading, and so on). In fact, if you have trouble deciding where to put headings, it may be a sign that your document needs to be reorganized.

Once you have determined where headings belong, make them as informative as possible and try to make headings at the same level parallel in structure (see Guideline 8 in Chapter 10 on using parallel structure). Headings should tell the reader something. A single word or short string of nouns is usually not informative. On the other hand, sentences — statements or questions — make particularly informative headings. The headings in the following table of contents are from a student's term paper. These short headings tell the reader nothing.

Table of Contents

Briefs must have headings, and the headings should be informative and persuasive. They cannot be single words or labels; they must spell out the lawyer's conclusion on each question addressed in the brief. If a brief is particularly long or complex, it should contain informative subheadings as well. The headings and subheadings, taken together, then serve as a table of contents that summarizes the lawyer's position. Below are the headings from a Supreme Court brief. In this case the respondent was indicted on charges of armed robbery of a bank and was jailed before trial in the Norfolk City Jail. An FBI agent asked an inmate who had previously acted as a paid informant to be especially alert to any statements made by the respondent and several other federal prisoners but not to initiate conversation or ask questions about the charges against them. The informant later told the FBI agent that the respondent had talked openly about the robbery. The informant testified at the respondent's trial. The respondent's conviction was appealed on the basis that the FBI had violated his Sixth Amendment right to counsel.

Table of Contents

Some attorneys like to use the parties' names in an issue statement in order to personalize the argument, to differentiate the actors if there are many of them or if the facts are complicated, and for other similar reasons. However, other attorneys do not favor this practice. They believe that headings should never be personalized because one function of an appellate brief is to give the court an opportunity to convert issue statements into rules of law that can be applied to anyone in the future. (*See* Chapter 5 on drafting issue statements narrowly or broadly.)

EXERCISES

1. "If John mows Fred's lawn on Tuesday, Fred will pay him $10.00." Based on this sentence, construct an agreement for Fred and John. Provide a context: for example, purpose, parties, location; provide for contingencies; add any missing information. Then group and organize all the material and supply informative headings.

2. Break up and reorganize the leash law below. Insert informative headings in appropriate places.

LEASH LAW

No animal of the dog kind shall be allowed to go at large without a collar or tag, as now prescribed by law, and no person owning, keeping, or having custody of a dog in the District shall permit such dog to be on public space in the District, unless such dog is firmly secured by a substantial leash not exceeding four feet in length, held by a person capable of managing such a dog, nor shall any dog be permitted to go on private property without the consent of the owner or occupant thereof.

3. Before trial, a party can ask an adversary to stipulate (agree to) certain things, such as that certain documents are genuine, or that certain pieces of evidence can be admitted into court, or that certain facts are not really in dispute. In other words, the parties can formally agree that certain things are not at issue. This way, trial time is not wasted on facts, evidence, or documents that are already accepted by both parties.

The adversary must meet with the party asking for the stipulation at a time that is determined by the date of the trial notice. (Trial notice is notice given by one party in an action to an adversary, stating that he or she intends to bring a cause to trial at the next term of the court. The adversary generally learns of the specific trial date by finding out from the court when the case has been set on the docket.)

If the adversary does not meet to stipulate as the party has requested, then the party can file an order for the adversary to show cause why the documents, evidence, or facts should *not* be accepted by the court. If the adversary ignores the show cause order, then the court will automatically accept the documents or facts.

Following is a rule that deals specifically with stipulations. Read the rule, then rewrite and reorganize the rule so that it is easier to read and follows a logical order. In addition, indicate what organizing principle you have chosen and explain why you think it is appropriate.

If a party, by the date of issuance of trial notice in any case pending in this court, or within ten days thereafter in the case of an expedited trial notice, fails, after having been duly served with a request by his adversary, to meet and confer for the purpose of stipulating to the genuineness of documents or to the admissibility of evidence or to undisputed facts, the party serving the request may within 50 days, but not less than 35 days, prior to the date set for the call of the case from the trial calendar, file with the court a motion for an order to show cause why the documents, evidence, or facts covered in the request should not be accepted as proved for the purposes of the case.

4. Below are the facts and law from an employment discrimination case filed in a federal court in the District of Columbia. This information is in no particular order. The plaintiff claims that he was denied employment by the defendant employer. Assume that you are the plaintiff's attorney and that you must use this information to write a brief. Begin by identifying the issue and rules. Then use the factual statements to create an application section and a conclusion. Create a strong argument that shows why the plaintiff's case should not be dismissed because of improper venue. Show the outline (IRAC) for your argument in the margin of your paper. If you do not have all of the information that you think you need, then make reasonable assumptions and argue on the basis of these assumptions.

Facts and law.   The defendant employer is a member of a joint apprenticeship committee of printing unions and employers. This committee consists of six people, three of whom are officers of printing unions and three of whom are officers of print shops that are members of the print shop trade association. The committee meets in the District of Columbia and engages in at least the following activities in the District.

1. interviewing apprenticeship candidates
2. evaluating apprenticeship candidates
3. selecting and recommending apprenticeship candidates to be employed by member companies

A person cannot be hired as an apprentice by a member company unless he or she has been approved by the joint apprenticeship committee.

The defendant employer runs a print shop.

Under Rule 12(b)(3) of the Federal Rules of Civil Procedure, the defendant has moved this court for an order dismissing the employment discrimination action against it on the grounds of improper venue under §706(f)(3) of Title VII of the Civil Rights Act of 1964, as amended, 42 U.S.C. §2000e-5(f)(3).

The defendant employer has all of its offices and facilities in Virginia. It hires, fires, and promotes all employees in Virginia.

There are four criteria for venue under §706(f)(3) of Title VII. In summary, the action may be brought

1. In any judicial district in the state in which an unlawful employment practice is alleged to have been committed *or*

2. In the judicial district in which the employment records relevant to the alleged practice are kept *or*

3. In the judicial district in which the plaintiff would have worked but for the alleged unlawful employment practice *or*

4. In the judicial district in which the defendant has his principal office, if the defendant is not found within any of the above districts.

The plaintiff sought to be hired as an apprentice by the defendant but failed to gain the approval of the joint apprenticeship committee.

The joint apprenticeship committee was created by a collective bargaining agreement entered into by all of the employees and all of the unions. This agreement was entered into in the District of Columbia.

In *Trucking Management, Inc.,* 20 FEP Cases 342 (D.D.C. 1979), the defendant companies were members of a trade association. The companies were not located in the same state as the association. Nevertheless, the court found that membership in a trade association that negotiated a collective bargaining agreement on behalf of its members provides a sufficient nexus among the out-of-state defendants to satisfy the venue requirements of Title VII. Specifically, the court stated:

> From the beginning of this litigation, the negotiation of the NMFA [trade association] in the District of Columbia was the only alleged "unlawful employment practice" providing a sufficient nexus among the defendants to satisfy the venue requirements.

5. Arrange the following disjointed pieces of information into a coherent whole, then come to a conclusion about the facts and law in the case. Be sure to supply a logical organization and transitions for your argument.

The elements for a prima facie case for conversion are:

1. An act by a defendant that interferes with the plaintiff's right to possess a particular chattel. The act must be serious enough to warrant that the defendant pay for the full value of the chattel. Interference is established if the defendant exercises control or dominion over the property for a substantial amount of time.

2. The defendant must intend to commit the *act* leading to conversion. The defendant does not have to intend to convert the plaintiff's property.

3. The defendant's act must cause the interference or set in motion those forces that interfere with the plaintiff's possession of the chattel.

Stealing, embezzling, selling, or destroying chattel all qualify as acts that interfere with the plaintiff's possession of chattel.

Harvey bought a tape deck from Larry.
Right after Harvey got the tape deck, he sold it.
Larry had stolen the tape deck from Mike.
Harvey did not know that the tape deck was stolen property.
Mike is suing Harvey for conversion.

Chattel is tangible personal property or is intangible property that has been reduced to some physical form (e.g., a stock certificate).

6. You are an associate working for the law firm of Smith, Smythe, and Smooth. Your senior partner has given you this client letter, which was written by one of your colleagues. The partner asks you to comment on how well it is written. He also wants to know whether you think Mrs. Burton will understand it. Make a list of all the problems you find in the letter, reorganize it, and rewrite it.

Smith, Smythe, and Smooth
Attorneys at Law
160 Pennsylvania Avenue, N.W.
Washington, D.C. 20001
Telephone: (202) 555-2318

August 5, 2000

Mrs. Marion Burton
1400 Ft. McNavy Drive
Bethesda, Maryland

Re: Alimony for medical bills

Dear Mrs. Burton:

You asked if there was a way to recover your medical expenses from Admiral Burton. The normal procedure would be to garnish his wages. That means that his employer would withhold money and pay it into the court.

The problem is that your ex-husband's employer is the United States Navy. Under a doctrine of law called "sovereign immunity," you cannot sue the Government unless they consent to it. Congress recently passed a law permitting garnishment for alimony or child support only.

Admiral Burton's obligation to pay your medical bills comes from your property settlement agreement. When your divorce became final, the settlement agreement became part of the decree. U.S. law defines alimony as "periodic payments of funds for the support and maintenance of the former spouse." The medical payments fall within the state scheme of spousal support.

We have presented this information to Judge Stern and now await his ruling. If he holds that the medical payments are in fact "alimony" within the meaning of U.S. law, you will be able to garnish Admiral Burton's pay until the bills are fully paid.

Of course, if you have any questions, please contact me.

Sincerely yours,
Robert C. Shaw

10

Writing

Clearly

This chapter contains 13 guidelines for clear legal writing. They have been selected because they are particularly useful for writing and reviewing all types of legal documents, including exams, memoranda, briefs, pleadings, client letters, legislation, contracts, and leases. These guidelines are tools for you to use when you want to write for a specific audience or audiences, accomplish a well-defined purpose or purposes, and create well-organized, logical legal documents.

Note that the sentences and paragraphs used as bad examples and exercises for revision were, for the most part, taken from real legal documents, modified to eliminate the identities of the attorneys who wrote them. You will thus be learning from the mistakes of others, and will—if you learn these guidelines well—be spared the shame of writing such embarrassing material yourself.

Thirteen Guidelines for Clear Legal Writing

1. Write short sentences.
2. Put the parts of each sentence in a logical order.
3. Avoid intrusive phrases and clauses.
4. Untangle complex conditionals.
5. Use the active voice whenever possible.
6. Use verb clauses and adjectives instead of nominalizations.
7. Use the positive unless you want to emphasize the negative.
8. Use parallel structure.
9. Avoid ambiguity in words and sentences.
10. Choose vocabulary with care.
11. Avoid noun strings.
12. Eliminate redundancy and extraneous words; avoid overspecificity.
13. Use an appropriate style.

A Guideline 1: Write Short Sentences

You will often see two-and three-hundred-word sentences in all forms of legal writing, from hornbooks to judicial opinions, briefs, and memos. Probably no other single characteristic does more to needlessly complicate legal writing than these long sentences.

Research in linguistics and psychology has shown that the average reader can hold only a few ideas at a time in short-term memory.[1] After two or three ideas, the reader needs to pause and put together what he or she has read. The period at the end of a sentence is one signal for such a pause. When there are no periods in long strings of thoughts, the reader will try to break up the sentence into smaller pieces in order to understand it. However, the reader may not know where to pause or which ideas to group together. Readers often get lost in very long sentences.

In addition to the burden imposed by sheer length, most long sentences violate other guidelines for writing clearly. Structural complexities such as complex conditionals, passive verbs, unclear references, and nonparallel constructions add to the reader's difficulties.

Although you see long sentences in all kinds of traditional legal writing, there is nothing in the nature of the law itself that requires you to express all of your thoughts in one sentence. Your writing can be legally accurate whether you use one sentence or several sentences. Legal convention, however, will sometimes require you to put a lot of information in one sentence. For example, you may have to put each issue statement in a brief in its own sentence. This convention has resulted in some of the longest, most cumbersome sentences you will see in legal writing.

Here are two examples of overly long sentences that we have revised. The first example is a subsection from a will that we have broken into several sentences.

POOR: The trustee may pay all or part of the income to or for the benefit of the beneficiary or may accumulate all or part of the income, distribute trust principal (even all of it if necessary) to or for the benefit of the beneficiary for the beneficiary's maintenance, support, education, comfortable living, business or professional needs, or general welfare, and if there is more than one beneficiary, pay income or distribute principal to or for the benefit of the beneficiaries as it determines (even excluding one or more of the beneficiaries) without regard to any principle of law requiring impartiality among beneficiaries of the trust.

BETTER: The trustee may pay all or part of the income to or for the benefit of the beneficiary or may accumulate all or part of the income. The trustee may distribute trust principal (even all of it, if necessary) to or for the benefit of the beneficiary for the beneficiary's maintenance, support, education, comfortable living, business or professional needs, or general welfare. If there is more than one beneficiary, the trustee may pay income or distribute principal to or for the benefit of the beneficiaries as it determines (even excluding one or more of the beneficiaries), without regard to any principle of law requiring impartiality among beneficiaries of the trust.

---

1. Miller, The Magical Number Seven, Plus or Minus Two: Some Limits on Our Capacity for Processing Information, 63 Psychological Review 81 (1956).

Notice that just dividing the passage into shorter sentences makes it easier to read. Breaking up the last sentence and making it into a new paragraph can further clarify the drafter's meaning.

> If there is more than one beneficiary, the trustee, in addition to the powers noted above, may pay income or distribute principal to or for the benefit of one or more of the beneficiaries, as the trustee determines. The trustee may exclude one or more of the beneficiaries from these payments or distributions, even if the law requires that the trustee treat all beneficiaries equally.

Sometimes breaking up a long sentence into shorter sentences makes the entire passage longer. There is nothing wrong with this: The goal is *clarity*, not brevity for its own sake.

The second example is an issue statement, which we have rewritten so that it is shorter and easier to understand. It can be very difficult to put an issue statement into one sentence. If you create a sentence that is very long and very complex, keep rewriting it until you have put the parts of the sentence in a logical order and have removed all extraneous words.

POOR: The district court was correct in holding that the statute of limitations for medical malpractice begins to run at the time of the tort or when treatment ceases which was prior to the plaintiff's conception thereby foreclosing the right for her to bring a cause of action.

BETTER: Since the district court was correct in holding that the statute of limitations for medical malpractice begins to run at the time of the tort or when treatment ends, and since the plaintiff was conceived after both of these events, the plaintiff has no right on which to base a cause of action.

EXERCISES

Break up the following long sentences into shorter sentences. Rearrange the parts of the sentences and add words if necessary.

1. To remit a controversy like this to the circuit court of appeals where it properly belongs is not to be indifferent to claims of importance but to be uncompromising in safeguarding the conditions which alone will enable this court to discharge well the duties entrusted exclusively to us.
2. Following the *Hirota* decision at the 1948 term, a series of motions for leave to file petitions in war crime cases were again denied by an evenly divided court, with four justices returning to their pre-*Hirota* ground of lack of original jurisdiction and the other four amending their notation to state the opinion that argument should be heard on the motions for leave to file the petitions in order to settle the issue of what remedy, if any, the petitioners have.

3. A court order forcing the student editor of the Lincoln Weekly Star to publish candidate Jones' advertisements would clearly violate and destroy the discretionary editorial privilege guaranteed to newspapers by the First Amendment and consistently upheld by the Supreme Court of the United States.

4. Where, upon the trial of such a case as is indicated above, there was evidence from which the jury was authorized to find that the defendant's agent went to the plaintiff's home and knowing that she, a child of 11 years of age, was at home alone, attempted to gain entrance to the home for the announced purpose of repossessing a television set, and when the child refused to admit him by the front door that he went to the rear door and wrote a note which he exhibited to the child through a window of the door and in which he threatened to go for the police and have her put in jail if she did not admit him so that he could take possession of the television set, and that the child became so frightened by this threat that she became extremely nervous, fearful of leaving the house, and unable to sleep at night, the jury would be authorized to find that the conduct of the defendant's agent, who was acting within the scope of his authority, was willful misconduct under the circumstances, and that the child's resulting nervousness and distress was a natural and probable consequence of such willful misconduct. (203 words)

5. In the case of a State Medicaid plan that the Secretary of Health and Human Services determines requires State legislation (other than legislation appropriating funds), in order for the plan to meet the additional requirements imposed by such amendment, the State plan shall not be regarded as failing to comply with the requirements imposed by such amendment solely on the basis of its failure to meet these additional requirements before the first day of the first calendar quarter beginning after the close of the first regular session of the State legislature that begins after the date of the enactment of this Act. For purposes of the preceding sentence, in the case of a State that has a two-year legislative session, each year of such session shall be deemed to be a separate regular session of the State legislature. (138 words)

B | Guideline 2: Put the Parts of Each Sentence in a Logical Order

Some sentences are ineffective or difficult to read because they lack internal logic. It is very important to put the parts of a sentence in a logical order. Start each sentence with information that is familiar to your audience or that will tell the reader where you are going with the sentence. If the sentence is the first in your document, begin it with information that will provide a context. If the sentence is in the middle of a document, begin the sentence by tying it to the information in the previous sentences or paragraphs. The following opening sentence from a letter provides the reader with a context that ties the content of the letter to the reader's own past action.

In response to your request of April 10, 2001, I am sending you copies of the pleadings and some additional documents.

Don't make your reader read through an entire sentence in order to discover its purpose.

Here is an example from a student memo. It is the opening paragraph of the student's Discussion section.

Since the instant action arose in Connecticut (the employer and employee are located in Virginia, but the alleged discrimination occurred in Connecticut), the initial issue to be resolved in determining what limitations period applies in a section 1981 action in federal court in Virginia is which state's law applies.

The main idea in this sentence — the initial issue that will be considered in the memo — is buried in the middle of the sentence. The student should have begun the sentence with a statement of the issue and then recounted the specific facts of the case.

The issue in this case is what limitations statute applies in a section 1981 action brought in federal court in one state if the cause of action arose in another state. In this case, the suit was brought in federal court in Virginia. The employer and the employees are located in Virginia, but the alleged discrimination occurred in Connecticut.

This guideline applies to groups of several sentences, or even paragraphs, as well. Look for a *logical sequence* — a time sequence, a cause-and-effect relationship, an order of priority — and arrange the sentences or paragraphs in that order. As with a single, longer sentence, begin with information that the reader already knows or that will explain where you are headed and use that as a context for information that follows. Tie the sentences to each other with the proper transitions (and, but, because, however, moreover, nonetheless, furthermore, therefore, thus, and so on).

EXERCISES

Put the parts of each sentence into a more logical order.

1. The fact that the *Rutgers* publication was a newspaper and the present publication is a law review and requires special selection of the type and quality of its articles is what distinguishes the two cases and will probably be the crucial factor in the court's decision.

2. The ultimate verification of the inquiries at the hospital was the damaging factor.

3. Whether or not the method of gathering data would be objectionable to the reasonable person is the question that must be asked by the court.

4. The court of appeals in holding that the doubt rule contravenes the Administrative Procedure Act, ruled correctly.

5. Whether the "true doubt" rule is identical to this view overruled by *Del-Vecchio v. Bowers, supra* and rejected by Congress in enacting F.R.Evid. 301 which, moreover, is fundamentally antagonistic not only to federal law but all American law, is not considered by the agency.

C Guideline 3: Avoid Intrusive Phrases and Clauses

One reason that a sentence can be too long is that it may contain a phrase or clause that has been inserted into the middle of the main clause. These additions, exceptions, or pieces of incidental material disrupt the logical flow of the sentence and make it difficult for readers to understand what is meant.

Sometimes even relatively short sentences contain intrusive phrases or clauses. The italicized words in the example below are not part of the main sentence. The date comes in the middle of the verb. The address comes between the verb and its object.

POOR: Interested attorneys may, *on or before (date),* submit *to the Clerk, (address),* written comments *regarding the proposed change in court procedures.*

Notice how much clearer even a short sentence can become when the intrusive phrases have been moved so that they no longer separate the parts of the main clause (subject, verb, and object).

GOOD: Interested attorneys who want to comment on the proposed change in court procedures may send comments in writing to the Clerk, (address), by (date).

Intrusive phrases occur in abundance in all kinds of legal documents. In the following example from a law student's memo, the student tried to cram too much information into one sentence.

POOR: One of the main questions presented in this memo is whether 28 U.S.C. §636(b)(1)(B), *which allows a district court to decide a suppression motion based on the record developed before a magistrate, the magistrate's proposed findings of fact and recommendations, and the defendant's written and oral objections before the district court,* violates the Due Process Clause.

The italicized information is inserted in such a way that it interferes with the continuity of the main part of the sentence. Because the subject of the sentence is separated from the verb by 37 words, the reader does not know where the sentence is going until the very end. The student should have broken up the sentence and reordered the information logically.

BETTER: One of the main questions presented in this memo is whether 28 U.S.C. §636(b)(1)(B) violates the Due Process Clause. This section allows the district court to decide a suppression motion based on the record developed before a magistrate, the magistrate's proposed findings of fact and recommendations, and the defendant's written and oral objections before the district court.

The reader of the rewritten version knows immediately what the point of the passage is. A related problem is illustrated by the following sentence.

POOR: Petitioner's argument *that exclusion of the press from the trial and subsequent denial of access to the trial transcripts is, in effect, a prior restraint* is contrary to the facts.

In this sentence, the subordinate clause, which is in italics, intrudes into the middle of the main clause. The verb phrase of the subordinate clause ("is . . . a prior restraint") is perilously close to the verb phrase of the main clause ("is contrary to the facts") and makes the sentence very confusing to read. This type of subordinate clause construction is called *self-embedding,* and psycholinguistic research[2] has shown that self-embedding is very difficult for readers' minds to process. The writer could easily have avoided self-embedding in that sentence.

BETTER: Petitioner argued that excluding the press from the trial and subsequently denying access to the trial transcripts is, in effect, a prior restraint. This argument is contrary to the facts.

In general, the best way to deal with any type of sentence with intrusive phrases is to remove the inserted material and put it into a new sentence.

---

2. Psycholinguistic research is the study of how language is perceived and understood, using the methods of experimental psychology. *See* Miller & Isard, Free Recall of Self-Embedded English Sentences, 7 Information and Control 292 (1964); and Schwartz, Sparkman, and Deese, The Process of Understanding and Judgment of Comprehensibility, 9 Journal of Verbal Learning and Verbal Behavior 87 (1970).

EXERCISES

Underline the intrusive phrase(s) and rewrite the sentence.

1. No outpatient health care, which is ordinarily available to people in this category and must be obtained through the HMO, will be available after this date.

2. Some people, especially those receiving services that are covered by insurance and who have to pay only a nominal copayment, overutilize certain services.

3. Moreover, the rule which without question was applied is invalid as petitioner, because it offers a substitute, must be assumed to agree.

4. On May 23, 2006, petitioners (hereafter plaintiffs), consisting of 16 minors, suing as public school students, and seven parents of students attending public schools, brought the underlying action against real parties in interest (hereafter defendants) in respondent superior court claiming a deprivation of rights in violation of the Elementary and Secondary Education Act of 1965.

5. In light of the prevailing jurisprudence, including that of the District of Columbia, contrary to our position that the district court should look to District of Columbia law (jurisdiction where the action arose), I conclude that a summary judgment motion relying on the applicability of the limitations provisions of the forum state (Maryland) is more likely to succeed than one relying on the law of the state in which the action arose.

6. The court held that the agreement whereby she would support him financially and provide household services while he wrote a German textbook, in return for which he would support her when he reestablished his professional career, was enforceable.

7. Although the Court stated that it need not reach the question of whether strict scrutiny was required because even under the most exacting standard of review the Minority Business Enterprises (MBE) provision passes constitutional muster, nowhere in the court's opinion is there any indication that it applied the strict scrutiny necessary to determine whether the MBE provision was in fact constitutional.

8. Moreover, although claimant's edema theory about which the fact finder expressed grave doubt and therefore indicated no difficulty in evaluating can be said to have been probative, independent of its believability, since any tendency to make the existence of a fact more probable, he made no finding that it was credible.

D Guideline 4: Untangle Complex Conditionals

A conditional is a statement that establishes an *if . . . then* relationship between pieces of information; a complex conditional is a conditional with many conditions (*if* statements) or many rules or consequences (*then* statements). A conditional or complex conditional may not always contain the word *if*. Some conditionals introduce a condition with *when, where, whether,* or other words or phrases. Many conditionals also lack the word *then* in the rule or consequence statement. For example,

> When both parties are residents of the same state, there is no diversity of citizenship.

This sentence could be rewritten:

> *If* both parties are residents of the same state, *then* there is no diversity of citizenship.

As long as the sentence states a condition and a rule or consequence, it is a conditional.

Readers often have problems understanding complex conditionals. The more conditions or rules and the more combinations of *ands* and *ors* that a sentence contains, the more difficult it is to understand.

Here is an example of a complex conditional from the Federal Rules of Civil Procedure, Rule 6(b).

Condition	**POOR:** *Enlargement.* When by these rules or by a notice given thereunder or by order of court an act is required or allowed to be done within a specified time, the court for cause shown may at any time in its discretion (1) with or without motion or notice
Rule or Consequence	order the period enlarged if request therefor is made before the expiration of the period originally prescribed or as extended by a previous order, or (2) upon motion made after the expiration of the specified period permit the act to be done where the failure to act was the result of excusable neglect.

To untangle a complex conditional like this one, it is often useful to list each provision. It can also help to physically separate each condition and rule on the page itself. This rule would be much easier to understand if it were rewritten with these suggestions in mind.

	GOOD: *Extending a time period.* This rule applies to acts that may or must be done within a certain time when that time is specified by:
Condition	• the Federal Rules *or* • a notice issued under the Federal Rules *or* • a court order.

If a party wishes to extend the time period, the party must show cause to the court to do so. The court may then, at its discretion, extend the time under two different sets of circumstances:

**Rule or
Consequence**

1. *If the request is made before the time period expires*, then the court may extend the original time period (or a previously extended time period) with or without motion or notice.
2. *If the request is made after the time period expires*, then the court may extend the original time period, but only if failure to act was the result of excusable neglect and if a motion is made.

EXERCISES

Rewrite the following complex conditionals so that they are easier to understand.

1. In a patent infringement action commenced in a district where the defendant is not a resident but has a regular and established business, service of process, summons, or subpoena upon such defendant may be made upon the defendant himself, his agent, or agent's representative conducting such business.

2. If a plaintiff who has once dismissed an action in any court commences an action based upon or including the same claim against the same defendant, the court may make such order for the payment of costs of the action previously dismissed as it may deem proper and may stay the proceedings in the action until the plaintiff has complied with the order.

3. When actions involving a common question of law or fact are pending before the court, it may order a joint hearing or trial of any or all the matters in issue in the actions; it may order all the actions consolidated; and it may make such orders concerning proceedings therein as may tend to avoid unnecessary costs or delay.

4. The court, in furtherance of convenience or to avoid prejudice, or when separate trials will be conducive to expedition and economy, may order a separate trial of any claim, cross-claim, counterclaim, or third-party claim, or of any separate issue or of any number of claims, cross-claims, counterclaims, third-party claims, or issues, always preserving inviolate the right of trial by jury as declared by the Seventh Amendment to the Constitution or as given by a statute of the United States.

5. When a presumption such as Longshore Act Section 20(a), which provides that it "shall be presumed in absence of substantial evidence to the contrary—[t]hat the claim comes within the provisions of the chapter" exists—if presumptions are "evidence," i.e., if they do not disappear upon presentation of proof sufficient to justify a contrary result but add

weight after rebuttal supporting a finding of any fact presumed—the burden of persuasion, because in every case opposing evidence must be stronger, is transferred from the party in whose favor the presumption was created (the claimant who therefore must be assumed to originally have had it) to the disfavored party (the employer).

E Guideline 5: Use the Active Voice Whenever Possible

The *passive voice* is an interesting grammatical construction. It is a way of changing the *focus* of a sentence without changing its meaning, by rearranging and adding words. Here are examples of active sentences and their passive counterparts.

> *Active:* John *hit* Morris.
> *Passive:* Morris *was hit* by John.
>
> *Active:* Alice *will eat* the entire pizza.
> *Passive:* The entire pizza *will be eaten* by Alice.

The passive voice allows the writer to focus on the object of the (original active) sentence rather than on the "doer" or the "agent" of the action. A passive construction can be in any tense; it can refer to a single action or to continuous action. For example:

> Those buildings *will have been destroyed* by flooding by the time the governor decides to act (future perfect tense).
>
> Even as we speak, the supplies *are being eaten* by rats (present continuous tense).

Because the passive voice does something unusual to the focus of a sentence, a passive sentence can be difficult for the reader to understand. Use the passive voice only when you want to focus on the object of the original active sentence.

When you use the passive voice, it is possible to *truncate* the sentence by leaving out the doer of the action. For example, the full passive sentence

> Morris was hit by John

can be made into the truncated passive

> Morris was hit [   ].

The full passive

> Those buildings will have been destroyed by flooding by the time the governor decides to act.

becomes the truncated passive

> Those buildings will have been destroyed [   ] by the time
> the governor decides to act.

Using a truncated passive allows a writer to speak in general terms in cases in which it does not matter who performed the action. For example:

> In most law schools, law is *taught* by means of the Socratic method.

The writer can also avoid stating who is responsible for the action when the identity of the actor does matter. The writer may intentionally "pass the buck" linguistically or may simply forget to identify the actor.

The effects of using the passive voice inappropriately can be particularly significant in legal writing. Much of legal writing deals with the rights and responsibilities that govern the past, present, or future actions of specific individuals or entities. A contract, for example, spells out the rights and responsibilities of individuals under certain carefully defined circumstances. However, this vital information can be obscured by the use of verbs in the passive voice, especially if the constructions are truncated.

The following passage is an example of a very familiar kind of contract: It is part of an insurance policy. One of its major purposes is to describe the rights and responsibilities of the insurer and of the insured. However, the passage fails to focus on this important information. It is unclear who "incurred," who "lost," who "earned," and who "made payments."

> The company will pay, in accordance with Chapter 670 of the Acts of 1970 of the Commonwealth of Massachusetts and all Acts amendatory thereof or supplementary thereto, subject to any applicable deductible, all reasonable expenses *incurred* within two years from the date of accident for necessary medical, surgical, X-ray, and dental services, including prosthetic devices, and necessary ambulance, hospital, professional nursing, and funeral services, and, in the case of persons employed or self-employed at the time of an accident, any amounts actually *lost* by reason of inability to work and earn wages or salary or their equivalent, but not other income, that would otherwise have been *earned* in the normal course of an injured person's employment, and for payments in fact *made* to others, not members of the injured person's household and reasonably *incurred* in obtaining from those others ordinary and necessary services in lieu of those that, had he not been injured, the injured person would have performed not for income but for the benefit of himself or members of his household (emphasis added).

Similarly, when an attorney describes the past actions of an individual in the fact statement or analysis section of a memo or brief, it is important that the reader know exactly who did what. The passive voice may do more than just confuse the reader about each individual's actions; the passive voice can dilute the impact the attorney is trying to achieve. A plaintiff's attorney should describe the actions of the defendant so that they seem real and direct. The attorney wants the court to know that a particular individual committed the act that caused injury to the plaintiff. If the attorney writes in the passive voice, the focus will be on the act instead of on the person who committed the act.

Here is an example: The plaintiff, Jean, is suing her mother's doctor because the doctor prescribed the drug DES for her mother, Mrs. M, six months before Mrs. M became pregnant with Jean. The fact statement in the plaintiff's brief contained the following passage:

> On January 15, 1958, the plaintiff's mother, Mrs. M, consulted the defendant about the medical complications that she had experienced as the result of a miscarriage in March of 1957. Since Mrs. M was again pregnant, the drug DES *was prescribed* for her to take orally to prevent another miscarriage. Assurances *were made* to Mrs. M that the drug was completely safe. The prescribed drug *was taken* from January 16, 1958, until approximately February 28, 1958, when another miscarriage occurred. In August of 1958, Mrs. M became pregnant with the plaintiff.

This passage becomes far more effective when the passive voice is replaced by the active voice. It becomes clear who did the prescribing and assuring and who took the prescription and acted on the assurance. As a result, the defendant is directly indicted.

> Since Mrs. M was again pregnant, *the defendant prescribed the drug DES* for her to take orally to prevent another miscarriage. The *defendant assured* Mrs. M that the drug was completely safe. Mrs. M took the prescribed drug from January 16, 1958, until approximately February 28, 1958, when Mrs. M had another miscarriage. In August of 1958, Mrs. M became pregnant with the plaintiff.

You can use the active voice as part of your strategy to persuade your audience when you write documents like briefs and memoranda. As you begin to consciously identify the passive voice in legal documents, you will see the subtle effects you can achieve with this grammatical construction. Be attuned to writers who use the passive indiscriminately, because these writers may be diluting the forcefulness of their arguments and analyses. Being aware of the passive is especially important when you analyze an opponent's brief.

Learn to make your own arguments more convincing by following these rules:

1. Use the active voice whenever possible.
2. Avoid truncated passives. Reveal who is responsible for a particular action and put this "doer" into the sentence.
3. Use the passive voice only when you are speaking in general terms, when you want to stress the receiver of the action and not the actor, or when you want to downplay the actor.

EXERCISES

Identify the passive verbs in the following sentences. Rewrite the sentences in the active voice. If the original sentence is ambiguous or just unclear, make a reasonable assumption and rewrite the sentence accordingly.

1. No request was made by the defendants for a separate trial of the federal claims nor was the judge asked to stay trial or to dismiss the state claims.
2. An opinion was rendered by the court after completion of the trial in which no evidence was found to support either the 10b-5 claim or the plaintiff's claim of violation of the margin requirements by the defendant.
3. It was held by the court that the requisite amount in controversy was lacking.
4. Dismissal for want of jurisdiction has been imposed where transparently inflated damages resulting from a minor injury, such as a minor whiplash, have been claimed by the plaintiff.
5. A renewal clause was incorporated into the contract by the parties as well as the changes that were made in the delivery dates.
6. It can be argued that since the building wasn't owned but was leased by our client, permanent occupancy was not intended.
7. An official file shall be established for each client. To the extent that retained copies of documents do not represent all significant actions taken, suitable memoranda or summary statements of such undocumented actions must be prepared promptly and retained in the file.

F Guideline 6: Use Verb Clauses and Adjectives Instead of Nominalizations

Another interesting construction that is overused in legal documents is known as nominalization—the creation of nouns from verbs and adjectives.

The verb	*can be made into the noun*
determine	determination
resolve	resolution
apply	application
enforce	enforcement
inquire	inquiry
reverse	reversal

The adjective	*can be made into the noun*
enforceable	enforceability
distinguishable	distinguishability

applicable	applicability
specific	specificity
important	importance

As with the passive voice, these constructions are grammatical and so are the sentences that contain them. But, as with the passive voice, writers who overuse nominalizations weaken their writing.

Nominalizations make sentences difficult to understand, because they do not communicate a scenario that the reader can picture. Like truncated passives, nominalizations eliminate information about who did what.

Nominalizations make sentences less persuasive. Because nominalizations are nouns, they are *static*, giving the reader little or no feeling that an *action* is involved. For the reader to fully grasp that someone *did* something, it is necessary to use verbs. Here are a few examples of sentences containing nominalizations. Notice how direct the sentences become once the nominalizations are replaced with verb clauses.

POOR: *Recovery* by our client is predicated upon *circumvention* of the current *interpretation* of the adultery statute.

GOOD: Our client can *recover* if he *circumvents* the current interpretation of the adultery statute. (Note that some nominalizations are appropriate, such as *interpretation* in this sentence, because it cannot easily be replaced with a verb clause.)

POOR: Appellant did not authorize the *compilation* or *dissemination* of her credit report expressly or by *implication* when she submitted her *application* for insurance.

GOOD: The appellant did not expressly or implicitly authorize [whom?] to *compile* or *disseminate* her credit report when she *applied* for insurance.

POOR: The case's *significance* is in the fact that it demonstrates the court's *recognition* of the great *importance* of the right to privacy.

GOOD: The case is *significant* because it demonstrates that the court *recognizes* the importance of the right to privacy. (Here, too, one nominalization, *importance,* is appropriate.)

As you can see in the second of these examples, nominalizations often lead to other awkward or wordy constructions. Here, the simple verb *applied* has become *submitted her application.* Similarly, *decide* may become *make a decision; interpret* may become *construct an interpretation; sign* may become *affix one's signature,* and so on. After making a noun out of the meaningful verb, the writer has to hunt around for another verb to make the sentence or clause grammatical. Often, the writer ends up using an "empty" verb, one that has no specific meaning: for example, *do, make, give, necessitate*. This type of writing makes the action seem remote from the actors in the sentence; this, in turn, makes it harder for the reader to picture the scene. If you find nominalizations in your own writing, try converting them into their original form as verbs or adjectives. In most cases this will make your sentence more direct, easier to understand, and more forceful.

EXERCISES

Identify the nominalizations in the following sentences. Rewrite the sentences to eliminate them.

1. We believe that the Act contains an underlying recognition that disclosure of the workings of a government bureaucracy can be of benefit to the public.
2. There are rules covering the preclusion of certain kinds of employment by the attorney after acceptance of these cases for purposes of the avoidance of any suggestion of a conflict of interest.
3. During the representation of a criminal defendant, an attorney must demonstrate an adherence at all times to the rules of professional conduct.
4. Disability arising at work or after years of employment due to employee susceptibility should not be the employer's liability.
5. The appellee and W. C. Frederick entered into a contract for the delivery of ice by the appellee to Frederick and, before the expiration of the contract, Frederick executed an assignment of the contract to the appellant; and on the refusal of the appellee to deliver ice to the assignee it brought an action on the contract against the appellee.

G Guideline 7: Use the Positive Unless You Want to Emphasize the Negative

Most people can easily understand a strong negative imperative ("Do not do that"). Negative statements, however, are generally more difficult for readers to process than positive statements. Furthermore, two negatives within a single clause are more than twice as difficult to understand as the corresponding positive statement.

Occasionally it is legitimate to use double negatives to capture subtleties of meaning. When you say that you are "not unhappy," for example, you do not necessarily mean that you are happy. The double negative expresses a state that is between happy and unhappy.

The words *unless, except,* and *until* are negatives, as are words such as *failure, absent,* and *deny.* Here is a very simple example.

POOR: Plaintiff contends that it could *not* properly demand an equitable adjustment *until* after the completion of the project.

GOOD: Plaintiff contends that it could properly demand an equitable adjustment only after the project is completed.

You may occasionally want to use double negatives to make a command or proscription more forceful. For example, in some circumstances you might use the double negative:

No client letter is to be sent out *unless* a senior partner has approved it.

Rather than the more positive form:

A client letter is to be sent out *only after* a senior partner has approved it.

In general, however, you should avoid using two negatives when you can make a positive statement.

More than two negatives make a clause exceedingly difficult or even impossible to understand. Yet legal writing is full of multiple negatives. Take a look at this example from a jury instruction:

POOR: *Failure* of recollection is common. Innocent *mis*recollection is *not un*common.[3]

BETTER: Failure of recollection is common. Innocent misrecollection is also common.

Following is an example of a triple negative from a law student's memo:

POOR: It is *un*likely that a Maryland district court would *ignore* the clear language of these opinions in the *absence* of convincing authority to the effect that a different rule applies where the action arose outside of the forum state.

GOOD: A Maryland district court would probably follow the clear language in these opinions unless there is convincing authority that a different rule applies where the action arose outside of the forum state.

Multiple negatives can be found in even longer passages than the above. Following is a penalty provision from a federal regulation.

---

3. California Jury Instructions — Civil — Book of Approved Jury Instructions §2.21 (1993).

POOR: The penalty provided in subsection (c) shall not apply to the disclosure of any information received under this subsection, except that such penalty shall apply to the disclosure (by the agency receiving such information) of any such information described in paragraph (1) unless such disclosure is made in a judicial, administrative, or other formal legal proceeding resulting from an investigation conducted by the agency receiving the information.

Untangling this type of sentence imposes a particularly heavy burden on the reader and can lead to misinterpretation and legal errors. The following revision deals with the multiple negatives (*not . . . except . . . unless*) by breaking up the passage into three separate sentences:

BETTER: The penalty provided in section (c) generally does not apply to the disclosure of information received under this subsection. However, the penalty does apply if an agency that received information described in paragraph (1) discloses any of it. But that agency may disclose the information without penalty in a judicial or administrative proceeding or other formal legal proceeding that resulted from the agency's own investigation.

Notice that untangling the multiple negatives and other difficult constructions brings to light a number of problems in the original clause. For example, the nominalization in "unless such *disclosure . . .* " leaves unclear whether, to avoid the penalty, the information must be disclosed only by the agency receiving the information or whether it could be disclosed by any one else in the course of the legal proceeding. These problems are far less likely to arise if you avoid convoluted constructions containing multiple negatives in the first place.

EXERCISES

Rewrite the following sentences in the positive, if possible.

1. We cannot but think that the Court in *Robson v. Drummond* went to the utmost length to which the principle can be carried.
2. A will shall not be valid unless it is signed by two witnesses.
3. There are few lawyers who would not agree that there are situations where "it is more important that the applicable rule of law be settled than that it be settled right."
4. With the vendor number being retroactively set to the original date of revocation, the agency cannot ascertain that the Company would not take responsibility for breach of the Vendor Standards.

H Guideline 8: Use Parallel Structure

Sentences or clauses that bear the same conceptual relationship to some major idea should have parallel grammatical structure, for example, all infinitives, all active voice, all gerunds (the *-ing* form of the verb, used as a noun), and so on. Sentences with parallel structure are much easier to read and remember. Here is a simple example:

POOR: To write a legal memo
- Identify the legal issues (imperative)
- Doing the correct research is your first priority (gerund and copula)
- You should make sure to read all cases and statutes with care (active sentence)
- Shepardize any cases that you use in your memo (imperative)
- It is important to use the correct citation form (stative sentence)

GOOD: To write a legal memo
(all
imperatives)
- Identify the legal issues
- Do the correct research
- Read all cases and statutes with care
- Shepardize any cases that you use in your memo
- Use the correct citation form

Parallel structure is important in lists. It is also important within a sentence and among sentences in a paragraph. Following is an example from a student memo. The student is discussing whether or not certain items in a rental property would be considered to be fixtures:

POOR: Mr. Smith *used* the carpeting in his store, the air conditioner *was used* to cool the store, and the toilet in the back room *was intended for use* in the store.

The student used both the active and passive voice. The sentence is more effective and easier to understand if all the verbs are simple active verbs.

BETTER: Mr. Smith *used* the carpeting in his store, *used* the air conditioner to cool the store, and *intended* to have the toilet in the back room available for use in the store.

Parallelism is one of the best devices for effective, persuasive writing. First, a writer can use parallelism to test the cogency of his or her reasoning. Putting ideas into a parallel structure can help reveal to the writer whether those ideas are actually parallel. Once several ideas are lined up in a series, with the same grammatical structure, the writer can often tell whether he or she has forced dissimilar ideas into the same framework.

Second, a repeated grammatical structure emphasizes important information. When the arrangement of words in one sentence is repeated in another sentence, the repeated structure tends to stand out. In fact, a writer can achieve an emotional impact by arranging words, phrases, or sentences in structurally similar groupings. By repeating these groupings, the writer can build a powerful statement.[4]

Here is an example of an artful use of parallelism. It is from a speech by Winston Churchill to the House of Commons at the start of World War II. Notice how Churchill used parallelism in the overall structure of the passage by asking a question and then answering it. This provides a powerful framework for his ideas. He also used parallelism within sentences to emphasize concepts and to build them to a climax. The parallel structures are italicized.

> *You ask, what is our policy? I will say:* It is *to wage* war, by sea, land, and air, *with all* our might and *with all* the strength that God can give us; *to wage* against a monstrous tyranny, never surpassed in the dark, lamentable catalogue of human crime. That is our policy. *You ask, what is our aim? I can answer* in one word: Victory—*victory* at all costs, *victory* in spite of all terror; *victory,* however long and hard the road may be; for without *victory,* there is no survival. Let that be realised; *no survival* for the British Empire; *no survival* for all that the British Empire has stood for, *no survival* for the urge and impulse of the ages, that mankind will move forward towards its goal. But I take up my task with buoyancy and hope. I feel sure that our cause will not be suffered to fail among men. At this time I feel entitled to claim the aid of all, and I say, "Come, then, let us go forward together with our united strength."[5]

EXERCISES

Correct the lack of parallelism in the following passages.

1. Upon vacating, the Tenant agrees to pay for all utilities services due and have same discontinued; to see that the property is swept out and all trash or other refuse is removed from the premises; that the doors and windows are properly locked or fastened; and that the key is returned to the Land-lord or Agent.

2. The test used in determining whether the bookcases could be removed from the rental property was whether or not they became a fixture under the tests used in determining fixtures:

    1. alterations made to the property to facilitate installations of equipment;
    2. who bore the cost of expense;

---

4. For more details on parallelism, *see* L. Oates, A. Enquist, & K. Kunsch, The Legal Writing Handbook 764-771 (1993), and the sample memorandum of points and authorities and accompanying discussion in Chapter 14 of this book.
5. Churchill, Speech to the House of Commons, May 13, 1940, reprinted in Their Finest Hour 22 (1977).

3. removal without damage to the premises;
4. whether the item is particularly adapted to the particular present use — in that it would not be equally useful elsewhere.

3. The trend is toward recognizing the rights of citizens to privacy and for punishing unwarranted intrusions thereon.

Guideline 9: Avoid Ambiguity in Words and Sentences

An ambiguous word or sentence is one that can be interpreted in more than one way. If you want to be certain the reader understands your meaning, you should know the causes of ambiguity and how to deal with them.

1. Ambiguity at the Word Level

There are many kinds of ambiguity. Ambiguity at the word level is prevalent in legal language because the law gives common, everyday words special legal meanings. For example, a motion in legal language is a particular type of pleading, not a movement or gesture, nor a proposal for action in a parliamentary setting.

When words have different meanings in different contexts, readers will understand exactly what is meant only when they are familiar with the context. This applies not only to legal language itself, but to technical words and phrases that you may use in drafting a legal document for a particular trade.[6] Shipping or construction contracts, for example, may use terms that mean something different in that trade than in everyday usage. It is important that the trade meaning be clear — not only for the benefit of the parties to the contract, but in case it is ever necessary to interpret rights and obligations under the contract.

Avoid using *shall.* One source of ambiguity is the use of the word *shall.* In writing legal documents, it is traditional to use *shall* to establish a legal obligation. However, many lawyers use *shall* incorrectly. They use it inconsistently — to mean both *must* (obligatory or mandatory action) and *will* (future action). This ambiguous use can cause legal problems.

---

6. *See* Frigaliment Importing Co. v. B.N.S. International Sales Corp., 190 F. Supp. 116 (S.D.N.Y. 1960), where one party to a contract thought that the word "chicken" in the contract referred only to broiling and frying chickens, while the other party insisted that in the trade the term also included stewing chickens. *See also* Nashville v. K. R. Co. v. Davis, 78 S.W. 1050 (Tenn. 1902) (holding that a goose was not "an animal," within the meaning of a state statute that required railroad engineers to take evasive action when "an animal or obstruction" appeared on the track).

To complicate matters further, lawyers sometimes use *shall* along with *must* and *will* in the same document. Because most people do not use *shall* in ordinary speech or writing and therefore do not use it properly in legal documents, we suggest that you do not use it at all. Use *must* when you mean the action is obligatory; use *will* when you intend future (nonobligatory) action; use *may* for permissible action. In the negative, use *must not; will not;* and *need not* or *does not have to. May not* is often ambiguous. It can mean either "must not" or "does not have to." For example, the following sentence can be interpreted in two ways.

> If you give incorrect information on your application to take the bar exam, we may not accept your application.

The sentence can mean "we are barred from accepting it" or "we have the option of refusing it."

Don't use elegant variation.   In legal documents it is important to use only one term for any concept. Call the car that struck your client "the car" every time you mention it; don't refer to it as "the car" in one place and as "the vehicle" in another place. As Mark Twain said, "Eschew elegant variation." Referring to the same thing by different names may confuse the reader; it may also create legal problems. For example:

> I conclude that we should argue that the limitations period of the forum state applies, rather than that of the *state where the action arose.* However, if we argue for the limitations period of the *accrual state,* we will have to rethink our strategy.

The writer assumed that the reader would understand that the state where the action arose and the accrual state are the same thing, but the reader may assume that they are two distinct states or become confused enough to give up trying to understand the passage.

2. Ambiguity at the Sentence Level

Misplaced words or unclear structure.   Ambiguity can also occur at the sentence level. If you misplace words or fail to indicate what a word or phrase refers to, you will confuse the reader.

---

6. *See* Frigaliment Importing Co. v. B.N.S. International Sales Corp., 190 F. Supp. 116 (S.D.N.Y. 1960), where one party to a contract thought that the word "chicken" in the contract referred only to broiling and frying chickens, while the other party insisted that in the trade the term also included stewing chickens. *See also* Nashville v. K. R. Co. v. Davis, 78 S.W. 1050 (Tenn. 1902) (holding that a goose was not "an animal," within the meaning of a state statute that required railroad engineers to take evasive action when "an animal or obstruction" appeared on the track).

Misplacing words such as *only* and *exclusively* can make a sentence ambiguous. For example:

> Describe the client's property only in section II of the will.

Does this mean describe the property and no other asset in section II, or describe the property in section II and nowhere else? *Only* is a useful word, but depending on where it is placed, it can create ambiguity.

You can also create ambiguity by using *more than* or *less than* carelessly. Be sure that the reader knows what is being compared. Consider, for example, this line from an old commercial:

> I love Devil Dogs more than Marcia.

It can mean either "more than I love Marcia" or "more than Marcia loves Devil Dogs." If the meaning of a sentence with *more than* or *less than* is not clear, fill in the missing words that will make it clear.

Pronouns. You must also be careful when you use pronouns. Make sure the reader will know which noun the pronoun refers to. If you have not made it clear which noun is the pronoun's antecedent, you can confuse the reader. For example:

> If the argument is made that the Secretary's regulation applies in our case, I believe that *it* will be attacked by our opponent.

The reader may be unsure whether the pronoun *it* refers to the Secretary's regulation (will the opponent attack the validity of the regulation) or to the argument that the regulation applies in the case at issue (will the opponent attack the validity of the argument?).

Here is a particularly egregious example, based on an actual federal statute:

> Physicians can invest in securities of corporations provided they meet the following standards.

It is not clear whether *they* refers to the physicians, the corporations, or the securities. Sentences like this not only manifest poor writing; they may also indicate fuzzy thinking.

You must also make sure each pronoun is in the same person (he, she, it) and number (he, they) as the noun it refers to. Not doing so will give readers a poor impression of you. For example, in the following sentence the pronouns *they* and *their* do not agree with the antecedent *one*.

> If one of the expert witnesses were to be used in this trial, they would be asked to show their qualifications.

Misplaced clauses.   Yet another type of ambiguity arises from misplacing subordinate clauses. Position a subordinate clause so that it is clear which words you want the clause to modify. For example:

> The second type of fringe benefit is the receipt of goods, services, or money, not as a salary, *which is indirectly related to the performance by the employee of his duties on his job.*

> Our client is questioning the $2,000 requested for heat treatments for the plaintiff's arm *based upon Dr. Smith's itemized medical report.*

In each of these sentences, it is unclear exactly what the subordinate clause refers to. Does "which is indirectly related" in the first sentence refer to "salary" or "receipt" or "benefit"? Does "based upon Dr. Smith's itemized medical report" in the second sentence modify "the $2,000" or "requested" or "heat treatments"? Each sentence should be rewritten so that only one interpretation is possible.

Conditionals.   Conditionals can be especially ambiguous if they contain both *ands* and *ors*. For example:

> If a client is receiving alimony or is receiving child support and has been divorced for more than one year, then this section of the rule does not apply.

This sentence can be interpreted two ways. It can mean:

> This section of the rule does not apply if the client
> 1. Is receiving either alimony or child support *and*
> 2. Has been divorced for more than one year.

Or the sentence can mean:

> This section of the rule does not apply if the client
> 1. Is receiving alimony *or*
> 2. Is receiving child support and has been divorced for more than one year.

Nothing in the original sentence tells the reader which conditions belong together.
   To avoid ambiguity in conditionals, make it clear where conditions begin and end. You can use punctuation, but that is not the best solution. A better solution is to use *syntax* to clarify the message. For example, you can repeat the subject of the sentence before each full condition.

> *If the client* is receiving either alimony or child support and *if the client* has been divorced for more than one year, then this section of the rule does not apply.

Or you can use *layout* to make the conditions clear. We used layout above to demonstrate the two possible interpretations of the alimony example. The best solution is to use a combination of syntax and layout to get your message across unambiguously.

Exceptions require even more care. Exceptions are negative conditions (if not . . . then; if . . . then don't). Exceptions cause confusion because the reader must shift gears from "apply this rule" to "don't apply this rule." A shift like this can be particularly confusing if the exception appears in the same sentence as the rule.

POOR: The same cost accounting period shall be used for accumulating costs in an indirect cost pool as for establishing its allocation base, *except* that the contracting parties may agree to use a different period for establishing an allocation base, provided:
1. The practice is necessary . . .
2. The practice . . . *etc.*

Rather than joining exceptions into the same sentence as the rule, you should state the rule and then start a new sentence with "However, if . . . " or "Nonetheless, if . . . " The above example would be much clearer if it were rewritten as follows:

BETTER: Use the same cost accounting period for accumulating costs in an indirect cost pool as for establishing the allocation base for that period. However, the contracting parties may agree to use a different period for establishing an allocation base, if all of (or any one of) the following conditions hold:
1. The practice is necessary
2. The practice . . . etc.

3. Intentional Ambiguity

Ambiguity can have a valid place in legal writing. Legislation is often designed to be ambiguous so that it will be flexible enough to cover unforeseen circumstances. Ambiguity can also be useful to the writer who *wants* to obscure his or her meaning, as in the case of an attorney who is answering interrogatories. However, using intentional ambiguity takes a great deal of skill and care: Inappropriate or unsophisticated use can backfire. A piece of ambiguous legislation, for example, could exclude or include the wrong conditions, situations, or people. Unskillfully drafted answers to interrogatories may obscure neutral pieces of information while revealing too much about sensitive issues.

EXERCISES

Find and eliminate the ambiguities in the following sentences. Also use the other guidelines to make the sentences clearer.

1. This statute applies to any individual who is at least 65 years of age or who is disabled and has a spouse living at home.
2. If you have taken into account all of your clients and their unique concerns when completing the interrogatories or conducting depositions, then it is likely that you have been successful with them.
3. No person shall be a representative who shall not have attained to the age of 25 years, and been 7 years a citizen of the United States, and who shall not, when elected, be an inhabitant of that state in which he shall be chosen.[7]

J # Guideline 10: Choose Vocabulary with Care

From law school onward, members of the legal profession often unthinkingly emulate the writing they encounter in legal treatises, opinions, and casebooks. And often the language used in these documents is ungrammatical, unnecessarily complex, or archaic. Choose your vocabulary carefully. Try not to indiscriminately follow the models you see just because they look and sound "legal."

1. Eliminate or Change Archaic or Unnecessary Words

There are a number of archaic words that commonly occur in legal documents. These words can often be left out entirely. If, for the sake of precision, you can't just leave them out, replace them with commonplace words or phrases (e.g., henceforth = from this day forward; hereinbefore = previously in this document).

---

7. *See* Art. I, §2, cl.2 and Art. I, §3, cl.3, Constitution of the United States. These clauses set the qualifications for Representatives and Senators, respectively. The meaning of these clauses was at the heart of the constitutional dispute over whether a state could impose term limits on members of its congressional delegation. *See* U.S. Term Limits, Inc. v. Thornton, 514 U.S. 779 (1995). One of the issues in Thornton was whether these clauses set out the exclusive qualifications or merely the minimum qualifications. The double negative ("No Person . . . who shall not have attained. . . . ") in each clause added to its ambiguity. Compare the language in Art. I, §2, cl.2 with the clearer language in Art. VI, cl.3, which states that "no religious Test shall ever be required as a Qualification to any Office or public Trust under the United States." Disagreements over the meaning of Art. I, §2, cl.2 persist. *See* Campbell v. Davidson, 233 F.3d 1229 (10th Cir. 2000) (holding that a state statute requiring congressional candidates to be registered voters in the congressional district in which the person seeks election violates Art. I, §2, cl.2).

The following is by no means an exhaustive list of words of this kind. You will no doubt come across others. Try to keep them out of your own writing.

aforesaid   hereinbefore
henceforth   hereinafter
herein   heretofore
hereafter   thereto
thereby   thereunto
   verbs ending in *-eth*
   said, same, such (when you mean *the*)
   one (before a person's name)

2. Replace Difficult Words or Legal Jargon with Words Your Readers Will Know

This principle is often stated as "use short words," but it is not really length that causes problems. It is unfamiliarity that causes problems. As it happens, of course, less familiar words tend to be longer than common words.

This principle should be tempered by your knowledge of your audience. The purpose of a document is to communicate to the people who must read it. When people write only for other people in their field, it is appropriate to use technical words and specialized ways of communicating. Brevity and precision are both served by the use of specialized language if the reader and the writer give the same interpretation to that language. However, even lawyers can have trouble understanding specialized legal terms. For example, a criminal lawyer might have trouble understanding a document meant for tax lawyers.

Furthermore, many of the documents that lawyers produce are meant to be read by nonlawyers, who are unlikely to understand legal vocabulary and terms of art. The lay audience may also be confused by words or phrases that look familiar but that have a special meaning to lawyers. The list shown in Table 10-1 will give you an idea of how you can substitute simpler terms for complex or specialized terms. The words in this list will not always be perfectly interchangeable. Nevertheless, it is a good rule of thumb to try the simpler term first to see if it works as well as the more difficult one. You will find that your audience will not be insulted if you use *after* instead of *subsequent to*, no matter how sophisticated that audience is.

TABLE 10-1

Some Words and Phrases You Can Change

Don't use this word	*if this word will work as well*	*Don't use this word*	*if this word will work as well*
accord	give	institute	begin
adequate amount	enough	in the event that	if
afford	give	maintain	keep, continue, support
aggregate	total	necessitate	require
allocate	give, divide	on or about	on
applicable	that applies	on or before	by
as to	about, relating to	on the part of	by
attain	reach	originate	start
attributable to	from, by	per annum	a year
by reason of	because of	prior to	before
cease	stop	procure	get
commence	begin	promulgate	issue
constitute	make up	provided that	however if
deem	consider	pursuant to	under
effectuate	carry out	retain	keep
exclusively	only	render	make, give
expiration	end	shall	must, may, will
for the duration of	during	solely	only, alone
for the purpose of	to, for	sufficient	enough
for the reason that	because	submit	send, give, contend
furnish	give, provide	subsequent to	after
has the option of	may	said, same, such	the, this, that
indicate	show	terminate	end, finish
in excess of	more than	unto	to
initiate	begin	utilize	use
in lieu of	instead of	without the United States	outside the United States

3. Define or Explain Technical Terms

There are times when you cannot eliminate or change technical terms or legal terms of art, even though you know that some part of your audience will not be familiar with those terms. A definition, explanation, or example can help. If the definition for a technical term is fairly short, you can insert it right after the technical term the first time that term appears. You can do this with or without parentheses.

The following excerpt from a bank's loan note includes two examples of technical terms that are defined or explained in the sentence ("refinanced" and "rule of 78").

Prepayment of Whole Note: Even though I needn't pay more than the fixed install-ments, I have the right to prepay the whole outstanding amount of this note at any time. If I do, or if this loan is *refinanced — that is, if I take out a new loan to pay off my old loan —* you will refund the unearned finance charge, figured by *the rule of 78 — a commonly used formula for figuring rebates on installment loans.* However, you can charge a minimum finance charge of $10.

You can provide a fuller explanation or example by making it a main part of the text itself, as in the following rewritten jury instruction.

There is a type of negligence that involves the conduct of the plaintiff, rather than the defendant. It is called *contributory negligence.*
　　If a plaintiff is negligent, and his negligence helps cause his own injury, we say that the plaintiff is contributorily negligent.
　　A plaintiff who is contributorily negligent cannot recover money for his injury.

The following explanation of *default* from the rewritten bank note also illustrates how a term can be defined or explained within the main part of the text.

Default:　I'll be in default
　　　　　1. If I don't pay an installment on time; *or*
　　　　　2. If any other creditor tries by legal process to take any money of mine in your possession.

EXERCISES

1. Underline the inappropriate or unnecessarily difficult vocabulary in this passage. Rewrite the passage.

CONSENT OF MINOR CHILD TO ADOPTION

I, Jane Smith, age 11, born on March 1, 1989, do hereby consent to my adoption by John Jones. I understand that if this adoption is granted, the relationship of parent and child will be established between myself and John Jones the same as if I had been born to him and further that all rights of my mother, Mary Jones, will be reserved unto her. I further consent to the change of my name to Jane Jones.

2. Underline and mark with the appropriate letter any words or phrases that you think are: a) totally unnecessary; b) necessary but need to be defined or translated.

KNOW ALL MEN BY THESE PRESENTS:

That the undersigned, individually and as parents or guardians of John Smith, a minor of the age of 12 years, residing at 1800 Oak Street, for and in consideration of the sum of Eight Thousand Dollars lawful money of the United States of America, to them in hand paid for and on behalf of said minor, the receipt whereof is hereby acknowledged, do hereby remise, release, and forever discharge Asa Luntz from any and all claims which are a result of a certain accident or event which occurred on or about June 5th, 1994, at 4700 Chestnut Street.

K Guideline 11: Avoid Noun Strings

In addition to allowing its users to create verbs from nouns and adjectives (nominalizations), the English language also allows the use of nouns as adjectives. For example, in the phrase *client interview form,* the first two nouns modify the final noun, *form.* Two or more nouns in a row are often called a noun string.

When a writer strings together more than two nouns, especially with an occasional adjective added to the string, it becomes difficult for the reader to understand the relationships among the nouns. Noun strings are (usually) grammatical, but the longer the string, the harder it is for the reader to understand what is going on. Some of the worst noun strings appear as the names of institutions or programs: consider *Family Planning Services Delivery Improvement Research Grants Program.* Here are other examples of noun strings from student memos and briefs:

- Qualified scholarship funding bonds
- The District of Columbia Human Rights Law limitations period
- Intrusive pretrial discovery methods

This is what one of these noun strings looks like in the context of a sentence:

> There is no precedent to support our position that the District of Columbia Human Rights Law limitations period applies to section 1981 actions.

Noun strings lack the "little words" — usually prepositions, sometimes the possessive *'s* — that clarify *how* the nouns are related. Noun strings may shorten a sentence, which may appear to simplify it, but removing the little words actually makes the sentence more complex. The reader has to laboriously untangle the noun string and reconstruct the original relationships. The reader puts back the prepositions or possessives mentally, and that takes time and energy. Noun strings can also make a sentence ambiguous, so that readers sometimes untangle them incorrectly. A good example is the name *International Ladies Garment Workers Union.* Is this a union of ladies who work on garments or a union of workers who work on ladies' garments? Are the ladies, the union, the workers, or the garments international?[8]

---

8. Another example is *Federal Employers Liability Act.* Is this an act that regulates federal employers or a federal act that regulates certain employers?

The solution is to unstring noun strings whenever possible. For example,

POOR: There is no precedent to support our position that the *District of Columbia Human Rights Law limitations period* applies to section 1981 actions.

GOOD: There is no precedent to support our position that the limitations period of the District of Columbia Human Rights Law applies to section 1981 actions.

POOR: Not all information is available to the consumer for *consumption or purchasing choice decisions.*

GOOD: Consumers do not have all the information they need to decide what to use or what to buy.

Notice that noun strings often include nominalizations. When you unstring the noun string, you should also look for the verb underlying the noun and make sure that it is necessary. In the last example, for instance, "consumption" comes from the verb *consume*, which really means to use up or to eat; "purchasing" comes from the verb *purchase*, which really means to buy; and "choice" comes from the verb *choose*, which is redundant here because it means the same as *decide*, which appears as the noun "decisions."

EXERCISES

Identify the noun strings in the following sentences and unstring them. Correct any other errors you may find.

1. The State bar client grievance committee is an attempt at a voluntary professional self-regulation program.
2. The Supreme Court held in *Ohralik v. Ohio State Bar Association*, 436 U.S. 447 (1978), that the state could prohibit attorney in-person client solicitations.
3. This is a request for public comment on a proposal for an industry self-regulated voluntary informational labeling program.
4. The company shall facilitate communication, collaboration, and coordination for Data Report Production activities within the group, as specified in its contract.
5. For section 508 compliance, it may be necessary for an agency to outsource accessibility efforts, such as PDF document and forms accessibility, and to install a Web-service enabled accessibility checker.

L ## Guideline 12: Eliminate Redundancy and Extraneous Words; Avoid Overspecificity

Legal drafters often use two words that have almost identical meanings where one is really enough (aid and abet, false and untrue). There is a historical reason for these pairs. One term is usually Anglo-Saxon, while the other is Latin-based, derived through Norman French. In the Middle Ages when British common law had to deal with English-speaking yeomen and French-speaking aristocrats, doublets like these may have been necessary. In twenty-first-century America, they usually only add redundancy. Here are some of the more common pairs to be aware of:

each and every	false and untrue
any and all	excess and unnecessary
aid and abet	final and conclusive
authorized and empowered	type and kind
full and complete	absolutely and completely
order and direct	null and void

Bureaucrats and academicians are also guilty of using two words where one will do. The temptation to say things twice is often very hard to fight, but extra words that do not add any information should be left out. For example:

personal opinion	honest opinion
next subsequent	positive benefits

Some of these examples are truly redundant. You could not use the opposite of the adjective and have a meaningful phrase. For instance, what are negative benefits? In other cases, the adjective is informative only if you are stressing that attribute, for example, "This is my personal opinion, not that of the group."

The use of extraneous words can also overload a sentence and obscure its meaning. Extraneous words often appear as meaningless sentence introductions.

It is possible that you may not be able to file your brief on time.
This is to inform you that your case has been put on the docket.
There are four people *who* would like to testify.
It was in the fall of 1990 *that* she revised her will.

You can tell that an introduction is extraneous if you can remove it and still communicate the same information.

Extraneous words can appear anywhere in a sentence. For example, one law student wrote:

The *matter presented* for this Court's *determination in the case at bar* is the *question* of *allowing* a cause of action for a preconception tort in Minnesota.

The student could have eliminated many of the italicized words and rewritten the sentence as follows:

The court must decide whether the plaintiff can recover under Minnesota law for negligence that occurred before the plaintiff was conceived.

A good way to edit out extraneous words is to think of how you would express the concept orally. Often this will enable you to eliminate words that only serve to pad your sentences.

Another, related problem is overspecificity—that is, listing every possible instance of a general concept. Some attorneys fear that they won't be "covered" unless they list every possibility.

KNOW ALL MEN BY THESE PRESENTS:

That John Smith, hereinafter designated as the Releasor, for and in consideration of the sum of $8,000, the receipt whereof is hereby acknowledged, has *remised, released, and forever discharged,* and by these presents *does remise, release, and forever discharge* the said Releasee *of* and *from* all *debts, obligations, reckonings, promises, covenants, agreements, contracts, endorsements, bonds, specialties, controversies, suits, actions, causes of actions, trespasses, variances, judgments, extents, executions, damages, claims, or demands,* in law or in equity, which against the said Releasee, the Releasor *ever had, now has,* or hereafter *can, shall, or may have, for, upon, or by reason of* any *matter, cause, or thing* whatsoever, from the beginning of the world to the day of the date of these Presents.

Not only is this overspecificity unnecessary, it can be dangerous: The drafter can easily leave out an important item or action, and because he or she has been so specific, the omission would probably be interpreted as intentional. If a litigated document contains such omissions, the omissions can be used by your opponents to their advantage.

Rather than specifying every instance, we suggest that you use a general term and perhaps one or two examples, or several general terms, for example, " . . . released from all obligations, suits and other claims . . . ." Remember that under the rule of ejusdem generis, courts will often construe general terms that follow terms of a particular or specific meaning as being defined or limited by these specific terms. That is, the general terms will be interpreted as applying only to things that fall into the same class as those specifically mentioned first. For example, if a list includes "dogs, cats, and other animals," "other animals" would probably exclude amoebas. The more general item is limited by the prior terms.

EXERCISES

Eliminate redundancy, superfluous words, or overspecificity in the following exercises. Also replace or eliminate any unnecessary legal jargon.

1. Any and all persons operating motor vehicles of any type and kind whatsoever in the District of Columbia shall obtain liability insurance.
2. The findings and determinations hereinafter set forth are supplementary and in addition to the findings and determinations previously made in connection with the issuance of the aforesaid order and of the previously issued amendments thereto; and all of the said previous findings and determinations are hereby ratified and affirmed, except insofar as such findings and determinations may be in conflict with the findings and determinations set forth herein.
3. §550.10 Trees, shrubs, plants, grass, and other vegetation. (a) General injury. No person shall prune, cut, carry away, pull up, dig, fell, bore, chop, saw, chip, pick, move, sever, climb, molest, take, break, deface, destroy, set fire to, burn, scorch, carve, paint, mark, or in any manner interfere with, tamper, mutilate, misuse, disturb, or damage any tree, shrub, plant, grass, flower, or part thereof, nor shall any person permit any chemical, whether solid, fluid, or gaseous, to seep, drip, drain or be emptied, sprayed, dusted or injected upon, about, or into any tree, shrub, plant, grass, flower, or part thereof, except when specifically authorized by competent authority; nor shall any person build fires, or station, or use any tar kettle, heater, road roller or other engine within an area covered by this part in such a manner that the vapor, fumes, or heat therefrom may injure any tree or other vegetation.

M Guideline 13: Use an Appropriate Style

It is important to choose the right style when you write legal documents. The style you use will depend on your audience and your purpose. Once you choose an appropriate style, stick with it throughout the document. Following are several guidelines to the style you should use when you write memos, briefs, letters, and other documents.

1. Use the Correct Point of View, Labels, and Pronouns

The point of view, labels, and pronouns you use in legal writing will depend on the type of document you are writing. For example, the rules are slightly different for briefs and memos. You should generally write briefs in the third person (he, she, or it) from the point of view of an observer of the facts and the law.

This will give the document a professional tone that will help convince your reader that you have drawn your conclusions from research and reasoning rather than by relying on your own biases and emotions.

This means that you should avoid referring to yourself with the personal pronoun *I* or *me* or to yourself and your client as *we* or *us*. Instead, formally refer to the client as petitioner, respondent, appellant or appellee, or, better still, use the client's last name. Also avoid using phrases that suggest that your statements are your personal observations: *I feel, It is my opinion, It is our belief.* Present your contentions more objectively by referring to yourself and your client in the third person: *Petitioner contends, Appellee suggests.* Be careful about being overly cautious in the way you present your contentions. Do not use phrases such as *It appears that, It seems likely that, It is suggested* to keep from committing yourself. Although cautious statements are occasionally necessary, they are usually used as a safety device, that is, the user of such a statement cannot later be proved wrong. The consequence of hedging your bet this way is that the reader perceives the statement as just what it is — an equivocation. Your assertion is robbed of force. This is especially undesirable in a brief, where you are trying to persuade your audience.

POOR: Now that I have reviewed the facts, it appears that the petitioners have failed to establish undue influence, overreaching, and misrepresentation.

GOOD: The evidence shows that the petitioners have failed to establish undue influence, overreaching, and misrepresentation.

You should use the same style when you write memos. Even though you are not writing for an adversary or for the court, you still want to convince your audience that your analysis is impersonal and well reasoned. However, because memos are often internal documents, you may have more leeway for informality. For example, a law firm may allow you, or even expect you, to express your conclusions or recommendations as your own opinions. For instance, you might offer the following conclusion:

> It is my opinion that the petitioners have failed to establish undue influence, over-reaching, and misrepresentation.

When you are writing letters to a client or a loan agreement for consumers, you can relax the rules presented above. In fact, it may be quite appropriate to present your document in the first person (I) or in the second person (you).

You can also use personal pronouns to give a document a tone of directness and personal interest. People may be more motivated to read a document that they feel is addressed to them. Using personal pronouns will also force you to write active rather than passive sentences (see Guideline 5). In a regulation or set of instructions, you can define *you* to mean all of the various participants. This can save space by making it unnecessary to repeat a cumbersome list many times.

In the revised regulations for Citizens Band (CB) radio operators (47 C.F.R. Part 95, Subpart D (1993)), the heading of each section is a question that the CB owner might ask. The body of each section is the answer. The first person pronouns (I, my) and the second person pronouns (you, your) refer to the CB owner in the questions and the answers, respectively.

> **§95.404 (CB Rule 4)   Do I need a license?**   You do not need an individual license to operate a CB station. You are authorized by this rule to operate your CB station in accordance with the rules in this subpart.

In some revised bank forms and insurance policies, the company is writing to the consumer. *We* refers to the company and *you* means the consumer. Compare these two versions from a homeowners' insurance policy:

BEFORE: *Company's options.* It shall be optional with this Company to take all, or any part, of the property at the agreed or appraised value and to repair, rebuild, or replace the property destroyed or damaged with other of like kind and quality within a reasonable time, on giving notice of its intention to do so within 30 days after the receipt of the proof of loss herein required.

AFTER: *Our option.* If we give you written notice within 30 days after your signed, sworn statement of loss, we may repair or replace any part of the property damaged with equivalent property.

Unfortunately, there is no standard way to use pronouns. Sometimes the consumer is *I* and the company is *you*. This lack of consistency in the use of pronouns from one document to the next may be confusing to readers. There is also some evidence that readers find it difficult to remember who is who as they get further and further into a document that has both *we* and *you* in it. For most documents a good solution is to call the reader *you* and refer to your firm, company, or agency by name or initials.

2. Use the Correct Tense

Legal writing has specific rules for when you should use the present and past tenses in memos and briefs.

1. If you are writing your own argument or analysis or if you are writing about your opponent's argument, use the present tense.

   > Petitioners *argue* that common sense *dictates* that respondent's activities be classified as commercial.

2. If you are writing about a rule or statute that is still in force, use the present tense.

> According to §2-513 of the Uniform Commercial Code, a person who *buys* goods *has* a right to inspect the goods before *accepting* or *paying* for them.

3. If you are writing about a case that the court has already decided, use the past tense.

> In *Weisberg v. Williams, Connolly & Califano*, 399 A.2d 992, 995 (D.C. 1978), the court *held* that the statute of limitations for legal malpractice will not run if the defendant fraudulently concealed improprieties.

4. If you are writing about the actions of the people involved in a case, use the past tense, unless the actions are still going on. Discuss ongoing actions in the present tense.

> While it *is true* that the respondent *might have profited* from her activities, this *was not* the respondent's primary motive.

3. Use a Formal but Not Pompous Style

Aim for a style that is neither too chatty and colloquial nor too formal or inflated. It is difficult to describe the happy medium between these two extremes. To get an idea of the proper style, look at the sample memos and brief presented later in this book. Here, however, we point out a few characteristics to avoid.

1. Avoid inappropriately "chatty" language.

> The most recent appellate court decision wasn't very good for our side. It will be a lot of trouble for us to argue around it.

2. Try to avoid inflated language. Using an inflated term like "telephonic communications" for telephone calls can give your writing a pompous tone.

> The attorney's subsequent *telephonic communications* were nothing more than the further dissemination of information to a special group.

3. Avoid cliches and mixed metaphors. You can damage your credibility if you use them. Cliches tell the reader that your thinking is not original. Metaphors are difficult to create, and if your metaphor doesn't work, or if you mix metaphors, you risk looking foolish. Here are examples from student memos that contain cliches and mixed metaphors. Note that in the second one the student also misquotes the metaphor, using *unchartered* instead of *uncharted*.

> A recurring theme in petitioner's appeal is that the courts have been flexible in their response to changing times. That flexibility is evidenced by *the slow and*

grudging wheels of Justice is but a romantic notion of Justice responding to *every hue and cry*.

Whether this small number of jurisdictions represents a trend or a *minority rushing blindly into unchartered waters* remains to be seen.

4. Use an Appropriate Approach

Begin your analysis or argument by dealing directly with the facts and law. Do not begin an analysis or argument with philosophical discussions, as in the following example from a memo.

> Since a lawyer's primary function is protecting and advising a client in the client's best interest, it is always of the utmost importance to first determine what it is, exactly, that the client needs or wants. Before assuming lawsuits and potential liability it is necessary to examine alternative procedures that may, in fact, serve the client as well or better than winning a particular day in court.

Legal briefs and memos are not term papers; don't write them like term papers. For term papers, students are usually expected to do library research on a topic and then write up all that they have discovered about that topic. The student may be encouraged to philosophize, cite people's opinions, or give a history of the topic. Here is an example in which a student used a term paper approach. The student was arguing that recognizing the specific tort of invasion of privacy is not necessary, because a plaintiff can currently use other tort actions and existing statutes to enforce the right of privacy.

> The right of privacy is an important value which has been gleaned from the Bill of Rights and developed throughout our nation's history. Arguing against it is like arguing against American notions of freedom, liberty, and justice.
>
> Historically, a tort action of privacy never existed in common law. Kalven, Privacy in Tort Law — Were Warren and Brandeis Wrong?, 31 L. & Contemp. Prob. 326, 327 (1978). The first major work done on the subject was motivated by the author's displeasure with stories of his daughter's marriage. Warren & Brandeis, The Right to Privacy, 4 Harv. L. Rev. 192 (1890). Out of this article arose the tort called invasion of privacy, which some courts began recognizing some thirty years later.

In the law, the reader's expectations are different, and hence the writer's approach must be different. The writer should include only information that is necessary for analyzing the facts and the law. The writer should leave out irrelevant material, no matter how interesting it may seem.

REVIEW EXERCISES

Identify all of the problems in each sentence and then rewrite the sentence.

1. Recent developments in Wisconsin law have made some progress in clearing up the problems encountered in the construction of the drunk driving statute and will aid the resolution of our client's problem.

2. In *Marsh v. Alabama*, 326 U.S. 501 (1946), it was found that the town was not unlike others in its accessibility and functions to the public.

3. In this determination, state membership or representation on policymaking bodies and state powers over institutional decision making would be important factors for examination.

4. To examine more closely the objectionable methods of data gathering, reflect upon the attainment of private mental records from a state entity.

5. The agency's argument for deference is as a result based upon claim that the "X" rule, which requires that the evidence be first determined to be "otherwise in equipoise" ("Question Presented") — or a prior version or versions thereof not significantly different — was created by the courts of appeals and has long been sound law; which, if true, would mean that deference to its determination concerning the statute which it administers is not relevant.

11

Writing
Effectively

A Step One: Developing a Logical Argument

As an attorney, you will be required to convince your audience to accept your point of view in documents ranging from letters to clients to briefs for the court. In this chapter, we present a variety of techniques for constructing and writing persuasive legal documents.

In law you will rarely work with unambiguous situations or rules because most real-life situations are ambiguous. Your job as an advocate is to persuade your readers that your description of the facts is the closest to what occurred, that the law or rule you have chosen to apply to a particular situation is the most appropriate one, that your understanding of the law is the most accurate, and that your overall interpretation of the situation is superior to any other interpretation, especially that of an adversary. To be persuasive, you must

1. Develop a logical argument.
2. Choose the most appropriate and effective information to emphasize in your argument.
3. Use writing techniques that will help you make the most of your position.

When you write a persuasive document, you must give that document a logical structure. For example, the IRAC framework (Issue, Rule, Application, Conclusion) that we discussed in Chapter 9 can help convince your readers that a tight, well-constructed thought process led you from your assertion in the issue statement to your conclusion.

You will probably not start out with a tight, well-constructed body of information when you sit down to compile a legal document. The process of creating a brief, for example, involves researching the facts and the law, thinking about the significance of the research, writing up the research, and then going back to do additional research before writing a final draft. In creating any document, research, thought, and writing are interactive: as you write, you realize that you need more research; as you do more research, you change what you have written.

How do you impose a structure on a process of this sort? Begin with the assumption that you do not want to walk your readers through the twists and turns you had to take to develop your argument. You want them to follow your reasoning along one straight path — and to think that the path you have chosen is sound and logical.

In order to create a logical structure, think about what you are trying to accomplish when you deal with a problem in law. You will often find that you are trying to establish that a specific set of facts fits within a well-settled rule of law. One way to do this logically and systematically is to use the principles of deductive reasoning to set up the skeleton of your legal analysis.

1. Deductive Reasoning in Law

You are probably familiar with the basic categorical syllogism. For example:

MAJOR PREMISE: All men are mortal.
MINOR PREMISE: Socrates is a man.
CONCLUSION: Socrates is mortal.

Deductive reasoning is the thought process that occurs whenever you set out to show that a minor premise (a specific situation, event, person, or object) fits within the class covered by a major premise (an established rule, principle, or truth) and to prove that, consequently, what applies to the class covered by the major premise must necessarily apply to the specific situation. In short, deductive reasoning allows you to prove that your particular case is covered by an established rule.

Deductive reasoning is a cornerstone of legal thought. Lawyers are often called upon to decide how a rule of law applies to a given case. Since the rule is usually stated in general terms and a client's problem is usually very specific, deductive reasoning can be used to bridge the gap between the general and the specific. For example:

Rule of Law (major premise): Courts have held that any agreement made in jest by one party and reasonably understood to be in jest by the other party will not be enforced as a contract.

Facts of our case (minor premise): Robert agreed to paint Lee's entire house, but both Robert and Lee understood that Robert was only joking.

Conclusion: Robert's agreement is not an enforceable contract.

These basic steps of deductive reasoning form the skeleton of a legal argument. In fact, the rule-application-conclusion sequence of IRAC forms a simple syllogism: The rule contains the major premise, the application contains the particular facts of the minor premise, and the conclusion sums up the information and provides an answer to the issue.

The order in which you present a syllogism may not be the order in which you accumulate the information or think through the problem. Thus, you may work in the order: conclusion, rule, application. If you do that, you begin by deciding what you want to accomplish for your client. Then you go over rules from analogous cases, statutes, or constitutions to find one that will serve as your major premise, or you propose a new rule from the information you have gathered in your research. Finally, you carefully review the facts of your case and present them in a way that fits the rule or law.

For example: What do I want to accomplish for my client? I want my client declared "not guilty." What rule or law can I use? Insanity is a defense — insane people are not guilty. What must I do to make a persuasive argument? I must demonstrate, in the way I present my facts, that my client is insane.[1]

We thought through this process as conclusion, rule, application. In a brief, however, we would present it as rule, application, conclusion: Insane people are not guilty. My client is obviously insane (because . . .). Therefore, my client cannot be considered guilty.

Another way to construct your argument is in the order application, rule, conclusion. You begin with the facts of your case, try to find or construct a rule that accommodates the facts, and then reach the best conclusion you can for your client.

In building your case, you can work on the parts of the syllogism in any order. You work with them interactively until you achieve a logical relationship among the three parts. Moving the parts around can help you to clarify your own thinking, while keeping the basic structure of the syllogism in mind tells you what your argument should look like when you present it to the reader.

No matter how you got to your conclusion, you should present it as rule, application, conclusion — a syllogism. This not only helps your readers to follow your argument, it may help persuade your readers that you reached the conclusion in favor of your client only *after* following the syllogism to its logical conclusion.

2. Expanding the Syllogism into a Legal Argument

The syllogism serves as the skeleton of a legal argument. Once you have created the skeleton, you must flesh it out. For example, once you have the major premise in a particular case, you must present evidence that your specific fact situation does indeed fit within the class covered by the major premise. In the example about painting Lee's house, you would have to show that there was a promise but that both parties knew that it had been made in jest, as "jest" has been interpreted by the courts.

---

1. Keep in mind that you may *present* facts in the way that will best fit a rule of law and serve your purposes, but you cannot *change* the facts of your case. It is perfectly permissible to interpret the ambiguities that exist in any factual situation in your own favor, but it is unethical to distort or to hide facts.

In the rest of this section, we discuss techniques for expanding the different parts of a syllogism. We present the parts in the order of the standard syllogism, even though you may not always work in this order when you construct your argument.

a. *The Major Premise*

In most cases, your major premise will either be a given (you are told what the rule of law is and you must apply it to a set of facts), or you must extract the rule from legal authorities such as constitutions, statutes, regulations, and reported cases. (See Chapter 6.) You must then draw the appropriate information from these authorities and present the information so that your rule is well substantiated. In addition, you must define the abstract terms in the rule in order to clarify the rule and make it easier to apply the rule to the facts in your case.

Using legal authority effectively. In many of the legal arguments you will make, the link between your assertion and conclusion will depend upon the credibility of the authority you use in your major premise. You will argue that your assertions are valid because your authority says they are, and your authority is worth following. Legal authority can take a number of forms. It can be *enacted law:*

- A constitution or charter
- A treaty
- A statute or ordinance
- An administrative regulation
- A rule of procedure

or it can be *case law:*

- An opinion based on an enacted law
- An opinion based on common law
- An opinion based on principles of equity
- An opinion involving a combination of enacted law, common law, and equity

Under certain circumstances, scholarly works and treatises can also be the legal authorities that you rely on.

You will learn, in time, how much weight is usually given to a certain authority under different circumstances and how authorities relate to one another. Once you understand these principles, you must learn to build them into your documents so that your assertions are well researched and completely substantiated. Here are several guidelines to follow.

1. Make sure that the authority actually supports your position. Do not take information from an authority and use it out of context so that it appears to support a position that it really does not.

2. Quote directly out of your sources of authority if the material you are quoting is effective and well written or if the quoted material is well known. This lends authenticity and directness to your argument which you could not achieve by paraphrasing. However, if the material is poorly written, paraphrase it.[2] Also, be careful not to overquote. Don't create a document that merely repeats what others have said when you should really be presenting legal analysis.

3. Make sure that you are quoting the relevant portions of your source.

Using definitions to clarify terms.   Some rules of law include abstract terms that need definition. Sometimes the key to using the authority you want to cite is to define one or more of its terms to show that your case fits into the definition.

For example, Article I §8(1) of the U.S. Constitution states that "The Congress shall have power to . . . lay and collect taxes, duties, imposts, and excises, to pay the debts and provide for the common defense and general welfare of the United States. . . . " The term "general welfare" is not defined. It is up to Congress and the courts to determine what specific situations the term covers, and it would be up to you to define this term if you wanted to use it as part of an argument.

Let's say you want to argue that Congress's giving federal money to a private corporation, *X* Auto Company, serves the general welfare of the country. You might begin by constructing a syllogism for this argument.

MAJOR PREMISE:	Congress can spend money for the general welfare.
MINOR PREMISE:	Giving federal money to economically distressed corporations such as the *X* Auto Company serves the general welfare of the country.
CONCLUSION:	The Congress can give federal money to *X* Auto Company.

In order to support your case, you should define "general welfare" so that your use of it in your minor premise fits within the term as it is used in your major premise.

Because legal definitions frequently have several layers, you can use these layers to build the definition you need. For the case of *X* Auto Company, you might argue

1. Congress can exercise broad discretion.
2. This means that Congress can provide revenues to specific groups and individuals as long as these allocations will benefit the entire country and not just a privileged few.
3. These specific groups and individuals can include the elderly, the unemployed, local disaster victims, and so on.

---

2. Always paraphrase with care so that you do not distort the meaning of the material. In addition, it is seldom a good idea to paraphrase a statute or other enacted laws, since each word may be essential to the meaning of the law.

You can show that your definition is accurate by citing these authorities:

1. In *Helvering v. Davis*, 301 U.S. 619, 640 (1937), the Supreme Court held that "[t]he discretion [regarding what constitutes general welfare] belongs to Congress, unless the choice is clearly wrong, a display of arbitrary power, and not an exercise of judgment." The Court interpreted the phrase "general welfare" very broadly.
2. The Supreme Court has held in a number of cases that Congress's broad discretion extends to legislation affecting specific groups and individuals.
3. This legislation has included the unemployment compensation scheme created by the Social Security Act of 1935, *Steward Machine Co. v. Davis*, 301 U.S. 548 (1937), the old-age benefit provisions of the Social Security Act, *Helvering v. Davis,* local disaster victims, and individuals with moral claims against the government.

Note that the first two layers include broad terms such as "welfare" and "discretion." You must continue to define until you have reached the level where the definition is illustrated by concrete facts. Once you have concrete examples, you must make them meaningful to your case. In the next section, we discuss how you can use analogy to tie the examples in your definition to the facts in your case.

Let's look at another example of a definition. Definitions that arise strictly from the common law rather than from a constitution or statute also frequently contain broad terms. For example, the tort of battery has been defined, in part, by the following elements:

1. An *act* by the defendant that *brings about harmful or offensive contact* to the *plaintiff's person.*
2. *Intent* on the part of the defendant to bring about harmful or offensive contact to the plaintiff's person.
3. *Lack of consent* from the plaintiff.

All of the italicized terms are in need of further explication. What behavior on the part of the defendant constitutes "an act"? What is "intent"? What is an "offensive contact"? What constitutes the "plaintiff's person"? How does the plaintiff give (or withhold) "consent"?

Let's pursue the layers of definition for "plaintiff's person."

1. The plaintiff's person has been construed to include the plaintiff's body and *anything that is connected* to the plaintiff's body.
2. In *Fisher v. Carousel Motor Hotel, Inc.*, 424 S.W.2d 627 (Tex. 1967), the plaintiff was a black man who was attending a buffet lunch at the defendant's hotel. While the plaintiff was waiting in line to be served, one of the defendant's employees snatched the plaintiff's plate and shouted that the plaintiff would not be served. The court held that the unpermitted and

intentional grabbing of the plate was a battery, even though the plaintiff himself was never touched.

b. *The Minor Premise*

The most important techniques for expanding your major premise are citing authority and defining terms. The most important technique for expanding your minor premise is analogy, either to the facts of other cases or to the policies underlying other decisions.

Arguing by analogy: similarity of facts. When you argue by analogy, you reason that if two or more situations are the same in some significant respect, they are likely to be the same in other significant respects as well, so they ought to be classified together. (If you want to *distinguish* your case from others, you show that it is *not* analogous.)

You could link the major and the minor premises of the general welfare case by using the following analogy: Funding should be provided for *X* Auto Company because the case is similar to cases in which the Court has approved Congress's funding in the past. Here is a way you might express this.

The facts in the *X* Auto Company case are very similar to the facts in cases that have already established the scope of "general welfare." In all of these cases, the courts agreed that

1. Private individuals or entities may receive funds from the federal government.
2. Individuals and entities may receive money that they did not personally contribute to the government.
3. Individuals and entities may receive money from the government when it helps them continue to earn money and spend money.

Arguing by analogy: similarity of policy considerations. Another way to link the major and minor premises is to show that the facts of your case are covered by a particular rule because your case furthers the same social goals as other cases already covered by the rule. For example, in the *X* Auto Company case, you might argue that your case and the previously decided cases all fulfill the following goals, regardless of the similarities or differences in their facts.

1. They keep individuals from turning to the state for support.
2. They keep the economy balanced and functioning.
3. They show people that the government will intervene if a segment of the population is about to experience an economic crisis.

The first step in making a policy argument is to identify what the authors of a rule intended when they created the rule. If you are investigating legislation, try looking at and analyzing legislative history or policy statements in the legislation itself. If you are investigating an opinion, try comparing your case with other cases that have been decided under the rule and showing that your case will help to further the same goals. You can look at any language in these opinions that sheds light on the objectives of the ruling.

Once you have established the purpose of the rule, i.e., what it was intended to accomplish, you can alter your major premise to include this purpose and emphasize the specific facts in your minor premise that suit the major premise. You would then argue that the authors of the rule intended that the rule cover cases like yours and that the principles behind the rule will be dangerously eroded if the court excludes your case.

If you were arguing that by analogy to the *Steward Machine* case X Auto Company should get federal funds, you might use this analogy on policy considerations:

> The courts have found that federal payments to particular groups or individuals such as the unemployed or the elderly can serve the general welfare because, in the long run, these payments benefit the entire nation. This idea is reflected in the words of Justice Cardozo in *Steward Machine,* 301 U.S. 548, 586-587 (1937):
>
>> During the years 1929 to 1936, when the country was passing through a cyclical depression, the number of the unemployed mounted to unprecedented heights. . . . The fact developed quickly that the states were unable to give the requisite relief. The problem had become national in area and dimensions. There was need of help from the nation if the people were not to starve. It is too late today for the argument to be heard with tolerance that in a crisis so extreme the use of the moneys of the nation to relieve the unemployed and their dependents is a use for any purpose narrower than the promotion of the general welfare.
>
> X Auto Company employs hundreds of thousands of employees. In addition, there are thousands of other employees who work in industries that depend on X Auto Company. Even though the problems of X Auto Company are not on the scale of the problems of the Great Depression, the loss of part of a major U.S. industry would have devastating effects on the U.S. economy as a whole. If federal funds can help X Auto Company continue to employ its workers, then thousands of private individuals will continue to earn and spend money. This will help protect the health of the nation's economy.

On the other hand, you could counter an argument based on similarity of policy considerations by showing that giving X Auto Company federal funds would widen the scope of the rule beyond the limits intended by those who derived the rule. This widening would have all kinds of adverse effects or troublesome consequences, such as opening the courts to a flood of frivolous litigation.

Setting up an analogy. To set up an analogy between two cases, using both the facts and the policy issues, begin by making a list of similarities and differences. Here is how you might expand the general welfare example to show that one case that has already been decided involving the old-age benefit provisions of the Social Security Act is or is not analogous to the X Auto Company case.

Similarities	*Differences*
In both situations the recipients may receive money that they only indirectly paid into the system. For example, Social Security recipients may receive funds in excess of the amount they actually put into the fund. The X Auto Company will receive funds that it indirectly paid in the form of taxes, etc.	The recipients of old-age benefits have paid into an insurance fund over the years, while the X Auto Company would be receiving money from a nonspecific tax fund that it has not contributed to. Taxes and insurance are not the same thing.
Many individuals who need support will benefit from the federal funds: employees in the case of X Auto Company, and older members of the population in the case of old-age benefits.	It is quite a different thing for the federal government to provide funds to a private corporation than it is to provide them to individuals. The government is set up to benefit members of the general population. It is not the government's purpose to benefit a large private corporation.
The X Auto Company funds will help keep the economy healthy because it will keep a major industry alive and will keep X's employees (and employees of other companies that depend on X) off of welfare and other forms of state subsidy. Similarly, the old-age benefits of Social Security assure citizens that they will have an opportunity to put money into a fund that they can draw on in their old age, provided they have worked the requisite amount of time to qualify. This keeps older people from having to turn to the state for support.	Giving funds to a private business may actually unbalance the economy, disturbing the free market and fair competition.

In section B of this chapter, we discuss writing techniques that emphasize favorable information and de-emphasize unfavorable information. You can use those techniques to stress either the similarities or differences between cases.

c. *The Conclusion*

After you have established and developed your major and minor premises, you are ready to reach a conclusion that follows logically from them. You may need to use a cause-and-effect argument to show *how* you came to the conclusion.

In law you will often be required to show that there is a cause-and-effect relationship between certain events or actions. For example, causation is an element of many torts and crimes. We will not go into the subtleties of causation here; however, you should know that when you set up a cause-and-effect relationship, you have to do so logically.

Here is an example of how a cause-and-effect relationship can be established within a deductive argument. First, set up the skeleton of your argument.

> *General rule* (major premise): Under the law of State *X*, the operator of a motor vehicle is liable for his or her wrongful act, neglect, or default if it causes death or injury to another person.

> *Specific facts* (minor premise): The plaintiff was riding in her car on the freeway when the defendant's car hit her from behind. Two days later, the plaintiff suffered severe back pains and headaches.

> *Conclusion:* Therefore, the defendant should be liable for the damages the plaintiff has suffered.

If you terminated your argument at this point, it would appear that you had based your conclusion on a faulty premise or assumption: "All pain that occurs within two days of an accident is necessarily caused by that accident." (For more on faulty premises, see subsection 3 below.) Or your conclusion may appear to result from a *post hoc* fallacy, in which you assert that because event *B* follows event *A* in time, event *A* has therefore caused event *B*. To avoid the appearance that your conclusion does not follow logically from the premises, you must articulate the causal link between events. You could do so by beginning your conclusion with the following information.

> There is a good deal of evidence that the plaintiff's injury was caused by the defendant's act of hitting the plaintiff from behind. First of all, the plaintiff's medical records show that the plaintiff did not have a history of back problems or headaches, so there is no possibility that her injuries are part of a recurrent or chronic problem. Also, she has not engaged in any activity or suffered any other injury within the last few years that might have led to back pain or headaches. In addition, Dr. Jones, the plaintiff's physician, has examined the plaintiff and will testify that the pain the plaintiff is experiencing is the kind that the plaintiff would be likely to feel several days after a rear-end collision in an automobile.

You would finish your argument by qualifying your conclusion to reflect the evidence you have presented:

> Because the evidence from medical records and from an expert demonstrates that, in all probability, the plaintiff's injuries were caused by the defendant's conduct, the defendant is liable for the damage the plaintiff has suffered as a result of that conduct.

When you are constructing a cause-and-effect argument, keep the subject matter in mind. If you are working with causation in a complex statistical argument, you must comply with the generally accepted principles of statistical analysis. For example, you may have to adhere to a scientific definition of causation. However, if you are writing about more common types of problems, try to appeal to your readers' sense of how the world works: Present a cause-and-effect relationship that your readers will recognize from their own experience. You can appeal to your readers' common sense and to the "common wisdom of the community." Remember that judges and other attorneys are part of the community and that they will share this sense of what probably did or did not happen in a given situation.

3. Faulty Logic

Logic can be faulty in a number of ways. We end this discussion by pointing out two of the most common faults.

Faulty premise. An argument can be perfectly logical but invalid. For example, you might have a syllogism like this, in which the major premise is false:

MAJOR PREMISE:	All witnesses are men.
MINOR PREMISE:	Lee is a witness.
CONCLUSION:	Therefore, Lee is a man.

In other words, an argument is sound only if both of its premises are true.

Undistributed middle. If your minor premise can occur outside the bounds of the major premise, it will not necessarily follow from your major premise. For example:

MAJOR PREMISE:	No one has been sentenced to death for murder in California in the last two years.
MINOR PREMISE:	Smith was convicted of murder last year, but he was not sentenced to death.
CONCLUSION:	Therefore, Smith must have been tried in California.

The major premise in this example is not faulty. The problem is that the minor premise can occur outside the bounds of the major premise, that is, Smith could have been tried in another state and still not have been sentenced to death.

EXERCISES

1. Under the equal protection clause of the Fourteenth Amendment, the Supreme Court has held that legislation that contains racially based classifications is subject to very strict review by the courts. However, legislation that

establishes gender based classifications receives a lesser level of review. Compare and contrast the cases of women and blacks in this country in terms of their history of being discriminated against and their present need for protection. Set up your comparison with two columns, one for similarities and one for differences.

2. Read the following excerpt from an appellate opinion and pull the syllogism out of it.

> The contract for the purchase of certain machinery recited that "[n]o representations or warranties, of any sort, express or implied, except warranty of title, have been made by Seller unless specifically set forth in writing in this contract." (There were no warranties set forth elsewhere in the contract.) An action was brought on the contract by the Seller seeking recovery of the balance of the purchase price. The purchaser, in defense thereto, sought to set up the defense that the contract was unconscionable under Code §109A-2-302, which defense was disallowed by the trial judge and the verdict and judgment were rendered in favor of the plaintiff. The defendant appealed. *Held:* The provisions of the contract contended by appellant to be unconscionable under Code §109A-2-302 are provisions which the law itself specifically permits. This contention is without merit.

B Step Two: Using Effective Writing Techniques

Now that we have discussed ways to construct a logical argument, we will discuss how to present the argument effectively. This section tells you how to assess the audience of a persuasive document, how to make the argument fit the audience's needs and expectations, and how to write to make the most of your position.

1. Assessing Your Audience

In writing a persuasive document, you must first try to find out what your audience needs to know and to believe in order to accept your argument. You can do this by putting yourself in the audience's place.

Decide how much your audience knows. When you write a persuasive document, you must decide how much the audience already knows about the subject you will be covering. If you assume too much, you will lose the reader at the outset. If you assume too little, the reader may have to read — or at least scan — extra material. However, it is far safer to explain too much than too little. Remember to assess both lay and legal audiences. A law professor or judge may not be as well acquainted with a topic as you might think.

Assess the role or position of your audience. Know what your reader must *do* with the information in your document. For example, if you are writing for a judge, determine what information he or she needs in order to decide in your favor. In general, a judge needs to know what other judges have done in cases similar to your case. Present the judge with the one reasonable solution to the problem in the case — the one your client needs — and characterize your position as one that any reasonable judge would accept.

Consider the interests of your audience. Think about the goals your audience may have. For example, is your audience interested in furthering certain social or political goals?

Consider the constraints of your audience. What constraints does your audience have? For example, judges are constrained by the previous judicial opinions that make up a body of law. Judges cannot easily deviate from earlier decisions. If you take this into account, you can state your position in a way that will make the judge feel comfortable with it. Your document should not ask the judge to make a great leap beyond an established position. Present your position as a small step in the same direction as judges have been going or as the smallest step possible in a new but necessary direction. Justify any move you are advocating. Convince the judge that he or she will be providing continuity and certainty by deciding in your favor.

Assess the fears of your audience. Show your audience that their fears are not justified, because undesirable side effects will not occur in your particular situation. Or show your audience that in your particular case, any undesirable side effects are overridden by more important considerations. For example, if you are trying to argue the advantages of a homosexual rights statute to an ultraconservative group, you may want to spend only a small amount of space on the advantages of the statute and a great deal of space allaying the group's fears about the changes the statute will bring.

2. Emphasizing Effective and Appropriate Information

You can tailor your argument to fit your purposes by emphasizing different components of the syllogism covered in section A. You might want to stress the importance of the rule you have stated as your major premise, arguing that the reader should heed the fine points of the rule and should adhere to established law. On the other hand, you might want to argue that the facts in your case are all-important or that the policy considerations in your case should take precedence over both rule and fact.

Here is an example: In *Gleitman v. Cosgrove*, 49 N.J. 22, 227 A.2d 689 (1967), the court relied on a rule in order to avoid discussing controversial policy issues. The child plaintiff in the case suffered severe birth defects because his mother had had German measles in the second month of her pregnancy. The mother testified that she had informed her doctor of her illness and that he had told her it would not harm her baby. Thus, she was denied an opportunity to decide whether she would have the child or have a legal abortion. Her lawyers sued on the basis of "wrongful birth." However, the court would not allow the child to sue for "wrongful birth" because it would be too difficult for courts to apply the normal rule for measuring damages in tort actions.

> Damages are measured by comparing the condition plaintiff would have been in, had the defendants not been negligent, with plaintiff's impaired condition as a result of the negligence. The infant plaintiff would have us measure the difference between his life with defects against the utter void of nonexistence, but it is impossible to make such a determination. This Court cannot weigh the value of life with impairments against the nonexistence of life itself.

49 N.J. at 49, 227 A.2d at 703.

If your case has human appeal, then present it in human terms, especially if the law is unsettled. Focus the court's attention on a very real problem, dilemma, or hardship faced by another human being — your client. The dissent in the *Gleitman* case illustrates the point:

> [Mrs. Gleitman] was told . . . that her child would not be at all affected. In reliance on that she permitted her pregnancy to proceed and gave birth to a child who is almost blind, is deaf and mute and is probably mentally retarded. While the law cannot remove the heartache or undo the harm, it can afford some reasonable measure of compensation towards alleviating the financial burdens.
>
> While logical objection may be advanced to the child's standing and injury, logic is not the determinative factor and should not be permitted to obscure that he has to bear the frightful weight of his abnormality throughout life.

49 N.J. at 50, 227 A.2d at 704.

3. Using Appropriate Writing Techniques

Once you have assessed your audience and chosen the argument you want to make, you need to know how to present your argument in a way that will convince your audience. For your document to be effective, you must achieve the appropriate tone. You can set the tone of your document by the information you choose to present and the order in which you present it, the grammatical constructions you use, and the vocabulary you choose. We have discussed some of these features earlier in this book; they are particularly important in persuasive writing.

The first thing you must do is to decide how you want to present yourself to your reader. When you write a research document such as an intraoffice memo, you want to come across as an individual who supports the position of the client but has not allowed this bias to cloud your reasoning or prevent you from gathering all of the facts and law in the case. You construct a balanced document for the scrutiny of a colleague — a document that presents the strengths and weaknesses of your client's case. If you are asked to make recommendations, then you should make them honestly, without allowing the tendency to favor your client influence your suggestions. It is in this way that a memo is a persuasive document: You strive to persuade your colleagues or your supervisors that you have written a document that contains scrupulous research, sound reasoning, and good judgment.

But when you are writing a brief, your major purpose is quite different: You are trying to persuade your audience that your argument is the correct one. Even so, you still want to appear as the scrupulous researcher and sound reasoner who is simply showing the judge the best way to analyze a situation or to resolve a dispute. In other words, you want to appear reasonable and logical: You want to argue your case without appearing strident or argumentative. However, because you must present information that is favorable to your client, you may need to mold the information to suit your purposes. You can accomplish much of this by emphasizing favorable information and de-emphasizing unfavorable information. There are a number of techniques that you can use to do this.

a. *Emphasizing Positive Information*

Put favorable information in a prominent place. Research shows that information that is presented either first or last tends to receive more attention than anything in between.[3] In many legal documents, you will want to put your most important or compelling information first. For example, if one of the purposes of your document is to serve as a reference, then the reader will want to get to the major issues immediately. If the purpose of your document is mainly to be persuasive, then you will want to win your reader over quickly by starting with your most impressive arguments.

Make sure that important information not only appears in a prominent place but is properly highlighted. When you are presenting facts, for example, it may not be advisable for you to present every detail as it occurred. Often students are afraid to leave any information out, so they end up burying critical facts in a detailed chronology. It is more valuable to isolate what is important, move facts out of chronological order if they are better emphasized that way, and leave out incidental information.

Describe favorable information in detail. A detailed description of the contents of a law or of the facts of a particular case can attract the reader's attention

---

3. *See* Atkinson & Shiffrin, Human Memory: A Proposed System and Its Control Processes, 2 The Psychology of Learning and Motivation: Advances in Research and Theory (Spence & Spence eds. 1967); K. Fernandes & A. Rose, An Information Processing Approach to Performance Assessment: An Investigation of Encoding and Retrieval Processes in Memory, Technical Report, November 1978, American Institutes for Research, Washington, D.C.

and, often, sustain the reader's interest — as long as the details are important ones. The plaintiff's attorney who wrote the following fact statement wanted to emphasize the defendant railroad's negligence. Notice the narrative quality of the description of the behind-schedule train, the employees' actions, the bright lights of the waiting room, and the poorly lit staircase. The reader can almost picture the scene.

> The train was running behind time. Several witnesses testified that the passengers were told by railroad employees to "hurry up." Mrs. Roberts emerged from the brightly lit waiting room, which naturally emphasized the darkness outside. Mrs. Roberts hurried down the unlighted outside staircase that leads to the train platform, missed a step, and fell beyond the narrow platform in front and down the slope beyond, incurring serious injuries. The fall aggravated Mrs. Roberts's existing health problems, which include diabetes and a thyroid condition.

Use effective sentence structures and grammatical constructions.   The guidelines in Chapter 10 will help you improve your writing, and clearer writing is more likely to be persuasive. Here we will discuss a few of the guidelines that are particularly relevant to persuasive writing because they give your arguments force without making them strident.

The grammatical constructions that you use can greatly affect how persuasive your document will be. Thus, when you use the active voice, your writing will be direct, and it will not be difficult to tell who did what. The passive voice will be less persuasive. For example, if your complaint on behalf of the plaintiff states that "The plaintiff was knocked to the ground and was repeatedly kicked" you have diluted the impact of the defendant's acts. However, if you rewrite this sentence in the active voice, you put life and action back into it, and you directly indict the defendant: "The *defendant knocked* the plaintiff to the ground and repeatedly *kicked* him."

You can also make your writing direct and forceful by using verb clauses and adjectives instead of nominalizations. For example, you might have stated that "The witness's *embezzlement* of company funds in 1992 is an example of his *untrustworthiness.*" The terms "embezzlement" and "untrustworthiness" are abstract; it is almost as though the defendant has committed concepts and not acts. The sentence can be rewritten into a direct and forceful statement: "The witness *embezzled* funds from the company in 1992; this shows that *he cannot be trusted.*"

Short sentences tend to be more forceful, and hence, more persuasive, than long ones. The more the reader has to remember when going through a sentence, the more likely he or she is to get bogged down. Thus, anything that makes a sentence less complicated is likely to result in a more effective sentence. Since intrusive phrases and complex conditionals tend to add length and complexity to sentences, following the guidelines for eliminating intrusive phrases and simplifying complex conditionals will help you produce more persuasive writing.

Choose your words with care.   Another device that enhances persuasiveness is the use of straightforward, unqualified language. Avoid excessive use of adjectives. For example, you will tip your reader off that you are trying too hard to be convincing if you write sentences such as this: "It took the plaintiff a *long, long time* to see a doctor about his injury." You could make this same point more effectively by stating the dates of the injury and the doctor's visit and by emphasizing the amount of time between the two.

Intensifiers or qualifiers such as *quite, rather, extremely*, and *very* can also dilute the forcefulness or persuasiveness of a sentence. Psycholinguistic research has shown that readers regard unqualified sentences as being much more forceful than sentences with adverbial qualifiers.[4] You are better off avoiding these qualifiers when you can, using instead appropriately strong nouns or verbs that don't need qualifiers. For example, you can replace *run very fast* with the much stronger *dash*. If you cannot eliminate qualifiers entirely, be sure to choose them carefully and use them sparingly.

Similarly, it is often a mistake to speak in absolutes. The law is seldom absolute. Most of your legal writing will consist of arguments or recommendations to apply established principles to new facts. Therefore, avoid words and phrases such as *clearly, without a doubt, undeniably,* and *obviously*. In addition, these words and phrases have been so overused and misused that they have lost their punch; they are usually little more than excess baggage.

On the other hand, be careful not to let the natural uncertainty of legal analysis force you into using a hesitant or tentative style. You should also avoid words like *somewhat, occasionally*, and *possibly*. Don't say "We think this is possibly the answer that the court is looking for in cases of this kind." You want to write forcefully and convincingly and make straightforward, affirmative or negative statements: "We think this is the answer that the court is looking for" or, better still, "This is the answer that the court seeks."

Use active, descriptive words. You can choose words that add persuasiveness to your writing by being aware of connotations and subtle shades of meaning. In the example below, the italicized words render the description flat and lifeless.

> The defendant *ran* down the street *toward* the plaintiff and *collided with* the plaintiff. The plaintiff *fell* to the ground. The defendant *picked up* the plaintiff's handbag, *opened* it, and *placed* the contents of the bag on the sidewalk. He *sorted through* the *contents* until he came upon the plaintiff's wallet. He then *picked up* the wallet and ran.

This example can be rewritten to be more effective. Although the words that are italicized in the rewrite below are close in meaning to the words in the original example, they convey action and some emotional impact.[5]

---

4. J.D. Feezel, A Qualified Certainty: Verbal Probability in Arguments, 41 Speech Monographs 348 (1974).
5. Research by Loftus & Palmer, Reconstruction of Automobile Destruction: An Example of the Interaction Between Language and Memory, 13 J. Verbal Ed. 585 (1974), showed that when the experimenter varied the verb in the question "How fast was the blue car going when it (contacted/collided

The defendant *charged* down the street *at* the plaintiff and *knocked* the plaintiff to the ground. The defendant then *grabbed* the plaintiff's handbag and *spilled* the contents on the sidewalk. He *rummaged* through the plaintiff's *belongings* until he found her wallet, then he *grabbed* the wallet and ran.

However, when you are trying to add life and emotional impact to your writing, do not go overboard. If you choose clichés or words that are emotionally overloaded, you risk tipping off your reader that you are struggling to convince. For example, an attorney wrote in a brief:

It is *difficult to conceive of a more graphic example* of the term "abandon" than that which is presented here, where *mere infants* were *rendered pitifully vulnerable* to the *dangers of the night* as a result of the preoccupation of a mother with her *personal pleasures.*

The attorney could have created a more convincing, forceful description if she had eliminated the italicized words and phrases and had presented more details. The facts tell the story; they do not need embellishing.

In this case, the mother was preoccupied with her own plans to attend a party that evening. She left her two infants, aged five and three, alone in her apartment, locked in the bedroom, until morning. No one else was in the apartment when the fire broke out. None of the neighbors could reach the children because their mother had bolted the front door. The children could not get out of the bedroom because their mother had wedged a chair under the outside of the bedroom door to keep the children from leaving.

b. *De-emphasizing Negative Information*

Your natural inclination in writing a persuasive document will be to present only those facts that are most favorable to your own side. However, legal documents are generally not one-sided accounts. You must deal with negative or damaging information for two reasons.

1. Your opponent will probably introduce the information. If you have not discussed damaging information, you will look, at best, careless and uninformed, and at worst, dishonest. If your audience thinks that you have told only part of the story, they may doubt your entire analysis.
2. You may have an ethical obligation to inform the court.[6]

---

with/smashed into) the red car?" different subjects who had seen the *same* film of the accident gave estimates of speed that increased significantly from "contacted" to "smashed into." This research was cited in an *amicus curiae* brief filed with the Supreme Court in Daubert v. Merrell Dow Pharmaceuticals, Inc., 509 U.S. 579 (1993).

6. Ordinarily there is no ethical duty to volunteer harmful facts. However, there is an exception: In an *ex parte* proceeding, where the adversary is not present, an attorney must inform the court of *all* material facts, "whether or not the facts are adverse." Rule 3.3(d), ABA Model Rules of Professional Conduct.

You can help give your document a more balanced, "scholarly" tone if you present negative as well as positive information. But do not state the negative information so well that you make your opponents' arguments for them. If your document seems too balanced, your readers will not know which side you are on. To avoid this, try to minimize the importance of negative information. Acknowledge the information, but arrange your analysis so that the points in your favor appear crucial, while the damaging information appears to be merely peripheral. There are several ways to accomplish this.

Put negative information in an obscure place.   Place damaging or unfavorable content in the middle of your document, where it is less likely to attract attention. If possible, bury negative information in the middle of paragraphs or sentences. If you are enumerating items or issues, place the least favorable information in the middle of the list.

You can also bury negative information by putting it in a subordinate clause. This will emphasize the information in the main clause and de-emphasize the information in the subordinate clause. In addition, you can bury negative or controversial material by juxtaposing it with neutral material.

Present negative facts broadly or in summary.   You can gloss over negative information by presenting it broadly or as a summary, leaving out the details that might capture and hold your reader's attention. If you look back at the example of the fact statement from the railroad station case discussed in the section on emphasizing favorable information (page 218), you will remember that details were used to highlight the negligence of the railroad. In the fact statement from the defendant's brief, the defendant emphasizes different facts and glosses over details about the railroad station. The reader will barely be able to picture the station, but will probably have a very good idea of what Mrs. Roberts looks like and how she behaved before she was injured.

> Mrs. Roberts, a corpulent woman weighing two hundred and fifty pounds, left the railway waiting room to catch her train. Witnesses testified that she was walking quickly and wearing shoes with very high heels. She apparently rushed onto the outside staircase without giving her eyes a chance to adjust to the light and tripped on one of the steps.

Use "ineffective" sentence structures and grammatical constructions.   You can also obscure negative information by reversing the language guidelines, that is, by using passives, nominalizations, embedded phrases and clauses, and "fuzzy" or ambiguous terms. However, be extremely careful when violating the guidelines. The sections you have selected to de-emphasize may stand out so much that you end up drawing attention to them instead.

Following is an example of how one attorney presented the facts in a memorandum of points and authorities in a way that emphasized certain facts and de-emphasized others. Notice how the attorney describes the petitioner's activities during the time the will was being probated.

FACTS

Luanne Cox died on April 3, 1976, leaving a last will and testament which she executed in New York as a resident of the Borough of Manhattan, City, County and State of New York on December 7, 1971. Arnold Squire, the executor nominated under the will, filed a petition for probate in Surrogate's Court, County of New York, on May 8, 1976. Petitioner John Cox, a son of the decedent, signed a waiver of citation and a consent to have the will admitted to probate, after consulting with his personal attorney. The probate court admitted the will to probate on June 16, 1976, without objection. The will was probated as a will of a New York domiciliary. Petitioner, as a beneficiary under the will, subsequently was paid a $10,000 bequest. On March 3, 1978, nearly two years after Squire offered the will for probate, John Cox filed a petition to (a) vacate his waiver of citation and the consent to admit the will to probate, and (b) vacate the decree admitting the will to probate.

Petitioner alleges that he executed the waiver believing that the will, although being probated in New York, would be probated as that of a Louisiana resident and that Louisiana law would apply. This would have allowed the petitioner to elect against the will and receive one quarter of the estate.

Notice how the author presents certain dates and activities with precision: Luanne Cox died on April 3, 1976; Arnold Squire, the executor, filed a petition for probate on May 8, 1976; and the probate court admitted the will to probate on June 16, 1976.

However, the dates on which John Cox supposedly found out certain information are very vague. We are not told *when* Cox signed the waiver and consent, except that it was sometime after consulting with his personal attorney. We are also not told when Cox received his bequest, except that it was sometime after the will was probated. However, the author suddenly becomes precise again: On March 3, 1978, John Cox filed a petition to vacate his waiver and consent. Note how the author emphasizes the fact that the date John Cox filed his petition was nearly two years after Squire offered the will for probate. The author argues later in the memo that the petitioner in this case was well informed about how his mother's will was being probated and that he failed to establish grounds to vacate the probate decree and set aside the waiver of citation and consent to probate.

The fact statement appears to present a precise chronology. Few readers would realize that the author has not told us in which order certain events occurred or how they relate to one another in time. The author has created the impression that the petitioner was greedy and filed the petition only when he became dissatisfied with the $10,000 bequest and found out that he could receive more under Louisiana law.

EXERCISE

Read through the facts presented below (based on *In re Hawley*, 67 Cal. 2d 824, 433 P.2d 919 (1967)). Imagine that you are the attorney representing the defendant at his murder trial. Write a fact statement for a brief. Then write a fact statement from the perspective of the prosecuting attorney. Be prepared to identify the differences in your approach to each.

The defendant is 29 years old. He had been drinking almost continuously from March 7, 1966, until the date of the homicide on March 19, 1966. On that day he met a woman in Sacramento's West End. They spent the morning drinking wine and in the evening decided to have intercourse. The defendant remembered seeing a mattress in an abandoned hotel. They entered the hotel and went into a small, dark room where decedent, Alejandro Lopez, also under the influence of liquor, was sleeping on the mattress. Defendant woke Lopez and asked him to leave. Lopez got up, said something in Spanish and tried to kick defendant, who knocked Lopez down with his fist. The defendant then had intercourse with his lady friend. Afterwards, Lopez made a remark that the defendant did not understand. The defendant grabbed a stick and hit Lopez with it until he stopped talking. He then dragged the still-alive Lopez into another room 50 feet away. He gathered papers and small sticks together around Lopez and lit them. The defendant says that he does not remember any of the details, nor does he remember dragging Lopez or lighting the fire. The defendant then went out of the building, his lady friend left him, and he met and started to drink with a male friend. The defendant noticed there was no fire in the building he had vacated and took his friend inside. The friend saw the body, and called the police. The two men waited until the officers arrived. The defendant then related some of these facts to the officers and signed a statement. An autopsy revealed that the fire caused Lopez's death. The only damage to the building was a charring of the floor by the body. The defendant was later indicted for murder and arson. He was represented by the public defender, who requested Dr. S. Green to prepare a psychiatric study of the defendant. In his report, Dr. Green reviewed the defendant's background. It showed that the defendant's mother, father, and girlfriend had all been killed in separate automobile accidents while they were intoxicated. The defendant had only completed the tenth grade in school. Since 1954 he spent about ten months of every year in prison, each incident resulting in his incarceration occurring while he was intoxicated. Dr. Green found physical deterioration and dilapidation with consequential impairment of retention, memory, and vocabulary. The defendant expressed no guilt about his actions and little concern over his fate. Dr. Green found him to be presently sane and responsible, but concluded as to his condition at the time of the crimes: "At the time of the alleged crime of arson, the effect of prolonged alcoholism would be so severe it would contaminate any intent he may have had. Furthermore, the amount of wilfulness and maliciousness would be severely restricted and he would be unable to comprehend such an action or govern himself."

12

Reviewing
and Editing

A Writing as a Process

Throughout this text we have characterized writing as a step-by-step process. If you approach writing as a process, you can build your documents in a careful and systematic way and still have the flexibility to accommodate different situations. For example, when you write a memorandum you need to be flexible in the way you order the tasks of doing research and writing. You would probably first do some research, then compile and write up your research; but once you have seen what you have accumulated, you might want to do more research and then revise what you have written.

Even though you may have to be flexible in the way you carry out various parts of the writing process, it is valuable to begin any writing task by articulating the steps you plan to take. It is also worthwhile to place the steps in a workable order, even if you end up moving the steps around or omitting some of them as you create the document. Look again at the writing plan we suggest on page 000.

B Reviewing, Revising, and Editing

Reviewing and revising appear in the diagram as post-writing steps, and indeed you should review and revise extensively and carefully once you have completed a draft of a document. However, you should also try to review and revise throughout the writing process. You can check what you have already written at any stage by looking at the legal sufficiency of the content of your writing and at the quality of the writing itself. In this chapter, we discuss a few techniques for reviewing and editing your writing for appropriateness, effectiveness, and (grammatical) correctness.

The techniques presented below are useful not only for reviewing and editing your own writing but also for reviewing and editing the writing of others. For example, if you serve on a law journal you may find yourself called on to edit the work of other students and of legal scholars who submit articles to the journal.

FIGURE 12-1

Prewriting Steps

Define *Purpose.*
Why do you need the document?

↕

Define *Audience.*
Who will use the document?

→

Determine *Constraints.*
What limits do you have on how you can write?

Writing Steps

Decide on *Content.*
What should go into the document?

→

Organize the document.
What is the most logical and effective order for the material?

→

Use the *language guidelines* for effective prose. What do you need to do to make your writing as clear as possible?

→

Use *persuasive techniques* where necessary. Which persuasive strategies make your writing most effective?

Post-Writing Steps

Review, revise, and edit.
How can you improve each draft of a document?

Eventually, when you are working as a lawyer, you will probably edit the work of your colleagues or of junior associates.

1. Checking for Appropriateness

Correctness is an important dimension of the reader's expectations, but it is not the only one. The reader also expects to be able to follow what is written. The assumptions underlying the two dimensions — correctness and appropriateness — are quite different. The reader's expectations about *correctness* are based on the assumption that professional writing should follow the rules of a dialect often called Standard American English. Grammatical structures and word forms that follow the rules of Standard American English are considered correct; those that do not are considered incorrect in professional writing.

The reader's expectations about *appropriateness* are based on the assumption that the pieces of information relate to one another in an orderly and comprehensible way. When a reader encounters a piece of information that does not seem to relate to what has come before, it violates the reader's expectation of what is appropriate. The violation can occur at any level, from a single word within a sentence to an entire argument within a brief. At whatever level the violation occurs, the reader pauses to try to make sense of what has been said — to try to create a relationship among the pieces of information that he or she has encountered. This relationship can be thought of as a link between what the reader already knows or has been told — *given* information — and the *new* information that the writer is introducing.

How the given-new concept works.   To understand the basic assumption that a reader expects to be able to relate pieces of information in a text, first look at these examples.

> The plaintiff had delivered a package just before lunch.

> The plaintiff had delivered a lecture just before lunch.

> The plaintiff had delivered a calf just before lunch.

Although your picture of the plaintiff changes from sentence to sentence (perhaps from the plaintiff's being a delivery person to a professor to a veterinarian or farmer), you can still easily make sense of each sentence. It is possible to relate the person (plaintiff) to the action (delivered) and the object.

When a reader cannot relate the pieces of given and new information to each other, the writer has seriously violated the reader's expectations. Look at this example:

> The plaintiff had delivered a store just before lunch.

A sentence like this is a complete stopper. The new information (store) simply does not fit into the given, the context of the sentence (plaintiff delivered). A reader cannot make sense of the sentence without assuming that words have been omitted (for example, "delivered *for* a store," or "delivered *something to* a store").

Although these sentences about the plaintiff delivering something are simple, they demonstrate the concept underlying the dimension of appropriateness: Readers expect pieces of information to relate to one another. More specifically, readers assume

1. That what appears first provides a context (i.e., is the given),
2. That what follows (new information) relates to the given (i.e., can be easily assimilated into the context),and
3. That any special relationship between the given information and new information will be made explicit by the writer.

These three assumptions form the basis of the reader's expectation of appropriateness. In this section, we will deal with the way the given-new concept works with regard to words within sentences.

How the given-new concept functions at the level of the word.   When a person is reading a sentence, each word in the sentence immediately becomes part of the reader's short-term memory and sets up expectations about what will follow. To see how strong the expectation for individual words can be, read the passage below. Fill in the three blanks in the last sentence. Put only *one* word in each blank.

A. *Statutory Entitlement to Homemaker Services Is Created by Federal and State Regulations*

To have a statutory entitlement, more than a unilateral expectation of benefit is required. *Board of Regents of State College v. Roth,* 408 U.S. 564 (1972) (non-tenured professor does not have statutory entitlement to position in absence of statute or contract). Instead, the property interest is both created and defined by "existing rules or understandings that stem from an independent source." Id. at 577. Plaintiff Clark has a statutorily created property interest in the homemaker services. This property _____ is conferred on her _____ Title XX of the _____ Security Act.

The correct words are *interest, by,* and *Social.* Each of these illustrates a type of appropriate information. You used information you had from the previous sentence, the other words in the sentence with the blanks, and your knowledge of English and law to fill in the blanks. As a reader, you would feel jarred by any other word in any of these positions; your expectations would be violated by words such as these:

This property (concern/issue/matter) is conferred on her (at/in/for) Title XX of the (Law/Tax/Compensation) Security Act.

Your expectation of the word *interest* (rather than *issue* or *matter*) comes from the information in the beginning of the passage that the legal issue here involves a "property interest." Your expectation of the word *by* comes from your knowledge of the English language (for example, things are conferred *on* people *by* other people, *by* statutes, etc.). Your expectation of the word *Social* in "Social Security Act" may come from the context of the case, perhaps from your knowledge of Title XX and homemaker services, or perhaps from your general knowledge that the primary "Security Act" is the "*Social* Security Act."

There is another language expectation about words that the entitlement passage did not illustrate: the use of the right word. A writer violates that expectation by using the wrong word, as in the following example with the wrong word italicized.

This is the only Maryland case where the court *intravened* with the distribution of property at the end of a meretricious relationship.

A wrong word like *intravened*, though close to the appropriate word (*intervened*), will jar the reader. Following is a list of several frequently confused words, with examples of their proper use.

imply/infer: By denying John's accusation, you *implied* that John is a liar. From that, the police *inferred* that John was the culprit.

affect/effect: The new ruling will not *affect* your ability to appeal. I expect our motion will have the desired *effect* on the defendant.

moral/morale: Alice is a very *moral* person. Her *morale* is low because she lost the case.

deter/defer: We attempted to *deter* him from pursuing the lawsuit, but he would not *defer* to our wishes.

ensure/assure: There was no way to *ensure* that they would win the case, but their lawyer *assured* them that she would do her best.

then/than: I said *then*, as I say now, that Dr. Smith was harder to cross-examine *than* Dr. Jones.

lie/lay: You assume the risk if you *lie* down on railroad tracks or if you *lay* a valuable object down on them. (Remember, however, that the past tense of *lie* is *lay*. The past tense of *lay* is *laid*.)

There are many other frequently confused words. Whenever you are uncertain of the spelling or meaning of a word, look it up before using it.

How the given-new concept functions for constructions longer than a phrase or sentence.   As we explained in Chapter 9, it is necessary to provide a context for all legal documents in the form of a heading, a sentence, a paragraph, or even an entire section. This is, in effect, the application of the given-new concept on a large scale. But it is often necessary to provide a context even for a paragraph or a short document. And you can confuse, or even lose, the reader by providing a context that is misleading or inappropriate. This is because it violates the reader's expectation of what will follow. Not providing a context would be like giving someone a recipe without any indication of what the recipe was for; providing an inappropriate context would be like giving someone a set of instructions labeled "Assembling Your Lawnmower" which turned out to be instructions for putting together a child's tricycle.

The given-new concept can also be violated in a piece of writing if it is so abstract that the reader has difficulty attaching it to his or her prior (given) knowledge or if the new information precedes the given information, requiring the reader to reread the entire passage several times to make sense of it. Following is an example of a violation of the given-new concept in a construction longer than a sentence.

> But if these dictates of reason are to have the force of law, there is need of a higher principle; for although their advantage is most manifest, still it alone could never lay so firm a restraint upon the spirits of men that they could not forsake such dictates if they could find satisfaction in disregarding this advantage, or believe that they could better consult their own advantage in some other way. Nor can a man's will be so thoroughly restrained by his mere intentions that he cannot go opposite it whenever he so pleases. And even if many men endowed with natural liberty should agree to keep these dictates, these will none the less, abide only so long as the agreement of those men continues in force. . . . It must, therefore, under all circumstances be maintained, that the obligation of natural law is of God.

In this argument regarding the motivating force behind natural law, sixteenth-century legal philosopher Hugo Grotius puts a couple of hundred words between his argument for the existence of a higher principle and the identification of that higher principle. While this rhetorical style may have been in vogue four hundred years ago, it no longer is, and should not be emulated. For the modern writer, this is a clear violation of the given-new concept.

EXERCISES

Each sentence contains at least one word that is inappropriate. Circle the inappropriate or wrong words in each passage and correct them. To correct an error, you may substitute another word or rewrite part of a sentence.

1. We can imply from these statistics the yearly cost of raising a child from infancy to 18 years of age.

2. We should also be able to establish a cause of action for breach of contract, if you can insure me that the following statements were made by Dr. Cooper on January 10, 2000.

3. To prove medical malpractice, Dr. Cooper's treatment on Mrs. Tall must have effected her health.

4. The carpet was put in the downstairs store, presumably for business reasons. A concrete floor would be somewhat out of decorum for a men's fashion boutique.

5. We asked our attorney about the rational behind the judge's decision.

2. Checking for Effectiveness

There are two major ways that you can check a document for effectiveness: by assessing the overall organization of the document and by assessing the style of the prose in the document.

You can examine the organization to make sure that it is logical and complete by making an outline of the headings and subheadings in the finished draft. This will help you determine whether the headings are parallel, whether sections are missing in the overall structure, or whether the document jumps from one topic to another without the proper transitions.

If you still cannot tell whether the structure of the document is sound, do a more detailed outline. Write a five-or six-word précis or summary of each paragraph in the document and arrange these units in order. This should help you determine whether the parts of the document fit together logically. For other organizational problems, use the checklist in the next section. Pay particular attention to item 15.

Once you have assessed the organization of the document, you should scrutinize the language and sentence structure. You can do this by using the language guidelines. We have provided a checklist that you can use to quickly ascertain whether the writer has followed the guidelines. Each item in the checklist has a number or letter that you can use as a code when referring to a problem you find in your own or another writer's work.

In general, when using this or any other editing system, keep in mind the following points.

1. *Praise* as well as criticize. A critique that is totally negative can dishearten or anger the writer. The writer might even shrug off the criticism, contending that the critic's comments are simply a difference of opinion. Try to avoid corrections that merely reflect a difference in taste.

2. *Describe*, don't judge. Instead of writing "poor organization" or "weak," describe the problems you encountered in reading the document. For example, "There is no transition between points three and four; therefore, I could not follow your argument."

3. *Be specific* regarding where the problems occur.

Editing Checklist

1. Are the sentences *too long*?
2. Are the parts of sentences in an *illogical order*?
3. Do the sentences in the document contain *intrusive phrases* or *clauses*?
4. Are there tangled *complex conditionals*?
5. Is the *passive* voice used inappropriately?
6. Are *nominalizations* used inappropriately?
7. Are there too many *negatives* or *multiple negatives*?
8. Is the *structure nonparallel*?
9. Is there unintentional *ambiguity*?
   a. at the *word* level
   b. at the *sentence* level
10. Is the *vocabulary* inappropriate?
    a. word or term needs definition
    b. word or term needs replacement
    c. archaic word
    d. inflated language
    e. incorrect use of legal terms
    f. wrong word
    g. jargon
11. Are there unwieldy *noun strings*?
12. a. Is there *redundancy*?
    b. Are there *extraneous* words?
    c. Is there *overspecificity*?
13. Is the *style* inappropriate?
    a. incorrect point of view
    b. parties, individuals, etc., labeled incorrectly
    c. incorrect use of pronouns
    d. incorrect tense
    e. language too colloquial
    f. language too pompous
    g. too much like a term paper
    h. too many clichés
14. Has the writer failed to write within his or her *constraints*?
    a. formal rules not followed
    b. informal rules not followed
    c. document too long
    d. document too short
    e. wrong content or information
15. Is the document *poorly organized*?
    a. no coherent organizing principle
    b. steps for a basic expository document missing
    c. steps for a complex legal document missing
    d. no context at the beginning of the document

e. no "roadmap" section

f. no table of contents in a long document

g. appropriate headings or subheadings missing

h. headings or subheadings not informative

i. organization of the document not made apparent

j. document not broken down into manageable sections

k. sections not parallel

l. good transitions needed

16. Does the writer need to rethink his or her *persuasive strategies*?

a. document too one-sided

b. too much prominence given to damaging material

c. information not ordered so that positive information stands out

d. information not ordered so that negative information is de-emphasized

e. more convincing vocabulary needed

EXERCISES

Use the language guidelines to edit the memo below. Also be prepared to make suggestions for improving the organization of the memo.

TO: Senior Partner

FROM: Associate

RE: Liability of Homeowner in Regard to Drowning of Minor

DATE: October 30, 2000

QUESTION PRESENTED

Whether a parent of a minor is entitled to recover against a private homeowner for the drowning death of a minor, when the homeowner is in compliance with local building codes.

BRIEF ANSWER

In pursuance to the state of Kentucky, the landowner would be liable for injuries as result of any injury or death that are incurred.

In regards to the above situation, Kentucky state law has recognized in certain situations like the above, from the finding that possessor of land is liable for physical harm if he creates or maintains an artificial condition which he realizes or should have realized will involve an unreasonable risk or serious bodily harm to children who would not have comprehend the risk of danger involved. Under Kentucky law a swimming pool is considered an artificial construction. Thus a landowner would be liable upon the finding that the Doctrine of Attractive Nuisance exists.

STATEMENT OF ALLEGATIONS

Harry Winston constructed a swimming pool. Winston enclosed his entire backyard with a six-foot high fence in compliance with the local building code. Melvin, who lives across the street, and is nine years old, climbed into Winston's yard. Melvin jumped into the pool, panicked and drowned.

ANALYSIS

There is no question but that the parents of the minor has a valid cause of action, if it can be shown that the doctrine of attractive nuisance is applicable.

"The Attractive Nuisance Doctrine provides that one who maintains upon his premises a condition, instrumentality, or other agency which are dangerous to children of tender years by reason of their inability to appreciate the peril therein, and which may reasonably be expected to attract children of tender years to the premises, is under a duty to exercise reasonable care to protect them against the dangers of the attraction." The Restatement of this principle has been applied to numerous cases involving actions for death of or injury to a child which was caused by a private residential swimming pool.

The evidence indicates that the minor was on a homeowner's property. However, the Attractive Nuisance Doctrine governs the liability of landowners to minors. Whether a minor is classified as a trespasser, licensee, or invitee is not a controlling consideration in the application of the Attractive Nuisance Doctrine. It could be argued that the Attractive Nuisance Doctrine is inapplicable, since the homeowner was in compliance with local building code requirements for maintaining an artificial structure in his backyard. That the homeowner is released of liability from injuries incurred to trespassing minors, because he had taken all necessary precautionary measures by erecting a six-foot fence. In the following case the Attractive Nuisance Doctrine is inapplicable *Hanners v. City of Ashland*, 331 S.W.2d 729 (Ky. 1960). The case involved a child eight years old who drowned while swimming on private property. The court held that Attractive Nuisance Doctrine did not extend to city's reservoir, which was filled with water, the city was not held liable for the death of the eight-year-old child drowned while swimming in the reservoir. The court's rationale behind its decision was that a reservoir is not considered the same as an artificial structure as in the case of a swimming pool. The principle of law is controlled by the decision and reasoning in *Schaufs' Admr. v. City of Paducah*, 106 Ky. 228, 50 S.W. 42 (1954). The principle of law was also controlled out of *Von Almen's Admr. v. City of Louisville*, 180 Ky. 441, 202 S.W. 880 (1918) and has not been departed from in this state. The facts from the above case are substantially similar to the facts in our present situation. Although in the above case the court denied the plaintiff the right to recover, the same underlining principle is applicable. The *City of Ashland* case further establishes the rule that ordinarily the landowner is liable for the action of minor, when physical harm results from artificial structures which the homeowner may anticipate constitutes unreasonable risk of serious injury to children who would not realize such danger.

It was also established in the leading case of *Louisville Trust Co. v. Nutting*, 437 S.W.2d 484 (Ky. 1968). Here, the court held that a homeowner is liable for the harm of trespassing minors, if he creates or maintains artificial condition which realize or should realize will involve unreasonable harm to children, and the instrumentality is one that would reasonably attract a child's attention to come on his premises.

While it appears to be a valid cause of action. It is important to take into consideration that the view is moderately restricting the application of the Doctrine of Attractive Nuisance theory. *Bentley v. South-East Coal Co.*, 334 S.W.2d 349 (Ky. 1960) considering the fact that the homeowner was in compliance with the local building codes will be our strongest contention. However, the theory behind the Doctrine of Attractive Nuisance is in our favor. Because of a child's immaturity and want of judgment, the "minor is presumed incapable of understanding and appreciating all of the possible dangers which he may encounter entering upon the land of another, or making his own decisions as to the chances he will take. Since it is not practical for the parents to chain to a bedpost. Thus if a child is to be protected at all, it will be the one upon whose land the child strays," Prosser fourth edition *Torts*. This view is the traditional social interest in the safety and welfare of children. The general rule is in our favor. Therefore it is a possibility of recovery under the Kentucky state Wrongful Death Statute 411-130:

> In a wrongful death action in which the decedent was a minor child, the surviving parent or parents may recover for loss of affection and companionship that would have derived from such child during its minority in addition to all other elements of damage usually recoverable in a wrongful death action, in negligence.

3. Checking for Correctness

After you have checked a document for appropriateness and effectiveness, you should also check it for correctness. This means that you should proofread your document for mechanical errors.

Proofreading is necessary, first, because human beings make mistakes, and second, because we are not especially tolerant of the mistakes that others make. When you write, you will probably make careless mistakes. Many of your readers will not overlook these mistakes and may not forgive you for them. Educated readers, such as law professors, senior partners, and judges, expect correctness. If your final copy contains frequent errors, even seemingly trivial ones, you jeopardize your credibility as a professional. If you find errors after filing a pleading with the court, you may have to follow up by filing errata sheets listing corrections.[1] Errors — either frequent small ones or occasional serious ones — can cause a reader to make negative inferences about you. Because of errors in a

---

1. Sometimes correcting errors may not be that easy. For example, a few years ago the Environmental Protection Agency issued a rule dealing with spills of polychlorinated biphenyls ("PCBs"). The rule that was published was not the rule that EPA intended to issue. Apparently, one of the drafters of the rule erroneously used the WordPerfect find/replace command. Since the error was discovered after the rule was published, EPA published a technical correction. An industry group immediately challenged the technical correction. The Court of Appeals agreed and set aside the technical correction. *See* Utility Solid Waste Activities Group v. Environmental Protection Agency, No. 99-1374 (D.C. Cir. Jan. 30, 2001). The court ruled that if a technical correction affects the substance of a rule, the agency may not freely publish the correction. Instead, according to the court, it must go through the formalities of the Administrative Procedure Act (e.g., notice-and-comment rulemaking).

document, a reader may conclude that you are lazy, uninterested in your work, illiterate, illogical, or incompetent.

As a professional, you cannot afford this "halo" effect of errors. Yet, if you simply reread one of your documents from top to bottom, you will probably not catch all the errors. The content is so familiar to you that you see what you expect to see or what you intended to put on the page. You may also have difficulty catching errors because you are reading word groups as quickly as you can comprehend them. Experienced readers do not read letter by letter or even word by word.

Good proofreaders do read slowly, often letter by letter, to be sure they are seeing each word as a word and not as a component of a thought. There are several ways to shift your focus away from the ideas to the words and letters. For most people, the trick is to slow down their normal reading speed. Here are a few ways to do this.

1. Use a computer "spell check" program on your document to catch any obvious misspellings.
2. Read your document out loud to someone who is proofreading a duplicate copy. The listener can concentrate on checking the accuracy of each word he or she hears rather than on absorbing the ideas.
3. Read your document backwards from the last sentence to the first, or, alternatively, read each page from the bottom to the top. These approaches slow down your reading considerably because you have to hunt for the beginning of each sentence.
4. Proofread each page line by line, placing a ruler under the line you are reading to keep your eyes from automatically moving ahead to the next word group.
5. Proofread each page line by line from *right to left* to maximize your review of each word. This method works particularly well as a final check for standard typographical errors such as dropped letters or transposed letters — provided that earlier readings have ensured that no words or punctuation are missing and that the overall flow is good.

Once you have selected a method and started proofreading, you will undoubtedly encounter errors that need to be marked for correction. If you plan to make all the corrections yourself, any mark will do. If, however, there is clerical staff available, it is good to know the accepted proofreading marks. Every dictionary has a page on proofreading marks; however, we have included the more common ones here for your convenience (*see* Figure 12-2). You will be able to use them with the exercises that follow.

A note about spelling and grammar-checking software.   Your first step in proofreading any document you produce on a computer will usually be to use the spell-checking software included with your word-processing program.

However, you cannot rely on your spell checker to catch all spelling errors — for example, in the cases of *there, their, and they're*; *meet and meat*; *or pair and pear*. You must still proofread your work, first on the screen and then on paper. You should do both because reading text on a screen is hard on the eyes, and this might cause you to miss errors that you would have spotted on paper.

Using grammar-checking software is even more problematic. Grammar checkers sometimes highlight as errors constructions that are not actually errors or suggest corrections that are themselves incorrect. Thus, you must know the correct grammatical or syntactic construction for what you wish to say in order to make the right choice. For example, as we were writing this book, our grammar checker erroneously labeled the following sentences as sentence fragments:

> U.S. law defines alimony as "periodic payments of funds for the support and maintenance of the former spouse."

> The plaintiff's mother, although nearby, neither saw nor heard the accident.

Our grammar checker also could not "understand" the following sentence and wrongly instructed us to change "ideas, that" to "ideas that" or "ideas, which."

> The sentence . . . has so much verbiage between the subject and verb, and such an unusual ordering of *ideas, that* it is painful to read.

Unfortunately, we cannot cede the parsing of a sentence to a piece of software. For guidance on grammar, see the Appendix, "An Overview of English Sentence Structure."

Proofreaders' marks are designed to communicate virtually any change with ease. To guarantee a perfect final product, be sure to use the correct mark, position it properly, and write it legibly.

If your document has been prepared with ample space between the lines, you can make corrections and insertions directly above the word or spot in question. If you don't have enough room there, however, you will need to treat your page and your corrections differently.

Draw an imaginary line down the center of the page. Any corrections needed to the left of that line will be written in the left-hand margin; any corrections to the right, in the right-hand margin. A caret (^) will mark the spot in the line where each correction is to be made. Use the margin space immediately to the left or right of the line to write the correction. Separate corrections with a forward slash. (*See* the examples of corrected pages in Figure 12-3 and Figure 12-4.)

FIGURE 12-2

	delete: the ~~the~~ court
	close up: law maker
	delete and close up: statuatory
^	insert: the bill passed
#	add space: S. Ct.
eq. #	space evenly / where / indicated
stet	let it ~~stand~~
tr.	transpose: justifee
	move right
	move left
	center
	move up
	move down
	begin new paragraph
sp.	spell out: U.S. United States
caps	set in capitals: CAPITALS
sc	set in small capitals: SMALL CAPITALS
lc	set in lowercase: lowercase
ital.	set in italic: *italic*
rom.	set in *roman:* roman (i.e., non-italic)
bf	set in boldface: **boldface**
=	insert hyphen: landlord-tenant
⅟M	insert em dash: Another lawyer—often a colleague—will review . . .
	superscript: footnote[1]
	subscript: H_2O
	comma
	apostrophe
	period
	semicolon
	colon
	quotation marks
	parentheses
/	used to separate two or more changes or at the end of an insertion

FIGURE 12-3

It is my opinion that you may recover from your doctor. Your
case offers clear evidence that Dr. cooper has breached his contract
with you. Your pregnancy and the subsequent delivery of your third
child were exactly the consequences that which you sought to avoid when
you contracted with Dr. Cooper to perform the tubal ligation. He
informed you and expressly stated that you would have no more children
after this operation. The birth of your third child after the preform-
ance of this operation is proof of the operations failure, and of Dr.
Cooper's breach of contract with you. The law in this state (Mass.)
allows one such as you to recover for a doctor's failure to perform
promises clearly made at the time he or she was hired.
Although it has been held generally that a contract to sterilize
a patient is not against public policy, the courts have reached a
different conclusion on the issue of damages for breach of contract.
Some courts have concluded that instead of being damaged, the patient
is blessed by the birth. It is our contention that the normal delivery
of a normal child following an unsuccessful sterilization operation
warrants compensable damages. Thus, following the recovery allowed in
the case stated, you should be reimbursed not only for out-of-pocket
expenses for the unsuccessful sterilization operation, but also for all
pain and suffering both mental and physical, attendant to the unexpected pregnancy. You told me that you had a conversation with Dr.
Cooper in which he made statements to the effect that a tubal ligation
was "a permanent thing" and said, "you are not going to have any more
children after this operation. These statements made by the doctor
did not create a contract. The words used by the doctor were designed
to make sure that you knew that the operation was nonreversible in

FIGURE 12-4

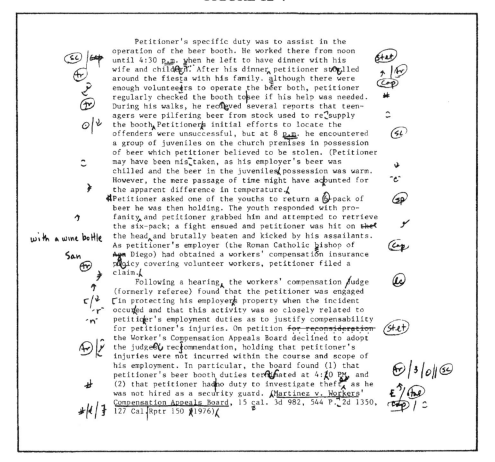

EXERCISES

To test your ability as a proofreader, proofread these exercises. The exercises contain a total of 20 careless errors. The errors include mistakes like transposed letters (*raed* for *read* or *form* for *from*), omitted or superfluous words or letters, substituted letters (*test* for *text*), wrong words (*then* for *than*), and omitted or unnecessary punctuation marks.

1. Brooks converted the store into a mens clothing store and converted the second floor into an apartment. He removed the original radiators and installed and electric heating system to heat both floors. A new carpet was placed on a wooden flame which was bolted to the frist floor, and an air conditioner was placed in a frist floor window. On the second floor he replaced the plumbing fixtures and installed a new toilet and shower.

2. Mr. Brooks may remove and sell the air conditioner. Since the unit is a window type, it is only tenuously annexed to the building an may be

removed without damage. It is not particularly adapted use in that location; that is, the unit would fit equally well in countless other window. Also, the very choice of such a model indicates Mr. Brooks intention to remove it later. Other jurisdictions have decided this point.

3. These two objects — the forced-air heat pump, including duct work, and the upstairs plumbing fixtures — can be consider together since they all under the same legal theory. The law that covers these two object is that of replacements, since the forced-air system and the newly-installed bathroom replace systems of the same type that were in existence when our client moved in. A fixture substituted for one that was on the premises at the time of the lease is generally not removable if the original has been damaged or permanently removed, since the effect of such action would be to leave the premises in a worse condition then when the lessee took the lease.

4. In that case the tenant, Jensen, took out a broken toilet, substituting a working toilet for the duration of his lease. On leaving the premises, Jensen remove the toilet he had installed and re-installed the original broken toilet, leaving the property in in substantially the same state in which he received it. The court ruled that the lessee has a right to remove the improvemnets and additions that he has made to the leased property, provided he leaves it in the state which it was received. It follows form that decision that if our client still has the old toiler, he may reconnect it and remove the new toilet as personal property.

PART III
Creating Specific
Legal Documents

13

Writing an
Intraoffice
Memorandum

A   What Is a Memorandum?

An *intraoffice memorandum* (memo) is an informative document that summarizes the research on the points of law or the facts of a particular case. The memo is an internal office document[1] that is usually requested by, and addressed to, another lawyer — often a colleague or supervisor in the writer's firm. The writer may be asked to resolve a predefined issue or set of issues or to first identify all of the issues in a problem and then to resolve them. In practice, a memo may be used for many purposes: to alert the reader that more information is needed either from the client or through discovery, to inform the reader about the status of the law, or to present the reader with recommendations on how to proceed with a case.

A memo is a research tool rather than a document advocating a particular point of view. It should provide the reader with a complete picture of the facts and law in a case, including both positive and negative information, so that the reader can use the memo to anticipate counterarguments and to make sound decisions about the case. Thus, while the writer of the memo should indicate which side he or she is on, the writer should also present both the strengths and weaknesses of the client's position.

This chapter consists of two parts: The first part is an outline of the structure of a memo with explanations of each of its sections. The second part of the chapter is made up of two sample memos.

Keep in mind that this outline is only a basic structure: Memo formats vary widely, depending on the preferences of a particular law professor, law firm, or agency. The writers of the sample memos, for instance, have organized their memos in their own way, following already established conventions. With our outline, however, we show you one useful way of organizing a memo when you have had little or no experience in writing one. Our outline will not only help you to organize your first attempts at writing a memo, it will also help you think about the kinds of information, arguments, and supporting evidence that should go into your memo. Remember that the order in which you present the

---

1. There are also external or advocacy memos that resemble briefs. We will discuss advocacy memos in the next chapter.

information in a memo may not be the order in which you research, think about, or write that information.

B The Structure of a Memo

1. Outline

Heading

Background and Purpose of the Memorandum
Statement of the Issues
    Question 1   (There may be one or several questions. These
    Question 2   questions are sometimes called issues.)
Short Answer
Statement of the Facts
Applicable Statutes
Discussion
    Analysis of Question 1
    Analysis of Question 2
Conclusion

2. Explanation of the Parts of a Memo

a. *Heading*

Most memos begin with a heading in caps, e.g., MEMORANDUM OF LAW, and a heading that includes an identification of the case (use your client's name or the names of the parties if you know who they are), the name of the person who requested the memo, the name of the person submitting the memo, and the date the memo will be submitted. It should look something like this.

MEMORANDUM OF LAW

TITLE:	Smith v. Jones
REQUESTED BY:	Professor Freedman
SUBMITTED BY:	H. Monroe
DATE SUBMITTED:	November 12, 2006

A memo may require a more informative title. The title above can be replaced by a description of the subject of the memo. This description helps the reader to identify a memo quickly and will also be helpful to anyone who uses the memo in the future. Here is one way to provide this information.

MEMORANDUM OF LAW

TO: Professor Freedman
FROM: H. Monroe
DATE: November 12, 2006
RE: Liability of an employer for an assault committed by an employee in *Tibits v. Northern Industrial Suppliers, Inc.*

b. *Background and Purpose*

Some memos open with a discussion of why the writer has been asked to produce the memo or with some background information. This kind of introduction can quickly orient the reader to the topic of the memo. This section may not have a formal title. Here is an example:

> You have asked me to develop arguments in support of a motion for summary judgment in *Smith v. Jones* on the grounds that the plaintiff's claim is barred by the statute of limitations. This memo discusses several ways in which we can move for summary judgment.

c. *Statement of the Issues*

This section may also be called *Questions Presented*. It lists the legal questions that are presented in the memo. A writer must analyze the problem carefully so that all of the questions or major issues in the problem are dealt with.

According to convention, each question should consist of one sentence, and one sentence only. This makes these questions very difficult to write. If a question comes out too long, is structurally very complex, and doesn't inspire the reader to agree with the writer's position, it should be rewritten. The question may need to be restated or broken down into several separate issues. Here is an example of a statement of the issues.

Statement of the Issues

1. When a lease gives a lessee the power to renew the lease for "additional terms," how many renewals is the lessee entitled to?
2. When a lessee attaches personal property to the leasehold and later wants to remove it, what test will the court use to determine whether the property has become a fixture and thus belongs to the lessor?

However, if the issues in a memo are complex or if there are many issues, this section may contain only a summary of those issues. Each specific issue statement or question then appears at the beginning of the section in which the issue is actually analyzed.

Summary of the Issues

This memorandum discusses the contract doctrines of mutuality of obligation and mutuality of remedy. The memo focuses in particular upon scholarly treatment of these principles and how the courts have recently applied these principles. The memo also analyzes how courts have applied contract law in deciding cases arising under 42 U.S.C. §1981, which prohibits racial discrimination when contracts are created or enforced.

d. *Short Answer*

This section contains a short answer to the questions presented in the statement of the issues. For example:

Short Answer

Our client should be entitled to an equitable increase in its fixed fee based on the cost of the eight-month extension of management and support services that it provided as a result of the government's change orders. In addition, the costs that our client incurred for 22 months of extended management and support services as a result of the government's delays provide a basis for an increase in fee. This increase is warranted because the contract establishes time of performance as a crucial element in defining the scope of work.

e. *Statement of the Facts*

This section contains a clear and concise statement of the pertinent facts of the case. These are the facts upon which the discussion and conclusion are based. The statement of facts should include both favorable and unfavorable facts, since the writer must analyze the legal significance of each. Here is an example from a memo written by a firm representing the defendant, John Deboe. The issue in this case is whether the plaintiff, Long, can collect directly from Deboe's insurance company that part of a judgment against Deboe that exceeds Deboe's insurance coverage. There is evidence that the insurer acted in bad faith by refusing to settle with Long.

Statement of Facts

On October 10, 2000, John Deboe was involved in a traffic accident in which Lillian Long and her daughter were injured. Long sued Deboe in a Minnesota court for property damage and personal injuries to herself and her daughter. Long obtained a judgment against Deboe in the amount of $63,000. Deboe had automobile insurance with Good Group Insurance Company in the amount of $23,000, $40,000 less than the judgment against him. Good Group has paid the full amount of its coverage under the policy to Long, but Long has not yet collected any of the judgment in excess of the $23,000 policy amount.

Good Group had several opportunities, before trial, to settle with Long for an amount within the limits of Deboe's policy. Good Group refused on each occasion.

f. *Applicable Statutes*

Some memos will include a section that lists citations for all of the statutes and regulations that have been cited in the memo. Some agencies or firms may also want the applicable portion of the law reproduced along with the citations.

g. *Discussion*

The *discussion* is the core of the memo. It restates each of the questions presented in the memo. Each question is followed by a discussion or analysis in which the writer shows how the law (pertinent cases, statutes, and so on) can be applied to the facts in the case to answer the question.

For a sample discussion, *see* the memos in Section C below.

h. *Conclusion*

A memo frequently includes a *conclusion* summarizing the conclusions the writer has drawn from the discussion and recommending actions the reader might want to take based on the analyses in the discussion.

C Writing a Memo: Two Examples

Now let's look at two sample memos to see how all of these sections go together. Both were written by practicing lawyers. They have been adapted somewhat and the names have been changed. The first sample memo was actually the basis for a memorandum of points and authorities, which we present in the next chapter.

To give you an idea of how a law firm operates, we begin this section with the document that initiated the first sample memorandum. It, too, is a memorandum, but it is simply a request, written by a senior partner in the firm to an associate, asking that the associate research and write the first sample memorandum.

MEMORANDUM

TO: Lawrence Goldman

FROM: David Berg

SUBJECT: *United States v. Nevada Institute of Technology et al.*, Civ. No. 123-90-B (D. Md.)

DATE: January 17, 1994

We represent Nevada Institute of Technology ("NIT"), four of its current faculty, and one former faculty member in a six-count False Claims Act suit begun by the government in 1990. The government amended the complaint a few weeks after it filed the original action. The government claims that research conducted in the early 1980s by one of those scientists, Mark Able, was fraudulent and that any time Able or other scientists at NIT referenced Able's research in any grant application to the National Institutes of Health (NIH), those scientists violated the civil False Claims Act, 31 U.S.C. §§3729 et seq. As you know, the False Claims Act permits the government to recover treble the amount of money paid to any person or institution that knowingly submits false information to obtain federal funds.

The basic issue in this case is whether Able's research was fraudulent. In developing its defense to the government's case, NIT asked one of its other scientists, Dr. Martin Brown, to try to repeat Able's research. Brown was not involved in the case and did not know the other scientists. Brown succeeded in repeating Able's research, and we believe that Brown's research will help us prove that everything Able did was proper scientifically. Unfortunately, Brown's entire laboratory operates under a federal contract from the Department of Energy (DoE). All of his equipment is actually owned by the government, and all of the scientists in his laboratory are paid by the DoE. A number of Brown's scientists helped him replicate Able's earlier research.

On January 14, 1994, the government sought leave to amend its original complaint to join Brown as a new defendant. In the proposed amended complaint, the government asserts that Brown violated the False Claims Act because he used federal property and federal funds to help NIT defend against the original complaint. The government alleges that it is improper to use federal funds under a government contract to defend against a complaint brought by the government.

Although we have meritorious defenses to the government's claims against Brown, we would prefer to try the two cases separately. Accordingly, we anticipate opposing the government's motion to amend its complaint. Please prepare a memorandum discussing the best arguments that we should use in opposing the government's motion for leave to amend.

Note that Able left NIT in 1984 and is now a professor at Southern Technical Institute. Southern Technical is also a party defendant because Able submitted grant applications while an employee of Southern referencing the problematic research he performed while at NIT. The other individual defendants are still researchers at NIT. The original action was filed in U.S. District Court in Maryland because that is where NIH is located and that is where the NIH grant applications were submitted. However, Brown's contract issued out of the DoE office in our state, which, as you know, is about 2,000 miles from Maryland.

Please stop by to pick up the case file, which contains more detailed information on the case. If you need additional information, please give me a call.

MEMORANDUM

TO: David Berg

FROM: Lawrence Goldman

SUBJECT: *United States v. Nevada Institute of Technology et al.*, Civ. No. 123-90-B (D. Md.)

DATE: January 21, 1994

This memorandum responds to your request of January 17 to discuss the best arguments that we might make in opposing the government's motion seeking leave to amend its False Claims Act complaint against Nevada Institute of Technology, four of its current faculty, and one former faculty member, Mark Able.

Facts

On February 14, 1990, the United States instituted a civil False Claims Act action against Nevada Institute of Technology, Southern Technical Institute, Mark Able, Lawrence Charles, Gary Davis, Edith Edwards, and Norris Fink. In the complaint, the government alleges that between 1981 and 1983, Able, while a research fellow at Nevada Institute of Technology, fabricated research data and reported those data in a series of four articles published in prestigious scientific journals. The articles were co-authored by Charles, Davis, Edwards, and Fink, all of whom were more senior researchers at NIT. The complaint goes on to allege that from 1982 to 1989, Charles, Davis, Edwards, and Fink submitted numerous grant applications to the National Institutes of Health and in those applications they referenced the work they had done with Able. The government contends that each of the four scientists should have known that Able's research was fraudulent and that by referencing Able's research in their grant applications they violated the False Claims Act.

In 1984, Able became a member of the Southern faculty and submitted various grant applications in which he referenced his allegedly fraudulent work while at NIT. Accordingly, Southern has also been named as a defendant.

In 1991, while discovery was underway, administrators at NIT asked Dr. Brown to attempt to replicate Able's experiments that the government contends were fraudulent. Brown's research and his entire laboratory are supported by a research contract from the Department of Energy. Brown succeeded in replicating all of Able's research.

Discovery closed on March 1, 1993. On June 1, 1993, all of the defendants filed a motion for summary judgment. That motion relied heavily on the fact that Brown had succeeded in replicating Able's research, and therefore, Able's research could not have been fraudulent. That motion is still pending.

On January 14, 1994, the government filed a motion pursuant to Fed. R. Civ. P. 15(a) for leave to amend its complaint to add a seventh count. The new count alleges that Brown and NIT violated the False Claims Act by using Department of Energy research money to defend against a suit instituted by the government. In its motion, the government contends that it did not learn that Brown was fully funded by a DoE contract until it completed an internal investigation in November 1993. At this point, we have no reason to doubt the accuracy of the government's contention. However, the government certainly could have learned about it earlier had it taken a more complete deposition of Brown.

Issues

1. Does Fed. R. Civ. P. 20 prevent the government from joining Brown as a party defendant?
2. Would the prejudice to the existing defendants caused by amending the complaint outweigh the prejudice to the government if its motion were to be denied?
3. Is venue proper in Maryland for the new claim against Brown?

Short Answer

A strong argument can be made that joining Brown in the current lawsuit would be inconsistent with Fed. R. Civ. P. 20, which precludes a plaintiff from joining various defendants in the same action unless (1) the claim against all the defendants arose out of the same transaction and (2) there is an issue of either fact or law common to all of the defendants. Although there is some uncertainty in the existing case law regarding how Rule 20 should be applied in a case such as this, I believe that our chances of prevailing on this argument are good. I also believe that a strong argument can be made that prejudice to the existing defendants if the motion is granted would outweigh the prejudice to the government if its motion is denied. As a general proposition, however, courts have liberally granted leave to amend. Finally, I believe that venue would be proper with regard to Brown if leave to amend were granted. Under the False Claims Act, venue is proper with regard to all defendants, if it is proper with regard to any one defendant. Here, the court has already held that venue is proper in Maryland for the original defendants. I believe we should still discuss the venue issue in our memorandum to indicate to the court how inconvenient it would be to litigate the claim against Brown in Maryland. This may help further bolster our other two arguments.

Analysis

I. DOES FED. R. CIV. P. 20 PREVENT THE GOVERNMENT FROM JOINING BROWN AS A PARTY DEFENDANT?

Fed. R. Civ. P. 20(a), which deals with joinder of parties, provides, in pertinent part, that a plaintiff may join in one action all persons as defendants

> if there is asserted against them jointly, severally, or in the alternative, any right to relief in respect of or arising out of the same transaction, occurrence, or series of transactions or occurrences and if any question of law or fact common to all defendants will arise in the action.

In essence, Rule 20(a) has two requirements that must be satisfied for all the defendants and all plaintiffs: (1) the transaction or occurrence test, and (2) the commonality test. Neither test would be satisfied if the complaint were amended to add Brown.

A. Transaction or Occurrence Test

To satisfy the transaction or occurrence test, a plaintiff's right to relief must arise out of the same transaction or series of transactions. In *Papagiannis v. Pontikis,* 108 F.R.D. 177 (N.D. Ill. 1985), for example, the defendants fraudulently induced two plaintiffs to purchase oil well leaseholds. The defendants used the same scheme to defraud each plaintiff. However, each plaintiff purchased a different oil well. The court concluded that the two plaintiffs could not be joined in the same lawsuit because each plaintiff's right to relief arose out of a different contract, i.e., transaction. *See Paine, Webber, Jackson & Curtis, Inc. v. Merrill Lynch, Pierce, Fenner & Smith, Inc.,* 564 F. Supp. 1358 (D. Del. 1983) (holding that joinder of two parties was improper even though both were alleged to have infringed the same patent); *Saval v. BL Ltd.,* 710 F.2d 1027 (4th Cir. 1983) (holding that common allegations of fraud and breaches of warranty do not satisfy the transaction or occurrence test).

Correspondingly, in *Trail Realty v. Beckett,* 462 F.2d 396 (10th Cir. 1972), plaintiff entered into a contract to purchase land from the defendant. The contract was contingent on the plaintiff's obtaining financing from a bank. When the plaintiff failed to obtain the necessary bank financing, the defendant withdrew its offer to sell the property. Plaintiff instituted a specific performance action against the defendant to force him to sell the land. Later, the plaintiff learned that the president of the bank that refused to provide the financing had purchased the property from the defendant. Plaintiff sought to amend his complaint to join the bank and its president, claiming that they had breached their fiduciary obligation and that the only reason they had refused to loan the money was that the bank president wanted the property. The trial court denied the motion to amend and on appeal the Tenth Circuit affirmed, noting that the plaintiff's right to relief against the original landowner, on the one hand, and the bank and its president, on the other hand, arose out of different transactions. *See Wilkinson v. Hamel*, 381 F. Supp. 766 (W.D. Va. 1974) (denying plaintiff leave to join two new defendants, when the cause of action against the original defendants arose four years before his cause of action against the new defendants).

Based on the express language of Fed. R. Civ. P. 20(a) and the above case law, it would appear that the government will not be able to satisfy the transaction or occurrence test. The six counts in the original complaint arose out of NIH grant applications submitted between 1982 and 1989. To prevail on those counts, the government must prove that Able's research was fraudulent. The new count arose in 1991 under a Department of Energy contract. That count does not depend on whether Able's research was fraudulent.

The government will likely argue that the above cases can be distinguished factually from this case. In particular, in each of those cases a party attempted to join new parties that were in no way involved in the original transaction. In our case, though, one of the parties in the proposed count VII, NIT, is already a party defendant. Under Fed. R. Civ. P. 18, a plaintiff can join as many claims as it wishes against a defendant. Thus, amending the complaint to allege a new claim against NIT would be entirely consistent with both Fed. R. Civ. P. 18 and 20. In *Kaminsky v. Abrams*, 41 F.R.D. 168 (S.D.N.Y. 1966), the court permitted a plaintiff to amend his complaint to add a new cause of action against some of the original defendants and against new defendants. In that respect, *Kaminsky* is factually similar to our case. However, the court gave no rationale for its decision, and the joinder permitted in *Kaminsky* would appear to be inconsistent with the language of Fed. R. Civ. P. 20, which requires that there must be at least one transaction or occurrence linking all of the defendants. Here, if the complaint were to be amended there would be no single transaction linking all of the defendants.

B. Commonality Test

The government must not only be able to satisfy the transaction or occurrence test, but also the commonality test. Under the commonality test, the government must allege issues of fact or law common to *all* defendants. The government may argue that there is a common issue of law linking all the counts, namely the False Claims Act. However, courts have consistently held that alleged violations of the same statute are not sufficient to satisfy the commonality test. *See Kenvin v. Newburger, Loeb & Comp.*, 37 F.R.D. 475 (S.D.N.Y. 1965).

The issues of law raised in Count VII against Brown are distinct from those raised in Counts I-VI against the other defendants. In particular, the government's claims in Count I-VI involve allegations of "scientific misconduct." Government's Opposition to Defendants' Motion for Summary Judgment 1 (June 20, 1993). In contrast, its claim against Brown has nothing to do with scientific misconduct or scientific norms. Instead, its action against Brown arises under the Federal Acquisition Regulations, the rules that govern how an institution bills the government for work performed under a government contract.

The issues of fact raised by the new count have nothing to do with those raised in the original complaint. The original complaint relates solely to NIH grant applications submitted between 1982 and 1989. The new count relates to the administration of a DoE contract in 1991. The original complaint depends on the validity of Able's original research conducted in the early 1980s. The outcome of the new count does not depend on the validity of Able's earlier research and, indeed, has nothing to do with the validity of that research.

In short, it would appear that the government will be unable to satisfy the commonality test.

II. WOULD THE PREJUDICE TO THE EXISTING DEFENDANTS CAUSED BY AMENDING THE COMPLAINT OUTWEIGH THE PREJUDICE TO THE GOVERNMENT IF ITS MOTION IS DENIED?

It is by now axiomatic that leave to amend should be liberally granted. *See Foman v. Davis,* 371 U.S. 178, 182 (1962). Thus, in deciding whether to permit a plaintiff to amend his or her complaint, a court should focus "on prejudice or futility or bad faith as the only legitimate concerns in denying leave to amend since only these truly relate to protection of the judicial system or other litigants." *Davis v. Piper Aircraft Corp.,* 615 F.2d 606, 613 (4th Cir. 1980). Thus, in *Island Creek Coal Comp. v. Lake Shore, Inc.,* 832 F.2d 274 (1987), the Fourth Circuit found that the trial court abused its discretion in denying plaintiff's motion to amend where the facts giving rise to the amendment had only been discovered three months before.

Although leave to amend is liberally granted, it is well settled that a court may properly deny a motion to amend when it would "unduly prejudice the nonmovant." *Deasy v. Hill,* 833 F.2d 38, 40 (4th Cir. 1987). *See Davis v. Piper Aircraft Corp.,* 615 F.2d at 613 ("[P]rejudice resulting to the opponent by a grant of leave to amend is reason sufficient to deny amendment"). Here, if the government's complaint were amended to add the new count, it would delay resolution of the other six counts against the original defendants. Interestingly, the government has taken the position in other settings that delay in resolving a case of scientific misconduct can severely prejudice the scientists who have been charged with misconduct. *See* 50 C.F.R. Part 50; Declaration of Jules Hallum, Director of the Office of Scientific Integrity, submitted in

McCutchen v. United States Department of Health and Human Services, Nos. 92-5372, 92-5389 (D.C. Cir. appeal pending) (pages 67, 75-76, J.A. on appeal, attached). The National Academy of Sciences has also expressly recommended that misconduct allegations should be handled with dispatch. *See* National Academy of Sciences, Responsible Science 149 (1992). In short, permitting the government to amend this complaint would arguably undermine the government's policy of swiftly resolving misconduct allegations.

While we expect that the government will rely heavily on *Island Creek*, the leading Fourth Circuit case dealing with amending complaints, that case is distinguishable from ours. Specifically, in *Island Creek* the court reversed in part because the plaintiff could only have brought its new cause of action as part of the original complaint. Here, in contrast, there is nothing that would foreclose the government from filing a separate action against NIT and Brown. Thus, the government would not be prejudiced if its motion is denied. The original defendants, though, would be prejudiced by the delay occasioned by the amendment.

III. IS VENUE PROPER IN MARYLAND FOR THE NEW CLAIM AGAINST BROWN?

As noted above, the venue provision of the False Claims Act is expansive and provides as follows:

> Any action under section 3730 [the False Claims Act] may be brought in any judicial district in which the defendant or in the case of multiple defendants, any one defendant can be found, resides, transacts business, or in which any act proscribed by section 3729 occurred.

31 U.S.C. §3732.

Soon after the government instituted this proceeding, NIT and Southern each moved to change venue on two grounds. First, we argued that venue was improper, and second, even if proper, venue would be more convenient in Nevada than in Maryland. The court, in denying the motion, noted that the transactions arose in Maryland, because the grant applications were submitted to the NIH, which is located in Maryland. The court also noted that all of the grant applications are stored at NIH and that many of the witnesses, including NIH scientists, are located in Maryland. Since the court has already held that venue is proper in Maryland for the original defendants, it would be proper under the above section for any additional defendants who may be added.

Nonetheless, I recommend discussing the inconvenience of venue in Maryland with regard to Brown as a way of highlighting the differences between the original complaint and the new count. Specifically, none of the factors that the court used in deciding that venue was proper and convenient for the original defendants are present with respect to Brown. The office of the Department of Energy that awarded the contract is not located in Maryland, none of the documents relevant to the claim against Brown is in Maryland, and none of the witnesses is located in Maryland.

MEMORANDUM

TO: Jack Armstrong
FROM: Harvey Gold
DATE: March 4, 1986
RE: Disqualification of Norris Carter, Plaintiffs' Counsel in *Parkman et al. v. Doberman, Inc.*, Civil No. 84-156 WAI (D. Del., filed January 3, 1985)

Introduction

This memorandum examines whether we should move to disqualify plaintiffs' counsel, Mr. Carter, from participating in litigation pending against our client, Doberman, Inc., in the United States District Court, Delaware.

As more fully outlined below, plaintiffs, a group of Delaware businessmen, instituted an action for breach of contract against Doberman, Inc. Plaintiffs are represented by Norris Carter, a local attorney and entrepreneur. You have asked me to evaluate the possibility of disqualifying Carter because of his intimate involvement in the contract negotiations that gave rise to the pending litigation. Because of that involvement it is likely that either plaintiffs or defendant will call Carter as a witness. Carter is also an individual plaintiff in the action. This complicates the analysis and may make it difficult, under the "advocate-witness" rule, to completely disqualify him from participating in the litigation.

On July 17, 1985, plaintiffs, six businessmen from Dover, Delaware, approached our client, a New Jersey Corporation whose business is waste management disposal, and offered to sell our client their interest in certain waste disposal sites situated in the northeast corridor of the United States. Because of the magnitude of the transaction, negotiations were complex and lengthy. Numerous issues were involved, including the safety of the facilities, the nature of the waste products stored at the various sites, and the price to be paid. As part of the negotiations, the parties agreed that they needed to commission an environmental study to determine the amount of various chemicals that each of the sites could safely accommodate. They would then use the results of the studies to fix the fair market value of each of the sites. The parties agreed that the cost of the studies would be borne by Doberman, if it purchased the sites.

Soon after that, the plaintiffs arranged to have the studies undertaken at a cost of $75,000. After the studies were completed, Doberman offered to purchase the sites for $250,000, an amount significantly less than the $2.5 million that the plaintiffs had hoped to receive. Plaintiffs rejected the offer and asked to be reimbursed for the cost of the studies. Doberman refused, arguing that it was only obligated to reimburse plaintiffs if it purchased the sites, and because plaintiffs had rejected its offer, it was not obligated to reimburse them. Plaintiffs maintain that during the course of the negotiations, Doberman indicated that if the results of the studies were satisfactory it would make a good faith offer. Plaintiffs also maintain that although the results of the studies were satisfactory, Doberman did not make an offer in good faith. Doberman rejects the contention that it reached such an understanding with plaintiffs during the negotiations and adheres to its position that its obligation to pay for the studies was contingent on its actually purchasing the sites.

Norris Carter, one of the plaintiffs, was present along with the other plaintiffs during the negotiations, and he actively participated in them. It is our understanding that the plaintiffs will corroborate each other. It is also our understanding that the corporation that conducted the environmental studies is owned by Carter and two of the other plaintiffs, and it is possible that the cost of the studies may have been artificially inflated.

Issues

1. What standards should be used in determining whether an attorney who is also a potential witness should be disqualified from participating in the trial?
2. If an attorney ought to be disqualified, would the attorney's pro se status affect the disqualification?
3. Can a client waive the disqualification rule?

Legal Standard

The applicable provisions of the American Bar Association's Model Code of Professional Responsibility state:

DR 5-101   *Refusing Employment When the Interests of the Lawyer May Impair His Independent Professional Judgment.* . . .

(B) A lawyer shall not accept employment in contemplated or pending litigation if he knows or it is obvious that he or a lawyer in his firm ought to be called as a witness, except that he or a lawyer in his firm may testify:

   (1) If the testimony will relate solely to an uncontested matter.

   (2) If the testimony will relate solely to a matter of formality and there is no reason to believe that substantial evidence will be offered in opposition to the testimony.

(3) If the testimony will relate solely to the nature and value of legal services rendered in the case by the lawyer or his firm to the client.

(4) As to any matter, if refusal would work a substantial hardship on the client because of the distinctive value of the lawyer or his firm as counsel in the particular case.

DR 5-102   *Withdrawal as Counsel When the Lawyer Becomes a Witness.*

(A) If, after undertaking employment in contemplated or pending litigation, a lawyer learns or it is obvious that he or a lawyer in his firm ought to be called as a witness on behalf of his client, he shall withdraw from the conduct of the trial and his firm, if any, shall not continue representation in the trial, except that he may continue the representation and he or a lawyer in his firm may testify in the circumstances enumerated in DR 5-101(B)(1) through (4).

(B) If, after undertaking employment in contemplated or pending litigation, a lawyer learns or it is obvious that he or a lawyer in his firm may be called as a witness other than on behalf of his client, he may continue the representation until it is apparent that his testimony is or may be prejudicial to his client.

Discussion

I. AN ATTORNEY MUST BE DISQUALIFIED IF (1) THE ATTORNEY OUGHT TO BE CALLED AS A WITNESS ON BEHALF OF HIS OR HER CLIENT OR (2) THE ATTORNEY'S TESTIMONY WOULD PREJUDICE HIS OR HER CLIENT.

The Model Code of Professional Responsibility (Code) delineates two situations in which an attorney is obligated to withdraw from pending litigation. First, the attorney is obligated to withdraw from conducting a trial if the attorney "ought" to be called as a witness on behalf of his or her client. *See* DR 5-102(A). Second, the attorney is obligated to withdraw if the attorney learns, or it is obvious, that he or she will be called as a witness by another party and that the attorney's testimony may prejudice his or her client. *See* DR 5-102(B). Although DR 5-102 addresses situations in which the attorney has already been retained, a parallel provision, DR 5-101, addresses the case in which the attorney has not as yet been retained. Note that the two disciplinary rules differ slightly. Under DR 5-101(B), an attorney is counseled to refuse to represent a client in contemplated or pending litigation if the attorney "ought to be called as a witness." In contrast, under DR 5-102(A) the attorney should withdraw only if the attorney "ought to be called as a witness on *behalf of his client.*" (Emphasis supplied.) This distinction between the two disciplinary rules, although of theoretical interest, is of no real significance. As a practical matter all reported cases have involved attorneys who were already representing the client. Courts have uniformly relied on the language of DR 5-102 in deciding whether an attorney should be disqualified, ignoring the broader language of DR 5-101.1

A. *Standards for Ascertaining When an Attorney "Ought" to Be Called to Testify on Behalf of His or Her Client.*

Before we move to disqualify Carter, we must determine whether he "ought" to be called to testify on behalf of his clients. Courts in various jurisdictions have formulated a variety of different tests for deciding whether an attorney ought to be called as a witness. Unfortunately, the Third Circuit has adopted the most restrictive test. In *Universal Athletic Sales Co. v. American Gym, Recreational & Athletic Corp.*, 546 F.2d 530, 539 n.21 (3d Cir. 1976), cert. denied, 430 U.S. 984 (1977), the court declared that an attorney ought to be called as a witness only when the attorney has "crucial information in his possession which must be divulged."

Other courts have given the word "ought" a broader meaning. The most liberal expression of the rule appears in *MacArthur v. Bank of New York*, 524 F. Supp. 1205 (S.D.N.Y. 1981). There Judge Sofaer stated: "defendant's argument that McNicol's testimony would merely corroborate other testimony, even if accurate, is unavailing. The test is whether the attorney's testimony could be *significantly useful* to his client; if so, he ought to be called." Id. at 1208-1209 (emphasis added). Judge Sofaer went on to conclude that, since "independent counsel would seem likely to call McNicol, both to supply his own account of the events in question (even if corroborative) and to prevent the jury from speculating about his absence," he was a witness who ought to be called. Id. The Sixth Circuit has also looked to what independent counsel would do to answer the question of whether a witness ought to be called. In *General Mill Supply Co. v. SCA Services*, 697 F.2d 704, 708 (6th Cir. 1982), the court stated, "we do not think it at all likely that any independent counsel for General Mill would feel safe in letting the case go to submission, without use of the material divulged in the affidavit [of General Mill's attorney]."

The Second Circuit also does not require testimony to be "crucial" in order to conclude that a witness ought to be called. In *J.P. Foley & Co. v. Vanderbilt*, 523 F.2d 1357 (2d Cir. 1975), the court ruled that because the attorney's testimony was "necessary" to his client's case he "ought" to appear as a witness.

Finally, the California Supreme Court has established what appears to be the only test that balances a number of factors to determine whether an attorney ought to be called as a witness.

Whether an attorney ought to testify ordinarily is a discretionary determination based on the court's considered evaluation of all pertinent factors including, inter alia, the significance of the matters to which he might testify, the weight his testimony might have in resolving such matters, and the availability of other witnesses or documentary evidence by which these matters may be independently established.

Comden v. Superior Court, 20 Cal. 3d 906, 913, 576 P.2d 571, 574, 145 Cal. Rptr. 9, 12 (1978).

Assuming that the court would apply the *Universal Athletic Sales* test, which requires testimony to be crucial in order for the court to conclude that a witness ought to be called, it is important to focus on the possible nature of Carter's testimony. On the issue of liability, Carter's testimony would probably be only corroborative. Each of the other five plaintiffs is in a position to testify about the course of the negotiations and to provide the finder of fact with pertinent evidence bearing on plaintiffs' claim. Because Carter's testimony would be only corroborative, it is unlikely that a court following the Third Circuit rule would find his testimony crucial to his client's case.

Indeed, even under the more liberal tests discussed above, a court might be reluctant to disqualify Carter. For instance, under the so-called independent counsel test used by the court in *MacArthur*, the court focuses on the significance of the attorney's testimony and on what a "detached" attorney would do under similar circumstances. Carter's testimony would merely corroborate that of five other witnesses; therefore it is unlikely that it would prove significant, and hence, it is unlikely that a detached attorney would call him as a witness. Five friendly witnesses testifying about the same events are more than enough. Indeed, it is perilous to call too many witnesses to testify about the same set of events. As most attorneys well know, the more eye witnesses that are called the more likely it is that discrepancies will arise. In short, the optimum trial strategy develops a sound and credible case while minimizing the likelihood of contradiction. Under such a strategy a detached attorney would probably call two or three plaintiffs to testify in their case in chief and reserve the others, excluding Carter, to testify in rebuttal.

Even if it develops in the course of litigation that Carter ought to testify and therefore could be disqualified under the "ought" rule, it is doubtful that a district court in the Third Circuit actually would disqualify him. As a practical matter, some courts defer to the attorney's judgment regarding whether he or she should in fact testify. The Third Circuit is a leader in deferring to an attorney's judgment about whether he or she is a necessary witness. *See Kroungold v. Triester*, 521 F.2d 763, 766 (3d Cir. 1975); *Beaver Falls Thrift Corp. v. Commercial Credit Business Loans*, 563 F. Supp. 68, 71 (W.D. Pa. 1983) ("It is not the job of this Court to second-guess the decision of plaintiff's counsel where, as here, it is not obvious that [the attorney] ought to be called as a witness and there is no indication that the decision not to call him will result in prejudice to the client"); *Zions First National Bank, N.A. v. United Health Clubs*, 503 F. Supp. 138, 141 (E.D. Pa. 1981) ("United is certainly in the best position to know whether [its attorney's] testimony is necessary to its case, and Zions has not made any specific allegations which cast doubt on United's position that it will have no need for his testimony"); *J. D. Pflaumer, Inc. v. United States Department of Justice*, 465 F. Supp. 746, 748 (E.D. Pa. 1979) ("[The] attorney and his client are in the best position to determine whether his testimony is in fact indispensable"). *See also Borman v. Borman,* 393 N.E.2d 847 (Mass. 1979) (court should defer to the counsel's decision that he not testify unless it is "obviously contrary" to the client's best interest).

Despite these precedents calling for trial judges to defer to the attorney's judgment regarding whether he or she should testify, one Third Circuit district court appears to be less restrained. "I harbor sincere doubts, however, whether the strictures of DR 5-102(A) may be avoided by the assertion that an attorney will not and need not testify on behalf of his client. This rule calls for disqualification where the attorney ought to testify, not where he will testify." *Commercial Credit Business Loans v. Martin,* No. 76-812, slip op. at 2 n.2 (E.D. Pa. June 11, 1984).

There is a great deal of law to support the court's doubts, though it is not from the Third Circuit. Numerous cases state that it is inappropriate to defer to the attorney's judgment in deciding the issue of disqualification under DR 5-101(B) or DR 5-102(A). *See, e.g., General Mill Supply Co. v. MacArthur Services,* 637 F.2d 704, 708 (6th Cir. 1982); *MacArthur v. Bank of New York,* 524 F. Supp. 1205, 1208 (S.D.N.Y. 1981) ("attorneys anxious to participate in the litigation might fail to step aside and testify even if their testimony could help the client; other attorneys might fail to step aside and testify because the client insists upon their continued representation"). *See also* ABA Model Code of Professional Responsibility, Ethical Consideration 5-10 ("Doubts should be resolved in favor of the lawyer testifying and against his becoming or continuing as an advocate").

In conclusion, it is unlikely that a motion to disqualify Carter on the grounds that he ought to testify would be successful. First, as a matter of law, the "ought" test cannot be satisfied because Carter's testimony would be merely corroborative of the testimony of five other witnesses. Second, courts in the Third Circuit have been reluctant to vigorously apply the disciplinary rule and instead have most often relied on the attorney's judgment about whether he or she should testify.

B. Standards to Be Used in Ascertaining Whether an Attorney's Testimony Would Be Prejudicial to His or Her Clients.

Carter could also be disqualified from acting as attorney for the other plaintiffs under the standards of DR 5-102(B). If it is likely that the defendants would call him to the stand and elicit testimony that "is or may be prejudicial" to Carter's clients, DR 5-102(B) requires that he be disqualified. Although there is relatively little case law under this rule, the law that does exist uniformly places a heavy burden on the movant. *See, e.g., Kroungold v. Triester,* 521 F.2d 763, 766 (3d Cir. 1975); *Zions First National Bank, N.A. v. United Health Clubs,* 565 F. Supp. 138, 140 (E.D. Pa. 1981). Courts are loath to allow counsel to disqualify opponents by calling them as witnesses.

Nevertheless, when it has been demonstrated that an attorney's testimony would be likely to be prejudicial to his or her client, courts have been quick to disqualify the attorney. *Freeman v. Kulicke & Soffa Industries*, 449 F. Supp. 974, 978 (E.D. Pa. 1978). One factor that courts have used in deciding whether an attorney's testimony would prove prejudicial is the likelihood that the attorney's credibility will be questioned during the examination. Courts have also focused on whether the attorney's testimony would contradict the testimony of other favorable witnesses or undercut the client's case. Id.

Here, there is a possibility that Carter's testimony, at least on the issue of damages, would prove prejudicial to his client's case. As noted above, Carter is part owner of the company that performed the favorable environmental studies. Although the accuracy of those studies is not in dispute, defendant is prepared to prove that the costs of those studies were unreasonably high and even inflated. Defendant may well call Carter to testify about the company's pricing policies and its profit margins. If the costs of those studies were in fact inflated, and Carter were to testify truthfully, then his testimony would prejudice his clients' damage claim. Moreover, his testimony, especially if it is developed through depositions, could also open him to suit by some of his current clients. If Carter is to be disqualified, the possibility that his testimony would be prejudicial to his clients appears to provide the only viable theory. Before this can be fully evaluated, however, we must have additional information about his potential testimony.

II. An Attorney's Pro Se Status May Not Necessarily Bar Him From Being Disqualified.

Even if Carter ought to be called, or if his testimony might prejudice his clients, there still exists a major roadblock in moving to disqualify him. Carter is a plaintiff in this action and under normal circumstances would be entitled at least to represent himself. In *O'Neil v. Bergan*, 452 A.2d 337, 344-345 (D.C. 1982), the court stated that when an attorney and the attorney's firm represent themselves, they have "not accepted 'employment' within the meaning of DR 5-101(B)," and hence, the disciplinary rule is not applicable. The rule does, however, still apply to Carter's representation of the other clients. In *Bottarc v. Hatton Associates*, 680 F.2d 895 (2d Cir. 1982), the court was slightly more restrained in outlining the permissible conduct of an attorney-litigant who ought to be called as a witness. *Bottarc* allowed the attorney to testify, to have his law firm represent him, and to assist in pretrial proceedings, so long as he was not the "advocate" from his firm. Thus, even under this restrictive approach, Carter's firm could remain in the case so long as Carter did not participate as an advocate. *See also Norman Norell, Inc. v. Federated Department Stores*, 450 F. Supp. 127 (S.D.N.Y. 1978) (attorney-witness allowed to participate in pretrial preparation).

We might argue against even this type of limited participation, however, based on *General Mill Supply Co. v. SCA Services*, 697 F.2d 704, 712 (6th Cir. 1982). In that case the court disqualified an advocate-witness who was also "in a realistic and not just a figurative sense, a party in interest."

> In these days of crowded dockets, settlement of civil suits, like plea bargains in criminal cases, are much desired by courts, which cannot force them. It is part of the duty an attorney owes the court to consider carefully all opportunities of settlement and report on them objectively to the client, with a fair and objective recommendation whether acceptance would be in the client's interest. This duty, an attorney in Mr. Garratt's situation would have extraordinary difficulty in performing.
>
> Courts likewise hope the counsel in civil cases will cooperate in discovery so it can proceed without day to day supervision by the court. . . . Hope for this from an attorney in Mr. Garratt's position would be a faint hope indeed.

These same settlement and discovery arguments can be made regarding Carter as advocate, witness, and litigant.

In short, courts appear to be split on how an attorney's pro se status affects his or her ability to participate in litigation when under normal circumstances the attorney would have been disqualified. As noted above, one court has held that pro se status insulates an attorney from DR 5-102, but the majority of courts have held that the disciplinary rule is applicable even when an attorney is a party to the proceedings. Even those courts have split on the issue of whether total disqualification is warranted.

Although the uncertainty in the law makes a definitive conclusion difficult, it appears that Carter's pro se status would insulate him from being totally disqualified. It is likely that Carter would be precluded from actively participating in the trial or from representing the other plaintiffs, but he would be permitted to assist in preparing for trial.

III. CLIENT MAY NOT WAIVE THE DISQUALIFICATION RULE.

Finally, the question remains whether a client may consent to his or her attorney's being both an advocate and a witness. There is limited authority for the proposition that a client should be able to consent to such a potential conflict of interest. *See, e.g.,* Note, The Advocate-Witness Rule: If Z, then X, but Why?, 53 N.Y.U.L. Rev. 1365 (1977). However, courts have uniformly rejected this proposition. In *Rosen v. NLRB,* 735 F.2d 564, 574-575 (D.C. Cir. 1984), the court stated:

> DR 5-102(A), unlike other rules in the Code of Professional Responsibility, . . . makes no provision for client waiver of its application. Moreover, part of the underlying rationale for the rule, namely that a lawyer's serving in a dual role of witness and advocate is unseemly, is directed at the *protection of the public interest in continued respect for the legal profession rather than any waivable private interest.* (Emphasis added.)

See also MacArthur v. Bank of New York, 524 F. Supp. 1205, 1209 (S.D.N.Y. 1981) ("Nor may the client waive the rule's protection by promising not to call the attorney as a witness. The ostensible paternalism of disregarding such waivers is justified by the circumstances in which the problem arises"); *Freeman v. Kulicke & Soffa Industries*, 449 F. Supp. 974, 978 (E.D. Pa. 1978) ("where a movant demonstrates that a lawyer's (or a firm member's) testimony will or is substantially likely to prejudice his or her client's case, the disciplinary rule is breached and our rules of court, which are concerned directly with the standards of the bar and only indirectly with the interests of litigants, are violated").

In short, the purpose of the rule is to preserve the distinction between advocacy, which is based on reason and is subject to objective evaluation, and testimony, which is based on the witness's moral qualities and is evaluated in terms of individual credibility. Therefore, client consent is irrelevant.[1]

Conclusion

A motion to disqualify counsel under the advocate-witness rule is dependent on the facts, and thus Carter's probable testimony must be flushed out. Based on current information, it is unlikely that a Third Circuit court would find that Carter ought to testify. Our ability to successfully move to disqualify appears significantly greater under the prejudice test. If Carter ought to testify on behalf of his clients or might testify prejudicially to his clients, it might still be possible to move to limit his participation to pro se representation. Moreover, it is possible that even his pro se representation could be barred, if not totally, then at least from trial advocacy.

---

1. None of the exceptions to DR 5-101(B) or DR 5-102(A) is applicable to this situation. The first three exceptions: uncontested matters, matters of formality, and the nature and value of legal services are clearly inapposite. A quick review of the case law under the fourth "substantial hardship" exception shows similar inapplicability as it relates to the "distinctive value" of Carter's services. *See, e.g.,* General Mill Supply Co. v. SCA Services, 697 F.2d 704, 713-715 (6th Cir. 1982) ("The hardship situation covered by subparagraph (4) is one where the lawyer-client team come unexpectedly upon a disqualification situation, against which they neither actually did nor could have safeguarded themselves. We do not think it was meant for a case where a possible dilemma was visible years before it arose, yet the parties went right on increasing the helpless dependence of client upon lawyer"); MacArthur v. Bank of New York, 524 F. Supp. at 1210 ("familiarity . . . with the client's case is not sufficient to permit an exception to the rule"); American Bar Foundation, Annotated Code of Professional Responsibility 218 (Maru ed. 1979) and cases discussed therein.

14

Writing a Memorandum of Points and Authorities

What Is a Memorandum of Points and Authorities?

A *memorandum of points and authorities*, as opposed to an intraoffice memorandum, is a persuasive document that is filed with a trial court. Most trial courts, for example, require a party to submit a memorandum of points and authorities whenever the party files a motion, for example, a motion to dismiss, a motion for summary judgment, or a motion for leave to amend a complaint. The memorandum is designed to convince the court that the party's motion should be granted. The party against whom that motion is filed is then given an opportunity to file a memorandum of points and authorities opposing the motion.

There is no universal format for a memorandum of points and authorities. Trial courts in each jurisdiction have their own rules governing memoranda submitted with motions. For example, many trial courts limit the number of pages that you may write, and in some jurisdictions, if the document exceeds 25 pages, it must contain a table of contents and table of authorities (a list of the cases, statutes, and other references cited in the memo). Therefore, before writing a memorandum of points and authorities, you should consult the local rules of the court.

In this chapter we present and discuss a sample memorandum of points and authorities that was crafted from the intraoffice memorandum presented in the previous chapter. By presenting both documents, we hope to highlight the differences between an informative document and a persuasive document.

B Sample Memorandum of Points and Authorities

As you will recall, the sample intraoffice memorandum in *United States v. Nevada Institute of Technology* discussed various arguments that the defendants could marshal in opposing the plaintiff's motion to amend its complaint. The attorney who drafted that intraoffice memorandum was then asked by the senior lawyer in the firm to transform his memo into a memorandum of points and authorities. The result of that effort is set out below. Next to each section of the memorandum, we discuss how and why the attorney drafted that section of the memorandum the way he did.

IN THE UNITED STATES DISTRICT COURT FOR THE DISTRICT OF MARYLAND

United States of America,	)	
	)	
Plaintiff,	)	
	)	
vs.	)	Civil No.
	)	123-90-B
Nevada Institute of	)	
Technology et al.,	)	
	)	
	)	
Defendants.	)	

Defendants' Memorandum in Opposition to Plaintiff's Motion to File Second Amended Complaint

Introduction

Plaintiff is seeking to amend its False Claims Act complaint four years after filing its original complaint, nine months after discovery has closed, and six months after dispositive motions have been filed, to join a new defendant, Dr. Martin Brown, and a new claim unrelated to those in its first amended complaint. Specifically, in the first amended complaint, Plaintiff contended that research funded by the National Institutes of Health ("NIH") and conducted by Mark Able at the Brain Tumor

In our opinion, the most important part of a memorandum of points and authorities is its introduction. The introduction sets the tone of the memo and outlines the legal arguments. It should be short, interesting, easy to understand, and convincing. The first sentence of the introduction conveys three ideas that form the backbone of the rest of the memo: (1) the plaintiff has waited a long time to amend the complaint; (2) the case is about ready for trial; and (3) the amendment would

Research Center ("BTRC") at Nevada Institute of Technology ("NIT") in the early 1980s had been incorrectly performed and that defendants violated the False Claims Act each time they referenced any of Able's results in subsequent grant applications submitted to NIH from 1982 through 1989. Plaintiff now seeks leave to join Brown.[1] Plaintiff does not claim that Brown was in any way involved in conducting or supervising Able's research. Plaintiff does not claim that Brown submitted grant applications referencing Able's research. Plaintiff does not claim that Brown's research was improperly performed. Nor does Plaintiff claim that Brown received funding from NIH. Instead, Plaintiff charges that in 1991-1992, Brown violated certain "allowable cost" principles in administering a contract with the Department of Energy. None of the other defendants, other than NIT, is named as a defendant in this new and unrelated count.

Plaintiff's motion for leave to amend should be denied for a variety of reasons. First, amendment is not appropriate under Fed. R. Civ. P. 20(a) when, as here, the new count is unrelated to the original counts and implicates only one of the original seven defendants (i.e., NIT). Second, the five individual scientists named in the original action would be seriously prejudiced by the delay caused by litigation of this new count. None of these scientists is even named in the proposed new count. And third, for the proposed new defendant, Martin Brown, venue is inconvenient in this district. None of the witnesses or parties is found in this district, and none of the transactions alluded to in Count VII occurred in this district.

change the character of the entire case and trial. These ideas are then further developed in the remainder of the first paragraph. The first paragraph is an interesting example of how an attorney can use the cold facts, unadorned by adjectives or adverbs, to convey an impression and build an argument. Specifically, notice how the attorney uses a series of four short sentences to highlight the differences between the plaintiff's case against Brown and its case against the other defendants. Each of these sentences stresses a particular fact that is relevant to the other defendants but not to Brown. To amplify these differences, the writer has used a series of parallel constructions ("plaintiff does not claim that Brown . . . "). To further drive these differences home, the writer then tells us what it is that the plaintiff is claiming Brown did (violated certain cost principles). The contrast between the major violations that the other defendants are alleged to have committed and the relatively insignificant act that Brown is alleged to have done is striking.

The first paragraph is fact oriented. The second paragraph sets out the three legal arguments that will be presented in the body of the memorandum. It is both a summary of and roadmap to the legal arguments that are to follow.

---

1. Brown is the director of the Laboratory of Radiobiology, a research facility at NIT, distinct from the BTRC where the other defendants are employed. *See* Second Amended Complaint at ¶22.

Argument

The Argument section of a memorandum of points and authorities corresponds to the Analysis section of an intraoffice memorandum, except that the purpose here is to be persuasive. This memorandum contains three principal headings, each of which summarizes a legal argument.

I.   LEAVE TO AMEND SHOULD BE DENIED BECAUSE JOINDER OF DR. BROWN IS IMPROPER UNDER FED. R. CIV. P. 20(a)

Fed. R. Civ. P. 20(a) provides, in pertinent part, than a plaintiff may join in one action all persons as defendants

> if there is asserted against **them** jointly, severally, or in the alternative, any right to relief in respect of or arising out of the same transaction, occurrence, or series of transactions or occurrences **and** if any question of law or fact common to **all defendants** will arise in the action. (Emphasis supplied.)

Rule 20(a) "does not contemplate joinder where, as here, an attempt is made to incorporate into an existing action a different action against different parties and presenting entirely different factual and legal issues." *Trail Realty, Inc. v. Beckett,* 462 F.2d 396, 400 (10th Cir. 1972). Amendment is only proper if the plaintiff can satisfy both the transaction or occurrence test and the commonality test for **all** the defendants. Neither test is satisfied by the proposed amendment. Indeed, the new count is so unrelated to the original action that the outcome of one will have no bearing on the outcome of the other.

The first paragraph both sets the stage for the Rule 20(a) argument and summarizes that argument. The organization and style of this paragraph are interesting. The writer glides from the objective (a pure statement of Rule 20(a)) to the subjective (his conclusion that the requirements of Rule 20(a) have not been met). First, the writer presents Rule 20(a). Second, he uses a quotation from an appellate court to emphasize the requirements of the Rule: "Rule 20(a) 'does not contemplate joinder where, as here, an . . . .' " Third, he summarizes the two tests that must be met to satisfy Rule 20 (a). Finally, he argues that neither test has been satisfied, and therefore, joinder is inappropriate.

The two requirements of Rule 20(a) form the organizing principle for the rest of the argument in this section.

A.   *Plaintiff's New Count Does Not Satisfy the Transaction or Occurrence Test*

Under the transaction or occurrence test, the plaintiff's right to relief must arise out of the same transaction or series of transactions. *Kenvin v. Newburger, Loeb & Company,* 37

The organization of this subsection is fairly representative of persuasive writing. The author first presents three cases to show how other federal courts have applied the "transaction or occurrence" test. Not surprisingly, the cases that have been chosen

F.R.D. 473, 475 (S.D.N.Y. 1965). In *Papa-giannis v. Pontikis,* 108 F.R.D. 177 (N.D. Ill. 1985), for example, plaintiffs alleged that they were victimized by the same defendants using the same scheme to fraudulently induce plaintiffs to purchase oil wells. Each plaintiff purchased a different oil well in the same leasehold. The court concluded that joinder was improper under Rule 20(a), even though the defendants used the same scheme and even though the wells were in the same leasehold, because each plaintiff's right to relief arose out of a different transaction. The court deemed that even though the scheme used was the same for both victims, that was insufficient to satisfy the Rule 20(a) transaction or occurrence test. *See Saval v. BL Ltd.,* 710 F.2d 1027 (4th Cir. 1983) (holding that common allegations of fraud and breaches of warranty do not satisfy the transaction or occurrence test).

Correspondingly, in *Paine, Webber, Jackson & Curtis, Inc. v. Merrill Lynch, Pierce, Fenner & Smith, Inc.,* 564 F. Supp. 1358 (D. Del. 1983), plaintiff instituted an action seeking a declaratory judgment that defendant's patent on a computer software system was invalid. Defendant counterclaimed, charging plaintiff with patent infringement, and sought to join another brokerage house, Dean Witter, as a third-party defendant. Even though Merrill Lynch alleged that both Paine Webber and Dean Witter infringed the same patent, the court held that that was not sufficient to satisfy the transaction or occurrence test of Fed. R. Civ. P. 20(a). "Allegations of infringement against two unrelated parties based on different acts do not arise from the same transaction. *See Siemens Aktiengesellschaft v. Sonotone Corp.,* 370 F. Supp. 970 (N.D. Ill. 1973)." *Paine, Webber, Jackson & Curtis, Inc. v. Merrill Lynch, Pierce, Fenner & Smith, Inc.,* 564 F. Supp. at 1371 (D. Del. 1983).

Similarly, in *Trail Realty v. Beckett, supra,* plaintiff entered into a contract for the purchase of land from defendant, but when plaintiff failed

are ones where courts have found that the test had not been satisfied and that joinder was therefore improper.

to obtain the necessary financing from a bank within the time specified in the contract, defendant withdrew its offer to sell and sold the property to the president of plaintiff's bank. Plaintiff instituted a specific performance action against defendant and sought to amend its complaint to allege a breach of fiduciary duty by the bank and its president. The trial court denied the motion to amend and on appeal the court affirmed, noting that plaintiff's right to relief against the seller on the one hand, and the bank and its president on the other hand, did not arise out of the same transaction.

Here, by no stretch of the imagination can one argue that plaintiff's claim against Dr. Brown arises out of the same transaction or set of transactions as the claims against the other individual defendants and the Southern Technical Institute. In particular, the claims against the original defendants were based on four experiments performed by Able in the early 1980s, which plaintiff alleges were improperly performed. The set of transactions consisted of NIH grant applications that referenced Able's challenged research. The last transaction in that set occurred in 1989. In contrast, the count against Brown relates to actions that occurred in 1991-1992 and, specifically, to whether he appropriately allocated costs under a Department of Energy contract. Brown's performance of an experiment similar to the one performed by Able is even less relevant to joinder than was the patent common to all third-party defendants in *Paine Webber*, the scheme and leasehold common to all defendants in *Papagiannis*, or sale of the parcel of property common to all defendants in *Trail Realty*. In those cases, at least, the transaction involved, while insufficient to satisfy the transaction test, was relevant to the disposition of the case against all the defendants. Here, though, the outcome of the experiment is not relevant to, and has no bearing on, plaintiff's claim against Brown.

The present case is analogous to *Wilkinson v. Hamel*, 381 F. Supp. 766 (W.D. Va. 1974), where

After presenting the three cases, the author builds a two-pronged argument. First, by using the facts of the present case, he shows how the plaintiff has failed to satisfy the "transaction or occurrence test." This is done once again by highlighting the differences between the action against Brown and the action against the other defendants. Second, the author acknowledges that there is one similarity arguably linking the original defendants and Brown. But he then uses the three cases that he discussed above to show how even that similarity cuts against joinder. Notice how he uses a single sentence to summarize all three cases.

The author concludes the subsection by discussing a case, *Wilkinson v. Hamel*, that is similar, in terms of the sequence of events, to the present case.

plaintiff unsuccessfully attempted to join new defendants as a result of conduct that occurred four years after the original occurrence. In *Hamel*, plaintiff's teaching contract with a state college was not renewed in 1970, and in 1974 he instituted a civil rights action against the college under 42 U.S.C. §1985. Also in 1974, he requested that the Governor of Virginia and the Attorney General of Virginia require binding arbitration and that his claims be settled for $10,000. When the Attorney General refused plaintiff's settlement offer, plaintiff sought leave to amend his complaint to join both officials. In denying the motion, the court noted that the original occurrences happened in 1970, while those involving the new defendants happened four years later. In so ruling, the court observed that

> [b]ecause plaintiff first contacted the additional defendants in 1974, any effort on their part to assist the plaintiff at that time could not have had any effect on plaintiff's alleged constitutional claims under §1985 in that any such claims matured four years earlier.

Wilkinson v. Hamel, 381 F. Supp. at 767.

Here, according to plaintiff, the last of its claims against the original defendants matured in 1989. However, its claim against Brown did not arise until 1991 and therefore, that claim, as in *Hamel*, has no bearing on the original six counts.

B. Plaintiff's New Count Does Not Satisfy the "Commonality" Test

Under Fed. R. Civ. P. 20(a), not only must plaintiff satisfy the transaction or occurrence test, it must also satisfy the commonality test. Specifically, under the commonality test, plaintiff must allege issues of fact or law common to *all* of the defendants. In other words, the resolution of an issue in Count VII must affect the resolution of an issue in the original action. As discussed below, the disposition of the claim against Brown in Count VII will have no bearing on the disposition of the claims against the other defendants in Counts I-VI.

Once again, the author begins by setting out the law concerning the "commonality" test and reminding the court that the plaintiff must satisfy both the "transaction or occurrence" test and the "commonality" test. In discussing the law, he states that the commonality test can be satisfied if there is either a question of fact or a question of law common to all of the defendants. Using this as an organizing principle, he then proceeds in the remainder of this subsection to show that there is neither a common

That claims in Count VII allege violations of the same statute is not sufficient to satisfy the commonality test. *See Kenvin v. Newburger, Loeb & Comp.*, 37 F.R.D. 475 (S.D.N.Y. 1965).

The issues of law raised in Count VII against Brown are distinct from those raised in Counts I-VI against the other defendants. Specifically, plaintiff has alleged in Counts I-VI that the defendants violated the False Claims Act by either improperly performing or improperly reporting the results of research to NIH under a series of NIH grants. Plaintiff has characterized its original action as one of "scientific misconduct." Plaintiff's Opposition to Defendants' Motion for Summary Judgment or in the Alternative, Partial Summary Judgment 1 (July 1, 1993). The plaintiff argues that the defendants violated scientific norms for conducting or reporting NIH-funded research. In contrast, its claim against Brown has nothing to do with either scientific norms or scientific misconduct. There is no claim that Brown's research was in any way flawed. Instead, plaintiff's action against Brown arises under the allowable cost principles of the Federal Acquisition Regulations ("FAR"), that corpus of rules that governs contracts but not grants. It is difficult to see how cost allocation principles under the FAR have anything in common with the ethics of science or the rules governing NIH grant applications. Moreover, the commonality requirement must be met for all of the defendants. Because NIT's Department of Energy contract administered by Brown has nothing in common legally with plaintiff's claims against the Southern Technical Institute, all of which involve NIH grants, the requirement is not met.

If there is no legal issue common to all defendants, plaintiff must allege a common factual issue. There are no factual issues common to all defendants. That Brown undertook an x-ray experiment is not relevant because plaintiff

question of law nor of fact linking all of the defendants.

To show that there is no common question of law, the author stresses the differences between the original action and the new one against Brown, namely that the original action involved questions of scientific norms while the new action involves questions of accounting for money. Notice how he uses the plaintiff's own words to characterize the original action as one involving "scientific misconduct."

The defendant's argument that there is no common question of fact is short, consisting of only two sentences. In essence, the writer is inviting the plaintiff to try to show that there is a common question of fact linking all the parties.

The author ends this subsection by emphasizing all of the differences between the original action and the new one.

does not claim that Brown improperly performed that experiment.[2]

In short, there are no questions of law or fact common to Brown and the other defendants. The allegations against Brown are not temporally related to those against the other defendants. The occurrences in the original complaint ended in 1989, while those in Count VII did not begin until 1991. They do not involve the same federal agency. The occurrences in the original complaint involve NIH while those in Count VII involve the Department of Energy. They do not involve the same form of funding. The occurrences in the original complaint involve grant funding, while those in Count VII involve a government contract. And finally, they do not involve the same genre of allegations. The allegations in the original complaint involve issues of scientific misconduct, while those in Count VII involve cost accounting principles under the Federal Acquisition Regulations.

II. PLAINTIFF'S MOTION TO AMEND SHOULD BE DENIED BECAUSE THE PROPOSED AMENDMENT WOULD NEEDLESSLY PREJUDICE THE ORIGINAL INDIVIDUAL DEFENDANTS

Plaintiff argues that its motion to amend ought to be granted because it neither acted in bad faith nor unreasonably delayed amending its complaint after completing Dr. Brown's deposition on March 19, 1993.[3] Plaintiff concluded its memorandum by asserting, without the benefit of either facts or analysis, that "[n]one

The argument in this section is organized similarly to the argument in the first section. There is a short discussion of the law. The author then applies that law to the facts to reach a result and ends by showing how the case relied upon by the plaintiff is really not relevant to the present case.

The legal argument is constructed in an interesting way. As you will recall from the intraoffice memorandum, courts generally permit parties to amend complaints even at a

---

2. The only factual link alleged by plaintiff is that Brown undertook an experiment in an attempt to replicate Able's earlier x-ray experiment. That factual link does not create an issue of fact common to the two actions. A common issue of fact is one that when resolved will affect the outcome of the two actions. However, whether the defendants violated scientific norms, as alleged in Counts I-VI, will in no way affect whether Brown violated allowable cost principles under the FAR, as alleged in Count VII. Conversely, whether Brown violated a provision of the FAR will have no effect on whether the other defendants breached scientific norms, as claimed by the plaintiff.

3. Plaintiff is seeking leave to amend under Fed. R. Civ. P. 15(a). The motion, however, "should have been filed as a motion to permit [Plaintiff] to serve a supplemental pleading under Fed. R. Civ. P. 15(d) rather than as a motion to amend [Plaintiff's] complaint under Fed. R. Civ. P. 15(a), because the events giving rise to the [new claim] . . . occurred subsequent to the filing of the original complaint." Knauer v. Johns-Manville Corp., 638 F. Supp. 1369, 1372 n.1 (D. Md. 1986).

of the present Defendants has been prejudiced by the timely filing of plaintiff's Second Amended Complaint. . . . " Memorandum at 11. As demonstrated below, each of the current individual defendants would in fact be severely prejudiced if the current complaint were amended to allege a cause of action unrelated to the counts in the pending action. In contrast, plaintiff would suffer no prejudice if its motion were denied since it would be free to file a separate action against Brown and NIT, thereby permitting the two cases to proceed to trial on their own schedules.

The Federal Rules are designed to function as "a means to the proper presentation of a case; . . . they are to assist, not deter, the disposition of litigation on the merits." *Deasy v. Hill*, 833 F.2d 38, 42 (4th Cir. 1987) (quoting 3 Moore's Federal Practice 15.02 [1] (1985)). Accordingly, the Rules "shall be construed to secure the just, speedy, and inexpensive determination of every action." Fed. R. Civ. P. 1. Thus, undue delay can constitute prejudice. And it is well settled that a court may properly deny a motion to amend if it would "unduly prejudice the non-movant." *Deasy v. Hill,* 833 F.2d at 40. *See Davis v. Piper Aircraft Corp.,* 615 F.2d 606, 613 (4th Cir. 1980) ("[P]rejudice resulting to the opponent by a grant of leave to amend is reason sufficient to deny amendment").

Such is especially the case here, where plaintiff, throughout these proceedings, has repeatedly characterized its complaint against the original defendants as "a case of scientific misconduct. . . . " Plaintiff's Opposition to Defendants' Motion for Summary Judgment or in the Alternative, Partial Summary Judgment 1 (July 1, 1993). The Department of Health and Human Services, NIH's parent agency, has expressly recognized that allegations of scientific misconduct, even when untrue, may damage an individual's reputation and career, undermine his or her ability to compete favorably for federal grant funds,

relatively late stage in the proceedings. The author does not mention this aspect of the law. Instead, he focuses on the one factor that courts have used in denying motions to amend, namely undue prejudice.

Having established that undue prejudice is a legitimate basis for denying a motion to amend, the author then must show that undue prejudice would occur in this case if the plaintiff were allowed to amend its complaint. It is normally difficult to prove undue prejudice. To overcome this difficulty, the author uses the government's (the plaintiff's) own words and regulations to show that undue prejudice arises if a case of scientific misconduct is not quickly resolved. He bolsters this proof with statements from a powerful member of Congress and from the prestigious National Academy of Sciences. The author then argues that if the complaint is amended, that would delay the resolution of the original action and would therefore prejudice the defendants.

Notice how the author uses the theme of prejudice to distinguish the one case that the plaintiff cited in its memorandum in support of its motion to amend. In particular, he argues that the appellate court in *Island Creek* permitted the plaintiff to amend its complaint because otherwise the plaintiff would have been severely prejudiced. The author then shows that if the plaintiff in the present case were denied the opportunity to amend, it would suffer absolutely no prejudice. In short, if the complaint were amended, the defendants would be prejudiced, but if the complaint were not amended, the plaintiff would suffer no prejudice.

and imperil tenure decisions. *See* Declaration of Dr. Jules Hallum, Director of the Office of Scientific Integrity, submitted in *McCutchen v. United States Department of Health and Human Services*, Nos. 92-5372, 92-5389 (D.C. Cir. appeal pending) (pages 67, 75-76, J.A. on appeal, attached as Exhibit A). In a recent hearing, Congressman John Dingell observed that "[misconduct] [c]ases were still taking too long to resolve, the result being unfair damage to both the reputation of the accused and the accuser." Transcript from *Hearing on Recent Actions Involving the Office of Scientific Integrity of the National Institutes of Health and Events Regarding the Cleveland Clinic*, House Committee on Energy and Commerce 2-3 (August 1, 1991) (pages 1-3, attached as Exhibit B).

Accordingly, the Department of Health and Human Services has adopted a series of regulations and procedures designed to minimize the untoward consequences associated with a misconduct proceeding. Central to those regulations is the requirement that misconduct inquiries and investigations be swiftly conducted. *See* 42 CFR Part 50. Moreover, the National Academy of Sciences has expressly recommended that misconduct allegations should be handled with dispatch. *See* National Academy of Sciences, Responsible Science 149 (1992). In short, the longer a misconduct proceeding lasts, the greater the risk that innocent scientists will be needlessly stigmatized. Such is the case here.

Discovery in the original action closed in March 1993. The parties deposed 17 witnesses whose testimony and exhibits span 29 volumes. Dispositive motions were filed by the defendants on June 1, 1993. The plaintiff, however, has now sought to further delay ultimate resolution of its charges against Drs. Charles, Davis, Fink, Able, and Edwards by seeking to amend its complaint to add a new count, against a new defendant, involving legal and factual issues unrelated to those in its first amended complaint. "Belated claims which change the character of the litigation are not favored." *Deasy v. Hill*, 833 F.2d at 42. *See Davis v. City of Portsmouth, Virginia*, 579 F. Supp. 1205, 1212 (E.D. Va. 1983) (leave to amend denied where plaintiffs sought to add new defendants and new "claims [which] are fundamentally different from the claims in the . . . original complaint"). Because the proposed Count VII involves issues of allowable costs under the Federal Acquisition Regulations, additional discovery will undoubtedly be needed and new dispositive motions will undoubtedly be filed. This will lengthen the current proceedings and needlessly delay resolution of the first six counts, thereby prejudicing the five defendant scientists.

Moreover, plaintiff's reliance on *Island Creek Coal Co. v. Lake Shore, Inc.*, 832 F.2d 274 (4th Cir. 1987) is misplaced. There, the court permitted plaintiffs to amend their complaint to allege a new cause of action against the original defendants. The plaintiffs did not, as here, seek to add a new defendant. Critical to the court's decision in *Island Creek* was the fact that if plaintiffs were denied the opportunity to amend "they would likely be confronted with the defense of res judicata, based on their failure to raise such claim in this case." *Island Creek Coal Co. v. Lake Shore, Inc.*, 832 F.2d at 281. In short, the plaintiffs would have been prejudiced had their motion to amend been denied. In contrast, here there is nothing that would preclude the plaintiff from instituting a separate action against Brown and NIT, and thus the plaintiff would suffer no prejudice if its motion to amend were denied. Similarly, in *Davis v. Piper Aircraft Corp.*, 615 F.2d 606, 613 (4th Cir. 1980), the court concluded that plaintiff's motion to amend ought to have been granted because "no finding of prejudice was made by the trial court," that "defendant was from the outset made fully aware of events" giving rise to the amendment, and that denying the motion effectively foreclosed plaintiff's right of action. Here, in contrast, there is strong evidence that the individual defendants would be severely prejudiced by the delay caused by the proposed, unrelated amendment, and plaintiff will not be prejudiced if its motion to amend is denied.

III.   AMENDMENT SHOULD BE DENIED BECAUSE VENUE IS MORE APPROPRIATE IN THE NORTHERN DISTRICT OF CALIFORNIA

In the original action, the NIT defendants sought to transfer the case to a more appropriate venue. In successfully opposing that motion, plaintiff argued that

> The National Institutes of Health, the federal agency defrauded by the defendants' conduct, is located in Maryland. The defendants submitted their grant applications to NIH, the grants were issued out of NIH, and the federal funds were paid to the defendants by NIH. As such, NIH is the repository for all the records of the grants at issue, as well as for all of the records relating to the proposal evaluation process. Moreover, potential witnesses, including all of the government witnesses, reside in this or neighboring districts.

Plaintiff's Memorandum in Opposition to Defendant NIT's Motion for Change of Venue 5-6 (April 18, 1991).

In sharp contrast, with respect to the proposed Count VII none of the events occurred in Maryland; they all occurred in the Northern District of Nevada. In particular, the DoE contract was issued out of the Department's Oakdale, Nevada, office, the contracting officer responsible for overseeing the contract is stationed in the Oakdale office, and all records relevant to the contract were submitted by NIT to, and are to be found in, that Oakdale office. Moreover, none of the witnesses, including any of the parties, is to be found in Maryland. The

The final section is not really an argument at all. The defendants are not asserting that venue would be improper in Maryland. Rather, they are discussing the issue of venue in order to highlight the differences between the original cause of action and the proposed action against Brown. In essence, the author is using logistical inconvenience as a way of bringing the court back to the original theme, discussed in the first section of the memorandum, that there are significant factual and legal differences between the two actions.

experiment that was allegedly improperly billed to the contract was performed in Nevada.

In short, none of the considerations that favored retaining the original action in Maryland are present with respect to Count VII. This is not surprising, since that count is entirely unrelated to the counts contained in the first amended complaint.

Conclusion

For the foregoing reasons, plaintiff's motion to file a second amended complaint should be denied.

Respectfully submitted,
BERG, PIERCE & MARTIN

_____

David Berg
Lawrence Goldman
1001 Pine Avenue
Pittsville, Nevada
(917) 624-2500
Attorneys for Defendants
   Nevada Institute of Technology,
   Mark Able, Lawrence Charles,
   Gary Davis, Edith Edwards,
   and Norris Fink

The memorandum of points and authorities (with the names of the parties changed) was actually submitted in a federal court case. How do you think the trial judge ruled? The trial judge denied the plaintiff's motion to amend because the judge believed that it would unduly prejudice the original defendants. The court relied heavily on the government's own statements and regulations that delay in a scientific misconduct case injures all concerned. The court declined to address the Rule 20(a) argument pressed by the defendants.

15

Writing an

Appellate Brief

In this chapter, we will examine three types of appellate briefs, each with a distinct purpose: (i) a traditional appellate brief, sometimes called a brief on the merits; (ii) a certiorari petition; and (iii) an *amicus* brief.

A   What Is an Appellate Brief on the Merits?

An appellate brief is a written argument designed to persuade an appellate court that your position on the case on appeal is the correct one. If you are the appellant, your brief argues that the lower court made errors in its decision in a particular case and that these errors were prejudicial. If you are the appellee, you argue that there were no prejudicial errors and that the lower court's decision should stand. A brief states the facts of the case, identifies the relevant issues, and presents an argument that is supported by statutes, regulations, or precedent. Every section of a brief is written to persuade: The facts of the case are written so that they present the writer's position in the best light, the issues are drafted so that they optimize the writer's argument, and so on. The entire brief must convince the court that the analysis of facts and law and the conclusions in the brief are sound and should be adopted. In addition, a brief serves as a reference for the court. It should contain a list of relevant cases and statutes and a well-documented analysis of the pertinent issues.

There is no rigid formula for the format of a brief. Courts in each jurisdiction have their own requirements, ranging from rules that briefs be highly structured and specific to rules allowing lawyers more discretion in structuring their briefs.

In this part, we first present an outline for a brief and then use excerpts from the three briefs submitted in *Smith v. Doe*, 538 U.S. 84 (2003) — Petitioners' brief, Respondents' brief, and Petitioners' reply — and on occasion, snippets from other briefs, to illustrate each section of the outline. Smith involved the constitutionality of Alaska's sex offender registration law. At issue in *Smith* was whether Alaska may (i) compel an individual convicted of sex-related crimes to register with the state and (ii) make information about the ex-offenders publicly available on the Internet, even though the individual committed the sex-related offense before the registration law was enacted. The Constitution prohibits states from "pass[ing] any . . . ex post facto Law[.]" U.S. Cont. art. I, § 10, cl. 1. An ex post facto law is one that retroactively either criminalizes conduct that had been previously lawful or increases the penalty for a given crime. In this case, Alaska's sex offender registration act applied to individuals who had been convicted of sex-related crimes before the registration act was passed. These individuals argued that the registration act, as applied to them, was an ex post facto law and therefore, invalid.

After presenting and discussing excerpts from the briefs in *Smith v. Doe*, we then present sections from each argument side-by-side to illustrate how each side attacks the other's argument while attempting to strengthen its own argument. Finally, we reproduce a significant portion of the brief submitted on behalf of the Petitioners, the State of Alaska and its officials. The Respondents' brief and the complete version of the Alaska brief can be obtained either on the Web (http://supreme.lp.findlaw.com/supreme_court/docket/2002/november.html01-729) or through Westlaw or Lexis.

We have chosen *Smith v. Doe* not only because the issue it presents is interesting, understandable, and of contemporary significance, but also because the Petitioners' briefs are very well written. They were the work of John Roberts, Jr., now Chief Justice of the United States and considered by many to have been one of the best Supreme Court advocates of his time. *Smith v. Doe* was the last case that Roberts argued in the Supreme Court before taking his seat on the United States Court of Appeals for the District of Columbia Circuit, about one month after *Smith* was decided.

Keep in mind that there are entire texts written on the subject of brief-writing and that there are many schools of thought on how an appellate case should be presented to a tribunal. The strategies used in brief-writing are as varied and complex as the strategies used in presenting a trial. Thus, you should regard this outline as a useful, but not necessarily universal, conceptual framework for a brief.

1. The Structure of a Brief

a. *Outline*

Cover page
Questions Presented
 Question 1
 Question 2
 Question 3
Parties to the Proceeding
Table of Contents
Table of Authorities
Opinions Below
Jurisdiction

Constitutional Provisions and Statutes Involved
Statement of the Case [Statement of Facts]
Summary of Argument
Argument
    Analysis of Question 1
    Analysis of Question 2
    Analysis of Question 3
Conclusion

b. *Explanation of the Parts of a Brief*

(1) Cover Page. The *cover page* should include the name of the appellate court, the number assigned to the appeal, the parties' names, the name of the lower court that rendered the decision that is being appealed, a description of the kind of brief that is being submitted (appellee's or appellant's brief), and a list of the attorneys who are submitting the brief. *See* Figure 15-1 for an example of a cover page from a brief that was submitted to the United States Supreme Court. In cases before the Supreme Court, the case number (here, 01-729) indicates the Term in which the first filing (usually a petition for certiorari, i.e., a petition for review) occurred. In *Smith v. Doe*, Alaska filed its certiorari petition on November 21, 2001. Supreme Court Terms start on the first Monday in October and end 365 days later. They are designated by the year in which the Term starts.

As you may notice, the name of the case changed between the time the briefs were submitted and the time the case was decided. When the briefs were submitted, Glenn G. Godfrey was the Commissioner of the Alaska Department of Public Safety and was the official responsible for implementing Alaska's Megan's Law. By the time the case was decided by the Court, Godfrey had been replaced as Commissioner by Delbert W. Smith and the name of the case changed accordingly.* This frequently occurs when governmental officials are involved in litigation in their official capacities. *See* Sup. Ct. R. 35.3 ("When a public officer who is a party to a proceeding in this Court in an official capacity . . . ceases to hold office . . . any successor in office is automatically substituted . . . .").

---

* It is interesting that when the certiorari petition was filed, the Commissioner was Ronald O. Otte. Job security does not appear to be a hallmark of that particular office.

FIGURE 15-1

No. 01-729

In The
Supreme Court of the United States

GLENN G. GODFREY AND BRUCE M. BOTELHO,
Petitioners,

v.

JOHN DOE I, JANE DOE, AND JOHN DOE II,
Respondents.

**On Writ of Certiorari to the
United States Court of Appeals for
the Ninth Circuit**

BRIEF FOR PETITIONERS

JOHN G. ROBERTS, JR.*
JONATHAN S. FRANKLIN
CATHERINE E. STETSON
HOGAN & HARTSON L.L.P.
555 Thirteenth Street, N.W.
Washington, D.C. 20004
(202) 637-5810

CYNTHIA M. COOPER
3410 Southbluff Circle
Anchorage, Alaska 99515
(907) 349-3483

BRUCE M. BOTELHO
Attorney General
STATE OF ALASKA
Department of Law
P.O. Box 110300
Juneau, Alaska 99811
(907) 465-3600

* Counsel of Record

Counsel for Petitioners

(2) Questions Presented. This section may also be called *Legal Issues* or *Issues Presented*. It focuses on the issues of the case that the writer wants the court to consider. The issues are framed as questions. Each question should be only one sentence long and should be concisely worded in a way that presents the writer's argument in the most favorable light. (*See* Chapter 11 for information on how to do this.) While each side is supposed to address the same questions, courts frequently permit the parties to restate the questions. Here is an example of the way Alaska framed the question presented in *Smith v. Doe.*

Question Presented

Alaska's sex offender registration act, Alaska Stat. §§ 12.63.010 *et seq.*, requires convicted sex offenders to register with the Alaska Department of Public Safety and makes offender information available to the public. The Department elected to publish the information on the Internet. Does the statute, on its face or as implemented by the Department of Public Safety, impose punishment for purposes of the Ex Post Facto Clause of the United States Constitution?

This is a very non-argumentative, almost matter-of-fact, way of stating the question. Some litigators prefer to pump into the "questions presented" as many facts as possible either to make the question either more appealing or to make its answer self-evident; others preface the questions presented with a short paragraph to provide context. Recently, the Court granted certiorari in a products liability case against Philip Morris USA. In the certiorari petition, Andrew Frey, an extraordinarily experienced Supreme Court advocate, presented Petitioner's questions as follows:

(I)
Questions Presented

In this case brought by the widow of a smoker, the jury held Philip Morris liable for fraud and awarded $79.5 million in punitive damages — 97 times the compensatory damages awarded by the jury. On remand from this Court for reconsideration in light of *State Farm Mutual Automobile Insurance Co. v. Campbell*, 538 U.S. 408 (2003), the Oregon Supreme Court upheld the trial court's refusal to instruct the jury that it could not punish Philip Morris for harms to nonparties, concluding that a jury may punish for such harms so long as the conduct that caused those harms is similar to the conduct that harmed the plaintiff. Then, construing the evidence in the light most favorable to the plaintiff, the court proceeded to hold that the punitive award was not unconstitutionally excessive, despite concluding that the punitive award was not reasonably related to the harm to the plaintiff. The questions presented, each of which is the subject of a conflict in the lower courts, are:

1. Whether, in reviewing a jury's award of punitive damages, an appellate court's conclusion that a defendant's conduct was highly reprehensible and

analogous to a crime can "override" the constitutional requirement that punitive damages be reasonably related to the plaintiff's harm.

2. Whether due process permits a jury to punish a defendant for the effects of its conduct on non-parties.

3. Whether, in reviewing a punitive award for excessiveness, an appellate court is permitted to give the plaintiff the benefit of all conceivable inferences that might support a finding of high reprehensibility even if the jury made no such specific factual findings.

Frey used an introductory paragraph to set the stage for the questions presented, highlighting two facts. First, he emphasized up front that the award of punitive damages was nearly one hundred times greater than the award of compensatory damages. Second, he noted that the Oregon Supreme Court upheld the award even though it acknowledged that there was no rational relationship between the punitive damage award and the underlying compensatory damages. And third, he noted that the state Supreme Court permitted punitive damages to be awarded for injuries that others had suffered who were not parties to the litigation.

(3) Parties to the Proceeding. Many courts, including the Supreme Court, require litigants to list all of the parties to the proceeding and also require each litigant to list its parent corporations, as well as related corporations (*e.g.*, those owning at least 10 percent of corporation's stock). This requirement enables the judges to readily determine whether they have a potential conflict of interest, as might arise if the judge owns stock in the corporate parent of one of the parties. There is one exception to this requirement — namely, when a party sues under fictitious name (*i.e.*, John Doe, Mary Roe), as is the case here. The use of a fictitious name, while exceptional, is permitted where there is a demonstrated need, usually for privacy reasons, to protect the identity of the party. For example, "abortion cases are, and always have been recognized to be, exceptional cases for anonymity purposes." *Roe v. Aware Woman Center for Choice, Inc.*, 253 F.3d 678, 685 n.8 (11th Cir. 2001). Even though a party proceeds under a fictitious name, the party's name is revealed to the other side.

Here is the listing of the parties in Alaska's brief.

(ii)

Parties to the Proceeding

Petitioners Glenn G. Godfrey (successor to Ronald O. Otte) and Bruce M. Botelho are, respectively, the Alaska Commissioner of Public Safety and the Alaska Attorney General. Otte and Botelho were defendants in the District Court and appellees before the Court of Appeals for the Ninth Circuit. Respondents John Doe I, Jane Doe, and John Doe II were plaintiffs in the District Court and appellants before the Court of Appeals for the Ninth Circuit.

(4) Table of Contents. The *table of contents* lists the major parts of the brief and shows the number of the page on which each part can be found. The list includes all of the section divisions of the brief, as well as the headings and subheadings of the writer's argument.

Not only does the table of contents serve as a reference tool for quickly finding information within the brief, but the informative headings and subheadings provide the reader with an overview of the writer's argument. Well constructed headings can do a great deal to persuade the reader, since they present a logical map of the steps in the writer's reasoning. Here is a sample table of contents from Alaska's brief.

Table of Contents

(5) Table of Authorities. The *table of authorities* lists, in separate categories, all of the cases, statutes, regulations, and miscellaneous sources (such as law review articles and treatises) used to support the attorney's arguments. These are listed with full citations and references to every page in the brief on which they appear. Some courts may require that the most important citations be starred. Here is an example of part of the table of authorities from Alaska's brief. The full table of authorities was considerably longer.

V
Table of Authorities

(6) Opinions Below. A brief may include a section that contains citations to the lower court opinions in the case. Many appeals courts require the petitioner (or appellant) to reproduce in an appendix the lower court opinions. In the example below from Alaska's brief, the opinions issued by the lower courts were reproduced by Alaska's counsel in the certiorari petition.

Opinions Below

The opinion of the Ninth Circuit, as amended, is reported at 259 F.3d 979 and reprinted in the appendix to the petition for certiorari ("Pet. App.") at 1a. The original opinion is reprinted at Pet. App. 33a. The opinions and orders of the United States District Court for the District of Alaska dated March 31, 1999, and August 12, 1999, are not reported; they are reproduced at Pet. App. 69a and 118a, respectively.

(7) Jurisdictional Statement. Briefs sometimes include a separate section for general information about the case. This section can include one or more of the following:

1. The statutory basis or the rule under which the court can hear the case;
2. The judicial history of the case (any rulings below that are now being appealed, dates of any judgments, etc.);
3. The general nature of the case or summary of the dispute;
4. How the case has come before the present court; and
5. The identity of the parties.

Here is the jurisdictional statement from the Alaska brief.

Jurisdiction

The judgment of the Ninth Circuit was entered on August 8, 2001. The Ninth Circuit denied petitions for rehearing and for rehearing en banc on August 23, 2001, and September 6, 2001. Pet. App. 124a, 123a. The petition for certiorari was filed on November 21, 2001, and granted on February 19, 2002. 122 S. Ct. 1062. The jurisdiction of this Court is invoked under 28 U.S.C. § 1254(1).

The jurisdictional statement is usually, but not always, short and to the point. Section 1254(1) vests the Supreme Court with jurisdiction to hear cases from a court of appeals via petition for certiorari.

(8) **Introduction.** A formal introduction, if properly written, can set the tone and stage for the brief. It should be short, provide necessary background, and avoid polemics. The introduction in the Alaska brief is set out below; the Respondents opted against having an introduction. As you will note, the Alaska introduction contains only seven sentences. Notice how the first sentence sets out the twin purposes of the Alaska law — to safeguard the public and to assist law enforcement. The second sentence builds on that theme by casting the law as one that provides "truthful" information to the public. The third sentence links this information with the finding of the lower court that the law had a non-punitive intent. This sentence is the key to the entire brief because it is very difficult to establish that a law is "penal," and hence subject to the ex post facto prohibition, if it is not a traditional criminal statute and was not enacted with a punitive intent. The next few sentences emphasize that the Court of Appeals is a lone voice and that the court got it wrong.

Introduction

The Alaska Sex Offender Registration Act ("ASORA") was enacted to protect the public and to assist law enforcement in investigating future crimes. It requires state law enforcement entities to gather truthful information about sex offenders and to make certain of that information available to the public. The State has chosen to make such information available on the Internet. Like all other courts to have considered sex offender registration laws, the Ninth Circuit concluded that the legislature acted with non-punitive intent when it passed the ASORA. The court of appeals erroneously departed from the overwhelming majority of courts, however, in holding that the ASORA was nonetheless so punitive in effect that it violated the Ex Post Facto Clause. We are aware of no case in which this Court has held that a law had a non-punitive intent and yet nonetheless violated the Ex Post Facto Clause. Nor has this Court ever held that regulatory requirements like those imposed on sex offenders by the ASORA amount to punishment; indeed, it has countenanced far more onerous burdens imposed by non-punitive regulatory statutes. The Ninth Circuit's decision should be reversed.

(9) **Statement of the Case (Statement of Facts).** The *statement of the case,* sometimes referred to as the *statement of facts,* may include the information that would otherwise be included in the jurisdictional statement if the format does not require that jurisdictional information be placed in its own separate section. In addition, this section must state the facts of the case. Some attorneys consider this the most important section of a brief, since it can set the tone for the rest of the document.

The facts should be presented thoroughly and accurately, but also concisely. The statement should include everything that is relevant, but it should emphasize favorable information and de-emphasize unfavorable information in order to present the facts in the light most favorable to the writer's position.

Here are excerpts from the statements of the case from the opposing briefs in *Smith v. Doe.*

Petitioners' Statement of the Case

STATUTORY BACKGROUND.

1. In 1994, after a series of sexual crimes against children committed by prior offenders made news across the country, Congress passed the Jacob Wetterling Crimes Against Children and Law Enforcement Act, 42 U.S.C. §§ 14071 *et seq.* The Wetterling Act directs the Attorney General to develop guidelines for state sex offender registration programs, *id.* § 14071(a), specifies registration requirements for individuals convicted of certain sex offenses and the duration of those requirements, and permits States to release registry information "to protect the public concerning a specific person required to register under [the Act]." *Id.* § 14071(e)(2). The Wetterling Act encourages States to adopt registration programs that conform to or exceed its terms by conditioning receipt of certain federal funds on the implementation of such programs. *Id.* § 14071(g)(2). In 1996, Congress amended the Wetterling Act to provide that offenders convicted of one "aggravated sex offense" or two or more triggering offenses be required to register for life, and to permit States to disclose registry information "for any purpose permitted under the laws of the State." *Id.* §§ 14071(b)(6), (e) (Supp. III 1997). Today, all fifty States and the District of Columbia have sex offender registration and notification statutes on their books. Approximately thirty States and the District of Columbia make their registries available on the Internet. *See* U.S. Dep't of Justice, Bureau of Justice Statistics, *Summary of State Sex Offender Registries, 2001* (2002) (noting that "a growing number of States use[] the Internet to fulfill notification requirements under Megan's Law"); http://www.meganslaw.org (collecting Internet sex offender registries).[2]

The rapid development of state sex offender statutes has led to a spate of lawsuits challenging their terms. A central question presented by many of those lawsuits is

---

2. Such laws are often called "Megan's Laws," after Megan Kanka, a seven-year-old New Jersey child who was sexually assaulted and murdered by a neighbor who unbeknownst to the Kanka family had two prior convictions for sexual offenses against children. *See* Wayne A. Logan, *Liberty Interests in the Preventive State: Procedural Due Process and Sex Offender Community Notification Laws,* 89 J. CRIM. L. & CRIMINOLOGY 1167, 1172 (1999).

whether sex offender registration and notification constitute retroactive punishment prohibited by the Constitution's Ex Post Facto Clause. The overwhelming majority of courts have answered that question in the negative. *See infra* n.11.

2. The State of Alaska became the thirty-second State to enact a sex offender registration law when, in 1994, its legislature enacted the ASORA. The ASORA requires convicted sex offenders to register with law enforcement authorities and authorizes public disclosure of certain information in the sex offender registry. Alaska Stat. §§ 12.63.010, 18.65.087.

The ASORA was enacted "at a time when the state legislature perceived that Alaska's high rate of child sexual abuse constituted a 'crisis.'" Pet. App. 6a. The State's legislature heard testimony that the rate of child sexual abuse in Alaska was the highest in the Nation — indeed, more than six times the national average. *See Minutes of Hearing Before Senate Judiciary Comm.* ("*Senate Judiciary Hearing*"), 18th Alaska Legis., 1st Sess. 9 (Apr. 14, 1993) (No. 505); *Minutes of Hearing Before Senate Finance Comm.* ("*Senate Finance Hearing*"), 18th Alaska Legis., 1st Sess. 3 (Apr. 28, 1993). The State's sexual assault rate in 1993 was the second highest in the Nation and had nearly doubled in the prior two years. *See Senate Judiciary Hearing* at 9, 13 (Nos. 505, 209); *Minutes of Hearing Before House Judiciary Comm.* ("*House Judiciary Hearing*"), 18th Alaska Legis., 1st Sess. 17 (Feb. 10, 1993) (No. 000). Legislators also heard testimony that about a quarter of Alaska's entire prison population was incarcerated for sexual offenses, and that studies had shown that sex offenders had high rates of recidivism. *See Minutes of Hearing Before House Finance Comm.* ("*House Finance Hearing*"), 18th Alaska Legis., 1st Sess. 7 (Mar. 3, 1993); *Senate Judiciary Hearing* at 9 (No. 505); *House Judiciary Hearing* at 9 (No. 612).

* * *

FACTS.

Respondent John Doe I was charged with three counts of first-degree sexual abuse of a minor. Ct. App. Sealed E.R. 113. He pled nolo contendere [equivalent for most purposes to a guilty plea] to one count of first-degree and one count of second-degree sexual abuse of a minor and was sentenced to twelve years' imprisonment, four years of which were suspended. *Id.* at 113-114. John Doe I was released from prison in December 1990. *Id.* at 114. He married respondent Jane Doe after his release from prison. *Id.* at 115. Respondent John Doe II was charged with first degree sexual abuse of a minor. *Id.* at 126. He pled nolo contendere to one count and was sentenced to eight years' imprisonment. *Id.* John Doe II was released from prison in May 1990. *Id.*

John Doe I and John Doe II were required to register as sex offenders under the ASORA because they were convicted after July 1, 1984 of offenses triggering application of the statute. *See* 1994 Alaska Sess. Laws ch. 41, § 12(a). Because both were convicted of an "aggravated sex offense," *see* Alaska Stat. § 12.63.100 (1), the Act required both to provide, on a quarterly basis, "written verification" of their current address and notice of any changes to their registry information. *Id.* §§ 12.63.010(d)(2), 12.63.020; 1998 Alaska Sess. Laws ch. 106, § 25 (new registration requirements for aggravated sex offenses apply retroactively).

Respondents' Statement of the Case

(A) THE RESPONDENTS.

Seventeen years ago, John Doe I was convicted of intra-family sexual abuse and sentenced to 8 years in prison. He was released from prison in 1990 to serve out a period of mandatory parole and supervised probation. Id. Citing his low risk for reoffense and his compliance with treatment program requirements, the Alaska Board of Parole released him two years early to serve out the remainder of his supervised probation. Id. He has long since completed his probation, and has been unconditionally discharged, with all of his civil rights restored. Id. He is not a pedophile, and treating professionals stated it was unlikely that he would commit another offense. CR 28.

After his release from prison, the Alaska Superior Court made a judicial determination that John Doe I was successfully rehabilitated, and it awarded him custody of his minor daughter. CR 18. He has since remarried, he has established a business, and he has reunited with his children, including the victim of his offense. Id.

Jane Doe is married to John Doe I. CR 18. Jane is employed in a professional capacity and she has never been convicted of a criminal offense. She married John Doe I after his release from prison, and was aware of his criminal history. Id.

John Doe II was convicted 18 years ago and sentenced to serve 8 years in prison. CR 18, Affidavit of John Doe II. He was released on mandatory parole in 1990, with no residual period of probation. Id. He complied with program requirements, successfully completed mandatory parole and was unconditionally discharged in 1992. All of his civil rights were restored, and he is gainfully employed. Id.

(B) PRE-1994 RIGHTS.

The Alaska Sex Offender Registration Act ["ASORA"] significantly diminished respondents' pre-existing rights under the Alaska Constitution and state law. After serving their sentences, the Does had the right to be unconditionally discharged with all civil rights restored. Alaska Stat. 12.55.185(15); Alaska Stat. 33.30.241.

Among these rights is the right under Article I, § 12 of the Alaska Constitution to be reintegrated into society, and to seek to become the object of respect, rather than the object of fear or loathing by their fellow citizens. *Abraham v. State*, 585 P.2d 526, 531 (Alaska 1978). This right to seek reintegration as a full member of society is a right guaranteed by the Alaska Constitution and protected by the Due Process Clause of the 14th Amendment. *Ferguson v. Department of Corrections*, 816 P.2d 134, 139-140 (Alaska 1991). Although the constitutional provision conveying this right was amended in 1994, 18th Legislature's Legislative Resolve No. 58, the right remains. Alaska Stat. 12.55.005 (2000); *Mathis v. Sauser*, 942 P.2d 1117, 1124 (Alaska 1997) citing, *Ferguson*.

The Does also had a specific right of privacy guaranteed by the Alaska Constitution, and protected by the Due Process Clause of the 14th Amendment. Alaska Const. art. I, § 22; Breeze v. Smith, 501 P.2d 159, 168 (Alaska 1972). This specific right of privacy was created in the 1970's when the State, using federal grant funds, was developing the Alaska Justice Information System, ["AJIS"] a computerized database of information on the criminal history of individuals. Inf. Op. Att'y Gen.

XXX-XX-0479, pp. 18-23 (Dec. 10, 1986). Fearful that such a system was the precursor of a "Big Brother" governmental information bureaucracy, legislators responded with Article I, § 22, which was overwhelmingly approved by the voters and which states: "The right of the people to privacy is recognized and shall not be infringed." Alaska Const. art. I, § 22. Inclusion of the right to privacy was intended to exert control over the AJIS system, prohibiting public disclosure of criminal records and other governmental records, and to avoid similar potential abuses with all future systems. Id. Responding to adoption of the right of privacy, the legislature adopted the Criminal Justice Information Systems Security and Privacy Act, which limits access to criminal history information. Alaska Stat., Title 12, Chapter 62.

Next, the Does had the right to be let alone, especially in one's home. See *Carey v. Brown*, 447 U.S. 455, 470-471 (1980); See generally Lewis, *The Jacob Wetterling Crimes Against Children & Sexually Violent Offender Registration Act: An Unconstitutional Deprivation of the Right to Privacy and Substantive Due Process*, 31 Harv. C.R.-C.L. L. Rev. 89 (Winter 1996). Encompassed within this important right is the right to be free from unwarranted governmental suspicion, and the right to be free from government initiated intrusions through vigilantism. Lewis, supra. This includes the right to personal safety. Lewis, 31 Harv. C.R.-C.L. L. Rev. at 106-07.

Additionally, the Does had the right to seek out and engage in employment, and to seek rewards of their own industry. *Hampton v. Mow Sun Wong*, 426 U.S. 88, 102 n. 23 (1976), citing *Truax v. Raich*, 239 U.S. 33, 41 (1915). The right to pursue employment is likewise a fundamental liberty interest. Id.

Although the Does were unconditionally discharged, reintegrated, productive citizens of Alaska, with all civil rights restored to them, the Alaska legislature decided that they were dangerous, they should be required to register with the police four times per year, they should be supervised for life and have their personal information and their status of "registered sex offender" announced to the world. 1994 Alaska Sess. Laws, ch. 41, § 1. The only factor triggering an invasion of protected rights and disenfranchising the Does by labeling them with a badge of infamy [a scarlet letter] is the past conviction. Alaska Stat. 12.63.100, 1994 Alaska Sess. Laws, ch. 41, §§ 12, 13.

(C) The ASORA.

In enacting the ASORA, legislative focus was on sex offenders, and the need to infringe this group's liberty interests, such as the right of privacy. 1994 Alaska Sess. Laws, ch. 41, § 1. Indeed, ASORA specifically diminishes the right of privacy by stating it is "less important than the government's interest in public safety." Id. The ASORA compels the Does to gather, collate and disclose information to the State so it may be included in a government information database labeling the Does as dangerous persons to be avoided.[2] Id. The ASORA requires a subclass of this select

---

2. It is not true that the ASORA merely allows collection and dissemination of "truthful" information so the public can make their own assessment as to dangerousness. Pet. Br. 25. The intent to declare all registrants as presently dangerous persons to be actively avoided is evident from certain amendments to Alaska Stat. 11.51.100(a)(2) [1998 Alaska Sess. Laws, ch. 99, § 5] Alaska Stat. 47.10.011(7) [1998 Alaska Sess. Laws, ch. 99, § 18], & Alaska Stat. 34.70.050 [1998 Alaska Sess. Laws, ch. 45 § 54]. Under these amendments, sale of a home requires disclosure of the registration list, a child in need of aid proceeding can commence if the registered sex offender lives in a home where a minor child resides,

group of reintegrated Alaska citizens to report the same information four times per year for the rest of their lives, and the Does are among this subclass. Alaska Stat. 12.63.020 (1998). The provisions compelling compliance, and creating the reporting requirements are codified in Title 12 of the Alaska Statutes, which are part of the State's criminal code, while the administrative and implementation provisions are placed in that section of the code governing the Department of Public Safety [State Police], the Agency charged with administering the sanctions imposed by the ASORA. See, e.g., Alaska Stat. 18.65.010-087 (2001).

Notice the difference in the organization and the emphasis of the two briefs. How paragraphs are organized can transform the text's emphasis. The organization of each party's Statement of the Case illustrates this point. For example, Petitioners' Statement of the Case starts by showing that every state has a law similar to the Alaska law at issue here and further, that Alaska was far from the first state to pass a law of this type. The Statement emphasizes that Alaska only enacted the legislation when sex crimes, and by implication sex crimes against minors, was at an all time high. The Statement lays out the findings of the legislature, because legislative findings are key to determining whether a law is penal or not. Roberts and his colleague then spent seven sentences discussing the cases of Doe I and Doe II; the discussion provides little information about either man. We are left with the sense that not only is the Alaska law a reasoned response to a dire situation, but also that overturning the Alaska law will effectively overturn the laws of every other state. Courts, including the Supreme Court, are generally reluctant to take action that will have ramifications well beyond the case before it. Petitioners' brief plays to that the proclivity.

By contrast, the Respondents start by discussing, in detail, the background of the individual Respondents, delineating how each Doe committed a crime, served his time, was reintegrated into society, is gainfully employed, and in one case, is not only married but has children, and gained custody over the child whom he molested. The vignettes also specify each of the rights restored to each Respondent after that Respondent had completed his respective sentence and that were nullified by the Alaska law. The purpose of this listing is to emphasize that the more rights that a law seeks to nullify, the more likely that law is really penal in character and hence subject to the ex post facto provision of the Constitution.

(10) Summary of Argument. Most appellate courts require the parties to present a concise summary of their entire argument up front. This provides an opportunity to emphasize the most salient features of your arguments with punch, weaving in those facts that help demonstrate that your legal theories are correct. A *summary of argument* should not be confused with an introduction. An introduction sets the tone for the brief; a *summary of argument* is really a summary of what you are going to argue, citing cases where appropriate.

---

and a person can be convicted of a Class C felony, subject to five years in prison, if they let the children go fishing, camping, or generally stay the weekend with their grandfather or grandmother, if either of those grandparents is a registered sex offender.

Compare the *Summary of Argument* from the Alaska brief with the one from Respondents' brief. Notice how the Summary of Argument in each brief relies on the same case and on the same spot cite—*Kansas v. Hendricks*, 521 U.S. 346, 361 (1997). Petitioners rely on *Hendricks* to support the proposition that where legislative intent is regulatory, a party arguing that the intent was really penal bears an extraordinarily heavy burden. Respondent relies on *Hendricks* to support its argument that merely because a state legislature labels a law as "regulatory" does not preclude a court from concluding that it is really punitive. The first paragraph of each party's Summary highlights an important difference in the way each approaches the case. Petitioners embrace the Court's holdings in other ex post facto cases and argue that those cases set a very high bar for anyone who seeks to label a state law as punitive when the state legislature has expressly noted that the law is regulatory. Respondents never challenge this formulation; instead they appear to accept it and argue that they have surmounted the high bar. Respondents' strategy is highly defensive, perhaps too much so. They never take issue with the burden of proof that they must shoulder; this becomes more evident in the argument section of the brief.

Petitioners' Summary of Argument

The ASORA is a regulatory law intended to help protect the public from future harm by collecting truthful information and making it available to those who choose to access it. It is not a penal law intended to punish people for past acts. To determine whether a law is penal within the meaning of the Ex Post Facto Clause, the Court employs a two-step test. First, the Court asks whether the legislature intended that the law serve legitimate regulatory purposes, rather than punitive ones. If so, the inquiry is at an end, except in extremely limited circumstances where the party challenging the law carries the "heavy burden" of showing by the "clearest proof" that the stated intent is merely a charade for punitive goals. *Hendricks*, 521 U.S. at 361.

This "clearest proof" requirement exists not only because of the inherent difficulties in ascertaining legislative intent other than through the statutory language itself, but also because of the purposes of the Ex Post Facto Clause. The Ex Post Facto Clause protects against vindictive or malicious legislation, an inquiry that necessarily turns on the intent of the legislature. Precisely the same sanction can be either civil or penal depending on the legislature's intent. Thus, once it is determined that the legislature's intent was not punitive, the ex post facto inquiry is all but over. Other constitutional provisions, such as the Due Process Clause, protect against legislation that is irrational or does not sufficiently serve its stated purposes.

As every court to have considered the issue (including the Ninth Circuit below) has held, the intent behind sexual offender registration and notification statutes is regulatory, not punitive. As the Alaska legislature expressly declared, the ASORA was intended to "protect[ ] the public" and "protect[ ] the public safety," by collecting and making available truthful information that people may find useful to safeguard themselves and their children from possible future harm. 1994 Alaska Sess. Laws ch. 41, § 1. The law was not intended to punish people for past acts, and in fact imposes only minimal regulatory requirements on those required to register. The legislative history confirms this express non-punitive intent.

The ex post facto inquiry is therefore over unless there is the clearest proof that the legislature's expressed intent masks a true punitive purpose. To locate such proof, the Court has traditionally looked to the factors set forth in *Mendoza-Martinez* as guideposts. Demonstrating the narrowness of that inquiry, however, the Court has never held that a law had a non-punitive purpose but nevertheless violated the Ex Post Facto Clause in light of the *Mendoza-Martinez* factors. Indeed, the Court has routinely upheld the retroactive application of laws far more onerous than the ASORA.

Contrary to the Ninth Circuit's holding, there is no proof, much less the required clearest proof, that the ASORA is so punitive in purpose or effect so as to negate the legislature's finding to the contrary. The Ninth Circuit correctly held that three *Mendoza-Martinez* factors indicated that the law is not punitive. First, registration and notification provisions have not historically been regarded as punishment. Registration requirements are commonplace in our regulated society, and provisions that make information about criminal records available to the public are likewise common and have never been considered additional punishment for the underlying crime. Second, the ASORA does not come into play only upon a finding of scienter. To the contrary, the law's provisions are triggered only by the fact of a conviction. Third, the law plainly has a non-punitive purpose that can rationally be assigned to it — protecting the public from future harm.

The Ninth Circuit erred, however, in concluding that the four other *Mendoza-Martinez* factors so outweighed the others and the legislature's intent as to render the ASORA punitive in fact. First, the ASORA imposes no affirmative disability or restraint. The registration and verification requirements are undemanding and, contrary to the Ninth Circuit, do not require that quarterly verifications be submitted in person. The notification provisions likewise impose no affirmative disability or restraint. Although notification could conceivably have negative collateral effects due to the actions of those who learn the information, those consequences accompany any disclosure of criminal records and are not an affirmative disability or restraint imposed by the law. Second, the ASORA does not further the traditional aims of punishment. It is not inherently retributive to collect truthful information and make it available to those who choose to access it as a means of safeguarding themselves and their families. And even if the law were seen as a deterrent, the Court has long held that deterrence is a civil, not simply punitive, goal. Third, while the ASORA applies only to behavior that is already criminal, that factor should be of little import in the ex post facto inquiry, and the Court has never held a law punitive simply because it applies to convicted felons. Finally, the ASORA is not excessive in comparison to its regulatory purposes, particularly when compared to far more onerous laws the Court has upheld in the past. Ex post facto analysis does not require a perfect fit between means and ends, and such inquiries are in any event better left to a due process analysis.[*]

---

[*] In referencing "due process," the Petitioners are really referencing a doctrine called "substantive due process" which has not been enforced by the Courts since the 1930s. Substantive due process requires that a state law have a rational relationship to a legitimate government purpose. *Authors' note.*

Respondents' Summary of Argument

1. The ASORA, a law which regulates the person rather than his participation in an activity or profession, and based solely on the past conviction, is punitive. This conclusion is supported by application of the "intent-effects" test, which test is employed by the Court to determine whether a purported civil, regulatory provision should be classified as criminal. *Hendricks*, 521 U.S. at 361.

2. In applying the "intent-effects" test, this Court first looks for a clearly stated preference on the part of the legislature. Hendricks, 521 U.S. at 361. If no clear preference exists, the Court examines the ASORA on its face to determine whether it is regulatory in both structure and design. Id. In doing so, factors such as codification, triggering events, and existence of procedural protections are some of the factors that guide the Court to its conclusion. *Hendricks,* 521 U.S. at 361. Indeed, in Hendricks, this Court found non-punitive intent because the Act was codified in the probate code, and because the Act was not triggered solely by conviction. In *United States v. One Assortment of 89 Firearms*, 465 U.S. 354, 363 (1984), this Court held that one of the most important characteristics of a regulatory law is adequate procedural protections.

3. The Court may also seek to determine whether the ASORA amends the criminal law, and whether it imposes additional sanctions generally imposed by laws that are decidedly penal. *See Mendoza-Martinez*, 372 U.S. at 168-169. Moreover, an important element in establishing an objective manifestation of intent is examination of the focus of the legislature in enacting the ASORA. *Flemming*, 363 U.S. at 613-614. If the legislature focused on an activity from which sex offenders should be barred because of relevant past conduct, a presumption may exist that the legislature intended the ASORA to be regulatory. Id. However, the contrary is true if the focus was on the person or class of persons to whom the ASORA applies. *Id.*

4. In applying this facial examination to the ASORA, every relevant factor points to punitive intent and the only conclusion that can be drawn is that the legislature intended the ASORA to be penal. Because there is sufficient risk that retroactive application will increase the punishment for past crimes, the ASORA may not be applied retroactively without violating the Ex Post Facto Clause.

5. Where facial examination is inconclusive, or results in a conclusion that the Act in question is decidedly civil, the Court inquires further to determine whether the challenged Act is so punitive either in purpose or effect that it transforms what was intended as a civil remedy into a criminal penalty. *Hudson*, 522 U.S. at 99. In making this determination, several factors are used as guideposts, including:

    Whether the sanction involves an affirmative disability or restraint, whether it has historically been regarded as punishment, whether it comes into play only on a finding of scienter, whether its operation will promote the traditional aims of punishment-retribution and deterrence, whether the behavior to which it applies is already criminal, whether an alternative purpose to which it may rationally be connected is assignable for it, and whether it appears excessive in relation to the alternative purpose assigned. *Mendoza-Martinez*, 372 U.S. at 168-169 (citations emitted).

6. Respondents need only show that any one of these factors, or any combination of two or more demonstrates that the ASORA is excessive in either its purpose or effect. *United States v. Ward*, 448 U.S. 242, 249 (1980); *United States v. One Assortment of 89 Firearms*, 465 U.S. at 365 n.7. The *Mendoza-Martinez* factors are not exhaustive or dispositive and the weight to be given each factor depends upon the context and type of sanction at issue. *Hudson, supra*.

7. The ASORA is not a regulatory law because it does not seek to regulate any activity from which respondents should be barred due to relevant past conduct. Rather, the ASORA is punitive in intent because the legislative focus was the group of persons previously convicted of sex offenses. Moreover, the ASORA is not only codified as criminal, its enactment resulted in substantive amendments to Alaska's criminal laws, demonstrating it was intended to be an integral part of the criminal law. Furthermore, the ASORA unduly infringes upon private interests, including fundamental rights. Because punitive intent is evidenced from the face of the ASORA, the effects need not be considered and it cannot be applied retroactively to persons whose offenses were committed prior to its effective date if there is a sufficient risk that it will increase the punishment for past offenses. *Lynce, supra*. If punitive legislative intent is not evident by examination of the ASORA, the court will nonetheless classify the law as penal if its objective features demonstrate that it is punitive in either purpose or effect. *Hendricks*, 521 U.S. at 361. In applying the seven *Mendoza-Martinez* factors to the ASORA, one results in ambiguous intent, six weigh in on the side of classifying the ASORA as criminal.

(11) Argument. The *argument* is the heart of the appellate brief and contains the writer's analysis of the issues that the writer identified in the questions presented. The argument is broken into sections, with each section devoted to a single legal issue. The sections are identified by headings or subheadings that present the writer's conclusions or assert an answer (either positive or negative) to the questions that were presented earlier in the brief.

Sometimes, the headings in petitioners' and respondents' briefs mirror each other. In our example, the Petitioners' brief has a section entitled:

> The Ninth Circuit's Assessment Of The *Mendoza-Martinez* Factors Was Critically Flawed And Did Not Support A Finding By The "Clearest Proof" That The ASORA Is Punitive.

The Respondents' corresponding heading reads:

> Application Of The *Mendoza-Martinez* Factors Compels The Conclusion That The ASORA Must Be Reclassified As Criminal Because It Is Excessive In Its Purpose And Effect.

On page 338, we present in its entirety the *Mendoza-Martinez* section of the Petitioners' brief in *Smith v. Doe*. For comparison, we have reproduced below the corresponding section of the Respondents' brief (footnotes omitted).

There is nothing fancy, at least organizationally, about the *Mendoza-Martinez* section of each brief. The issue is whether *Mendoza-Martinez* requires a court to view the Alaska statute as penal. Both Petitioners and Respondents agree that *Mendoza-Martinez* applies to this case. Both look to the seven factors in *Mendoza-Martinez* and organize their arguments around those factors. In discussing the seven factors, each side follows the same familiar and very basic organizational pattern: IRAC. The major difference between the two briefs is how each applies those same seven factors.

Arguably the most critical factor in *Mendoza-Martinez* is "affirmative disability or restraint." Because of its importance, the subsection in both parties' briefs addressing that factor are presented side-by-side below. The Petitioners define the phrase "affirmative disability or restraint," and indicate how it has been applied by other courts in other settings. They then show that, by applying the factor as other courts have done supports the finding that Alaska's law is not penal in effect. The Respondents, oddly, never really define the term and never remind the reader that the lower court found in their favor on this factor. The Respondents speak about privacy, about the scarlet letter and other historical illustrations and problems, but they never show how the Alaska law imposes a restraint or affirmative disability on them. In sharp contrast, the Petitioners' brief tends to be remains concrete and focused. In general, however, we consider both to be well written.

Respondents' Argument: *Mendoza-Martinez* Section

C. Application of the Mendoza-Martinez factors compels the conclusion that the ASORA must be reclassified as criminal because it is excessive in its purpose and effect.

Factor 1, Affirmative disability or restraint.

The ASORA imposes an affirmative disability or restraint because it places registrants at a serious disadvantage and it limits or prevents the exercise of fundamental rights. Moreover, the ASORA labels registrants with a scarlet letter, subjects them to community scorn, and outrage, and it subjects registrants to a lifetime of governmental supervision and monitoring, which is the fundamental equivalent to a lifetime on parole or probation. See Brief of Public Defender Service, D.C., As *Amicus Curiae*.

It is not true that disability or restraint only equates to incarceration. Pet. Br. 37-38. Disability or restraint includes inflicting deprivations on an individual in order to prevent his future misconduct. *United States v. Brown*, 381 U.S. at 458-459. In *Cummings*, the Court disagreed that a disability or restraint only exists when the sanction involves physical restraint on the individual. *Cummings*, 71 U.S. at 322. The Court recognized that restraint takes many forms and "[t]he deprivation of any rights, civil or political, previously enjoyed, may be punishment. . . . " *Id.*

Moreover, the Court noted that counsel for the government did not include within his definition of liberty, freedom from outrage on the feelings, and the Court held that deprivation of rights or privileges vested under prior law could constitute punishment. *Id.* The most important determinative factor was "the circumstances attending and the causes of the deprivation." *Id.*

Here, the Does had a right under Alaska law to reintegrate into society and to be left alone. *Abraham*, 585 P.2d at 531. This right is fundamental and protected by the Due Process Clause of the 14th Amendment. *Ferguson*, 816 P.2d at 139-140. Moreover, the Does had the right to unconditional release after service of their sentences and the right to have all their civil rights restored. Alaska Stat. 33.30.241, Alaska Stat. 12.55.185(15). Compelling the Does to register, coupled with the imposition of conditions such as the duty to report a change of residence, a change in employer, hair color, type of vehicles, etc., all deprives them of rights and privileges existing under prior law. The circumstance attending a deprivation of these rights is the State's desire to fulfill one of the stated goals of penal administration in Alaska, and the cause of the deprivation is the prior conviction because the ASORA only applies after conviction for a sex offense. Alaska Stat. 12.63.100 (1998).

Pasting a scarlet letter on the offender through public notification places the offender at risk of violence, and clearly imposes an affirmative disability and restraint. Examples of violent community response continue to mount and add to the reams of evidence which weigh heavily against criminal registration and public notification. Jerusalem: A Framework for Post-Sentence Sex Offender Legislation, "Perspectives on Prevention, Registration, and the Public's 'Right' to Know," 48 Vand. L. Rev. 219, 245-46 (1995). This retributive, stigmatizing community environment has the opposite effect of rehabilitative treatment, which is the second proposed policy goal of these registration laws. *Id.* Public notification laws have created an atmosphere where vigilantism, and public condemnation is the norm, rehabilitation is the exception. Silva: Dial, 1-900-PERVERT, and Other Statutory Measures That Provide Public Notification of Sex Offenders, 48 SMU. L. Rev. 1962, 1983-84 [1995]. Under the guise of protecting the public, these laws have been the cause of homes being burned, *id.*, at 1983; of beatings, and of families being run out of town. *Id.*, at 1983-1984. Even small children have been harassed merely because their parent was once convicted of crime. *Id.*, p. 1984. Empirical studies show that these laws do not protect the public, they do not reduce the incidence of crime and in fact, they may be part of the cause of the recent rise in criminal activity. *Id.*, pp. 1979-1980. See also Note: Battling Sex Offenders: Is Megan's Law An Effective Means Of Achieving Public Safety?, 19 Seton Hall Leg. J. 519, at 546-549 (1995). Finally, there are ever increasing reported incidents of the wrong person being attacked because the public believed a criminal lived at that address. *Id.*, pp. 558-560. The empirical evidence continues to mount and these case histories show that these offense-based registration and public notification laws do indeed impose an affirmative disability and restraint. See generally, Brief of New Jersey Public Defender Agency As Amicus Curiae.

Factor 2, Whether the sanction has historically been regarded as punishment.

Public notification, shaming, ostracism, and community obloquy have historical roots and have traditionally been nothing but punishment. A. Earle, Curious

Punishments of Bygone Days, 1-2 (1896) (Applewood reprint 1995). The lower court erred in concluding otherwise. Pet. App. 18a. While it is true that regulatory laws are not historically regarded as punishment Pet. Br. 35, that truth does not stand where the law regulates the individual, rather than an activity.

Earle, a social historian of the 19th Century noted that "our far-away grandfathers" were most afraid of ridicule and this sensitiveness which made a "lampoon, a jeer, a scoff, [or] a taunt, an unbearable and inflaming offense was of equal force when used against men of the day in punishment for real crimes and offenses." *Id.* Earle's historic account of punishment shows that "contemptuous publicity and personal obloquy" was incorporated into all forms of punishment, and that public exposure as well as public mocking by the whole community was thought to be the most effective form of punishment. *Id.*, at 3. Moreover, the motivation for imposition of publicity and public exposure as a form of punishment is nearly identical to the reasons given for these offense-based Megan's laws — because the public wanted to know who were the criminals, and where they could be found. A. Earle, at 87. It was "characteristic of the times," every little community sought to know the offenses and offenders that could hinder the growth and prosperity of their new communities. *Id.*

Not only is publicity regarding one's crime historically regarded as punishment, but forced registration itself has punitive roots — although the historic form of that registration was somewhat different than the modern day computer database. In those historic times discussed by Earle, forced registration took the form of wearing a badge that gave the information required, such as the place of residence. A. Earle, pp. 89-90.

In more recent times, registration of criminals was never thought to be anything other than punishment. Note: *Criminal Registration Ordinances: Police Control Over Potential Recidivists*, 103 U. OF PA. L. REV. 60, 61 (1954). This 1930's attempt at criminal registration was not unlike the current trend. Conviction of a crime was the single element that triggered the application of these laws to the individuals affected. *Id.*, at 65. Additionally, the conviction for the covered offenses would trigger the duty to register, regardless of the jurisdiction in which the conviction occurred. *Id.* at 68, 75. These outdated criminal registration laws required those persons to be fingerprinted, photographed, and they required reports as to the changes in one's residence. *Id.* Like the ASORA, these registration laws all carried significant penalties that could be imposed upon those persons who failed to comply with the registration requirements. *Id.*, at 79. Unlike the ASORA, however, these registration laws were never touted as being anything other than punishment. *See In re Allen Eugene Reed on Habeas Corpus*, 663 P.2d 216, 218 (California 1983).

Clearly, registration of convicted offenders and public notification about their crimes must be historically regarded as punishment, and nothing but punishment.

Factor 3, Applies only upon a finding of scienter.

The ASORA applies only after conviction for a sex offense and thus, applies only after a finding of scienter [i.e., intent]. In adopting this element of the effects test, this Court intended a finding of scienter if the intent, bad faith or knowing conduct of the party was at issue in the original crime to which the new sanction is applied. *Mendoza-Martinez*, 372 U.S. at 169 n.24, citing *Helwig*, 188 U.S. at 610-612. In *Helwig*, the sole question presented was whether a statute, which imposed an additional monetary payment for importations constituted a penalty. *Helwig*, 188 U.S. at 611. In reaching its conclusions, the Court held that there could be no question that the statute in question imposed a penalty, "[i]t is because of the action of the importer with relation to the importation in question" that the sanction is applied. *Id.* Thus, if the offense triggers application of the statute, the sanction only comes about upon a finding of scienter. It is not true that scienter can only be found if the ASORA itself requires such a finding, and the underlying offense triggering the ASORA is relevant. Pet. Br. 36.

The lower court based its conclusion on interpretation of Alaska's sexual abuse statutes, and the lack of any "intent" requirement. Pet. App. 18a. However, scienter can include bad faith or knowing conduct. *See Kurth Ranch*, 511 U.S. at 774. In Alaska, knowing conduct is an element of sexual abuse. *See Van Meter v. State*, 743 P.2d 385, 389 (Alaska App. 1987). Because scienter is an element of the crime triggering the ASORA's application, the ASORA operates upon a finding of scienter.

Factor 4, Whether the ASORA promotes the traditional aims of punishment-retribution and deterrence.

The ASORA promotes traditional aims of punishment — retribution and deterrence. Pet. Br 44, Pet. App. 21a. The lower court found the ASORA primarily retributive because of the lifetime registration requirement, quarterly verification of the same information four times per year, excessive notification and because there was no way to escape the ASORA's effect, and not merely because of a misstatement of the law. Pet. App. 21a. Here, petitioners admit that the ASORA is intended to deter future crime, although they wrongly contend that retributive and deterrent goals are insufficient to classify the ASORA as penal. Pet. Br. 44, *See Kurth Ranch, supra* (law was penal due to its excessive effect and deterrent goals).

Factor 5, Whether the ASORA applies to conduct which is already a crime.

This factor is highly relevant to the Ex Post Facto inquiry. Pet. Br. 44-45. It makes little difference whether double jeopardy or retroactive punishment is at issue, the question to be answered is whether the law is criminal, and not civil. *Hudson*, 522 U.S. at 93-94. Thus the question whether the ASORA applies to behavior which is already criminal is relevant to this inquiry. Pet. Br. 44-45. That question must be answered in the positive because the ASORA only applies after conviction for a sex offense. Hence, it applies only to conduct which is already a crime.

Factor 6, Whether an alternative purpose may rationally be assigned.

The alternative purpose assigned by the legislature is protection of the public through deterrence of future sex offenses. Pet. Br. 37, 44. Although, this alternative purpose is valid, and rational, it does not compel the conclusion that the ASORA is civil rather than penal. *New York v. Burger*, 482 U.S. 691, 693, 712 (1987). Regulatory laws may have the same purpose as penal laws, but regulatory laws are generally distinguishable because they are narrowly drawn to accomplish the stated purpose. *Id.* Thus, although the lower court held that a valid alternative purpose could be assigned to the ASORA, this factor should be given little weight in determining whether the ASORA is penal or civil. Pet. App. 23a. It is respectfully asserted that protection of the public through deterrence of future criminal behavior is a constitutionally insufficient purpose to justify such a broad offense-based registration and public notification law that labels the individual with a badge of infamy. At best, the alternative purpose assigned to the ASORA is ambiguous. Hence, evaluation of the ASORA under this factor does not compel the conclusion that the ASORA was intended to be civil.

Factor 7, Whether the ASORA is excessive in relation to its assigned purpose.

In determining whether the ASORA is excessive in relation to its asserted purpose, comparison of the ASORA to laws which regulate the qualifications for the practice of medicine is completely unreasonable. Pet. Br. 46, citing, *Hawker.* *[Authors' note: The Respondents never state why is it not reasonable to use qualifications for practice of medicine.].* Moreover, it is unreasonable to compare the ASORA to the civil remedial statutes challenged in *Hendricks,* because the ASORA provides no procedure whatsoever to determine future dangerousness based on current evidence. Pet. Br. 47. The ASORA does that, which this Court in Hendricks said should not be done-it predicts future dangerousness based solely on the past conviction. *Hendricks,* 521 U.S. at 360.

The question whether the ASORA is excessive is not more pertinent to a due process inquiry because the process due under a particular statute depends upon whether the statute in question is regulatory or penal. Pet. Br. 47-48. *Cf., United States v. Salerno,* 481 U.S. 739, 746 (1987). Furthermore, where fundamental rights are abridged by the challenged act, the State must do more than show a reasonable relationship between the purpose and the means employed to achieve the desired purpose. Pet. Br. 48. Instead, the State must show both a compelling State interest and that the Act is narrowly tailored to achieve that compelling interest. *Roe v. Wade,* 410 U.S. 113, 155 (1973).

In this instance, fundamental rights are infringed and the legislature knew that to be true when the ASORA was enacted — the legislative findings recognized a specific right of privacy and recognized that the right of privacy was being infringed by the ASORA. 1994 Alaska Sess. Laws, ch. 41, § 1. Additionally, the right to rehabilitation and reintegration, which is a right protected by due process in Alaska, is infringed as are other rights discussed previously herein. *Ferguson,* 816 P.2d at 139. Hence, petitioners have the burden of showing that the ASORA is narrowly tailored to meet the goal of protection of the public through deterrence of future conduct.

The registration provisions of the ASORA are excessive in relation to the alternative purpose assigned because if a registrant provides the myriad of information demanded under the ASORA, and all of the information is accurate and does not change, then why should the individual be forced to provide the same information four times per year for the rest of his life? The only purpose for demanding that the registrant provide the same information, four-times per year for the rest of his life and to, each time, swear upon oath that it is true, is to punish. There could be no other legitimate purpose for such a demanding provision. The stated goals of the ASORA are far outweighed by the stigmatic and punitive effects associated with forced registration and public notification. Indeed, the empirical evidence shows that in attempting to protect the public, these offense-based Megan's laws put a large segment of the public at substantial risk. Brief of New Jersey Pubic Defender Agency as *Amicus Curiae.* See also CR 107, Exhibit 9-11, CR 101, Exhibit 12-16. That portion of the public who may be housing registrants, providing employment to registrants, or related to registrants by blood or marriage are clearly at substantial risk solely because of the State's action. The assertion that the cause of vigilantism against innocent members of the public is public response and not State action lacks merit. *NAACP v. Alabama*, 357 U.S. 449, 463 (1958). "[I]t is only after the initial exertion of state power represented by the . . . [disclosure], that private action takes hold." *Id.*

In attempting to protect the public through deterrence of future conduct, the ASORA violates fundamental rights, lacks procedures for determining future dangerousness, impedes the ability to find and maintain a home, interferes with the ability to seek and maintain employment, invades the personal relationships of the registrant, and places the registrant, their families and other members of the public at substantial risk of vigilantism. CR 107, Exhibits 9-11, CR 101, Exhibits 12-16; Brief of New Jersey Public Defender As *Amicus Curiae*. The ASORA labels the offender with a badge of infamy, a label expositive of the crime and tells the public the individual is dangerous and should be ostracized into an inner-community banishment as a new class of citizen.

The ASORA is also excessive because it operates to infringe upon fundamental liberties of persons convicted of a sex offense who pose no threat whatsoever to the public. *See McKune v. Lile*, 536 U.S. 24, 122 S.Ct. 2017, 2024 (2002). Although the rate of recidivism for sex offenders varies depending upon the number of, and category of sex offender studied, *see generally*, Brief of N.J. Public Defender, As *Amicus Curiae*; Brief of United States, As *Amicus Curiae*, it is reasonable to conclude that the average recidivism rate is less than 20 percent. *Id.* Even if the government's asserted rates are considered, that means that 50 to 80 percent of the individuals compelled to register and labeled for life are not likely to re-offend and do not pose a threat to public safety. *See* Brief of United States As *Amicus Curiae*. In Alaska, thousands of individuals, including family, friends, employers, and associates of the registered offender, are unnecessarily subjected to the harmful and punitive effects of the ASORA. Nationally, hundreds of thousands of lives will be destroyed if this Court sanctions enactment and enforcement of broad-based registration and notification laws like the ASORA. Nearly every sex offender and public notification law upheld by the federal courts have tailored the provisions imposed to the actual risk posed by the offender. *See Cutshall v. Sundquist*, 193 F. 3d 466, 474 (6th Cir. 1999); *Roe v. Office of Adult Probation*, 125 F. 3d 47, 54 (2d Cir. 1997); *E.B. v. Verniero*, 119 F. 3d 1077, 1098 (3d Cir. 1997); *Doe v. Pataki*, 120 F.3d 1263, 1269-70 (2d Cir. 1997). Rather than have professionals assess the degree of risk, Alaska chose to let the untrained, uninformed public, some of whom will and have engaged in vigilantism, make that determination for themselves. Resp. App. 8a-9a. Because the ASORA applies to all persons previously convicted, regardless of degree of risk actually posed, it imposes its stigmatizing effect on persons who pose no threat to the public, and it is excessive in relation to the assigned purpose of protecting society through deterrence of future conduct. *See Salerno*, 481 U.S. at 747-749.

Side-by-Side of "affirmative disability or restraint" sections from each brief

To highlight the differences between the two argument sections, the subsections from each party's brief discussing "the affirmative disability or restraint" factor appear side-by-side starting on p. 306. A third column contains the Petitioners' reply to the Respondents' argument, and a fourth column sets out some of our observations about the main arguments of each side.

Petitioners' Argument —	*Respondents' Argument* —
Mendoza-Martinez Factors: The factor below is the fourth factor discussed by the Petitioners; the Ninth Circuit found in Petitioners' favor on the first three factors discussed by Petitioners.	*Mendoza-Martinez* Factors: Factor 1 below is the first factor discussed by the Respondents; they prevailed on this factor in the Ninth Circuit.

Affirmative Disability Or Restraint. [*Underlining added.*]	**Factor 1, Affirmative disability or restraint.** [*Underlining added.*]
1. The ASORA does not impose an "affirmative disability or restraint" on registrants. *See Mendoza-Martinez*, 372 U.S. at 168. This Court in *Hudson* likened that term, as "<u>normally understood</u>," to the " '<u>infamous punishment</u>' of imprisonment." 522 U.S. at 104 (quoting *Flemming*, 363 U.S. at 617); *see also Seling v. Young*, 531 U.S. 250, 272-273 (2001) (Thomas, J., concurring in the judgment) (<u>equating</u> "<u>affirmative disability or restraint</u>" with "<u>confinement</u>"); *compare Hendricks*, 521 U.S. at 362 (noting that civil commitment scheme "<u>does involve an affirmative restraint</u>," but finding that disability outweighed by legislature's non-punitive purpose). The ASORA imposes on registrants <u>no</u> physical restraint of any kind. It does not restrict their freedom of movement, does not require pre-clearance before they can switch jobs or residences, and does not restrict them from living or working in any part of the community. *See, e.g., Femedeer*, 227 F.3d at 1250 (offenders are "free to live where they choose, come and go as they please, and seek whatever employment they may desire"); *Cutshall*, 193 F.3d at 474; E.B., 119 F.3d at 1102.	The ASORA imposes an affirmative disability or restraint because it places registrants <u>at a serious disadvantage and it limits or prevents the exercise of fundamental rights</u>. Moreover, the ASORA labels registrants with a scarlet letter, subjects them to community scorn, and outrage, and it subjects registrants to a lifetime of governmental supervision and monitoring, which is <u>the fundamental equivalent to a lifetime on parole or probation</u>. See Brief of Public Defender Service, D.C., As *Amicus Curiae*.
2. According to the Ninth Circuit, however, the Act's registration provisions "impose a significant affirmative disability" because they "subject[] offenders to onerous conditions" — namely, the requirement that certain sex offenders, like respondents, "re-register at police stations four times each year every year of their lives." Pet. App. 13a-14a. The court viewed the requirement that offenders "appear in person at a police station on each occasion" as the critical factor making the law impermissibly "onerous." Id. at 14a.	<u>It is not true that disability or restraint only equates to incarceration.</u> Pet. Br. 37-38. Disability or restraint includes inflicting deprivations on an individual in order to prevent his future misconduct. *United States v. Brown*, 381 U.S. at 458-459. In *Cummings*, the Court disagreed that a disability or restraint only exists when the sanction involves physical restraint on the individual. *Cummings*, 71 U.S. at 322. The Court recognized that restraint takes many forms and "[t]he deprivation of any rights, civil or political, previously enjoyed, may be punishment. . . . " *Id.* Moreover, the Court noted that counsel for the government did not include within his definition of liberty, freedom from outrage on the feelings, and the Court held that deprivation of rights or privileges vested under prior law could constitute punishment. *Id.* The most important determinative factor was "the circumstances attending and the causes of the deprivation." *Id.*
The court's holding was based on a persistent misapprehension of the relevant provision of the ASORA. The ASORA specifically permits registrants to submit "written verification" of their registry information quarterly or yearly. *See* Alaska Stat. §§12.63.010(d)(1) (annual verification), (d)(2) (quarterly verification). The Alaska Code provisions implementing the ASORA similarly make clear that registrants may verify their information by mail, rather than in person. The relevant Code provision	Here, the Does had a right under Alaska law to reintegrate into society and to be left alone. *Abraham*, 585 P.2d at 531. This right is fundamental and protected by the Due Process Clause of the 14th Amendment. *Ferguson*, 816 P.2d at 139-140. Moreover, the Does had the right to unconditional release after service of their

Petitioners' Reply	Authors' Comments

Affirmative Disability Or Restraint.

Petitioners' Reply	Authors' Comments
The ASORA does not impose physical restraints on registrants and does not constrain registrants' freedom of movement. Nor does the law on its face or of its own force curtail their employment, housing, or educational opportunities. Respondents do not dispute any of this. They have also abandoned the Ninth Circuit's erroneous and persistent statements that the ASORA's registration requirements require offenders to "register in person four times each year every year of their lives" — an error forming the centerpiece of the court's conclusion that the law imposed an "affirmative disability" and was "excessive." *See* Pet. App. 13a-14a, 7a, 19a, 20, 27a, 28a; Resp. Br. 32 n.16 (acknowledging that "the panel may have relied on a misstatement of Alaska law"). Respondents contend instead that the law imposes an "affirmative disability or restraint" because registrants are exposed to "community scorn[] and outrage" and because private citizens in the community might take unlawful action against them. *See* Resp. Br. 31-33, 41; D.C. Pub. Def. Br. 13-27; ACLU Br. 18-21; N.J. Pub. Def. Br. 6-21. The ASORA does not impose those consequences; they "(1) are wholly dependent on acts by private third parties, (2) result from information most of which was publicly available prior to the [Act], and (3) flow essentially from the fact of the underlying conviction." *Doe v. Pataki,* 120 F.3d at 1280; *see Meadows v. Board of Parole & Post-Prison Supervision,* 47 P.3d 506, 512 (Or. App. Ct. 2002) (unwelcome societal consequences "are the result of the offender's crimes and not of the designation and disclosure statutes"); *see also* N.J. Pub. Def. Br. 9, 15 (giving examples of negative community response to sex offender where *no* government-sponsored notification was conducted). As the Third Circuit recognized in *E.B. v. Verniero,* information relating to criminal convictions, publicized as a matter of course in our judicial system, may be the source of a wide range of adverse consequences for the convicted defendant, running from mild personal embarrassment to social ostracism and/or vigilante retribution. Employment may be lost, and the opportunity for future employment may be dramatically reduced. * * * Nevertheless, our laws' insistence that	Each side started its *Mendoza-Martinez* argument by discussing the factor or factors on which it prevailed on in the Ninth Circuit. The first two sentences of each opening brief highlight the fundamental issue of the case, namely what constitutes "punishment." The Petitioners immediately build on prior Supreme Court decisions. The Petitioners are telling the Court what the law is; the Respondents appear to be telling the Court what the law ought to be. This is a subtle but important distinction, one based not on interpretation of the law but on the attorneys' writing styles and rhetorical choices. However, it can have important ramifications because arguing what the law "ought" to be implies that that is not the current state of the law. The Respondents delay discussing prior Court decisions until the second paragraph and then do not emphasize the holdings of those cases as much as they could have done. Respondents rely on *Cummings v. Missouri,* 71 U.S. 244 (1866). In that case, Missouri amended its Constitution to require those seeking to practice various professions, including lawyers, teachers, ministers and the like, to take an oath that they had not taken arms against the Union during the Civil War. Those who fought for the Confederacy could not honestly take the oath and were thereby barred from the professions. The Court held that the Missouri law was an ex post facto law. *Cummings* does stand for the proposition that "punishment" can take forms other than incarceration. Was the Alaska law as offensive as the Missouri law? Did the Missouri

Petitioners' Argument —	*Respondents' Argument —*
specifies that "When an offender submits a registration form to a registration agency without appearing in person, the registration agency shall review the form. If the form or any document submitted in connection with the form has obvious discrepancies *** the registration agency will notify the offender of the need for corrections and may not accept the form until the offender makes all necessary corrections". [13 Alaska Admin. Code §09.025(d) (emphasis added).]	sentences and the right to have all their civil rights restored. Alaska Stat. 33.30.241, Alaska Stat. 12.55.185(15). Compelling the Does to register, coupled with the imposition of conditions such as the duty to report a change of residence, a change in employer, hair color, type of vehicles, etc., all deprives them of rights and privileges existing under prior law. The circumstance attending a deprivation of these rights is the

See also id. §09.025(e) (information is considered submitted "on the date *** it is postmarked, if mailed").

To be sure, the State bears significant responsibility for the panel's initial confusion. Asked at oral argument whether registrants must "go to the police station" to verify their registry information, counsel for the State responded, "under the current law, yes." *See* Pet. App. 7a n.4. The State's rehearing petition, however, corrected the misstatement. But the Ninth Circuit's amended opinion nonetheless persisted in placing heavy reliance on the supposed requirement of quarterly or annual "in-person" verification. *See id.* at 7a, 14a, 19a, 20a, 27a, 28a. The panel based its holding entirely on counsel's statement at oral argument. *Id.* at 7a n.4. Thus, in the face of the plain text of the statute, its implementing code provisions, and the State's corrective statement in its petition for rehearing, the Ninth Circuit panel opted to retain its demonstrably erroneous interpretation of the ASORA's requirements.

That was wrong. The principles that courts are not bound by stipulations of law, *see, e.g., Swift & Co. v. Hocking Valley Ry. Co.*, 243 U.S. 281, 289 (1917), and that estoppel does not typically run against the government, *see, e.g., Illinois ex rel Gordon v. Campbell*, 329 U.S. 362, 369 (1946), converge to make clear that the court should have decided the case under the correct view of what the ASORA provides. The court of appeals had an independent obligation to determine the meaning of the controlling statute, *see Kamen v. Kemper Fin. Servs., Inc.*, 500 U.S. 90, 99 (1991) (court "retains the independent power to identify and apply the proper construction of governing law"), and a misstatement by counsel during oral argument cannot override the language of the statute. The Act's registration requirement is, as other courts correctly have found, nothing like the "infamous

---

(Respondents' Argument, continued)

State's desire to fulfill one of the stated goals of penal administration in Alaska, and the cause of the deprivation is the prior conviction because the ASORA only applies after conviction for a sex offense. Alaska Stat. 12.63.100 (1998).

Pasting a scarlet letter on the offender through public notification places the offender at risk of violence, and clearly imposes an affirmative disability and restraint. Examples of violent community response continue to mount and add to the reams of evidence which weigh heavily against criminal registration and public notification. Jerusalem: *A Framework for Post-Sentence Sex Offender Legislation, "Perspectives on Prevention, Registration, and the Public's 'Right' to Know,"* 48 VAND. L. REV. 219, 245-46 (1995). This retributive, stigmatizing community environment has the opposite effect of rehabilitative treatment, which is the second proposed policy goal of these registration laws. *Id.* Public notification laws have created an atmosphere where vigilantism, and public condemnation is the norm, rehabilitation is the exception. Silva: *Dial, 1-900-PER-VERT, and Other Statutory Measures That Provide Public Notification of Sex Offenders*, 48 SMU. L. REV. 1962, 1983-84 [1995]. Under the guise of protecting the public, these laws have been the cause of homes being burned, *id.*, at 1983; of beatings, and of families being run out of town. *Id.*, at 1983-1984. Even small children have been harassed merely because their parent was once convicted of crime. *Id.*, p. 1984. Empirical studies show that these laws do not protect the public, they do not reduce the incidence of crime and in fact, they may be

Petitioners' Reply	*Authors' Comments*
information regarding criminal proceedings be publicly disseminated is not intended as punishment and has never been regarded as such. [119 F.3d at 1100.] Nor does Alaska foster or condone unlawful attacks on registrants by making registry information available to the public by way of the Internet. Alaska's electronic registry, like others of its kind, contains a stern warning: "This information is made available for the purpose of protecting the public. Anyone who uses this information to commit a criminal act against another person is subject to criminal prosecution." Alaska Dep't of Public Safety, *Sex Offender Registration Central Registry*, http://www.dps.state.ak.us/ nSorcr/ asp (last visited August 29, 2002). And contrary to the New Jersey Public Defender's suggestion, Br. 11, the availability of prosecution against those who harass or injure registered offenders is not an empty threat. *See* PD 25a, 39-40 (lodged by N.J. Public Defender) (noting that two men were charged with assault after attacking a man believed to be a registered sex offender). Respondents also claim that the ASORA and other such laws "do not protect the public" and may result in a "rise in criminal activity." Resp. Br. 33; *see also* N.J. Pub. Def. Br. 21; Mass. Comm. for Pub. Counsel Servs. Br. 18. How this supports their claim that the laws impose an "affirmative disability or restraint" on registrants is not immediately apparent. And respondents are wrong to boot: registration and disclosure statutes help prevent and solve crimes. *See* States' Amicus Br. 27-28; U.S. Br. 18 & n.15, 19-20 & n.17	law have any regulatory purpose, or was it merely enacted to extract an ounce of revenge following the Civil War? Does the fact that *Cummings* is nearly 150 years old affect its persuasive power? Here the Petitioners' main brief is quite interesting. They are telling the Court that one possible reason that the Ninth Circuit ruled the way that it did was that the attorney for the State incorrectly conveyed the scope of the Alaska law during oral argument and made it appear worse than it really is. The Respondents' rhetorical flourish, *i.e.*, "pasting a scarlet letter," over-dramatizes and, in our view, trivializes their argument. Notice how a three word sentence — "That was wrong" — can pack a real punch.

Petitioners' Argument —	*Respondents' Argument —*
punishment" of imprisonment. *See Cutshall*, 193 F.3d at 474; *Doe v. Pataki*, 120 F.3d at 1285; *E.B.*, 119 F.3d at 1102. The Act's requirement that certain offenders verify their information quarterly is in keeping with the federal Wetterling Act, which encourages States to require sex offenders to "verify the[ir] registration every 90 days after the date of the initial release or commencement of parole." 42 U.S.C. §14071(b)(3)(B). *See also* U.S. Dep't of Justice, Center for Sex Offender Management, Sex Offender Registration: Policy Overview and Comprehensive Practices (Oct. 1999) (http://www.csom. org/pubs/sexreg.html) (noting that "22 states require sexually violent predators to update their address information quarterly with law enforcement"). Quarterly (or more frequent) reporting requirements are a common feature of everyday life. *See Lambert v. California*, 355 U.S. 225, 229 (1957) ("Registration laws are common and their range is wide.").	part of the cause of the recent rise in criminal activity. *Id.*, pp. 1979-1980. *See also* Note: *Battling Sex Offenders: Is Megan's Law An Effective Means Of Achieving Public Safety?*, 19 SETON HALL LEG. J. 519, at 546-549 (1995). Finally, there are ever increasing reported incidents of the wrong person being attacked because the public believed a criminal lived at that address. *Id.*, pp. 558-560. The empirical evidence continues to mount and these case histories show that these offense-based registration and public notification laws do indeed impose an affirmative disability and restraint. *See generally*, Brief of New Jersey Public Defender Agency As *Amicus Curiae*.
<u>Even if it were true</u>, moreover, that the ASORA required quarterly in-person, rather than written, verification for those convicted of certain offenses, that would not transform the registration requirement into an "affirmative disability or restraint." If Kansas's statute permitting indefinite civil commitment of certain sexual predators does not impose an unduly punitive "affirmative disability or restraint," in light of the non-punitive purpose of the civil commitment statute, *see Hendricks*, 521 U.S. at 362-363, requiring offenders convicted of aggravated or multiple sex offenses to verify their information every 90 days — whether in person or not — similarly cannot qualify as an unduly punitive restraint, given the concededly non-punitive purposes of the ASORA. *See Doe v. Pataki*, 120 F.3d at 1284-85 (rejecting ex post facto challenge to New York law requiring quarterly in-person verification for certain offenders for at least ten years and potentially for life).	
3. The Ninth Circuit also found that the Department of Public Safety's practice of posting its sex offender registry on the Internet imposed a "substantial" and "burdensome" "affirmative disability or restraint" on registrants, because it exposed them to widespread "community obloquy and scorn that damage them personally and professionally." Pet. App. 17a, 13a, 14a. But the posting of the registry on the Internet imposes no affirmative disability or restraint at all on a registrant, and certainly nothing akin to the "'infamous punishment' of imprisonment." *See Flemming*, 363 U.S. at 617. The Internet	

Petitioners' Reply	*Authors' Comments*
	The Petitioners argue that the Ninth Circuit misunderstood ASORA. ASORA did not, according to Petitioners, require in-person registration. They then argue in the alternative, *i.e.*, "Even if it were true. . . . "

Petitioners' Argument—	*Respondents' Argument —*

is simply the most efficient — and an increasingly common — way of making truthful information available to the public. *See Ashcroft v. ACLU*, 122 S. Ct. 1700, 1703 & n.2 (2002). As the Tenth Circuit observed in *Femedeer*, posting public information on the Internet "works merely a technological extension, not a sea change, in our nation's long history of making information public regarding criminal offenses." 227 F.3d at 1251. It is a particularly useful means of making that information available to the far-flung reaches of our largest State, and of ensuring — through daily updates — that the information is current and accurate.

Information about criminal records is routinely made available to the public; indeed, criminal trials must be open to the public. Yet even though that information has always had the potential for negative collateral consequences as a result of the actions of those who learn it, making the information available to the public has never been considered additional "punishment" for the crime itself. *See E.B.*, 119 F.3d at 1099-1100. This Court has never held that a law imposes an "affirmative disability or restraint" as a result of actions that members of the public — not the State — may or may not take.

Nor, moreover, is passive notification on the Internet as invasive as other active steps States may take to notify communities of the presence of sex offenders. Some States, for example, permit law enforcement officials to go door-to-door in an offender's neighborhood to inform community members of his presence, *see* Del. Code Ann. tit. 11, §4121(a)(1) (2001); *see also* D.C. Code §22-4011(b)(1)(A), or to publish offenders' names in newspapers, in fliers, or through local television outlets. *See Russell*, 124 F.3d at 1082; Susan D. Oakes, *Megan's Law: Analysis on Whether ItIs Constitutional to Notify the Public of Sex Offenders via the Internet*, 17 J. Marshall J. Computer & Info. L. 1133, 1142 (1999) (citing statutes). One State requires offenders to announce their presence in the community by personally notifying, by mail, "'[a]t least one person in every residence or business' " within a one-mile radius of the offender's residence. *See State ex rel. Olivieri*, 779 So. 2d at 739 (quoting La. Rev. Stat. Ann. §15:542(B)(1)(a)). Under all those notification schemes, community members may receive notice of an offender's presence in the neighborhood whether they ask for it or not. In contrast, as this Court recently recognized in *Reno v. ACLU*, 521 U.S. 844, 869 (1997), the Internet is

Petitioners' Reply	Authors' Comments

Petitioners' Argument—	*Respondents' Argument —*
"not as 'invasive' as radio or television." For an Internet user to obtain information, he or she must take "a series of affirmative steps more deliberate and directed than merely turning a dial." *Id.* at 854 (quotation omitted). And as the Tenth Circuit has observed, the fact that Internet users in far-off places can access a State's registry does not mean that they will, or that they would have any interest in doing so. *See Femedeer*, 227 F.3d at 1253. Alaska's scheme of Internet notification — shared by some thirty other States — thus does not impose an "affirmative disability or restraint" on Alaska registrants even remotely akin to imprisonment or confinement; it is today simply the most expedient method of conveying information to members of the public who are interested in that information. The purposes of the ASORA are constitutional, and they are not rendered unconstitutional because the State elects to implement the Act in the most efficient and economical way. *See Seling v. Young*, 531 U.S. at 263 ("The civil nature of a confinement scheme cannot be altered based merely on vagaries in the implementation of the authorizing statute."); *id.* at 270 n.* (noting "irrelevance of subsequent executive implementation" to ex post facto analysis) (Scalia and Souter, JJ., concurring); *Mendoza-Martinez*, 372 U.S. at 169 ("factors must be considered in relation to the statute on its face"); *supra* n.6.	

Petitioners' Reply	*Authors' Comments*

2. Writing an Appellate Brief: An Example

Following is a significant portion of the Petitioners' brief submitted in *Smith v. Doe*. We have included all of the sections of the brief in their entirety, other than the Argument section. In the Argument section, we present only the second argument, which deals with the *Mendoza-Martinez* factors. The first argument was edited out in the interest of brevity. We have also omitted the "Statutory and Regulatory Addendum," which sets out the Alaska law at issue in the case and some of its implementing regulations. The complete briefs for both parties are available online.

No. 01-729

In The
Supreme Court of the United States

GLENN G. GODFREY AND BRUCE M. BOTELHO,
Petitioners,

v.

JOHN DOE I, JANE DOE, AND JOHN DOE II,
Respondents.

On Writ of Certiorari to the
United States Court of Appeals for
the Ninth Circuit

BRIEF FOR PETITIONERS

JOHN G. ROBERTS, JR.*
JONATHAN S. FRANKLIN
CATHERINE E. STETSON
HOGAN & HARTSON L.L.P.
555 Thirteenth Street, N.W.
Washington, D.C. 20004
(202) 637-5810

CYNTHIA M. COOPER
3410 Southbluff Circle
Anchorage, Alaska 99515
(907) 349-3483

BRUCE M. BOTELHO
Attorney General
STATE OF ALASKA
Department of Law
P.O. Box 110300
Juneau, Alaska 99811
(907) 465-3600

* Counsel of Record

Counsel for Petitioners

(i)
Question Presented

Alaska's sex offender registration act, Alaska Stat. §§ 12.63.010 *et seq.*, requires convicted sex offenders to register with the Alaska Department of Public Safety and makes offender information available to the public. The Department elected to publish the information on the Internet. Does the statute, on its face or as implemented by the Department of Public Safety, impose punishment for purposes of the Ex Post Facto Clause of the United States Constitution?

(ii)
Parties To The Proceeding

Petitioners Glenn G. Godfrey (successor to Ronald O. Otte) and Bruce M. Botelho are, respectively, the Alaska Commissioner of Public Safety and the Alaska Attorney General. Otte and Botelho were defendants in the District Court and appellees before the Court of Appeals for the Ninth Circuit. Respondents John Doe I, Jane Doe, and John Doe II were plaintiffs in the District Court and appellants before the Court of Appeals for the Ninth Circuit.

iii
Table Of Contents

TABLE OF AUTHORITIES

No. 01-729

In The
Supreme Court of the United States

GLENN G. GODFREY AND BRUCE M. BOTELHO,
Petitioners,

v.

JOHN DOE I, JANE DOE, AND JOHN DOE II,
Respondents.

**On Writ of Certiorari to the
United States Court of Appeals for
the Ninth Circuit**

BRIEF FOR PETITIONERS

Opinions Below

The opinion of the Ninth Circuit, as amended, is reported at 259 F.3d 979 and reprinted in the appendix to the petition for certiorari ("Pet. App.") at 1a. The original opinion is reprinted at Pet. App. 33a. The opinions and orders of the United States District Court for the District of Alaska dated March 31, 1999, and August 12, 1999, are not reported; they are reproduced at Pet. App. 69a and 118a, respectively.

Jurisdiction

The judgment of the Ninth Circuit was entered on August 8, 2001. The Ninth Circuit denied petitions for rehearing and for rehearing en banc on August 23, 2001, and September 6, 2001. Pet. App. 124a, 123a. The petition for certiorari was filed on November 21, 2001, and granted on February 19, 2002. 122 S. Ct. 1062. The jurisdiction of this Court is invoked under 28 U.S.C. § 1254(1).

Constitutional, Statutory, and Regulatory Provisions Involved

Article I, section 10 of the United States Constitution provides, in pertinent part: "No State shall   *** pass any *** ex post facto Law."

The Alaska Sex Offender Registration Act, Alaska Stat. §§ 12.63.010-.100 and § 18.65.087, and pertinent regulatory provisions, are reprinted in the addendum hereto.

Introduction

The Alaska Sex Offender Registration Act ("ASORA") was enacted to protect the public and to assist law enforcement in investigating future crimes. It requires state law enforcement entities to gather truthful information about sex offenders and to make certain of that information available to the public. The State has chosen to make such information available on the Internet. Like all other courts to have considered sex offender registration laws, the Ninth Circuit concluded that the legislature acted with non-punitive intent when it passed the ASORA. The court of appeals erroneously departed from the overwhelming majority of courts, however, in holding that the ASORA was nonetheless so punitive in effect that it violated the Ex Post Facto Clause.

We are aware of no case in which this Court has held that a law had a non-punitive intent and yet nonetheless violated the Ex Post Facto Clause. Nor has this Court ever held that regulatory requirements like those imposed on sex offenders by the ASORA amount to punishment; indeed, it has countenanced far more onerous burdens imposed by non-punitive regulatory statutes. The Ninth Circuit's decision should be reversed.

Statement of the Case

STATUTORY BACKGROUND.

1. In 1994, after a series of sexual crimes against children committed by prior offenders made news across the country, Congress passed the Jacob Wetterling Crimes Against Children and Law Enforcement Act, 42 U.S.C. §§ 14071 et seq. The Wetterling Act directs the Attorney General to develop guidelines for state sex offender registration programs, id. § 14071(a), specifies registration requirements for individuals convicted of certain sex offenses and the duration of those requirements, and permits States to release registry information "to protect the public concerning a specific person required to register under [the Act]." Id. § 14071(e)(2). The Wetterling Act encourages States to adopt registration programs that conform to or exceed its terms by conditioning receipt of certain federal funds on the implementation of such programs. Id. § 14071(g)(2). In 1996, Congress amended the Wetterling Act to provide that offenders convicted of one "aggravated sex offense" or two or more triggering offenses be required to register for life, and to permit States to disclose registry information "for any purpose permitted under the laws of the State." Id. §§ 14071(b)(6), (e) (Supp. III 1997).

Today, all fifty States and the District of Columbia have sex offender registration and notification statutes on their books.[1] Approximately thirty States and the District of Columbia make their registries available on the Internet. *See* U.S. Dep't of Justice, Bureau of Justice Statistics, Summary of State Sex Offender Registries, 2001 (2002) (noting that "a growing number of States use[] the Internet to fulfill notification requirements under Megan's Law"); http://www.meganslaw.org (collecting Internet sex offender registries).[2]

The rapid development of state sex offender statutes has led to a spate of lawsuits challenging their terms. A central question presented by many of those lawsuits is whether sex offender registration and notification constitute retroactive punishment prohibited by the Constitution's Ex Post Facto Clause. The overwhelming majority of courts have answered that question in the negative. *See infra* n. 11.

2. The State of Alaska became the thirty-second State to enact a sex offender registration law when, in 1994, its legislature enacted the ASORA. The ASORA requires convicted sex offenders to register with law enforcement authorities and authorizes public disclosure of certain information in the sex offender registry. Alaska Stat. §§ 12.63.010, 18.65.087.

The ASORA was enacted "at a time when the state legislature perceived that Alaska's high rate of child sexual abuse constituted a 'crisis.'" Pet. App. 6a. The

---

1. *See* Ala. Code §§ 13A-11-200, 15-20-21(1), 15-20-25(b) (2001); Alaska Stat. §§ 12.63.010-.100, 18.65.087 (2001); Ariz. Rev. Stat. §§ 13-3821 et seq. (2001 & Supp. 2002); Ark. Code Ann. §§ 12-12-901 et seq. (West 2001); Cal. Penal Code §§ 290 et seq. (West 1999 & Supp. 2002); Colo. Rev. Stat. § 18-3-412.5 (1999 & Supp. 2002); Conn. Gen. Stat. §§ 54-250 et seq. (2001); Del. Code Ann. tit. 11, §§ 4120, 4121, 4336 (2001 & Supp. 2002); D.C. Code Ann. §§ 22-4001 et seq. (2001); Fla. Stat. Ann. §§ 943.043(1), 943.0435(1) (West 2001); Ga. Code Ann. § 42-94-4.1 (2001); Haw. Rev. Stat. §§ 846E-1 et seq. (2001); Idaho Code §§ 18-8301 et seq. (2001 & Supp. 2002); 730 Ill. Comp. Stat. §§ 150/1 et seq. (1997 & Supp. 2002); Ind. Code §§ 5-2-12-1 et seq. (West 2001 & Supp. 2002); Iowa Code Ann. §§ 692A.1 et seq. (West 2002); Kan. Stat. Ann. §§ 22-4901 et seq. (2001); Ky. Rev. Stat. Ann. §§ 17.500 et seq. (West 2001); La. Rev. Stat. Ann. §§ 15:540 et seq. (West 2001 & Supp. 2002); Me. Rev. Stat. Ann. tit. 34-A, §§ 11201 et seq. (West 2001 & Supp. 2002); Md. Ann. Code §§ 11-701 et seq. (2001 & Supp. 2002); Mass. Gen. Laws ch. 6, §§ 178C-178P (2002); Mich. Comp. Laws Ann. §§ 28.721 et seq. (West 2002); Minn. Stat. §§ 243.166, 244.052 (1992 & Supp. 2002); Miss. Code Ann. §§ 45-33-21 et seq. (2001); Mo. Rev. Stat. §§ 589.400 et seq. (West 2002); Mont. Code Ann. §§ 46-23-501 et seq. (2001); Neb. Rev. Stat. §§ 29-4001 et seq. (2001); Nev. Rev. Stat. §§ 179D.350 et seq. (2001); N.H. Rev. Stat. Ann. § 651-B (2001); N.J. Stat. Ann. § 2C:7 (1995 & Supp. 2002); N.M. Stat. Ann. § 29-11A (Michie 2000); N.Y. Correct. Law § 168 (McKinhey 2001 & Supp. 2002); N.C. Gen. Stat. §§ 14-208.5-208.31 (2001); N.D. Cent. Code § 12.1-32-15 (2001); Ohio Rev. Code Ann. §§ 2950.01 et seq. (West 2001); Okla. Stat. Ann. tit. 57, §§ 581 et seq. (West 1991 & Supp. 2002); Or. Rev. Stat. §§ 181.585 et seq. (2001); 42 Pa. Cons. Stat. Ann. §§ 9791 et seq. (West 1998 & Supp. 2002); R.I. Gen. Laws § 11-37.1 (2001); S.C. Code Ann. §§ 23-3-400 et seq. (2002); S.D. Codified Laws §§ 22-22-30 et seq. (Michie 2001 & Supp. 2002); Tenn. Code Ann. §§ 40-39-101 et seq. (2001 & Supp. 2002); Tex. Crim. Proc. Code Ann. §§ 62.01 et seq. (Vernon 2001); Utah Code Ann. § 77-27-21.5 (2001 & Supp. 2002); Vt. Stat. Ann. tit. 13, §§ 5401 et seq. (2001); Va. Code Ann. §§ 19.2-298.1 et seq.,-390.1 (Michie 2002); Wash. Rev. Code Ann. §§ 9A.44.130 et seq., §§ 4.24.550 et seq., § 4.24.5501 (2001 & Supp. 2002); W. Va. Code §§ 15-12-1 et seq. (2001); Wis. Stat. Ann. §§ 301.45 et seq. (West 2001 & Supp. 2002); Wyo. Stat. Ann. §§ 7-19-301 et seq. (Michie 2000).

2. Such laws are often called "Megan's Laws," after Megan Kanka, a seven-year-old New Jersey child who was sexually assaulted and murdered by a neighbor who—unbeknownst to the Kanka family—had two prior convictions for sexual offenses against children. *See* Wayne A. Logan, *Liberty Interests in the Preventive State: Procedural Due Process and Sex Offender Community Notification Laws*, 89 J. CRIM. L. & CRIMINOLOGY 1167, 1172 (1999).

State's legislature heard testimony that the rate of child sexual abuse in Alaska was the highest in the Nation — indeed, more than six times the national average. *See* Minutes of Hearing Before Senate Judiciary Comm. ("Senate Judiciary Hearing"), 18th Alaska Legis., 1st Sess. 9 (Apr. 14, 1993) (No. 505); Minutes of Hearing Before Senate Finance Comm. ("Senate Finance Hearing"), 18th Alaska Legis., 1st Sess. 3 (Apr. 28, 1993). The State's sexual assault rate in 1993 was the second highest in the Nation and had nearly doubled in the prior two years. See Senate Judiciary Hearing at 9, 13 (Nos. 505, 209); Minutes of Hearing Before House Judiciary Comm. ("House Judiciary Hearing"), 18th Alaska Legis., 1st Sess. 17 (Feb. 10, 1993) (No. 000). Legislators also heard testimony that about a quarter of Alaska's entire prison population was incarcerated for sexual offenses, and that studies had shown that sex offenders had high rates of recidivism. See Minutes of Hearing Before House Finance Comm. ("House Finance Hearing"), 18th Alaska Legis., 1st Sess, 7 (Mar. 3, 1993); Senate Judiciary Hearing at 9 (No. 505); House Judiciary Hearing at 9 (No. 612).

When it enacted the ASORA, the legislature stated its conclusions that:

(1) sex offenders pose a high risk of reoffending after release from custody;

(2) protecting the public from sex offenders is a primary governmental interest;

(3) the privacy interests of persons convicted of sex offenses are less important than the government's interest in public safety; and

(4) release of certain information about sex offenders to public agencies and the general public will assist in protecting the public safety. [1994 Alaska Sess. Laws ch. 41, § 1.]

The ASORA requires people convicted of a "sex offense" or "child kidnapping" — as defined by the statute — who are physically present in the State of Alaska to register with the Department of Corrections if they are incarcerated, or with their local state trooper post or police department if they are at liberty. Alaska Stat. § 12.63.010(b).[3] A person required to register under the ASORA must provide various information, including his name, address, place of employment, and information about vehicles to which he has access. He must also allow the police department to take a photograph and a set of fingerprints. *Id.* §§ 12.63.010(b)(1)-(2).

The Act requires offenders covered by its terms to notify their local police department when they change addresses. *Id.* § 12.63.010(c); see 13 Alaska Admin. Code § 09.040. Offenders convicted of an "aggravated sex offense" or of two or more sex offenses are further required to provide quarterly "written verification" to their local police department of their current address and of any changes to their registry information, for the rest of their lives. Alaska Stat. §§ 12.63.010(d)(2), 12.63.020(a). Those convicted of one non-aggravated

---

3. Those convicted before July 1, 1984 of one sex offense or child kidnapping do not have to register under the ASORA. See 1994 Alaska Sess. Laws ch. 41, § 12(a); 1998 Alaska Sess. Laws ch. 106, § 25(a).

offense covered by the Act must provide annual "written verification" of their current address and of any changes to their registry information, for fifteen years. Id. § 12.63.010(d)(1). See also 13 Alaska Admin. Code § 09.025(d)-(e) (detailing procedures for receiving written submissions from registrants).[4] Registrants may request the Department of Public Safety to correct or review information maintained in the registry and may appeal adverse responses to the Commissioner of Public Safety. *Id.* § 09.060. A person who knowingly fails to register, to file an address change notice, or to file the required annual or quarterly written statement is subject to criminal prosecution. *See* Alaska Stat. §§ 11.56.835, 11.56.840.

The ASORA designates most registration information as "nonconfidential" and requires that the State's Department of Public Safety make nonconfidential information available to the public. *See* Alaska Stat. § 18.65.087.[5] Until June 1997, the Alaska state troopers maintained a complete list of the State's registered sex offenders at each trooper post. Anyone who wished to could look at the list at the state trooper post, purchase a complete list of registered sex offenders, or request that a specific search be conducted. In June 1997, the Department of Public Safety made the sex offender registry available on the Internet. Pet. App. 73a.[6] The site displays a prominent warning: "This information is made available for the purpose of protecting the public. Anyone who uses this information to commit a criminal act against another person is subject to criminal prosecution." Alaska Dep't of Public Safety, Sex Offender Registration Central Registry (http://www.dps.state.ak.us/nSorcr/asp/). Alaska, like some twenty other States, see infra n.27, takes a categorical approach to notification; the State does not individually assess the risk of recidivism posed by each registered sex offender before posting registry information on the Department of Public Safety website.

FACTS.

Respondent John Doe I was charged with three counts of first-degree sexual abuse of a minor. Ct. App. Sealed E.R. 113. He pled nolo contendere to one count of first-degree and one count of second-degree sexual abuse of a minor and was sentenced to twelve years' imprisonment, four years of which were suspended. *Id.* at 113-114. John Doe I was released from prison in December

---

4. The Department of Public Safety may instruct an offender to appear in person to be photographed if five or more years have passed since a registration photograph was taken or there is reason to believe an offender's appearance has changed significantly. *Id.* § 09.030(b).

5. The following information provided by the registrant is kept confidential: fingerprints, driver's license number, anticipated changes of address, whether the registrant has been unconditionally discharged from the conviction, the date of the unconditional discharge, and whether the registrant has had treatment for a mental abnormality or personality disorder since the date of the conviction. *Id.* §§ 12.63.010(b), 18.65.087(b).

6. The ASORA does not specify the means of making registry information public, and the regulations simply state that such information be provided "by posting or otherwise making it available for public viewing in printed or electronic form." Alaska Admin. Code § 09.050(a). The statute allows public access to information regarding motor vehicles to which the registrant has access and to information about the length and conditions of the registrant's sentence, but the Department of Public Safety does not post this information on the Internet. Compare Alaska Stat. § 18.65.087(b) with http://www.dps.state.ak.us/nSorcr/asp/.

1990. *Id.* at 114. He married respondent Jane Doe after his release from prison. *Id.* at 115. Respondent John Doe II was charged with first-degree sexual abuse of a minor. *Id.* at 126. He pled nolo contendere to one count and was sentenced to eight years' imprisonment. Id. John Doe II was released from prison in May 1990. *Id.*

John Doe I and John Doe II were required to register as sex offenders under the ASORA because they were convicted after July 1, 1984 of offenses triggering application of the statute. *See* 1994 Alaska Sess. Laws ch. 41, § 12(a). Because both were convicted of an "aggravated sex offense," see Alaska Stat. § 12.63.100 (1), the Act required both to provide, on a quarterly basis, "written verification" of their current address and notice of any changes to their registry information. See id. §§ 12.63.010(d)(2), 12.63.020; 1998 Alaska Sess. Laws ch. 106, § 25 (new registration requirements for aggravated sex offenses apply retroactively).

PROCEEDINGS BELOW.

1. The Does sued petitioners — the state Commissioner of Public Safety and the state Attorney General — under 42 U.S.C. § 1983, claiming, inter alia, that the ASORA was an ex post facto law. Ruling on summary judgment, the District Court explained that the ex post facto issue turned on "whether the registration and/or notification provisions of ASORA constitute punishment." Pet. App. 76a. To answer that question, the court applied the two-step "intent-effects" test. *See Kansas v. Hendricks*, 521 U.S. 346, 361 (1997) (describing test); *United States v. Ward*, 448 U.S. 242, 248-249 (1980) (same). The District Court concluded that the legislature's intent was regulatory, not punitive, and that in particular the "legislative findings make plain that the 'release of certain information about sex offenders to public agencies and the general public will assist in protecting the public safety' " — clearly a non-punitive objective. Pet. App. 91a (quoting 1994 Alaska Sess. Laws ch. 41, § 1).

Turning to the effects prong, the court explained that plaintiffs were required to demonstrate by the "clearest proof" that despite the legislature's regulatory intent, the statutory requirements were "so punitive in effect as to prevent the court from viewing [them] as regulatory or civil in nature." *Id.* at 85a, 77a (quotation omitted). Reviewing several considerations set forth by this Court in *Kennedy v. Mendoza-Martinez*, 372 U.S. 144, 168-169 (1963), the District Court concluded that the plaintiffs had not satisfied that heavy burden. Pet. App. 90a, 94a, 99a. Plaintiffs appealed.

2. THE NINTH CIRCUIT REVERSED.

On the first step of the inquiry the panel found that the legislature sent "conflicting signals" about its intent. Pet. App. 42a. Acknowledging that the legislature's express findings indicated that the Act had "a non-punitive purpose — protection of the public through the collection and release of information" — the court found those findings "by no means conclusive," stating that the "structure and design of the Alaska Act" supported the conclusion "that the legislature intended that the statute be punitive." *Id.* at 45a-46a.

Turning to the "effects" prong of the ex post facto inquiry, the Ninth Circuit recognized that "[w]hen a legislature plainly states its intent that a statute is not punitive, courts must 'reject the legislature's manifest intent only where a party challenging the statute provides the clearest proof that the statutory scheme is so punitive either in purpose or effect as to negate the State's intention.'" *Id.* at 46a (quoting Hendricks, 521 U.S. at 361) (emphasis in original). The court held, however, that it would not employ that strict standard in this case but would instead apply only "ordinary and customary legal standards" in examining the statute's effect, because the legislature's intent was "unclear." *Id.* at 47a.[7]

The Ninth Circuit found the Act punitive in effect. Applying the seven *Mendoza-Martinez* "factors," *see* 372 U.S. at 168-169, the court concluded that three factors weighed against, and four in favor of, finding the Act punitive. The court recognized that sex offender registration and notification statutes "have not historically been regarded as punishment." Pet. App. 65a. The Ninth Circuit also recognized that the Act's provisions did not take effect only on a finding of scienter, which likewise weighed against finding the statute punitive. *Id.* at 53a-54a. And the Ninth Circuit acknowledged that the Act undoubtedly had the "alternative non-punitive purpose" of "public safety, which is advanced by alerting the public to the risk of sex offenders in their communities." *Id.* at 58a-59a. The court found that non-punitive purpose to "unquestionably provide[] support, indeed the principal support, for the view that the statute is not punitive." Id. at 59a.

The court, however, found four *Mendoza-Martinez* considerations to weigh in favor of finding the statute punitive. First, it concluded that the ASORA "imposed an affirmative disability on the plaintiffs." *Id.* at 48a. The court viewed the Act as requiring plaintiffs and others convicted of aggravated sex offenses to "appear in person at a police station" four times each year to verify their information, which the court concluded was so "onerous" a requirement as to constitute an affirmative disability. *Id.* at 48a-49a.

The Act's notification provisions also imposed an "affirmative disability," the panel held, because "by posting the appellants' names, addresses, and employer addresses on the Internet, the Act subjects them to community obloquy and scorn that damage them personally and professionally" and may "make the plaintiffs *completely* unemployable." *Id.* at 49a-50a (emphasis in original). Emphasizing again that the "standard of proof we apply here is different" than the exacting "clearest proof" standard, the court found that "[c]onsidered as a whole, the Alaska statute's registration and notification provisions[] impose a significant

---

7. *See also id.* at 48a n.8 ("in *Russell [v. Gregoire*, 124 F.3d 1079 (9th Cir. 1997), *cert. denied*, 523 U.S. 1007 (1998),] we required a showing of the 'clearest proof' because we determined that the legislature's manifest intent was that the statute not be deemed punitive, while here, because the legislative intent is unclear, we do not apply so burdensome a standard"); *id.* at 52a (noting that "the standard of proof we apply here is different than in [Russell]"); *id.* at 59a n.12 (again distinguishing the standard applied in Russell); id. at 61a n. 14 (distinguishing "clearest proof" standard applied by the Tenth Circuit in *Femedeer v. Haun*, 227 F.3d 1244 (10th Cir. 2000)).

disability on the plaintiffs," and thus "clearly favor[] treating the Act as punitive." *Id.* at 52a.

The court found that another *Mendoza-Martinez* consideration, whether the statute promotes the "traditional aims of punishment-retribution and deterrence," also weighed "on the side of finding the Act punitive." Id. at 54a. The Act's registration obligations — which, the court reiterated, imposed on those convicted of aggravated sex offenses a "duty *** to report quarterly to their local police stations" — appeared to the court to be "inherently retributive." *Id.* at 55a. The duration of the reporting requirements — and the fact that they were tolled in years of noncompliance — also gave the court pause. In its view, "requiring the offender actually to go to the police station and register 15 times (even if it takes more than 15 years when the offender skips some years)" exacted an additional penalty. *Id.* at 56a. The Act thus "appears to further the fundamental aims of punishment" and its requirements "suggest that they serve as retribution." *Id.* at 57a.

The court next concluded that because the Act "applies only to behavior that is already criminal," that weighed in favor of finding the statute punitive. *Id.* at 57a. Finally, the Ninth Circuit concluded that the ASORA "appears excessive in relation to [its] alternative purpose" of protecting the public. *Id.* at 59a (quotation omitted). The statute was "exceedingly broad," the court concluded, because it was not "limited to those who the state determines pose a future risk to the community;" rather, all sex offenders convicted after July 1984, no matter the risk they posed, were listed on the registry. *Id.* at 63a, 60a. Emphasizing again that the statute "forced" even a "successfully rehabilitated" offender "to submit to in-person registration at his local police department four times a year, every year," the court of appeals found that the ASORA's "unlimited public disclosure of sex offender information in all cases in which a defendant has ever been convicted of a sex offense" weighed "strongly in favor of a determination that its effect is punitive." *Id.* at 63a.

Weighing "all the *Mendoza-Martinez* factors together," under the "ordinary" standard of review it had held applicable, the court concluded, "on balance, *** the effect of the Alaska statute is punitive." *Id.* at 66a. It accordingly found that the statute's application to John Doe I and John Doe II violated the Ex Post Facto Clause. Id.

3. The State Sought Rehearing and Rehearing en Banc.

It challenged the panel's conclusion that the legislature's intent in enacting the ASORA was ambiguous, pointing out that Alaska's Act closely followed the structure and design of the Washington State sex offender law the Ninth Circuit had upheld in Russell. The State also pointed out that a critical factual error had permeated the panel's decision: no one was required to re-register "in person" at local police stations under the Act, as the opinion (six times) stated; registrants need only submit quarterly or yearly "written verification" of their information. Alaska Stat. § 12.63.010(d).

Without ruling on the petition for rehearing, the panel issued an amended opinion. Pet. App. la. The panel's amended decision made a U-turn from its initial conclusion on legislative intent: where it had once found the legislature's intent ambiguous, the panel now agreed that the Alaska statute was "remarkably similar" in structure to the Washington statute it had upheld in Russell, and it held that "the legislature acted with a non-punitive intent" when it passed the Alaska Act. Id. at 1la; *see id*. at 12a.

This meant that the court's analysis of the effect of the statute became subject to the "clearest proof" standard, and the court recognized as much. *Id.* at 12a-13a. But the panel simply reinstated almost verbatim its earlier analysis of the effect of the ASORA—except for deleting its earlier repeated statements to the effect that the "standard of proof we apply here is different" than the "clearest proof" standard.[8] Thus, whereas the panel had initially found that various factors indicated a punitive purpose and effect under "ordinary" standards of review, it now found that those same factors provided the "clearest proof" of the law's punitive nature.

The panel also held fast to its conclusion that the ASORA required offenders to re-register "in person" at police stations quarterly or annually — despite the plain language of the statute permitting "written verification" of information. *See id.* at 7a. In a new footnote, the court opined that the statute "on its face, does not clearly specify that these registrations must be made in person at local police stations," but stated that "the government represented at oral argument that periodic in-person registration at local police stations is required by the Act." *Id.* at 7a n.4.

The State again sought rehearing en banc. The court of appeals denied both the original petition for rehearing and the petition for rehearing from its amended opinion. Pet. App. 123a-124a. This Court granted certiorari. 122 S. Ct. 1062 (2002).

Summary of Argument

The ASORA is a regulatory law intended to help protect the public from future harm by collecting truthful information and making it available to those who choose to access it. It is not a penal law intended to punish people for past acts.

---

8. The alterations in the amended opinion are telling. For example, the court initially concluded that the Act "appears to further the fundamental aims of punishment," and that its requirements "suggest that they serve as retribution," Pet. App. 57a (emphases added); the amended decision states that the Act affirmatively did "further[] the fundamental aims of punishment" and that the requirements "show that they serve *** as retribution." *Id.* at 21a (emphasis added). *Compare also* Pet. App. 64a (original) ("the *Mendoza-Martinez* test leads us to hold that the Act's effect is sufficiently punitive that notwithstanding the legislature's ambiguous intent, the Alaska statute should be classified as punitive") with id. at 28a (amended) ("the *Mendoza-Martinez* test leads us to hold that the effects of the specific provisions of the Alaska Act provide the 'clearest proof' that, notwithstanding the legislature's non-punitive intent, the statute must be classified as punitive"); and id. at 66a (original) ("When we weigh all the *Mendoza-Martinez* factors together, we conclude, on balance, that for purposes of the Ex Post Facto Clause, the effect of the Alaska statute is punitive") with *id.* at 30a (amended) ("[W]eighing all of the *Mendoza-Martinez* factors together, the effects of the Act provide the clearest proof that it is punitive").

To determine whether a law is penal within the meaning of the Ex Post Facto Clause, the Court employs a two-step test. First, the Court asks whether the legislature intended that the law serve legitimate regulatory purposes, rather than punitive ones. If so, the inquiry is at an end, except in extremely limited circumstances where the party challenging the law carries the "heavy burden" of showing by the "clearest proof" that the stated intent is merely a charade for punitive goals. *Hendricks*, 521 U.S. at 361.

This "clearest proof" requirement exists not only because of the inherent difficulties in ascertaining legislative intent other than through the statutory language itself, but also because of the purposes of the Ex Post Facto Clause. The Ex Post Facto Clause protects against vindictive or malicious legislation, an inquiry that necessarily turns on the intent of the legislature. Precisely the same sanction can be either civil or penal depending on the legislature's intent. Thus, once it is determined that the legislature's intent was not punitive, the ex post facto inquiry is all but over. Other constitutional provisions, such as the Due Process Clause, protect against legislation that is irrational or does not sufficiently serve its stated purposes.

As every court to have considered the issue (including the Ninth Circuit below) has held, the intent behind sexual offender registration and notification statutes is regulatory, not punitive. As the Alaska legislature expressly declared, the ASORA was intended to "protect[ ] the public" and "protect[] the public safety," by collecting and making available truthful information that people may find useful to safeguard themselves and their children from possible future harm. 1994 Alaska Sess. Laws ch. 41, § 1. The law was not intended to punish people for past acts, and in fact imposes only minimal regulatory requirements on those required to register. The legislative history confirms this express non-punitive intent.

The ex post facto inquiry is therefore over unless there is the clearest proof that the legislature's expressed intent masks a true punitive purpose. To locate such proof, the Court has traditionally looked to the factors set forth in *Mendoza-Martinez* as guideposts. Demonstrating the narrowness of that inquiry, however, the Court has never held that a law had a non-punitive purpose but nevertheless violated the Ex Post Facto Clause in light of the *Mendoza-Martinez* factors. Indeed, the Court has routinely upheld the retroactive application of laws far more onerous than the ASORA.

Contrary to the Ninth Circuit's holding, there is no proof, much less the required clearest proof, that the ASORA is so punitive in purpose or effect so as to negate the legislature's finding to the contrary. The Ninth Circuit correctly held that three *Mendoza-Martinez* factors indicated that the law is not punitive. First, registration and notification provisions have not historically been regarded as punishment. Registration requirements are commonplace in our regulated society, and provisions that make information about criminal records available to the public are likewise common and have never been considered additional punishment for the underlying crime. Second, the ASORA does not come into play only upon a finding of scienter. To the contrary, the law's provisions are triggered only by the fact of a conviction. Third, the law plainly has a non-punitive purpose that can rationally be assigned to it — protecting the public from future harm.

The Ninth Circuit erred, however, in concluding that the four other *Mendoza-Martinez* factors so outweighed the others and the legislature's intent as to render the ASORA punitive in fact. First, the ASORA imposes no affirmative disability or restraint. The registration and verification requirements are undemanding and, contrary to the Ninth Circuit, do not require that quarterly verifications be submitted in person. The notification provisions likewise impose no affirmative disability or restraint. Although notification could conceivably have negative collateral effects due to the actions of those who learn the information, those consequences accompany any disclosure of criminal records and are not an affirmative disability or restraint imposed by the law. Second, the ASORA does not further the traditional aims of punishment. It is not inherently retributive to collect truthful information and make it available to those who choose to access it as a means of safeguarding themselves and their families. And even if the law were seen as a deterrent, the Court has long held that deterrence is a civil, not simply punitive, goal. Third, while the ASORA applies only to behavior that is already criminal, that factor should be of little import in the ex post facto inquiry, and the Court has never held a law punitive simply because it applies to convicted felons. Finally, the ASORA is not excessive in comparison to its regulatory purposes, particularly when compared to far more onerous laws the Court has upheld in the past. Ex post facto analysis does not require a perfect fit between means and ends, and such inquiries are in any event better left to a due process analysis.

Argument

II. THE EFFECT OF THE ASORA IS NOT PUNITIVE.

A. *The Mendoza-Martinez Factors.*

When this Court has examined whether the effect of a law is punitive, it has looked to the following factors:

> Whether the sanction involves an affirmative disability or restraint, whether it has historically been regarded as a punishment, whether it comes into play only on a finding of scienter, whether its operation will promote the traditional aims of punishment — retribution and deterrence, whether the behavior to which it applies is already a crime, whether an alternative purpose to which it may rationally be connected is assignable for it, and whether it appears excessive in relation to the alternative purpose assigned ***.
> [*Mendoza-Martinez*, 372 U.S. at 168-169 (footnotes omitted).]

The *Mendoza-Martinez* factors are culled from cases variously addressing whether a law is "punishment" under the Fifth, Sixth,[20] and Eighth[21] Amendments, and the constitutional prohibition against bills of attainder,[22] as well as the Ex Post Facto Clause.[23] Because the *Mendoza-Martinez* considerations were gathered from a number of different constitutional contexts, some prove more useful than others in an Ex Post Facto Clause inquiry. The question "whether the behavior to which [the new law] applies is already a crime," for example, is doubtless relevant to an inquiry under the Double Jeopardy Clause, *see Mendoza-Martinez*, 372 U.S. at 168 (*citing La Franca*, 282 U.S. at 572-573), but less so in determining whether a law exacts retroactive punishment in violation of the Ex Post Facto Clause. Because the factors are designed to apply across a variety of constitutional contexts, this Court has recognized that they are "neither exhaustive nor dispositive" and are meant for "guidance" only. *Ward*, 448 U.S. at 249; *see also United States v. One Assortment of 89 Firearms*, 465 U.S. 354, 365 n.7 (1984).

And while this Court's "intent-effects" test looks to the *Mendoza-Martinez* factors under the "effects" prong, one of the seven factors is itself aimed at legislative intent: "whether an alternative purpose to which [the law] may rationally be connected is assignable for it." 372 U.S. at 168-169. While this Court has cautioned that no one *Mendoza-Martinez* factor should be elevated to "dispositive" status, *Hudson*, 522 U.S. at 101, the Court has also noted that this "alternative purpose" inquiry is "[m]ost significant." *Ursery*, 518 U.S. at 290; *see also Moore*, 253 F.3d at 873 (same); *Russell*, 124 F.3d at 1091 (same).[24]

---

20. See Mendoza-Martinez, 372 U.S. at 168 (citing, *inter alia, United States v. La Franca*, 282 U.S. 568, 572-573 (1931) (invalidating punitive monetary penalty as violating the Double Jeopardy Clause) and *Wong Wing v. United States*, 163 U.S. 228, 237-238 (1896) (striking down law requiring illegal aliens to serve one year's hard labor in prison before deportation, on Fifth and Sixth Amendment grounds)).
21. *See Mendoza-Martinez*, 372 U.S. at 168 (citing *Trop*, 356 U.S. at 96 (striking down law stripping citizenship on Eighth Amendment grounds)).
22. *See Mendoza-Martinez*, 372 U.S. at 168 (citing *Trop*, 356 U.S. at 96 (striking down law stripping citizenship on Eighth Amendment grounds)).
23. *See Mendoza-Martinez*, 372 U.S. at 168 (citing, *inter alia, Flemming*, 363 U.S. at 617, and *Cummings*, 71 U.S. at 320-321).
24. The Court has on occasion articulated different approaches to the question whether a statute inflicts forbidden punishment, but legislative intent remains the paramount inquiry under these formulations as well. In *Salerno*, for example, the Court cited *Mendoza-Martinez* but formulated the test this way:

    > To determine whether a restriction on liberty constitutes impermissible punishment or permissible regulation, we first look to legislative intent. Unless Congress expressly intended to impose punitive restrictions, the punitive/regulatory distinction turns on "'whether an alternative purpose to which [the restriction] may rationally be connected is assignable for it, and whether it appears excessive in relation to the alternative purpose assigned [to it].'" [481 U.S. at 747 (quoting *Schall v. Martin*, 467 U.S. 253, 269 (1984) (quoting *Mendoza-Martinez*, 372 U.S. at 168-169)).]

    And in *Selective Service System v. Minnesota Public Interest Research Group*, 468 U.S. 841, 852 (1984), the Court articulated

    > three necessary inquiries: (1) whether the challenged statute falls within the historical meaning of legislative punishment; (2) whether the statute, "viewed in terms of the type and severity of burdens imposed, reasonably can be said to further nonpunitive legislative purposes"; and (3) whether the legislative record "evinces a congressional intent to punish." [quoting *Nixon v. Administrator of Gen. Servs.*, 433 U.S. 425, 475-476, 478 (1977).]

    Like the intent-effects test itself, each of these tests highlights the importance of legislative intent in the Ex Post Facto Clause inquiry.

The Ninth Circuit ignored all this when it examined the allegedly punitive effects of the ASORA. The court instead gave scant weight to the "clearest proof" standard, a point confirmed by the fact that the change to that standard in the amended opinion produced no change whatever in the substantive analysis. *See supra* n.8.

B. *The Ninth Circuit's Assessment Of The Mendoza-Martinez* Factors Was Critically Flawed And Did Not Support A Finding By The "Clearest Proof" That The ASORA Is Punitive.

The Ninth Circuit correctly found three of the *Mendoza-Martinez* factors to weigh against a finding of punitive effect.

Historical Punishment.   First, the panel recognized that registration and notification provisions like those in the ASORA are not historically regarded as punishment. Pet. App. 18a. As the same court earlier put it in Russell, registration is "typically and historically a regulatory measure." 124 F.3d at 1089. *See also Doe v. Pataki*, 120 F.3d at 1285 (registration "does not resemble any measures traditionally considered punitive").

The Act's notification provisions likewise are a far cry from the historical punishments to which *Mendoza-Martinez* referred. *See* 372 U.S. at 168 (citing, *inter alia*, *Wong Wing*, 163 U.S. 228 (one year's imprisonment at hard labor constitutes "punishment"), *Mackin v. United States*, 117 U.S. 348 (1886) (two years' imprisonment), and *Ex Parte Wilson*, 114 U.S. 417 (1885) (15 years' imprisonment)). Notification provisions cannot be compared with physical public punishments like whipping, branding, or the pillory, all of which required "the physical participation of the offender, and typically required a direct confrontation" — orchestrated and encouraged by the government — between the offender and the public. *Russell*, 124 F.3d at 1091-92; *see also Femedeer*, 227 F.3d at 1250-51; *Doe v. Pataki*, 120 F.3d at 1284 ("traditional shaming penalties such as branding or the stocks enlisted the offender's physical participation in his own degradation;" notification "imposes no physical pain, mark, or restraint on the offender"). As the court recognized in Russell, sex offender notification provisions are more akin to "'wanted' posters and warnings about escaped prisoners;" such notices have never been regarded as punishment. 124 F.3d at 1092.

Scienter.   The Ninth Circuit also correctly found that the ASORA did not come into play "only on a finding of scienter." *Mendoza-Martinez*, 372 U.S. at 168; see Pet. App. 18a-19a. The panel reached that conclusion, however, by the wrong route. It recognized that "[a] defendant must be convicted of a sex offense before the Alaska statute's provisions become applicable, and those offenses generally require a finding of scienter." Pet. App. 18a. But because the panel viewed some of the offenses triggering the ASORA as "strict liability" offenses — i.e., those requiring no proof that the offender knew the victim's age — the panel concluded that the ASORA did not come into play "*only* upon a finding of scienter." Id. at 19a (emphasis in original).

But whether the underlying offenses triggering application of the ASORA require a finding of scienter is irrelevant. The question is whether application of the ASORA itself — the challenged law — requires such a finding. It does not. The ASORA is triggered not upon a finding of scienter, but upon the existence of a predicate fact: conviction of one of the sex offenses specified under the statute. *See Hudson*, 522 U.S. at 104 (law authorizing debarment from banking industry did not come into play on a finding of scienter; the law applied to "any person 'who violates' any of the underlying banking statutes, without regard to the violator's state of mind"). Other courts of appeal to have addressed the scienter factor have adopted this approach. *See Femedeer*, 227 F.3d at 1251-52 (sex offender statute "on its face * * * does not impose a scienter requirement"); *Cutshall*, 193 F.3d at 475 (state sex offender registration act "applies to persons convicted of any one of the sex offenses listed in the statute, without inquiry into the offender's state of mind"); *cf. Doe v. Pataki*, 120 F.3d at 1281 (prior conviction used "'solely for evidentiary purposes'" under the statute) (quoting *Hendricks*, 521 U.S. at 362).

Alternative, Non-Punitive Purpose. Finally, the Ninth Circuit found that the "[m]ost significant" *Mendoza-Martinez* factor, *Ursery*, 518 U.S. at 290 — whether the law has an alternative non-punitive purpose that can rationally be assigned to it-weighed against finding the ASORA punitive. The panel recognized that the non-punitive purpose connected to the Act, "of course, is public safety, which is advanced by alerting the public to the risk of sex offenders in their communities." Pet. App. 23a. All the other courts to have considered the issue agree. *See, e.g., Femedeer*, 227 F.3d at 1253; *Cutshall*, 193 F.3d at 476; *Russell*, 124 F.3d at 1089, 1091; *E.B.*, 119 F.3d at 1097.

Despite having found three factors — in addition to the legislature's clear non-punitive intent — to weigh against a finding that the ASORA was punitive, the Ninth Circuit nonetheless concluded that the other four *Mendoza-Martinez* factors collectively provided the "clearest proof" of the ASORA's punitive effect. Pet. App. 28a. Its analysis of those factors was deeply flawed.

Affirmative Disability Or Restraint. 1. The ASORA does not impose an "affirmative disability or restraint" on registrants. *See Mendoza-Martinez*, 372 U.S. at 168. This Court in *Hudson* likened that term, as "normally understood," to the "'infamous punishment' of imprisonment." 522 U.S. at 104 (quoting *Flemming*, 363 U.S. at 617); *see also Seling v. Young*, 531 U.S. 250, 272-273 (2001) (Thomas, J., concurring in the judgment) (equating "affirmative disability or restraint" with "confinement"); *compare Hendricks*, 521 U.S. at 362 (noting that civil commitment scheme "does involve an affirmative restraint," but finding that disability outweighed by legislature's non-punitive purpose). The ASORA imposes on registrants no physical restraint of any kind. It does not restrict their freedom of movement, does not require pre-clearance before they can switch jobs or residences, and does not restrict them from living or working in any part of the community. *See, e.g., Femedeer,* 227 F.3d at 1250 (offenders are "free to live where they choose, come and go as they please, and seek whatever employment they may desire"); *Cutshall,* 193 F.3d at 474; *E.B.,* 119 F.3d at 1102.[25]

2. According to the Ninth Circuit, however, the Act's registration provisions "impose a significant affirmative disability" because they "subject[] offenders to onerous conditions" — namely, the requirement that certain sex offenders, like respondents, "re-register at police stations four times each year every year of their lives." Pet. App. 13a-14a. The court viewed the requirement that offenders "appear in person at a police station on each occasion" as the critical factor making the law impermissibly "onerous." Id. at 14a.

The court's holding was based on a persistent misapprehension of the relevant provision of the ASORA. The ASORA specifically permits registrants to submit "written verification" of their registry information quarterly or yearly. *See* Alaska Stat. §§ 12.63.010(d)(1) (annual verification), (d)(2) (quarterly verification). The Alaska Code provisions implementing the ASORA similarly make clear that registrants may verify their information by mail, rather than in person. The relevant Code provision specifies that

> When an offender submits a registration form to a registration agency *without appearing in person*, the registration agency shall review the form. If the form or any document submitted in connection with the form has obvious discrepancies * * * the registration agency will notify the offender of the need for corrections and may not accept the form until the offender makes all necessary corrections. [13 Alaska Admin. Code § 09.025(d) (emphasis added).]

See also id. § 09.025(e) (information is considered submitted "on the date * * * it is postmarked, if mailed").

To be sure, the State bears significant responsibility for the panel's initial confusion. Asked at oral argument whether registrants must "go to the police station" to verify their registry information, counsel for the State responded, "under the current law, yes." *See* Pet. App. 7a n.4. The State's rehearing petition, however, corrected the misstatement. But the Ninth Circuit's amended opinion nonetheless persisted in placing heavy reliance on the supposed requirement of quarterly or annual "in-person" verification. See *id.* at 7a, 14a, 19a, 20a, 27a, 28a. The panel based its holding entirely on counsel's statement at oral argument. *Id.* at 7a n.4. Thus, in the face of the plain text of the statute, its implementing code provisions, and the State's corrective statement in its petition

---

25. Contrary to the Ninth Circuit's conclusion, quarterly or annual verification is not "in some respects * * * similar to probation or supervised release." Pet. App. 13a; see also id. at 19a-20a. Probation conditions are more burdensome and generally include participation in treatment programs, performance of community service, and restrictions regarding alcohol consumption, leaving the jurisdiction, and persons with whom the probationer can associate. *See* Alaska Stat. §§ 12.55.090-.101. Unlike the requirements of the ASORA, probation is quite plainly an alternative criminal sentence. Thus, violating a condition of probation can result in revocation and the imposition of a suspended period of imprisonment.

for rehearing, the Ninth Circuit panel opted to retain its demonstrably erroneous interpretation of the ASORA's requirements.

That was wrong. The principles that courts are not bound by stipulations of law, *see, e.g., Swift & Co. v. Hocking Valley Ry. Co.*, 243 U.S. 281, 289 (1917), and that estoppel does not typically run against the government, *see, e.g., Illinois ex rel Gordon v. Campbell*, 329 U.S. 362, 369 (1946), converge to make clear that the court should have decided the case under the correct view of what the ASORA provides. The court of appeals had an independent obligation to determine the meaning of the controlling statute, *see Kamen v. Kemper Fin. Servs., Inc.*, 500 U.S. 90, 99 (1991) (court "retains the independent power to identify and apply the proper construction of governing law"), and a misstatement by counsel during oral argument cannot override the language of the statute.

The Act's registration requirement is, as other courts correctly have found, nothing like the "infamous punishment" of imprisonment. *See Cutshall*, 193 F.3d at 474; *Doe v. Pataki*, 120 F.3d at 1285; *E.B.*, 119 F.3d at 1102. The Act's requirement that certain offenders verify their information quarterly is in keeping with the federal Wetterling Act, which encourages States to require sex offenders to "verify the[ir] registration every 90 days after the date of the initial release or commencement of parole." 42 U.S.C. § 14071(b)(3)(B). *See also* U.S. Dep't of Justice, Center for Sex Offender Management, Sex Offender Registration: Policy Overview and Comprehensive Practices (Oct. 1999) (http://www. csom.org/pubs/sexreg.html) (noting that "22 states require sexually violent predators to update their address information quarterly with law enforcement"). Quarterly (or more frequent) reporting requirements are a common feature of everyday life. *See Lambert v. California*, 355 U.S. 225, 229 (1957) ("Registration laws are common and their range is wide.").[26]

Even if it were true, moreover, that the ASORA required quarterly in-person, rather than written, verification for those convicted of certain offenses, that would not transform the registration requirement into an "affirmative disability or restraint." If Kansas's statute permitting indefinite civil commitment of certain sexual predators does not impose an unduly punitive "affirmative disability or restraint," in light of the non-punitive purpose of the civil commitment statute, *see Hendricks*, 521 U.S. at 362-363, requiring offenders convicted of aggravated

---

26. *See, e.g.*, 2 U.S.C. § 434 (requiring candidates and campaign committees to file monthly or quarterly reports of campaign contributions); 7 U.S.C. § 6f (authorizing CFTC to require futures merchants to file quarterly reports detailing their financial activities); 15 U.S.C. § 78o-5(b)(2)(A) (authorizing SEC to require registered government securities brokers and dealers to file quarterly reports of their financial and securities activities); 17 U.S.C. § 1003(c) (requiring distributors of digital audio recording devices to file quarterly statement of accounts with Register of Copyrights); 26 U.S.C. § 527(j)(2) (requiring political organizations that accept contributions or make expenditures for electioneering functions to file election-year quarterly reports listing contributors and detailing expenditures); 30 U. S.C. § 1267(b)(1) (requiring mining permittees to make monthly reports of data required by the Department of the Interior); id. § 1232(c) (requiring coal mine operators to submit quarterly production statements); 42 U.S.C. § 1320b-7(a)(3) (requiring employers in States participating in social welfare programs to file quarterly wage reports with state agencies); 42 U.S.C. § 7671b (requiring those trading in ozone depleting substances to file annual or quarterly reports with EPA setting forth amount produced, imported, or exported); 49 U.S.C. § 30120(d) (requiring car manufacturers who have sold defective cars to provide quarterly reports on progress of the resulting notification programs).

or multiple sex offenses to verify their information every 90 days — whether in person or not — similarly cannot qualify as an unduly punitive restraint, given the concededly non-punitive purposes of the ASORA. *See Doe v. Pataki*, 120 F.3d at 1284-85 (rejecting ex post facto challenge to New York law requiring quarterly in-person verification for certain offenders for at least ten years and potentially for life).

3. The Ninth Circuit also found that the Department of Public Safety's practice of posting its sex offender registry on the Internet imposed a "substantial" and "burdensome" "affirmative disability or restraint" on registrants, because it exposed them to widespread "community obloquy and scorn that damage them personally and professionally." Pet. App. 17a, 13a, 14a. But the posting of the registry on the Internet imposes no affirmative disability or restraint at all on a registrant, and certainly nothing akin to the "'infamous punishment' of imprisonment." *See Flemming*, 363 U.S. at 617. The Internet is simply the most efficient — and an increasingly common — way of making truthful information available to the public. *See Ashcroft v. ACLU*, 122 S. Ct. 1700, 1703 & n.2 (2002). As the Tenth Circuit observed in *Femedeer*, posting public information on the Internet "works merely a technological extension, not a sea change, in our nation's long history of making information public regarding criminal offenses." 227 F.3d at 1251. It is a particularly useful means of making that information available to the farflung reaches of our largest State, and of ensuring — through daily updates — that the information is current and accurate.

Information about criminal records is routinely made available to the public; indeed, criminal trials must be open to the public. Yet even though that information has always had the potential for negative collateral consequences as a result of the actions of those who learn it, making the information available to the public has never been considered additional "punishment" for the crime itself. *See E.B.*, 119 F.3d at 1099-1100. This Court has never held that a law imposes an "affirmative disability or restraint" as a result of actions that members of the public — not the State — may or may not take.

Nor, moreover, is passive notification on the Internet as invasive as other active steps States may take to notify communities of the presence of sex offenders. Some States, for example, permit law enforcement officials to go door-to-door in an offender's neighborhood to inform community members of his presence, *see* Del. Code Ann. tit. 11, § 4121(a)(1) (2001); see also D.C. Code § 22-4011(b)(1)(A), or to publish offenders' names in newspapers, in fliers, or through local television outlets. *See Russell*, 124 F.3d at 1082; Susan D. Oakes, *Megan's Law: Analysis on Whether It Is Constitutional to Notify the Public of Sex Offenders via the Internet*, 17 J. Marshall J. Computer & Info. L. 1133, 1142 (1999) (citing statutes). One State requires offenders to announce their presence in the community by personally notifying, by mail, "'[a]t least one person in every residence or business'" within a one-mile radius of the offender's residence. *See State ex rel. Olivieri*, 779 So. 2d at 739 (quoting La. Rev. Stat. Ann. § 15:542(B)(1)(a)). Under all those notification schemes, community members may receive notice of an offender's presence in the neighborhood whether they ask for it or not. In contrast, as this Court recently recognized in *Reno v. ACLU*, 521 U.S. 844, 869 (1997), the Internet is "not as 'invasive' as radio or television." For an Internet user to obtain information, he or she must take "a series of affirmative steps more deliberate and directed than merely turning a dial." *Id.* at 854 (quotation omitted). And as the Tenth Circuit has observed, the fact that Internet users in far-off places can access a State's registry does not mean that they will, or that they would have any interest in doing so. *See Femedeer*, 227 F.3d at 1253.

Alaska's scheme of Internet notification — shared by some thirty other States — thus does not impose an "affirmative disability or restraint" on Alaska registrants even remotely akin to imprisonment or confinement; it is today simply the most expedient method of conveying information to members of the public who are interested in that information. The purposes of the ASORA are constitutional, and they are not rendered unconstitutional because the State elects to implement the Act in the most efficient and economical way. *See Seling v. Young*, 531 U.S. at 263 ("The civil nature of a confinement scheme cannot be altered based merely on vagaries in the implementation of the authorizing statute."); *id.* at 270 n.* (noting "irrelevance of subsequent executive implementation" to ex post facto analysis) (Scalia and Souter, JJ., concurring); Mendoza-Martinez, 372 U.S. at 169 ("factors must be considered in relation to the statute on its face"); *supra* n.6.

Traditional Aims of Punishment. The Ninth Circuit also concluded that the ASORA "furthers the traditional aims of punishment — retribution and deterrence," and counted that *Mendoza-Martinez* factor as weighing in favor of finding the statute punitive. Pet. App. 21a. The court based its conclusion that the ASORA was "inherently retributive" on its erroneous assumption that the Act required in-person quarterly or annual registration. Id. at 19a-20a. Moreover, the fact that the ASORA may have a deterrent effect does not make the statute punitive. This Court has long recognized that deterrence "'may serve civil as well as criminal goals,'" and thus "the mere presence of this purpose is insufficient to render a sanction criminal." *Hudson*, 522 U.S. at 105 (quoting *Ursery*, 518 U.S. at 292); *see also Garner*, 221 F.3d at 827 ("That a statute serves to deter future conduct does not automatically render it punitive, particularly where its overriding goal is remedial"). To hold that every statutory scheme with a deterrent purpose "renders such sanctions 'criminal' * * * would severely undermine the Government's ability to engage in effective regulation." *Hudson*, 522 U. S. at 105. The ASORA may deter future crime by causing those subject to its provisions to appreciate that public awareness may make it more difficult for them to commit future crimes undetected, but that does not make the law punitive.

Application To Behavior That Is Already Criminal. The Ninth Circuit also concluded that the fact that the ASORA "applies to behavior that is already criminal" gave additional support to the "conclusion that its effect is punitive."

Pet. App. 21a. That finding is of dubious merit for two reasons. First, as noted, while it may be appropriate in a Double Jeopardy Clause inquiry to ask whether a law attempts to criminalize behavior that is already subject to criminal penalties under another statute, *see La Franca*, 282 U.S. at 573, it is less apparent how this factor assists in resolving the question presented by the Ex Post Facto Clause: whether a law seeks to impose retroactive punishment. The Ex Post Facto Clause inquiry does not turn on whether the law in question exacts a second criminal punishment for an act already criminally punishable; it asks only whether the law unfairly exacts punishment for past acts — whether or not criminal when done. *See Calder*, 3 U.S. at 390; *Cummings*, 71 U.S. at 325-326.

Nor, moreover, can it be enough to render a statute punitive to find that it is triggered by a criminal violation. "By itself, the fact that a *** statute has some connection to a criminal violation is far from the 'clearest proof' necessary to show that a proceeding is criminal." *Ursery*, 518 U.S. at 292. *See also Ward*, 448 U.S. at 250 ("'Congress may impose both a criminal and a civil sanction in respect to the same act or omission'") (quoting *Helvering v. Mitchell*, 303 U.S. 391, 399 (1938)).

Excessiveness.   Finally, the Ninth Circuit concluded that the ASORA was too "excessive" — the final *Mendoza-Martinez* factor — to be non-punitive. "Most important" to its conclusion on this factor was the court's finding that the statute authorized release of "information as to all sex offenders," not just those who had been individually screened and found to "pose[] a risk of recidivism." Pet. App. 24a. Noting that some States individually classify offenders by "risk category" and restrict public notice to those offenders deemed most likely to reoffend, *id.* at 26a, the panel concluded that Alaska's categorical approach to public notice was "exceedingly broad." *Id.* at 27a.[27]

The Ninth Circuit failed to acknowledge, however, that many laws that impose regulatory burdens on convicted felons — and that make no risk assessment at all — have been upheld against Ex Post Facto Clause challenges. In

---

27. The federal guidelines implementing the Wetterling Act provide that "States *** are free under the Act to make judgments concerning the degree of danger posed by different types of offenders and to provide information disclosure for all offenders (or only offenders) with certain characteristics or in certain offense categories." 64 Fed. Reg. 572, 582 (1999). The guidelines emphasize that States "retain discretion to make judgments concerning the circumstances in which, and the extent to which, the disclosure of registration information to the public is necessary for public safety purposes." *Id.*
   More than twenty other States follow Alaska's categorical approach. *See, e.g.,* Ala. Code §§ 15-20-21 (1), 15-20-25(b) (2001); Fla. Stat. Ann. §§ 943.043(1), 943.0435(1) (West 2001); Ga. Code Ann. § 42-9-44.1 (2001); 173 Ill. Comp. Stat. Ann. § 152/115, 152/120(c) (West Supp. 2002); Ind. Code Ann. § 5-2-12-11(b) (West 2001); La. Rev. Stat. Ann. § 15:546 (West 2001); Md. Code Ann. § 11-717 (2001); Mich. Compl. Laws Ann. § 28.728(2) (West 2002); Miss. Code Ann. § 45-33-49 (2001); Mo. Ann. Stat. § 589.417.2 (West Supp. 2002); N.M. Stat. Ann. § 29-11A-5.1 (Michie 2000); N.C. Gen. Stat. § 14-208.15 (2001); Okla. Stat. Ann. tit. 57, § 584(E) (West Supp. 2002); Or. Rev. Stat. § 181.592 (2001); S.C. Code Ann. Rev. § 23-3-490 (2001); S.D. Codified Laws § 22-22-40 (Michie 2001); Tenn. Code Ann. § 40-39-106(f) (2001; Tex. Crim. Proc. Code Ann. § 62.08 (West Supp. 2002); Utah Code Ann. § 77-27-21.5 (2001 & Supp. 2002); Va. Code Ann. § 19.2-390.1(B)-(D) (Michie 2002); W. Va. Code § 151-2-2(h) (2001); Wis. Stat. Ann. § 301.46(5) (West 2001). Hawaii's categorical notification law, Haw. Rev. Stat. § 846E-3, was found to violate the Due Process Clause in *State v. Bani*, 36 P.3d 1255 (Haw. 2001).

Hawker, for example, this Court upheld against an ex post facto challenge a state law barring convicted felons from practicing medicine. The law contained no exception for "reformed" felons, nor did it provide a method for obtaining an exemption from its terms. The law's categorical application did not trouble this Court:

> It is no answer to say that this test of character is not in all cases absolutely certain, and that sometimes it works harshly. Doubtless, one who has violated the criminal law may thereafter reform and become in fact possessed of a good moral character. But the legislature has power in cases of this kind to make a rule of universal application, and no inquiry is permissible back of the rule to ascertain whether the fact of which the rule is made the absolute test does or does not exist. Illustrations of this are abundant. [170 U.S. at 197 (citing cases).]

Sixty years later, in *De Veau*, 363 U.S. 144, this Court upheld against an ex post facto challenge a law effectively banning convicted felons from serving as officials of waterfront unions. The Court rejected the suggestion that the law could have been tailored more closely to exclude only those likely to commit further criminal violations as union officials: "Duly mindful as we are of the promising record of rehabilitation by ex-felons *** it is not for this Court to substitute its judgment for the [legislature] regarding the social surgery required by a situation as gangrenous as [this]."[28] As this Court similarly noted in Hendricks, particularly where the legislature is addressing an intractable social problem susceptible to a variety of remedial approaches, state legislatures have "the widest latitude in drafting" civil remedial statutes. 521 U.S. at 360 n.3 (citing *Jones v. United States*, 463 U.S. 354, 365 n.13 (1983)).[29]

The courts of appeal, too, have recognized that the Ex Post Facto Clause does not demand a "perfect fit between ends and means." *Femedeer*, 227 F.3d at 1253 (upholding Internet notification). Similarly rejecting the contention that Louisiana's sex offender registration law was punitive because it "d[id] not condition neighborhood notification on carefully calibrated, individualized determinations of dangerousness," the Fifth Circuit noted:

> "A perfect fit between ends and means" need not exist for the legislature's objective intent to be other than punitive: "If a reasonable legislator motivated solely by the declared remedial goals could have believed the means chosen were justified by

28. *Cf. United States v. Hemmings*, 258 F.3d 587 (7th Cir. 2001) (statute prohibiting felons from possessing firearms not ex post facto law); *United States v. Mitchell*, 209 F.3d 319 (4th Cir.) (same), *cert. denied*, 531 U.S. 849 (2000).

29. As was explained in hearings on the ASORA, studies demonstrate that sex offenders have high rates of recidivism. See supra n.12; *see also* Grant T. Harris, *et al.*, *Appraisal and Management of Risk in Sexual Aggressors: Implications for Criminal Justice Policy*, 4 PSYCHOL. PUB. POL'Y & L. 73, 107 (1998) (noting "considerable risk" of recidivism among sex offenders); U.S. Dep't of Justice, Bureau of Justice Statistics, Child Victimizers: Violent Offenders and Their Victims 9 (1996). But determining to any degree of certainty whether a particular offender is likely to re-offend is far from an exact science. *See, e.g.*, John Monahan, THE CLINICAL PREDICTION OF VIOLENT BEHAVIOR (1995). It is in precisely such circumstances that the legislature should be given the most rein in crafting a remedial regulation that adequately protects public safety, giving due weight not only to judgments concerning likelihood of recidivism and the ability to make individual determinations on that score, but also to the extent of the harm caused by such recidivism that may occur.

those goals, then an objective observer would have no basis for perceiving a punitive purpose in the adoption of those means." [*Moore,* 253 F.3d at 873 (quoting E.B., 119 F.3d at 1098).]

See also Doe v. Pataki, 120 F.3d at 1282-83 ("The legislature is not required to act with perfect precision, and its decision to cast a net wider than what might be absolutely necessary does not transform an otherwise regulatory measure into a punitive sanction.").

The panel's conclusion that the statute was unduly broad in application is in any event more pertinent to a due process inquiry than to the question whether the law inflicts impermissible retroactive punishment. The question whether a statute unnecessarily captures offenders who are not dangerous or likely to commit sexual offenses in the future does not turn on whether the law applies retroactively; it turns on whether it is rational to categorize all sex offenders as subject to the same registration and notification provisions. That is a due process question. The Ninth Circuit erred in importing that inquiry into its Ex Post Facto Clause analysis.

The Ninth Circuit ultimately concluded that its analysis of four *Mendoza-Martinez* factors trumped the legislature's acknowledged non-punitive intent — not to mention three other *Mendoza-Martinez* factors weighing against a finding that the ASORA was punitive. Pet. App. 30a-31a. The court was wrong in its analysis of those four factors and wrong in its ultimate conclusion. This Court has time and again held that even statutes that impose heavy regulatory burdens will not be found to violate the Ex Post Facto Clause if they are enacted with a non-punitive purpose. The ASORA plainly was. Its provisions do not exact punishment; they are intended to protect the public, and ancillary burdens on registrants are an acceptable part of that vital regulatory effort.

Conclusion

For the foregoing reasons, the judgment below should be reversed.

Respectfully submitted,

JOHN G. ROBERTS, JR.*
JONATHAN S. FRANKLIN
CATHERINE E. STETSON
HOGAN & HARTSON L.L.P.
555 Thirteenth Street, N.W.
Washington, D.C. 20004
(202) 637-5810

CYNTHIA M. COOPER
3410 Southbluff Circle
Anchorage, Alaska 99515
(907) 349-3483

BRUCE M. BOTELHO
Attorney General
STATE OF ALASKA
Department of Law
P.O. Box 110300
Juneau, Alaska 99811
(907) 465-3600

* Counsel of Record

Counsel for Petitioners

B What Is a Petition for a Writ of Certiorari?

A Petition for a Writ of Certiorari is a brief aimed at convincing the Supreme Court of the United States (or a State Supreme Court) that a case is sufficiently important to warrant appellate review by the Court. As we discussed earlier, the Supreme Court takes only a relatively few cases each year. In its Rules, the Court spells out some of the factors it uses in deciding whether to grant a writ of certiorari (*i.e.*, whether to take up a case). *See* Sup. Ct. R. 10. Thus, for example, the Court considers whether on an important federal issue there is a conflict among the courts of appeals (i.e., a so-called "circuit split") or between a court of appeals and a state supreme court. An effective certiorari brief usually concentrates more on showing the importance of the legal issues in the case and less on errors made in the courts below. The respondent's brief in opposition emphasizes that the case is not worthy of the Court's attention. The respondent in an "op. cert.," as it is called, may argue, among other things, that there really is not a circuit split or that the issue is transient and not likely to recur. Given the extraordinarily low number of cases heard each year by the Court, the likelihood that any given petition will granted is low. Some advocates believe that where the case involves an unimportant issue and does not involve the federal government, the best course is not to file an op. cert. These advocates believe that a well written op. cert. can only make the case more interesting and improve the likelihood that a petition would be granted.

A good certiorari brief is difficult to write; the lawyer must curtail his or her usual desire to tout the merits of his or her case in favor of touting its importance.

Below is a portion of a certiorari petition submitted to the Supreme Court in *Anza v. Ideal Supply Corp.* Although the page limit for a certiorari petition is 30 pages (*see* Sup. Ct. R. 33), the Petitioners' brief in *Anza* is barely 14 pages. It is short, to the point, and well written. More revealing of its quality, however, is the fact that the Court granted certiorari. Following full briefing and oral argument, the Court reversed in part, vacated in part, and remanded the case to the Second Circuit. *See Anza v. Ideal Steel Supply Corp.*, __U.S.__, 126 S.Ct. 1991 (2006).

No. _____

In The
Supreme Court of the United States

JOSEPH ANZA, VINCENT ANZA, AND
NATIONAL STEEL SUPPLY, INC.

Petitioners,

v.

IDEAL STEEL SUPPLY CORP.,

Respondents.

On Writ of Certiorari to the United States
Court of Appeals for the Second Circuit

PETITION FOR WRIT OF CERTIORARI

HARRY FIRST
40 WASHINGTON SQUARE SOUTH
NEW YORK, NY 10012
(212) 998-6211.

Of Counsel

RICHARD L. HUFFMAN
  Counsel of Record
WILLIAM M. BRODSKY
FOX HORAN & CAMERINI LLP
825 THIRD AVENUE
11TH FLOOR
New York, NY 10022
(212) 480-4800

Counsel for Petitioners

i

Question Presented

Whether a competitor is "injured in his business or property by reason of a violation" of the Racketeer Influenced and Corrupt Organizations Act ("RICO") where the alleged predicate acts of racketeering activity were mail fraud but the competitor was not the party defrauded and did not rely on the alleged fraudulent behavior.

ii

Statement Pursuant to Supreme Court Rule 29.6

Petitioner National Steel Supply, Inc. is a privately owned entity. It has no parent corporation and there is no publicly held company that owns 10% or more of their stock.

iii
Table of Contents

v

Table of Authorities

1
Opinions Below

The ruling of the United States Court of Appeals for the Second Circuit dated July 2, 2004 reversing the decision of the District Court is officially reported at 373 F. 3d 251 and is reproduced at App. A at 1a.

The decision and order of the United States District Court for the Southern District of New York dismissing the plaintiff's complaint dated April 1, 2003 is reported at 254 F.Supp. 2d 464, and is reproduced at App. B at 27a.

Jurisdiction

The order of the United States Court of Appeals for the Second Circuit sought to be reviewed was entered on July 2, 2004. This petition is timely under 28 U.S.C. § 2101 and Supreme Court Rule 13.1 because it is being filed within 90 days of the entry of the order sought to be reviewed. This court has jurisdiction to review the order of the United States Court of Appeals for the Second Circuit pursuant to 28 U.S.C. § 1254.

Statutory Provisions Involved

The relevant statutory provisions are the Racketeer Influenced and Corrupt Organizations Act, 18 U.S.C. §§ 1961-1968, set out at App. C at 38a.

Statement of the Case

The jurisdiction of the district court was invoked under 28 U.S.C. § 1331 (general federal question jurisdiction). The plaintiff's two federal claims are based upon allegations that the defendants violated the Racketeer Influenced and Corrupt Organizations Act, 18 U.S.C. §§ 1962-1968 ("RICO"). The complaint having been dismissed by the district court on plaintiff's Rule 12 (b)(6) motion, the Record consists only of the plaintiff's amended complaint.

A. Summary of Allegations in the Amended Complaint

Plaintiff Ideal Steel Supply Corp. ("Ideal") and defendant National Steel Supply, Inc. ("National") are competitors. They sell "steel mill products (such as steel bars and sheets) and related hardware, supplies and services, to ornamental iron workers and small steel fabricators," as well as to "do-it-yourself homeowners." (Plaintiff's Amended Complaint, ¶ 16). They are the "principal competitors in New York City for the types of products they each sell" (*id.*, ¶ 15). The "overall demand" for their products "is dependent primarily upon economic activity in the real estate and construction businesses" and the general demand for "ornamental security or other ironworks" (*id.*, ¶ 22).

Sales made for resale, and sales made to tax-exempt entities (such as schools, churches, or other not-for-profit purchasers), are not subject to New York State sales tax; sales made to other purchasers are. *See id.*, ¶ 18. Ideal alleged that National did not collect sales tax on sales to those of its customers who were "cash-paying [and] non-exempt" (*id.*, ¶ 4) and that National's alleged failure to report such sales to the New York State Department of Taxation and Finance constituted "fraudulent misrepresentations" to that agency (*see id.*, ¶ 5). Plaintiff alleged that the New York State Department of Taxation and Finance "has relied and continues to rely" on the alleged fraudulent misrepresentations in defendant's sales tax returns (*see id.*, ¶ 30).

Ideal further alleged that National's failure to collect sales tax from these customers created "an improper competitive advantage for National over Ideal" (*id.*, ¶ 32). More specifically, Ideal alleged that after National opened a new facility in the Bronx in 2000 — "just eight minutes by automobile from Ideal's Bronx location" (*id.*, ¶ 20) — Ideal experienced "a steep drop in taxable cash sales . . . disproportionate to the effect that National's new Bronx location had on Ideal's overall sales" (*id.*, ¶ 35).

Ideal alleged that "each occasion" of National's false filing of its New York State sales tax returns ("at least since 1998 if not before") violated the federal mail and wire fraud statutes, 18 U.S.C. §§ 1341, 1343, and that each violation was a predicate act of racketeering under the Racketeer Influenced and Corrupt Organizations Act. *See* Plaintiff's Amended Complaint, ¶¶ 45-47. Ideal further alleged that National's alleged scheme "directly injures Ideal because defendants' conduct is aimed at increasing National's market share and overall profits at the expense of its principal competitor, Ideal." (*Id.*, ¶ 49.) Ideal thus sought damages for lost profits arising from the "substantial volume of its taxable cash business" which it lost to National (*see id.*, ¶¶ 50, 51).

Ideal also alleged that National had invested the "racketeering income" gained from its alleged tax avoidance when opening its new facility in the Bronx and that this gave rise to a separate violation of RICO (under § 1962(a)). As a result of this investment, Ideal alleged, it had "lost significant business and market share" (*id.*, ¶ 57). Ideal accordingly sought additional damages for this loss.

B. THE DECISIONS BELOW

District Court Judge Richard Berman dismissed the complaint, holding that Ideal had failed to plead that National's actions were both the proximate cause of Ideal's damages and that Ideal itself relied upon National's misrepresentations. The court reasoned that when a RICO claim is based upon the alleged racketeering activity of mail or wire fraud, the RICO plaintiff must be able to show it relied upon the fraudulent misrepresentations. 245 F. Supp. 464, at 468-69.

The Court of Appeals reversed, remanding the case for further proceedings. Judge Kearse, thoroughly reviewing Second Circuit precedent as well as precedent from the Fourth Circuit, wrote that it was appropriate to grant standing to a "competitor alleging injury to its business resulting from racketeering activity,"

373 F.3d 251, at 260, "even where the scheme depended on fraudulent communications directed to and relied on by a third party rather than the plaintiff." *Id.* at 263. It was enough that Ideal was "a competitor directly targeted by defendants for competitive injury." *Id.* at 264. Accordingly, the Court of Appeals held that Ideal's complaint adequately stated a claim under § 1962 (c) for conducting an enterprise through a pattern of racketeering activity, and under § 1962 (a) for investing racketeering income in the opening of its new store in the Bronx.

Reasons for Granting the Petition

This case presents an important issue of federal law on which the Circuits are split. The Second Circuit's willingness to expand standing under RICO to protect competitors when it was another party who was defrauded threatens to create a federal law of unfair competition, in which treble damages might be available for conduct that this Court would have viewed as procompetitive in the context of antitrust litigation. The result may be to undermine this Court's carefully crafted jurisprudence in the antitrust area, a result not likely intended by Congress when it placed the antitrust treble-damages remedy in the RICO statute.

I. THE CIRCUITS ARE SPLIT

In *Holmes v. Securities Investor Protection Corp.*, 503 U.S. 258 (1992), this Court established the basic approach for determining when a party is "injured in his business or property by reason of a violation" of the Racketeer Influenced and Corrupt Organizations Act ("RICO"), as required by Section 1964(c) of the Act. Drawing on decisions from the treble-damages provision of the antitrust laws, on which the RICO provision was modeled, *Holmes* held that plaintiffs are required to prove not just "but for" causation, but also "proximate" cause. *See id.* at 265-68. The Court used "proximate cause" to "label generically the judicial tools used to limit a person's responsibility for the consequences of that person's own acts." *Id.* at 268. Although the decision in *Holmes* did not adopt any particular bright-line statement of what that limit might be, the decision did stress the importance of "some direct relation between the injury asserted and the injurious conduct alleged," adding that a plaintiff complaining of harm "from the misfortunes visited upon a third person by the defendant's acts" is generally thought "to stand at too remote a distance to recover." *Id.* at 268-69.

The Second Circuit's decision in the instant case reads Holmes expansively, allowing a competitor to sue under RICO even though it is not the defrauded party and even though the alleged fraudulent conduct was "directed to and relied on by a third party rather than the plaintiff." 373 F.3d at 263. On this point there is a clear split in the Circuits.

On a formal level, this split has been expressed in the question whether "reliance" by the plaintiff is necessary, with the Circuit Courts for the Sixth and Eleventh Circuits requiring reliance and the First Circuit clearly rejecting the requirement (as did the Second Circuit in the instant case). *Compare, e.g.,*

Vandenbroeck v. CommonPoint Mortgage Co., 210 F.3d 696, 701 (6th Cir. 2000) (for a cognizable claim for fraud under RICO, plaintiffs must show a material misrepresentation and "that plaintiffs in fact relied upon that material misrepresentation") and *Sikes v. Teleline*, 281 F.3d 1350, 1360 (11th Cir. 2002) (to prove injury "in a civil RICO case predicated upon mail or wire fraud," plaintiff must prove that he was "'a target of the scheme to defraud' and that he 'relied to his detriment on misrepresentations made in furtherance of that scheme.'") (supporting citations omitted), *cert. denied*, 537 U.S. 884 (2002), *with Systems Management, Inc. v. Loiselle*, 303 F. 3d 100, 103, 104 n.3 (1st Cir. 2002) (although noting that some courts have required proof that the plaintiff "relied upon the deception," court holds that plaintiff workers, who did not receive the fraudulent communications, need not show reliance because "a reasonably predictable consequence" of the fraud was to enable the defendant "to continue to underpay his workers") (dismissing suit on other grounds); *cf. Poulos v. Caesars World, Inc.*, 379 F.3d 654, 666 n.3 (9th Cir. 2004) (although declining to reach question whether reliance is required in a civil RICO claim based on mail fraud, court recognizes that "[o]ur sister circuits have split on this issue") (citing examples of the split).

The heart of the disagreement in the Circuits, however, is over the question whether RICO will be read expansively to permit the recovery of damages by competitors who believe themselves disadvantaged by an alleged fraud. On this the Fourth Circuit agrees with the Second, and allows such suits, but the Sixth and Seventh do not.

In *Mid Atlantic Telecom, Inc. v. Long Distance Services, Inc.*, 18 F.3d 260 (4th Cir.), *cert. denied*, 513 U.S. 931 (1994), relied on by the Second Circuit in the instant case, the Fourth Circuit permitted a reseller of long-distance telecommunications service to sue its competitor under RICO on the grounds that the competitor had defrauded the competitor's customers by tricking them into thinking they were getting a better deal than they were, and that this fraud made it more difficult for the plaintiff to compete. Even though it was the defendant's customers who were the "direct victims" of the defendant's schemes, the court gave the plaintiff the opportunity to show that "the artificially low billings were purposefully devised" to hurt the plaintiff's business, thereby allowing the plaintiff to collect the "lost revenue due to the necessity of offering lower rates to match LDS's fraudulent ones." *Id.* at 263-64.

By contrast, in *Central Distributors of Beer, Inc. v. Conn*, 5 F.3d 181 (6th Cir. 1993), *cert. denied*, 512 U.S. 1207 (1994), the Sixth Circuit did not allow a beer distributor to sue its supplier and a competing distributor under RICO for fraudulently supplying beer to the competitor, in violation of Michigan law, thereby "usurping sales" that the plaintiff would otherwise have made. *Id.* at 182. Under RICO, the court held, the fraud "must involve misrepresentations or omissions flowing from the defendant to the plaintiff." *Id.* at 184. "Central Distributors has not produced a shred of evidence showing that any of the defendants made any false statements or omissions to Central Distributors or that Central Distributors relied on any statement or omission to its detriment." *Id.* at 184.

More to the point is the Seventh Circuit's decision in *Israel Travel Advisory Service, Inc. v. Israel Identity Tours, Inc.*, 61 F.3d 1250 (7th Cir. 1995), *cert. denied*, 517 U.S. 1220 (1996), a suit brought by a travel agency against its competitor, under both the Sherman Act and under RICO, for allegedly fraudulent statements made to customers in the course of promoting tours to Israel. After agreeing with the district court that the antitrust claim was without merit, the court of appeals considered the "more substantial RICO claim." The district court had dismissed the RICO claim on the ground that the plaintiff's injury was indirect, because the fraud involved consumers rather than the plaintiff-competitor. *See id.* at 1257. Judge Easterbrook, writing for the court of appeals, reviewed the decision of the Fourth Circuit in *Mid Atlantic Telecom* that RICO "allows suits when the predicate offenses influence customers and, derivatively, injure business rivals." Asserting that "[a] conflict among the circuits on such a question would be regrettable," the court decided to "accept *Mid Atlantic*." *Id.* at 1257.

Nevertheless, "like a troll under the bridge," to use Judge Easterbrook's colorful simile, *see id.* at 1257, there was another theory available for why the plaintiff-competitor lacked standing to bring its RICO claim. Drawing on Justice Scalia's "zone of interests" approach to standing articulated in *Holmes, see id.* at 1258, the court held that a plaintiff "must show not only that the defendant violated the law but also that the plaintiff is among the persons protected by the law." Id. The plaintiff, as a vendor to the persons deceived, was not "among the persons protected" by the Mail Fraud statute. The "essential point," Judge Easterbrook wrote, "is that the victims of the fraud are the object of solicitude; § 1341 [the Mail Fraud statute] does not establish a regimen of truth-telling without regard to details like who is losing out and why." *Id. Cf. Newton v. Tyson Foods, Inc.*, 207 F.3d 444, 447 (8th Cir. 2000) (zone of interests test suggests that only consumers have standing to sue chicken producer for alleged fraud in connection with government poultry inspections) (dismissing RICO suit by plaintiff beef producers for lack of standing). In taking this approach to standing, the Seventh Circuit clearly placed competitors who are not the victims of the fraud and who are, therefore, only injured "derivatively," outside the coverage of Section 1964(c) of the RICO statute. "[F]irms suffering derivative injury from business torts therefore must continue to rely on the common law . . . ." *Id.* at 1258.

The Second Circuit in the instant case has taken an approach to standing that differs from the approach taken by Judge Easterbrook and the Seventh Circuit in *Israel Travel Advisory Service*, and differs as well from the Sixth and Eleventh Circuits with regard to the need for reliance. Given the conflicting views on this question of standing for competitors who are not the direct victims of a fraud, and who have not relied on any fraudulent statements, it is critical that this Court provide further guidance to the federal courts on the limits that RICO places on

"a person's responsibility for the consequences of that person's own acts."
Holmes, supra.

II. The Court Should Limit Competitor Standing in Rico Mail Fraud Cases

The concept of fraud under the federal Mail Fraud statute has proven to be extremely elastic. *See, e.g., Gregory v. United States*, 253 F.2d 104, 109 (5th Cir. 1958) (scheme to defraud is judged by a standard that is a reflection of "moral uprightness, of fundamental honesty, fair play and right dealing in the general and business life of members of society"). As this Court has recognized as well, falsehoods can have anticompetitive effect. *Cf. California Dental Association v. Federal Trade Commission*, 526 U.S. 756, 773 n.9 (1999). If these falsehoods are litigated under the antitrust laws, the courts will give them careful attention to be certain that they are truly anticompetitive. *See Israel Travel Advisory Service, supra*, 61 F.3d at 1256 ("It is an abuse of the antitrust laws to invoke them to stifle nascent competition"). Providing treble-damages under RICO for Mail Fraud violations that might harm competitors, however, is a great incentive for those competitors to bring their complaints under RICO and thereby avoid the careful antitrust analysis that this Court has given to such complaints in recent years. This helps explain why Judge Easterbrook was so careful to cabin competitor standing in *Israel Travel Advisory Service.*

Two recent cases in which this Court has carefully limited antitrust recovery suggest the danger posed by the approach adopted by the Second Circuit in the instant case. One is *NYNEX Corp. v. Discon, Inc.*, 525 U.S. 128 (1998), involving a suit by a competitor for conduct which defrauded New York state regulators. Discon sued NYNEX for engaging in a boycott of its premises equipment removal services. The Second Circuit had held that boycott to be per se unlawful, but this Court reversed, holding that the boycott should be assessed under a rule of reason. The Court wrote (525 U.S. at 136-37):

> To apply the per se rule here—where the buyer's decision, though not made for competitive reasons, composes part of a regulatory fraud — would transform cases involving business behavior that is improper for various reasons . . . into treble-damages antitrust cases. And that per se rule would discourage firms from changing suppliers—even where the competitive process itself does not suffer harm. . . .

The freedom to switch suppliers lies close to the heart of the competitive process that the antitrust laws seek to encourage. *Cf. Standard Oil*, 221 U.S., at 62, 31 S.Ct. 502 (noting "the freedom of the individual right to contract when not unduly or improperly exercised [is] the most efficient means for the prevention of monopoly"). At the same time, other laws, for example, "unfair competition" laws, business tort laws, or regulatory laws, provide remedies for various "competitive practices thought to be offensive to proper standards of business morality." . . .

The other case is *Verizon Communications Inc. v. Law Offices of Curtis V. Trinko, LLP*, 540 U.S. 398, 124 S.Ct. 872 (2004). In *Trinko* this Court upheld the dismissal of a suit by a consumer of telecommunications services who alleged that Verizon had violated Section 2 of the Sherman Act by breaching its duty under the Telecommunications Act of 1996 to share its facilities with its competitors. Verizon's conduct had been examined by the FCC and the New York Public Service Commission, both of which had imposed financial penalties for noncompliance and had required remediation measures. *See* 124 S.Ct. at 873. In finding no violation of the antitrust laws this Court noted that antitrust analysis "'must sensitively recognize and reflect the distinctive economic and legal setting of the regulated industry to which it applies,'" *id.* at 881, and that "[t]o safeguard the incentive to innovate, the possession of monopoly power will not be found unlawful unless it is accompanied by an element of anticompetitive conduct." *Id.* at 879.

The care with which this Court approached the allegedly anticompetitive behavior in Discon and Trinko would not be duplicated were the litigation brought as a RICO/Mail Fraud case. The regulatory fraud in Discon is readily translatable into a fraud complaint, but it would then not be weighed under a rule of reason approach. The only question would be the financial impact on the competitor, not the impact on competition as tested under a rule of reason. Similarly, it would be easy for a competitor of Verizon to allege misrepresentations in Verizon's statements to regulators and seek treble damages for lost revenue, as the plaintiff sought in Mid Atlantic, supra. *See* Brief for Covad Communications Company, Inc. as Amicus Curiae in Support of Respondent, *Verizon Communication Inc. v. Law Offices of Curtis V. Trinko LLP*, 540 U.S. 398 (No. 02-682), 2003 WL 21755938 (competitor of Verizon alleging misrepresentations by Verizon to state commissions regarding availability of space in central offices for collocating facilities). Whether such conduct was anticompetitive and the impact of such liability on incentives to invest in new facilities, however, would go unexplored in a RICO suit.

The danger posed by a broad standing rule is confirmed by the Second Circuit's decision in the instant case. One of the arguments made by the defendant's competitor is that the advantage the defendant received through the alleged fraud generated profits which, in turn, were used by the defendant to open a store close to the plaintiff and to compete more effectively. The investment of the "racketeering income," plaintiff alleged, caused it to "'los[e] significant business and market share' (Complaint ¶ 57) resulting in damages in excess of $2,000,000 (*see* Complaint ¶ 58)." 373 F.3d at 255. The Second Circuit upheld this part of the plaintiff's claim, *see id.*, at 264, but whether this "loss of market share" caused by the investment in the defendant's new store is pro-or anticompetitive will not be tested in the RICO litigation. The focus will be on the proof of fraud, the investment of the income, and the consequent monetary injury.

The Second Circuit's extension of RICO standing to non-defrauded competitors threatens to turn RICO into a federal law of unfair competition, complete with treble damages and attorneys fees. It seems doubtful that the "background practice against which Congress legislates," *Holmes, supra*, 503 U.S. at 287 (Scalia, J., concurring), would lead to such an interpretation of the RICO private damages provision. Indeed, it would be ironic for RICO's private treble-damages provision, modeled as it was on the antitrust laws, to be interpreted in a way that end-runs those very laws. Review and reversal of the Second Circuit's approach to standing under RICO will thus advance the legislative purpose of both the RICO statute and the antitrust laws.

CONCLUSION

The petition for a writ of certiorari should be granted.

Respectfully Submitted,

RICHARD L. HUFFMAN
Counsel of Record
WILLIAM M. BRODSKY
FOX HORAN & CAMERINI LLP
825 THIRD AVENUE
11TH FLOOR
New York, NY 10022
(212) 480-4800

Of Counsel:

HARRY FIRST
40 WASHINGTON SQUARE SOUTH
New York, NY 10012
(212) 998-6211

C What Is an *Amicus Curiae* Brief?

An *amicus curiae* brief is submitted by a person or organization that wishes to bring to the Court's attention helpful material not likely to be presented by either party. *See* Sup. Ct. R. 37. An *amicus* brief can be submitted in support of the petitioner (appellant) or of the respondent (appellee). It can also be neutral — many *amicus* briefs are submitted in support of neither party. *Amicus* briefs tend to be less argumentative than the briefs submitted by the parties and, in many cases, are more academic in content and style.

We reproduce the *amicus* brief submitted by a group retired generals and admirals, former high ranking defense department officials, and Senators in the University of Michigan affirmative action cases — *Grutter v. Bollinger*, 539 U.S. 306 (2003) (law school admissions policy) and *Gratz v. Bollinger*, 539 U.S. 244 (2003) (undergraduate admissions policy). This brief proved to be unusually influential for an amicus brief because of the identities of the *amici*. A 5-4 Court upheld the law school's admission policy in *Grutter*, but by the same margin, struck down affirmative action policy for the undergraduate program. Justice O'Connor, the swing vote, appeared to be swayed by the Military amici brief that we have reproduced below. In writing for the Court in *Grutter*, 539 U. S. at 331, she stated:

> What is more, high-ranking retired officers and civilian leaders of the United States military assert that, "[b]ased on [their] decades of experience," a "highly qualified, racially diverse officer corps . . . is essential to the military's ability to fulfill its principle mission to provide national security." Brief for Julius W. Becton, Jr., et al. as Amici Curiae 5. The primary sources for the Nation's officer corps are the service academies and the Reserve Officers Training Corps (ROTC), the latter comprising students already admitted to participating colleges and universities. *Ibid.* At present, "the military cannot achieve an officer corps that is *both* highly qualified and racially diverse unless the service academies and the ROTC used limited race-conscious recruiting and admissions policies." *Ibid.* (emphasis in original). To fulfill its mission, the military "must be selective in admissions for training and education for the officer corps, *and* it must train and educate a highly qualified, racially diverse officer corps in a racially diverse educational setting." *Id*, at 29 (emphasis in original). We agree that "[i]t requires only a small step from this analysis to conclude that our country's other most selective institutions must remain both diverse and selective." *Ibid.*

No. 02-241, 02-516

In The
Supreme Court of the United States

BARBARA GRUTTER,

Petitioner,

v.

LEE BOLLINGER, *et al.*,

Respondents.

On Writs of Certiorari to the
United States Court of Appeals for the Sixth Circuit

CONSOLIDATED BRIEF OF LT. GEN. JULIUS W.
BECTON, JR., ADM. DENNIS BLAIR, MAJ. GEN.
CHARLES BOLDEN, HON. JAMES M. CANNON, LT.
GEN. DANIEL W. CHRISTMAN, GEN. WESLEY K.
CLARK, SEN. MAX CLELAND, ADM. ARCHIE
CLEMINS, HON. WILLIAM COHEN, ADM. WILLIAM
J. CROWE, GEN. RONALD R. FOGLEMAN, LT. GEN.
HOWARD D. GRAVES, GEN. JOSEPH P. HOAR, SEN.
ROBERT J. KERREY ET AL. AS *AMICI CURIAE*
IN SUPPORT OF RESPONDENTS

JOSEPH R. REEDER
ROBERT P. CHARROW
KEVIN E. STERN
GREENBERG TRAURIG
800 Connecticut Avenue
Suite 500 1501
Washington, D.C. 20006
(202) 331-3125

CARTER G. PHILLIPS
VIRGINIA A. SEITZ*
ROBERT N. HOCHMAN
SIDLEY AUSTIN BROWN &
WOOD LLP
K Street, N.W.
Washington, D.C. 20005
(202) 736-8000

Counsel for Amici Curiae

February 19, 2003

* Counsel of Record

[Additional *Amici Curiae* Listed on Inside Cover]

Additional *Amici Curiae* Represented by Above Counsel:
Adm. Charles R. Larson
Sen. Carl Levin
Hon. Robert "Bud" Mcfarlane
Gen. Carl E. Mundy, Jr.

Gen. Lloyd W. Newton
Lt. Gen. Tad J. Oelstrom
Hon. William J. Perry
Adm. Joseph W. Prueher
Sen. Jack Reed
Hon. Joseph R. Reeder
Gen. H. Norman Schwarzkopf
Gen. John M.D. Shalikashvili
Gen. Hugh Shelton
Gen. Gordon R. Sullivan
Gen. Anthony Zinni

i
Table of Contents

ii
Table of Authorities

SCHOLARLY AUTHORITIES

Interest of AMICI

Amici are former high-ranking officers and civilian leaders of the Army, Navy, Air Force, and Marine Corps, including former military-academy superintendents, Secretaries of Defense, and present and former members of the U.S. Senate.[1] They are deeply interested in this case, because its outcome could affect the diversity of our nation's officer corps and, in turn, the military's ability to fulfill its missions. *Amici*'s judgment is based on decades of experience and accomplishment at the very highest positions in our nation's military leadership. The responsibilities highlighted below do not begin to describe the full scope of their service. Lieutenant General Julius W. Becton, Jr. served in the U.S. Army for 40 years. He served five years as president of Prairie View A&M University, and subsequently served as Superintendent of the Washington, D.C. Public Schools. Admiral Dennis Blair, retired 4-star, served as Commander in Chief, U.S. Pacific Command (1999-2002), where he directed all Army, Navy, Marine Corps and Air Force operations across more than 100 million square miles. Major General Charles Bolden, retired astronaut and 2-star, was the nation's first African-American Marine astronaut. He flew four space shuttle missions, commanding two, including the mission placing the Hubble telescope into earth orbit. Honorable James M. Cannon served as Chairman of the U.S. Naval Academy Board of Visitors under Presidents Reagan and George H.W. Bush (1989-93).

Lieutenant General Daniel W. Christman, retired Army 3-star, was Superintendent of the U.S. Military Academy (1996-2001), where he had overall responsibility for admissions criteria at West Point.

General Wesley K. Clark served as Supreme Allied Commander, Europe (1997-2000), and Commander in Chief, U.S. Southern Command (1996-97).

Senator Max Cleland served as a combat officer in Vietnam and as Administrator of the U.S. Veterans Administration (1977-81). As U.S. Senator from Georgia (1997-2003), he chaired the Armed Services' Subcommittee on Personnel.

Admiral Archie Clemins, retired 4-star, served as Commander in Chief, U.S. Pacific Fleet (1996-99), the world's largest combined-fleet command.

Honorable William Cohen was the 20th Secretary of Defense (1997-2001). As U.S. Senator from Maine (1979-97), he chaired the Armed Services Committee's Seapower and Force Projection Subcommittee.

Admiral William J. Crowe, retired 4-star, was the 11th Chairman of Joint Chiefs of Staff (1985-89). He also commanded U.S. Naval Forces in the Persian Gulf and NATO Forces in Southern Europe and served as U.S. Ambassador to the United Kingdom (1993-97).

General Ronald R. Fogleman, retired 4-star, was Air Force Chief of Staff (1994-97) with overall responsibility for organizing and training the 750,000

---

1. Pursuant to Rule 37, letters of consent from the parties have been filed with the Clerk of the Court. In accordance with Rule 37.6, *amici* state that no counsel for either party has authored this brief in whole or in part, and no person or entity, other than *amici*, has made a monetary contribution to the preparation or submission of this brief.

active duty, Guard, Reserve and civilian members. He also served as Commander in Chief of U.S. Transcom (1992-94).

Lieutenant General Howard D. Graves, retired Army 3-star, was Superintendent of the U.S. Military Academy (1991-96), with responsibility for admissions criteria. Since 1999, he has served as Chancellor of the Texas A&M University system.

General Joseph P. Hoar, retired Marine 4-star, served as the Commander in Chief, U.S. Central Command (1991-94).

Senator Robert J. Kerrey received the Congressional Medal of Honor serving in the U.S. Navy SEAL special forces. He served as Nebraska governor (1983-87), U.S. Senator (1989-2001), and is the President of New School University.

Admiral Charles R. Larson, retired 4-star, was Commander in Chief, Pacific Fleet (1990-91), and Commander in Chief, U.S. Pacific Command (1991-94). He was also Superintendent of the Naval Academy (1983-86, 1994-98).

Senator Carl Levin is the Ranking Member of the Senate Armed Services Committee and, until January 2003, chaired that Committee, with oversight responsibilities for the armed services.

Honorable Robert "Bud" McFarlane, a retired Marine Corps officer, was President Reagan's National Security Advisor (1983-85), and also served as Deputy Director of the National Security Council.

General Carl E. Mundy, Jr., retired Marine Corps 4-star, was the Marine Corps Commandant (1991-95), and also served as Marine Corps Director of Personnel Procurement.

General Lloyd W. Newton, retired Air Force 4-star, commanded the Air Education and Training Command, where he was responsible for recruiting, training and educating all Air Force personnel, including the Air Force Recruiting Service, 13 bases, and the Air Force University.

Lieutenant General Tad J. Oelstrom, retired 3-star, was Superintendent, U.S. Air Force Academy (1997-2000), and is currently Director, National Security Program, Kennedy School, Harvard University.

Honorable William J. Perry was the 19th Secretary of Defense (1994-97), Deputy Secretary of Defense (1993-94) and Under Secretary of Defense for Research and Engineering (1977-81). He is currently a Professor of Engineering at Stanford University.

Admiral Joseph W. Prueher, retired 4-star, served as Commander in Chief, U.S. Pacific Command (1996-99), Commandant of Midshipmen, U.S. Naval Academy, and U.S. Ambassador to China (1999-2001).

Senator Jack Reed is an Army veteran. As U.S. Senator from Rhode Island, he serves on the Armed Services Committee and chairs the U.S. Military Academy Board of Visitors.

Honorable Joseph R. Reeder, the 14th Under Secretary of the Army (1993-97), had oversight responsibility for admission criteria for the U.S. Military Academy and the ROTC programs at our nation's universities.

General H. Norman Schwarzkopf, retired 4-star, served as Commander in Chief, U.S. Central Command (1988-91), and overall Commander of Allied Forces during the Gulf War.

General John M.D. Shalikashvili, retired 4-star, was the 13th Chairman of the Joint Chiefs of Staff (1993-97), and served as Supreme Allied Commander, Europe (1992-93).

General Hugh Shelton, retired 4-star, was the 14th Chairman of Joint Chiefs of Staff (1997-2001). He also served as Commander in Chief, U.S. Special Operations Command (1996-97).

General Gordon R. Sullivan, retired 4-star, served as Army Chief of Staff (1991-95), with overall responsibility for organizing and training over 1 million active duty Guard, Reserve, and civilian members.

General Anthony Zinni, retired Marine 4-star, served as the Commander in Chief, U.S. Central Command (1997-2001), and as Special U.S. Peace Envoy to the Middle East (2002).

Summary of Argument

Based on decades of experience, *amici* have concluded that a highly qualified, racially diverse officer corps educated and trained to command our nation's racially diverse enlisted ranks is essential to the military's ability to fulfill its principal mission to provide national security. The primary sources for the nation's officer corps are the service academies and the ROTC, the latter comprised of students already admitted to participating colleges and universities. At present, the military cannot achieve an officer corps that is *both* highly qualified *and* racially diverse unless the service academies and the ROTC use limited race-conscious recruiting and admissions policies. Accordingly, these institutions rely on such policies, developed to comport with this Court's instruction in *Regents of the University of California* v. *Bakke*, 438 U.S. 265 (1978).

The military has made substantial progress towards its goal of a fully integrated, highly qualified officer corps. It cannot maintain the diversity it has achieved or make further progress unless it retains its ability to recruit and educate a diverse officer corps. This Court and others have recognized that in certain contexts, the government may take race conscious action not only to remedy past discrimination, but to further other compelling government interests. *See Bakke*; *Wittmer* v. *Peters*, 87 F.3d 916 (7th Cir. 1996) (penological benefits justify consideration of race in selecting correctional officers; collecting similar cases). The rules should not be changed. The military must be permitted to train and educate a diverse officer corps to further our compelling government interest in an effective military.

More than 50 years ago, President Truman issued an executive order ending segregation in the United States armed services. That decision, and the resulting integration of the military, resulted not only from a principled recognition that segregation is unjust and incompatible with American values, but also from a practical recognition that the military's need for manpower and its efficient, effective deployment required integration. Since that time, men and women of all races have trained and fought together in our armed services, from Korea to Vietnam to Afghanistan. Today, almost 40% of servicemen and women are minorities; 61.7% are white, and the remaining almost 40% are minorities, including 21.7% African-American, 9.6% Hispanic, 4% Asian-American and 1.2% Native American. Dep't of Def. ("DoD"), Statistical Series Pamphlet No. 02-5, *Semiannual Race/Ethnic/Gender Profile By Service/Rank of the Department of Defense & Coast Guard* 4 (Mar. 2002) ("*DoD Report*").

In the 1960s and 1970s, however, while integration increased the percentage of African-Americans in the enlisted ranks, the percentage of minority officers remained extremely low,[2] and perceptions of discrimination were pervasive. This deficiency in the officer corps and the discrimination perceived to be its cause led to low morale and heightened racial tension. The danger this created was not theoretical, as the Vietnam era demonstrates. As that war continued, the armed forces suffered increased racial polarization, pervasive disciplinary problems, and racially motivated incidents in Vietnam and on posts around the world. "In Vietnam, racial tensions reached a point where there was an inability to fight." D. Maraniss, *United States Military Struggles To Make Equality Work*, Wash. Post, Mar. 6, 1990, at A01 (quoting Lt. Gen. Frank Petersen, Jr.). By the early 1970s, racial strife in the ranks was entirely commonplace. B. Nalty, *Strength For The Fight: A History Of Black Americans In the Military* 308-10 (1986). The lack of minority officers substantially exacerbated the problems throughout the armed services. LTC E.J. Mason, U.S. Army War Coll. Strategy Research Project, *Diversity: 2015 and the Afro-American Army Officer* 2-3 (1998). The military's leadership "recognized that its racial problem was so critical that it was on the verge of self-destruction. That realization set in motion the policies and initiatives that have led to today's relatively positive state of affairs." *Id.* at 3. "It is obvious and unarguable that no governmental interest is more compelling than the security of the Nation." *Haig* v. *Agee*, 453 U.S. 280, 307 (1981) (internal quotations omitted). The absence of minority officers seriously threatened the military's ability to function effectively and fulfill its mission to defend the nation. To eliminate that threat, the armed services moved aggressively to increase the number of minority officers and to train officers in diverse educational environments. In full accord with *Bakke* and with the DoD Affirmative Action Program, the service academies and the ROTC have set goals for minority officer candidates and worked hard to achieve those goals. They use financial and tutorial assistance, as well as recruiting programs, to expand the pool of highly qualified minority candidates in a variety of explicitly race-conscious ways. They also employ race as a factor in recruiting and admissions policies and decisions. These efforts have substantially increased the percentage of minority officers. Moreover, increasing numbers of officer candidates are trained and educated in racially diverse educational settings, which provides them with invaluable experience for their future command of our nation's highly

---

2. For example, at the end of the Vietnam War, only 3% of Army officers were African-American. Office of the Undersec'y of Def. Personnel & Readiness, *Career Progression of Minority and Women Officers* v (1999) ("*Career Progression*").

diverse enlisted ranks. Today, among active duty officers, 81% are white, and the remaining 19% are minority, including 8.8% African-American, 4% Hispanic, 3.2% Asian American, and .6% Native American. *DoD Report* at 4. A substantial difference between the percentage of African-American enlisted personnel (21.7%) and African-American officers (8.8%) remains. The officer corps must continue to be diverse or the cohesiveness essential to the military mission will be critically undermined. See *infra* at 17.

In specific contexts, the courts have approved race conscious action to achieve compelling, but non-remedial government interests. For example, the government's interest in "the promotion of racial diversity has been found sufficiently 'compelling,' at least in the context of higher education, to support the use of racial considerations in furthering that interest." *Wygant* v. *Jackson Bd. of Educ.*, 476 U.S. 267, 286 (1986) (O'Connor, J., concurring in part); *Metro Broad., Inc.* v. *FCC*, 497 U.S. 547, 568 (1990) (same) (citing *Bakke*). *Amici* submit that the government's compelling interest in promoting racial diversity in higher education is buttressed by its compelling national security interest in a cohesive military. That requires both a diverse officer corps and substantial numbers of officers educated and trained in diverse educational settings, including the military academies and ROTC programs. *See Haig*, 453 U.S. at 307; *Sweatt* v. *Painter*, 339 U.S. 629, 634 (1950) (students in racially-homogenous classrooms are ill-prepared for productive lives in our diverse society). President George Washington eloquently underscored the vital importance of direct association among diverse individuals in education and in the profession of arms:

> [T]he Juvenal period of life, when friendships are formed, & habits established that will stick by one; the Youth, or young men from different parts of the United States would be assembled together, & would by degrees discover that there was not that cause for those jealousies & prejudices which one part of the Union had imbibed against another part. . . . What, but the mixing of people from different parts of the United States during the War rubbed off these impressions? A century in the ordinary intercourse, would not have accomplished what the Seven years association in Arms did.
>
> [Letter from Pres. George Washington, to Alexander Hamilton (Sept. 1, 1796), *reproduced in* J. Ellis, *Founding Brothers: The Revolutionary Generation* 960-61 (2001).]

The crisis that mandated aggressive integration of the officer corps in the service academies and in ROTC programs is a microcosm of what exists in our society at large, albeit with potentially more severe consequences to our nation's welfare. Broad access to the education that leads to leadership roles is essential to public confidence in the fairness and integrity of public institutions, and their ability to perform their vital functions and missions. At present no alternative exists to limited, race-conscious programs to increase the pool of high quality minority officer candidates and to establish diverse educational settings for officers. The armed services must have racially diverse officer candidates who satisfy the rigorous academic, physical, and personal prerequisites for officer training and future leadership. It is no answer to tell selective institutions such as the service academies or the ROTC automatically to admit students with a specified class rank, even if such a system were administratively workable and would result in a diverse student body. This one-dimensional criterion forces the admission of students with neither the academic nor physical capabilities nor the leadership qualities demanded by these institutions, damaging the corps and the military mission in the process. The military must *both* maintain selectivity in admissions *and* train and educate a racially diverse officer corps to command racially diverse troops. The device of admitting a top percentage will not simultaneously produce high quality and diversity.

Like numerous selective educational institutions, the military already engages in aggressive minority recruiting programs and utilizes the service preparatory academies and other programs to increase the pool of qualified minority candidates. These important steps are vital to the continuing integration of the officer corps. The fact remains: Today, there is no race-neutral alternative that will fulfill the military's, and thus the nation's, compelling national security need for a cohesive military led by a diverse officer corps of the highest quality to serve and protect the country.

Argument

The Government's Compelling National Security Interest in a Diverse Officer Corps Requires Race-Conscious Admissions Policies for Officer Training Programs.

The United States armed forces were ordered to desegregate more than 50 years ago. Today the enlisted ranks are fully integrated, and the military has confronted the absolute imperative of integrating its officer corps in furtherance of the compelling national security interest in an effective military. To that end, the services have programs that consider race *both* in selecting participants who broaden the pool of qualified individuals for the service academies and the ROTC *and* in admission to the service academies and ROTC scholarship programs. Currently, no alternative means to field a fully qualified, diverse officer corps exists. This limited use of race in furtherance of the compelling governmental interest it serves is, accordingly, constitutional.

1. Integration of the Military

African-Americans have fought for the United States in every war. F.M. Higginbotham, *Soldiers for Justice: The Role of the Tuskegee Airmen in the Desegregation of the American Armed Forces*, 8 Wm. & Mary Bill Rts. J. 273, 277 (2000). During peacetime, however, the United States once excluded or limited the number of African-Americans in the military. With the urgent need for manpower occasioned by war, numerical restrictions were lifted, but African-Americans were relegated to racially-segregated units and often to manual labor positions. *Id.* at 279; see also C. Moskos & J. Butler, *All That We Can Be: Black Leadership and Racial 11 Integration the Army Way* 16-29 (1996); M. MacGregor, Jr., *Integration of the Armed Forces 1940-1965*, at 412 (1980). This situation began to change during World War II, when President Roosevelt revised racial policies for the armed services. Higgenbotham, *supra*, at 286-88. It was, however, President Truman's Executive Order 9981, signed on July 26, 1948, that set the United States military on its path to integration. See 13 Fed. Reg. 4313 (1948). On October 30, 1954, the armed forces announced that the last segregated unit had been abolished. Higgenbotham, *supra*, at 317. Early on, President Truman's Committee on Equality of Treatment and Opportunity in the Armed Services had made the case that integration was a military necessity and that it would ensure efficiency and combat readiness. See MacGregor, *supra*, at 351-52, 355. "[S]ince maximum military efficiency demanded that all servicemen be given an equal opportunity to discover and exploit their talents, an indivisible link existed between military efficiency and equal opportunity." *Id.* at 355. Indeed, the history of the integration of the armed services demonstrates that integration was driven by the urgent need to recruit and effectively utilize military manpower.

The Army initially resisted President Truman's command to integrate, until heavy casualties and slow troop replacement during the Korean War required that African-American soldiers be assigned to fight with undermanned white units. Moskos & Butler, *supra*, at 30; MacGregor, *supra*, at 433-34. The Marines simultaneously integrated based on the same imperative. MacGregor, *supra*, at 460. The Air Force saw significant gains in efficiency with integration, because "problems of procurement, training, and assignment always associated with racially designated units [were] reduced by an appreciable degree or eliminated entirely." *Id.* at 409. With the move to the All Volunteer Force in 1973, the military necessity of "includ[ing] all Americans in the pool of potential recruits took on added urgency." Dep't of Justice, *Review of Federal Affirmative Action Programs, Report to the President* § 7.5.1 (1995) ("*President's Report*").

Today, the military is one of the most integrated institutions in America. See, *e.g.*, Maraniss, *supra*, at A01. The modern military judgment is that full integration and other policies combating discrimination are essential to good order, combat readiness, and military effectiveness. DoD Directive 1350 requires the military to formulate, maintain, and review affirmative action plans with established objectives and milestones. Dep't of Def., Directive 1350.2 § 4.4 (Aug. 18, 1995). Instruction 1350.2 describes such programs as a "military necessity," critical to "combat readiness and mission accomplishment." Each service, accordingly, has its own regulations and instructions implementing the DoD mandate, and each service has goals for officer accessions. *See Career Progression* at 19.[3]

---

3. See also, *e.g.*, Dep't of the Navy, *Navy Affirmative Action Plan* (1991) ("*Navy Affirmative Action Plan*"), *enclosed in* Dep't of the Navy, OPNAV Instruction 5354.3D (Aug. 29, 1991) (setting goals for minority officer population and accessions); Dep't of the Navy, OPNAVINST 5354.1E, Equal Opportunity Policy § 4(a) (Jan. 22, 2001) (discrimination "adversely affect[s] good order and discipline,

As of March 2002, of the 1.1 million enlisted in the active duty forces, 61.7% were white, 21.7% African-American, 9.6% Hispanic, 1.2% Native American, 4.0% Asian American, and 1.8% were classified as "other." *DoD Report* at 4. In 1990, 24% of those who fought in Desert Shield/Desert Storm were African-American, and 30% of Army troops were African-American. Moskos & Butler, *supra*, at 35. Plainly, the missions of the United States military services cannot be accomplished without the minority men and women who constitute almost 40% of the active duty armed forces. Moreover:

> the current leadership views complete racial integration as a military necessity — that is, as a prerequisite to a cohesive, and therefore effective, fighting force. In short, *success with the challenges of diversity is critical to national security.* Experience during the 1960s and 1970s with racial conflict in the ranks was an effective lesson in the importance of inclusion and equal opportunity. As a senior Pentagon official told us, "Doing affirmative action the right way is deadly serious for us — people's lives depend on it."
>
> [*President's Report* § 7.1 (emphasis supplied).]

2. Integration of the Officer Corps

Fully integrated enlisted ranks made integration of the officer corps essential to the effective operation of our military. But, the military did not learn this lesson without first experiencing the dangerous and destructive environment of a racially diverse enlisted corps commanded by an overwhelmingly white officer corps. As a direct result of the lessons learned in the 1960s and 1970s, the military is now fully committed to officer corps integration. And while the armed forces have made remarkable strides in achieving racial integration, the military cannot lose ground. It must continue actively to foster representation of minorities in the officer corps by recruiting the most promising members of minority communities so that the service academies and the ROTC programs can train and educate officers who fulfill our national security requirements.

(a) The Lesson of History.

Almost as soon as President Truman ordered the integration of the armed forces, some in the military recognized the importance of integrating the officer corps.[4] After integration, however, the armed forces did not produce a

---

mission readiness, and prevent[s] our Navy from attaining the highest level of operational readiness"); Air Force Instruction 36-2706, at 1 (Dec. 1, 1996) (implementing DoD Instruction 1350.3); Dep't of the Army, Pamphlet 600-26, *Army Affirmative Action Plan* § 2-3 (May 23, 1990) (setting goals for officer accessions based on DoD 1350.3).

4. For example, in its final report to President Truman, the committee charged with overseeing integration expressed "dissatisf[action] with the small number of [black] officers in the [N]avy," and urged the Navy to increase minority participation in the ROTC and to recruit aggressively in minority communities. President's Comm. on Equality of Treatment & Opportunity in the Armed Servs., *Freedom to Serve: Equality of Treatment and Opportunity in the Armed Services (1950), reprinted in Blacks in the Military: Essential Documents* 275-76 (B. Nalty & M. MacGregor, Jr. eds., 1981).

substantial number of minority officers for more than a generation. Both lingering discrimination and the formal educational qualifications for officers precluded quick racial integration of the officer corps. As a result, over time, the armed forces became a racial mix of diverse enlisted ranks commanded by an overwhelmingly white officer corps. In 1962, a mere 1.6% of all commissioned military officers were African-American. Nalty, *supra*, at 313.

The chasm between the racial composition of the officer corps and the enlisted personnel undermined military effectiveness in a variety of ways. For example, military effectiveness depends heavily upon unit cohesion. In turn, group cohesiveness depends on a shared sense of mission and the unimpeded flow of information through the chain of command. African-Americans experienced discriminatory treatment in the military, even during integration, but the concerns and perceptions of African-American personnel were often unknown, unaddressed or both, in part because the lines of authority, from the military police to the officer corps, were almost exclusively white. *Id.* at 228-29; MacGregor, *supra*, at 579-80. Indeed, "communication between the largely white officer corps and black enlisted men could be so tenuous that a commander might remain blissfully unaware of patterns of racial discrimination that black servicemen found infuriating." Nalty, *supra*, at 282.

The military's pre-Vietnam racial problems generally were suppressed during battle (*e.g.*, in Korea). During peacetime, violent incidents were met with attempts to improve military life for African-Americans, but minority representation in the officer corps remained static. For example, in 1963, a special committee appointed by President Kennedy recommended that every military organization appoint an officer with authority to address issues raised by African-American servicemen. President's Comm. on Equal Opportunity in the Armed Forces, *Equality of Treatment and Opportunity for Negro Military Personnel Stationed Within the United States* 27-32 (June 13, 1963) (Initial Report), *reprinted in* 13 *Blacks in the United States Armed Forces: Basic Documents*, item 10 (M. MacGregor, Jr. & B. Nalty eds., 1977) ("*Basic Documents*"). This recommendation proved woefully inadequate. Nalty, *supra,* at 291, 329; Report by House Special Subcomm. on Disciplinary Problems in the U.S. Navy, H.A.S.C. Rep. No. 92-81, at 17,671, 17,690 (1973) ("*Special Subcommittee Report*"). During the 1960s and 1970s, the military experienced a demoralizing and destabilizing period of internal racial strife. Hundreds of race-related incidents occurred. For example, in the 1960s, racial violence among the Marines at Camp Lejeune was not uncommon. White officers were simply unaware of intense African-American dissatisfaction with job assignments and the perceived lack of respect from the Marine Corps. Nalty, *supra*, at 306-07. In the early 1970s, the Navy endured similar racial violence on board the *Constellation*, the *Kitty Hawk* and the *Hassayampa*. See generally *Special Subcommittee Report* at 17,674-79; Adm. E. Zumwalt, Jr., *On Watch* 217-32 (1976). In each case, the officer corps was caught off guard, unable to bring the situation under control, due to the absence of trust and communication between the predominantly white officer corps and frustrated African-American enlisted men.

Throughout the armed forces, the overwhelmingly white officer corps faced racial tension and unrest. "Fights between black and white soldiers were endemic in the 1970s, an era now remembered as the 'time of troubles.'" Moskos & Butler, *supra*, at 33. "In Vietnam, racial tensions reached a point where there was an inability to fight." Maraniss, *supra*, at A01 (quoting Lt. Gen. Frank Peterson, Jr.). African-American troops, who rarely saw members of their own race in command positions, lost confidence in the military as an institution. Mason, *supra*, at 2-3. And, African-American servicemen concluded that the command structure had no regard for whether African-Americans would succeed in military careers. 1 Dep't of Def., *Report of the Task Force on the Administration of Military Justice in the Armed Forces* 38-48, 59-66 (Nov. 30, 1972), *reprinted in* 13 *Basic Documents*, item 66.[5]

Making matters worse, many white officers had no idea how serious the problem was. "Violence and even death proved necessary to drive home the realization that the various assistant secretaries, special assistants, and even commanding officers had only the faintest idea what the black man and woman in the service were thinking." Nalty, *supra*, at 317. Ultimately, "[t]he military of the 1970s recognized that its race problem was so critical that it was on the verge of self-destruction." Moskos & Butler, *supra*, at 142.

The painful lesson slowly learned was that our diverse enlisted ranks rendered integration of the officer corps a military necessity. M. Neiberg, *Making Citizen-Soldiers: ROTC and the Ideology of American Military Service* 166 (2000) ("[t]he military came . . . to understand that having African American noncommissioned officers . . . and regular officers was critical to both the operational efficiency of the military and to the creation of the more just and equal environment that military leaders . . . wanted to create"); Nalty, *supra*, at 338 ("[b]y the time the draft ended . . . the services had realized that discipline had to be maintained and that councils and committees, although helpful in easing racial tensions and otherwise promoting harmony within a unit, could not shoulder the responsibilities that rightly devolved upon the commander"). "Racial conflict within the military during the Vietnam era was a blaring wakeup call to the fact that equal opportunity is absolutely indispensable to unit cohesion, and therefore critical to military effectiveness and our national security." *President's Report* § 7.5.1.

---

5. African-American servicemen were looking for African-American officers both for support and as a visible indication that the military recognized African-Americans as valuable contributors. *Hearings By the House Special Subcomm. on Disciplinary Problems in the U.S. Navy*, H.A.S.C. No. 93-13, at 595 (1972) (testimony of Commander B. W. Cloud); J. Foner, *Blacks and the Military in American History: A New Perspective* 211 (1974) ("[t]he scarcity of black officers intensified black grievances."); *id.* at 223 ("[b]lack servicemen told the [NAACP] . . . that if black officers were placed in command positions with white junior officers accountable to them, it would be a major step toward overcoming racial discrimination in the army"); Moskos & Butler, *supra*, at 33 (asking "[w]here was the black officer corps" of the late 1960s and early 1970s).

(b) Current Commitment To Racial Diversity In The Officer Corps.

Spurred by the lessons of the 1960s and 1970s, the armed forces have steadily integrated the officer corps since the end of the Vietnam conflict. In 1973, when the nation instituted its all-volunteer force, 2.8% of military officers were African-American. *Career Progression* at v. By March 2002, 8.8% of officers were African-American. *DoD Report* at 4. The representation of other minorities — Hispanics, Asian Americans and Native Americans — increased at an even faster rate over the same period. Minorities now comprise roughly 19% of all officers. *Id.* The modern American military candidly acknowledges the critical link between minority officers and military readiness and effectiveness. "[T]he current leadership views complete racial integration as a military necessity — that is, as a prerequisite to a cohesive, and therefore effective, fighting force. In short, success with the challenge of diversity is critical to national security." *President's Report* § 7.1. The military's continuing, race-conscious efforts to increase the percentage of minority officers have achieved some results, but this progress must continue. See Dep't of Def., *Population Representation in the Military Services* 4-8 (Nov. 1998). Accordingly, the armed forces strive to identify and train the best qualified minority candidates to serve as officers. *Infra* at 18-27. As we show, these efforts include race-conscious recruiting, preparatory, and admissions policies at the service academies and in ROTC programs — efforts that underscore the military's resolve to do what is necessary and effective to integrate the officer corps.

3. RACE-CONSCIOUS ADMISSIONS PROGRAMS FOR OFFICER EDUCATION AND TRAINING

Our armed forces therefore have focused their efforts on expanding the pool of qualified minority applicants for the academies and the ROTC — the primary sources for officers. Increases in minority enrollment in these institutions obviously will increase the numbers of highly qualified, minority officers. *Career Progression* at 31. The service academies and ROTC employ limited, race-conscious admission programs and policies, both to expand the pool of minority applicants and to increase the number of minority participants. Moreover, increased minority representation in the officer corps enhances our ability to recruit highly qualified minorities into the enlisted ranks.

A. Army.

In 1973, testimony by Army leaders before the House Appropriations Subcommittee confirms that integration of the officer corps was essential to address the Army's race-related turmoil. The witnesses identified "[i]ncreasing the number of minority cadets at [West Point] and in the ROTC program" as a critical component of improving the Army's race relations. *DoD Appropriations of 1974: Military Personnel: Hearing Before the Subcomm. on the Dep't of Def.*

of the House Comm. on Appropriations, 93d Cong., 308-09 (1974). The first program that succeeded in increasing minority representation was at West Point. In 1968, there were 30 African-American cadets at the Academy; by 1971, there were almost 100. T. Crackel, *West Point: A Bicentennial History* 238 (2002). The Army's successful integration of West Point continues. In 1993, minorities made up 16.5% of cadets, and the Class of 2005 is 25% minority, including 8% African-American (100 cadets) and 6% Hispanic (70 cadets). USMA Admissions Office, *Academy Getting Ready For Influx of New Cadets* (June 2001), *at* http://www.USNA.edu/PublicAffairs/R//010629/ influx.html. Today, there are more than 300 African-American and 150 Hispanic cadets.

In order to integrate itself, and hence the Army officer corps, the U.S. Military Academy has self-consciously attempted "to balance the Corps" and therefore has "develop[ed] goals for each class for desired percentages of scholars, leaders, athletes, women, blacks, Hispanics and other minorities." U.S. GAO, GAO/NSIAD-94-95, *Military Academy: Gender and Race Disparities* 13 (Mar. 17, 1994) ("*USMA GAO Report*"). West Point's Superintendent sets yearly targets for minority admissions. *Career Progression* at 20. As Director of Admissions Colonel Michael L. Jones stated, "'We like to represent the society we come from in terms of the student body's undergraduate experiences. [H]aving a diverse student body allows personal growth in areas where people may not have gotten it otherwise. We want people to understand the society they will defend.'" A. Clymer, *Service Academies Defend Use of Race in Their Admissions Policies*, N.Y. Times, Jan. 28, 2003.

The Academy's specific percentage goals for minorities are based upon their "representation in the national population and in the national pool of college bound people, and their representation in the Army." *USMA GAO Report* at 13. See also Col. M. Jones, Dir. of Admissions, *USMA Admissions: The Corp Starts Here*, *at* http://www.USMA.edu/PublicAffairs/ClubConference02./wppcp res0402.ppt (USMA seeking 20-25% minorities). In pursuit of these goals, "minorities [are] consistently offered admission [to West Point] at higher rates than whites [despite] lower academic predictor scores and lower academic, physical education, and military grades." *USMA GAO Report* at 2. This reflects the Academy's need to extend a greater number of offers to qualified minority candidates to achieve diversity. *Id.* In so doing, the Academy ensures that each minority candidate is highly qualified and has the potential to be an outstanding officer in the Army based on a broad range of factors.

(B) Navy.

Like West Point, the U.S. Naval Academy aggressively recruits minority applicants and employs a limited race-conscious admissions policy. The instructions implementing the Navy Affirmative Action Plan directed the Navy to achieve "a minority officer inventory of six percent Blacks by end of FY2000, [and] three percent Hispanics by end of FY99." *Navy Affirmative Action Plan* at 10. They set a Significant Action Step of monitoring the "United States Naval Academy

(USNA) actions to commission at least seven percent Black Navy officers annually starting with USNA Class of 1994" and ensuring "continued commissioning of at least four percent Hispanic Navy officers annually." *Id.* Additional Instructions issued in 1996 specifically stated that the "Naval Academy admissions procedures must support the primary objectives of selecting candidates who . . . [r]epresent women and minorities in appropriate numbers in support of the Equal Opportunity Program of the Department of the Navy." Dep't of the Navy, SECNAVINST 1531.2A, U.S. Naval Academy Curriculum & Admissions Policy 1-2 (Feb. 2, 1996). As Naval Academy Dean of Admissions David Vetter stated, " 'We want to build an officer corps that reflects the military services of which we are a part.' " Clymer, *supra.* Substantial human and financial resources are devoted to recruiting and admitting minority students to the Academy. The *Naval Academy Information Program Handbook* 23-25 (2000) (internal working document) guides Academy affiliated individuals who recruit high-school students, making clear that minority recruitment is a high priority. See *id.* at 23-25. Each recruiting region and the admissions office itself has a minority recruitment specialist. Critically, a GAO Report, U.S. GAO, GAO/NSIAD-93-54, *Naval Academy: Gender and Racial Disparities* 8 (Apr. 1993) ("*Naval Academy GAO Report*"), stated:

> The Academy also considers desired class composition of minorities and women in its selection of applicants. The Academy uses the "Chief of Naval Operations' goals" as a basis for establishing targets. Its targets for Blacks are 7 percent and 4 percent for Hispanics, which are the same as for the fleet. . . . The Academy accepts a greater percentage of women and minorities to allow for attrition and still achieve the Chief of Naval Operations' accession goals.

The *Naval Academy GAO Report* further found that "a higher percentage of minorities who did qualify were admitted to the Academy than their white counterparts" and that "[a]verage success predictor scores were significantly higher for whites than for minorities." *Id.* at 37. The Report therefore concluded that "*[b]ecause of the lower qualification rate of minorities, the Academy makes offers of appointment to the majority of qualified minorities to achieve the Chief of Naval Operations' commissioning goals for minorities.*" *Id.* at 38 (emphasis supplied).[6]

---

6. The Coast Guard has numerous programs to recruit minority applicants, including the Minority Introduction to Engineering Program (a free week-long program for minority students interested in engineering and otherwise eligible for the Academy). U.S. Coast Guard Acad., MITE: Minority Introduction to Engineering, *at* http://www.cga.edu/admissions/ summerprogramforjuniors/mite.htm (last visited Feb. 4, 2003). Minorities represent 18% of the Academy's class of 2004. See U.S. Coast Guard Acad., Diversity & Retention (Oct. 2001) *at* http://www.members. aol.com/_ht_a/lyndahaley/ academy/statistics.htm. In addition, the Coast Guard operates the College Student Pre-Commissioning Initiative, which provides training, tuition and stipends to college students enrolled in historically African-American colleges and universities, Hispanic Association of Colleges and Universities schools, and other approved institutions. See U.S. Coast Guard, College Student Pre-Commissioning Initiative (CSPI), *at* http://www.uscg.mil/jobs/cspi.html (last visited Feb. 4, 2003). The program is designed to increase minority junior officers in the Guard. See L. Healy, *Learning to Lead*, Military News, June 18, 2001. As of March 2002, minority officers constituted 13.7% of the Coast Guard officer corps. See *DoD Report* at 4.

(C)   Air Force.

Like other services, the Air Force has adopted a Policy Directive, instructing that "the Air Force will develop affirmative action programs which represent minorities, women, and persons with disabilities at all grade levels, in every employment category and in every major organizational element." Air Force Policy Directive 36-2 ¶ 2 (Oct. 1, 1996). See also Air Force Instruction 36-2706 § 1.1., at 7 (Dec. 1, 1996) (Air Force Equal Opportunity and Treatment Program improves mission effectiveness by combating discrimination and allowing "Air Force members [to] ris[e] to the highest level of responsibility possible"). The admissions policy of the Air Force Academy is set out in its catalog and in U.S. GAO, GAO/NSIAD-93-244, *Air Force Academy: Gender and Racial Disparities* (Sept. 1993) (*"Air Force GAO Report"*). The Academy compiles a list of candidates who meet minimum admission standards and then determines which eligible candidates will receive an offer. See U.S. Air Force Acad., *2001-2002 Catalog* 14 (2001). The *Air Force GAO Report*, at 33, states that "[o]n average, minorities had comparable physical fitness scores but lower academic admissions scores." From 1991-1995, 18% of minority applicants were deemed qualified for admission, compared with 28% of white applicants; but 76% of qualified minority candidates received offers, compared with 51% of white applicants. *Id.* at 35-36. Clearly, then, the Academy has an admissions policy that takes some limited account of race. See *id.* at 37-38 fig. 3.4 (admission score for minority students roughly 3000 points and for white students roughly 3200 points); Clymer, *supra* (quoting associate dean of admissions Rollie Stoneman, "'[race] certainly [is] one of any number of factors we consider'"). For 2000, 18% of enrolled students were members of a minority group. U.S. Air Force Acad., Information Sheet (2000) (unpublished) (on file with author).

(D)   Service Academy Preparatory Schools.

The service academy preparatory schools demonstrate both the importance the services place on integrating their officer corps and the race-conscious measures they employ to achieve that urgent need. Each service academy is associated with a federally-funded preparatory academy that is the single most significant source of minority candidates for that academy. See *Career Progression* at 35, 37; Moskos & Butler, *supra*, at 86; U.S. GAO, GAO/NSIAD-92-57, *DoD Service Academies: Academy Preparatory Schools Need A Clearer Mission and Better Oversight* 11 (Mar. 1992) (*"Academy Preparatory Schools GAO Report"*). For example, the Military Academy Preparatory School accounts for 20-40% of African-American students and 20-30% of Hispanic students at West Point, and these students are highly successful after admission. *Career Progression* at 37.[7] See also R. Worth, *Beyond Racial Preferences*, Washington Monthly, Mar. 1998, at 28 ("[b]ecause blacks score on average almost 200 points lower on the

---

7. Army preparatory school graduates "leave West Point with somewhat lower than average GPAs, but with better ratings on various other leadership measures that military academies prize. And 78 percent of [preparatory school] alumni graduated from West Point in four years, a half-percentage point higher

SAT than whites, [the Army preparatory school] has become an indispensable pipeline for bringing [blacks] into the officer corps"). Similarly, "[a]bout one-third of the minority midshipmen came from [the Naval Academy Preparatory School]." *Career Progression* at 38. See also B. Brubaker, *Prepping to Play Football for Navy*, Seattle Times, Apr. 21, 1996, at D3.

"Almost all Coast Guard students at [the Navy's preparatory school] are minorities." Am. Council on Educ., *Service Academy Preparatory Schools Project, Final Report* 89 (June 15, 1993) ("*Am. Council on Educ. Report*"). Fully one-third of minority cadets at the Air Force Academy attend its preparatory school. P. Grier, *The Case for Academics*, Air Force Mag., July 1993, at 60.

The current mission of the preparatory schools is to prepare minorities, as well as enlisted men, women, and athletes, for the service academies. *Academy Preparatory Schools GAO Report* at 3 (the preparatory schools are important "because they prepare minorities and women for academy admission, and therefore promote diversity in the officer corps"); H.R. Rep. No. 103-357, at 676 (1993) (same). Each preparatory academy uses a race-conscious admission policy.

The Army preparatory school sets specific numeric goals. See *Am. Council on Educ. Report* at 41. Both the Navy and Air Force preparatory schools enroll about 40% minority students. *See* Brubaker, *supra*, at D3 (quoting J. Renard, Naval Academy Dean of Admission, calling the preparatory school "'truly an affirmative action success story'" because "[w]ithout [the prep school] he could not possibly meet Navy goals to boost minority representation at the academy to 29 percent"); *Am. Council on Educ. Report* at 28-29 (the Air Force Preparatory school is roughly 40% minority and is providing 30-50% of minority students at the Academy). The Coast Guard, too, sends students to the Navy's preparatory school to "expand the pool of minorities applying to the Coast Guard Academy." U.S. GAO, GAO/RCED-94-131, *Coast Guard: Cost for Naval Academy Preparatory School and Profile of Minority Enrollment* (Apr. 12, 1994) (the preparatory school has "improved the minority profile" at the Coast Guard Academy which is its "primary purpose").

(d)   ROTC Scholarships.

The ROTC produced 48% of active duty officers as of 2000.[8] Like the service academies, it is considered a prime pathway for a career as a military officer. *Career Progression* at 15, 17. Because Academy classes are small, the armed services initially saw the ROTC as the "obvious solution" to the problems created by the lack of minority representation in the officer corps. Neiberg, *supra*, at 167 (quoting Ben Cassiday, *Report to the AFROTC Advisory Panel* (Sept. 18, 1972)). For minorities, the ROTC continues to be a particularly

---

than average." D. Dickerson, *How To KeepElite Colleges Diverse*, U.S. News & World Rep., Jan. 5, 1998, at 15.

8. *See* Office of the Assistant Sec'y of Def., *Population Representation in the Military Servs.*, tbl. 4.3 (Nov. 2001), *available at* http://www.dod.mil/prhome/poprep2000/html/chapter4/chapter4_3.htm. This number excludes so-called direct appointments for professionals (medical and legal professionals and clergy).

significant vehicle for increasing representation in the officer ranks. Moskos &
Butler, *supra,* at 84.

Like the service academies, the ROTC employs an aggressive race-conscious
admissions program. Each service's ROTC program is tasked to meet its service's
minority goals for commissioning officers. As a result, the ROTC's recruiting
programs and strategies are overtly race conscious. For example, the Air Force
"Gold Bar" program uses newly commissioned, minority ROTC graduates full
time in an effort to recruit minorities for its ROTC. *Career Progression* at 42.
The Navy ROTC tripled the number of African-Americans applying for a scholarship after the Secretary of the Navy set specific goals for minority officer
accession in 1993. *Id.* In addition to their targeted recruiting efforts, the ROTC
"administer[s] compensatory programs in an attempt to broaden the pool of
minority candidates." *Id.* at 31. For example, the Junior ROTC purposefully
targets inner city high schools and provides a program to address the special
needs of this population as a way to increase the pool of minority officer
candidates. *Id.* at 39-40. See also L.M. Hanser & A.E. Robyn, *Implementing
High School JROTC Career Academies* (2000).

To obtain an ROTC scholarship, a candidate must be admitted to the hosting
college or university. The pool of minority candidates at any given ROTC
member institution is thus limited to the number of minority students admitted.
In addition, the military services issue regulations that determine the number of
scholarships allotted to each school (although there are a certain number of
scholarship recipients not included in any school's allocation). See L. Morris,
U.S. Army, CBSP Fact Sheet 02, ¶ 2 (Sept. 26, 2002), *at* http:// www.rotc.
monroe.army.mil/scholarship__HPD/Scholarship% 20information%20TOC/
fact%20sheets.htm. To increase the number of minority ROTC participants,
the ROTC makes substantial numbers of scholarships available at historically
African-American colleges and universities ("HBCUs") and at institutions with
high Hispanic enrollment ("HMIs"). *Career Progression* at 34, 94. This allocation, by itself, ensures that a certain percentage of ROTC scholarships will be
awarded to minority college students.

The program's limited race-conscious policies are also reflected in the gap
between the SAT scores of minority scholarship recipients and average scholarship recipients. For example, the mean SAT score of recipients in 2001 was 1236
with an average high school GPA of 3.6, compared to the mean SAT score for
HBCU scholarship recipients of 920 and average high school GPA of 2.9. See
Cadet Command Headquarters, U.S. Army, Scholarship Fact Sheets: 2001 Pro-
files, figs. 1-2, *at* http://www.rotc.monroe.army.mil/scholarship_ HPD/Scholar-
ship%20information%20TOC/fact%20sheets.htm (last updated Oct. 2, 2002).
See also Moskos & Butler, *supra*, at 84.

The U.S. military's collective judgment is perhaps best summed up by General
Colin Powell, in confirming his strong support for affirmative action: "In the
military, we . . . used Affirmative Action to reach out to those who were
qualified, but who were often overlooked or ignored as a result of indifference

or inertia." Commencement Address, Bowie State University (1996), *reprinted in* 142 Cong. Rec. S9311, S9312 (daily ed., July 31, 1996).

4. Race Conscious Admissions Are Constitutional

The race-conscious admissions policies at the service academies and in the ROTC program serve compelling governmental purposes and are narrowly tailored to serve those purposes. Limited race-conscious admissions policies at civilian universities are constitutional for the same reason. This Court and others have recognized that in certain contexts, race-conscious action that furthers compelling, nonremedial government interests is constitutional. The government's interest in racial diversity in higher education is compelling and supports the use of racial considerations in furthering that interest. *Wygant*, 476 U.S. at 286 (O'Connor, J., concurring in part); *Metro Broad., Inc.*, 497 U.S. at 568 (same) (citing *Bakke*). Because racial diversity in higher education also is necessary to integrate the officer corps and to train and educate white and minority officers, it is essential to ensuring an effective, battle-ready fighting force. This is indisputably a compelling government interest. "It is obvious and unarguable that no governmental interest is more compelling than the security of the Nation." *Haig*, 453 U.S. at 307 (internal quotations omitted).

As noted, the service academies and the ROTC are the primary sources of our officer corps, including those in the highest ranks. Entry through these avenues gives an officer a relative advantage for promotion and assignment. *Career Progression* at 25; *id.* at 62-63 ("minorities from selective colleges have significantly higher performance ratings" on officer reviews than their cohorts from less selective colleges). History has proven that these institutions must provide substantial numbers of minority officers for the services to field the diverse corps that is essential to military efficiency and effectiveness. Indeed, just as compelling public safety and penological benefits justify consideration of race in the selection of police and correctional officers, even more compelling considerations of national security and military mission justify consideration of race in selecting military officers. Cf. *Wittmer*, 87 F.3d at 920.

Integration of the service academies and the ROTC also provides white and minority officers with the training and educational experience necessary to lead enlisted ranks that are 40% minority. In this connection, ROTC officer candidates are selected from those *already admitted* to host colleges and universities. These institutions must have sufficient minority enrollment so that their ROTC programs can, in turn, train and educate substantial numbers of qualified minority officers and provide officer candidates with a racially diverse educational experience. The military employs ROTC programs at HBCUs and HMIs to recruit high quality minority applicants in sufficient numbers, but preparing officer candidates for service, let alone *command*, in our racially diverse military is extraordinarily difficult in a racially homogenous educational setting. To paraphrase *Sweatt*, a future officer's most effective training and education cannot take place at an institution "in isolation from the individuals and institutions" that he or she will command. 339 U.S. at 634. "[T]he 'nation's future depends upon leaders trained through wide exposure' to the ideas and mores of students as diverse as this Nation of many peoples." *Bakke*, 438 U.S. at 312-13 (Powell, J., concurring) (quoting *Keyishan* v. *Board of Regents*, 385 U.S. 589, 603 (1967)). The crisis that resulted in integration of the officer corps is but a magnified reflection of circumstances in our nation's highly diverse society. In the 1960s and 1970s, the stark disparity between the racial composition of the rank and file and that of the officer corps fueled a breakdown of order that endangered the military's ability to fulfill its mission. That threat was so dangerous and unacceptable that it resulted in immediate and dramatic changes intended to restore minority enlisted ranks' confidence in the fairness and integrity of the institution. In a highly diverse society, the public, including minority citizens, must have confidence in the integrity of public institutions, particularly those educational institutions that provide the training, education and status necessary to achieve prosperity and power in America.

There is presently no workable alternative to limited, race conscious programs to increase the pool of qualified minority officer candidates and establish diverse educational settings for officer candidates. Plainly, as respondents' briefs show, the alternative proposed by the United States — admission of students who achieve a specified class rank — is no alternative for private universities and colleges or for graduate schools or for any public institution with a national student body. Equally to the point, the armed services must have racially diverse officer candidates who *also* satisfy the rigorous academic, physical, and personal prerequisites for officer training and future leadership. It is no answer to tell selective institutions, such as the service academies or the ROTC, automatically to admit students with a specified class rank, even if such a system were administratively workable. This lone criterion mandates the admission of students unable to satisfy the academic, physical, and character-related demands of the service academies or the officer training curriculum. Moreover, even if the pool of minority ROTC candidates remains quantitatively stable, such a policy will reduce the number of high quality minority candidates for ROTC scholarships. Minority candidates are not fungible in the way the government's proposed alternative suggests.

In the interest of national security, the military must be selective in admissions for training and education for the officer corps, *and* it must train and educate a highly qualified, racially diverse officer corps in a racially diverse educational setting. It requires only a small step from this analysis to conclude that our country's other most selective institutions must remain both diverse and selective. Like our military security, our economic security and international competitiveness depend upon it. An alternative that does not preserve both diversity and selectivity is no alternative at all. Nor does telling the military to work harder to recruit high quality minority candidates make sense. Each service already has numerous aggressive minority recruiting programs and expends significant funds and human resources on service preparatory academies and other programs in efforts to increase the pool of qualified minority candidates. As the growing percentage of minority officers reveals, the military services are making substantial progress toward diverse, highly qualified leadership – progress envied by other institutions in our society. That progress must be protected and must continue. The admissions policies of the service academies and the ROTC reflect a collective military judgment – that the carefully tailored consideration of race in the admission and training of officer candidates is essential to an integrated officer corps and hence to our fighting force. Today, there is no race-neutral alternative that will fulfill the military's and the nation's compelling need for a diverse officer corps of the highest quality to serve the country.

CONCLUSION

The court of appeals' decision that racial diversity in higher education is a compelling state interest should be affirmed.

Respectfully submitted,

JOSEPH R. REEDER
ROBERT P. CHARROW
KEVIN E. STERN
GREENBERG TRAURIG
800 Connecticut Avenue
Suite 500
Washington, D.C. 20006
(202) 331-3125

Counsel for Amici Curiae

February 19, 2003

CARTER G. PHILLIPS
VIRGINIA A. SEITZ*
ROBERT N. HOCHMAN
SIDLEY AUSTIN BROWN &
WOOD LLP
1501 K Street, N.W.
Washington, D.C. 20005
(202) 736-8000

* Counsel of Record

Appendix A

An Overview

of English

Sentence Structure

Professors, judges, and other educated readers expect documents to be correct. When they see errors, these readers may make negative inferences about the writer's intelligence and ability. One way to minimize the danger of being considered incompetent as a writer (and as a lawyer) is to eliminate errors. However, not all errors are equally easy to identify and correct. To correct spelling, you need only motivation and access to a dictionary or computer spell check program; to correct typographical errors, you need only plan well enough to allow time for proofreading. But to correct other problems such as incomplete or garbled sentences, you need to understand sentence structure well enough to determine what, if anything, is wrong with sentences or phrases that don't "sound quite right."

To understand how English sentences work, you need to master the concept of sentence patterns. The basic pieces (or elements) that can make up a sentence pattern fall into four categories: subject, verb, object, and complement. These basic pieces can only appear in certain combinations and orders. For example, in English the subject almost always comes before the verb and the object generally follows the verb. Other, less essential pieces—modifiers such as adverbs and adjectives and phrases that act as adverbs and adjectives—can appear in many more places.

The purpose of this section is to review with you the pieces that make up English sentences and to give you practice in recognizing correct and incorrect sentence patterns. This, in turn, will help you to avoid grammatical errors in your own writing and to recognize errors when editing your writing or the writing of others.

In this chapter, we will deal with patterns first and use them to explain the pieces that make up the patterns.

A   Common Sentence Patterns

1. The Active Voice

a. *Subject → Verb (S → V)*

The most basic pattern for English sentences is subject-verb; you cannot have a sentence without these two elements. The subject is the person or thing that the

385

sentence is about: hence, "subject." (Note that some grammarians have also called the subject the "topic.") Examples of subjects are nouns such as *cat, person, defendant, Canada, imagination, divorce.* Subjects can be more complex, as well, such as *trench warfare, an uncontested divorce, the thing stuck to my foot, people who live in glass houses.* In English, the subject almost always appears at the beginning of the sentence (or clause), before the verb.

The verb is the action of the sentence. Examples of verbs are *run, eat, find, defend, prosecute, sleep, swagger, be, seem.*

Note that in the pattern Subject → Verb, or **S → V**, for short, the arrow points from the S to the V. This is a grammatical convention to show that the subject is doing the action (as opposed to those sentence patterns in which the subject is the thing to whom the action is done). This type of sentence pattern, in which the subject is also the *actor*, is called an *active sentence.* Here are three simple sentences that illustrate this pattern:

> Lawyers litigate.
> Judges adjudicate.
> Clients remunerate.

One tip in identifying sentence patterns: Always look for the verb — the main action — first, then look for the subject of that verb. Try that on this longer sentence:

> She filed for a hearing before the California Department of Human Services.
> $$S \quad \rightarrow \quad V$$

The basic pattern of **S → V** still exists: she → filed. All of the other words in the sentence simply modify the basic pattern. "Filed" is the main action, and "she" is doing the action.

Note that in the **S → V** sentence, the verb does not perform its action on anything; in grammatical terms, the verb has no *object.* In the above sentence, there is no noun immediately following the verb — *she* did not file *papers,* or *a motion. She* filed *for something,* but that does not constitute the object of the sentence, as we will explain below. In an **S → V** sentence, the subject and the verb constitute the entire main idea of the sentence; everything else in the sentence merely describes or modifies the subject and verb.

Note: You may recall having been taught that active sentences in which the verb *cannot* normally take an object — verbs such as sleep, saunter, complain — are known as *intransitive sentences* and that those types of verbs are known as *intransitive verbs.*

b. *Subject → Verb → Object (S → V → O)*

This sentence pattern, S → V → O for short, differs from the S → V pattern in that it contains another piece, the object.

The object of a sentence is the person or thing that receives the action of the verb—the person or thing that answers the question "What/who is the verb doing its action to?" Objects most commonly occur in **active sentences**—that is, sentences in which the person or thing doing the action is the **subject** of the sentence. Also, for a sentence to have an object, the verb must be the type of verb that normally can take an object. Thus, a sentence such as "She slept" cannot take an object because one cannot sleep *something*. On the other hand, sentences like the following have verbs that can normally take objects:

S → V → O
Criminals commit crimes.
S → V → O
The state prosecutes criminals.

Here, again, the direction of the arrow is a graphic representation of the direction of the action (verb) toward the object. As in the S → V sentence, even if modifying words are added to the sentence, the basic pattern remains the same. And as in the S → V sentence, you should look for the verb first, then the subject, then the object.

S   V   O
Particularly unsavory criminals commit particularly heinous crimes.

Note: You may recall having been taught that sentences containing verbs that take an object are called *transitive sentences* and that verbs that can take objects are called *transitive verbs*. S → V → O sentences are probably even more common than S → V sentences.

Now that we have described active sentences with and without objects, we would like to provide a few additional pointers to help you identify the more complicated S → V sentences. Sometimes an S → V sentence looks as though it might be an S → V → O sentence because there is a person or thing (noun) soon after the verb. Look carefully. In general, if the noun after the verb has a preposition in front of it (for example, "in," "on," "for," "about," "to," "with," "by"), that noun is **not** the object of the verb, and the sentence is **not** an S → V → O sentence. It is an S → V sentence.

In the above sentence, "She filed for a hearing . . . " the words "for a hearing" are not the object of the verb because there is a preposition ("for") before them. In terms of the meaning of the sentence, the hearing is not the thing she filed; she filed papers, or a motion. There is no **direct** relationship between the verb and the following noun; the verb, in fact, has no object. On the other hand, a sentence that begins

She filed papers . . .

is an S → V → O sentence because "papers" is a noun with no preposition between it and the verb. The noun directly follows the verb and answers the question "What is the verb doing its action to?" — and is thus the object of the verb.

EXERCISES

1. For each of these sentences, circle the subject. Indicate whether the pattern is S → V or S → V → O. (The complete verbs appear in capital letters.)

   a. The homemaker services program of Senior Citizens, Inc., RECEIVED only a 30 percent reduction in funding.
   b. From these decisions certain characteristics of property interests protected by due process EMERGE.
   c. Again the Louisiana system HAS SOUGHT to minimize the risk of error.
   d. To provide adequate notice, the notice of termination of services MUST INCLUDE the reasons for the intended agency action.
   e. Within ten days of receiving the notice, Mrs. Clark COMPLIED by having Ms. Burns contact the local agencies.
   f. In response to the review, Puett INITIATED several reforms within the social services system, including the termination of several services provided by county offices and local agencies.
   g. In *Mathews*, the state agency RECEIVED medical reports from the recipient, from his physician, and from a psychiatric consultant.
   h. The Georgia suspension procedures FAIL to reflect a balance of Reverend Farewell's interests with interests of the state and the private party.

2. In these sentences, circle the subject and underline the complete verb once. Indicate whether the sentence is S → V or S → V → O.

   Example: This liberal (treatment) of trade fixtures <u>has</u> not <u>been</u> <u>confined</u> to Maryland. S → V

   a. The Georgia Department of Public Safety further erred in acting as a trial court, a violation of the Supreme Court's ruling in *Mitchell*.
   b. Because of the nature of the fixtures, damage to the realty and to the plumbing and heating equipment might result if they are removed.
   c. A state has only allowed outright seizure of property under special circumstances.

   d. In order to convert the first floor to a men's clothing shop and the second floor to an apartment, Brooks made several alterations to the premises.

   e. In all probability, our client will not prevail on the issue of renewal of the lease.

   f. They sent the manual (Procedure for Complaints, Appeals and Fair Hearings, Volume 4) to all regional, county, and area offices of the Tennessee Department of Human Services.

2. The Linking Verb

a. *Subject = Linking Verb = Complement (S = LV = C)*

This pattern is a variation on the first pattern ($S \rightarrow V$), but it contains a different type of verb, one often referred to as a "linking verb" or a "copula verb."

A linking verb expresses a state of being, or an appearance of reality. It does not express an action. Examples of linking verbs are all forms of the verb "BE" — is, am, are, was, were, would be, etc. — and verbs such as "seem" and "appear." For example,

> Example 1. The cases are distinguishable.

Because linking verbs do not express an action, they cannot have an object, that is, a receiver of the action. They can, and almost always do, however, have a *complement.*

> A complement describes the subject. A complement can thus be either a noun or an adjective.

It may help to think of the linking verb as an equal sign, and the **S = LV = C** sentence as an equation. The subject of the sentence is on the left side of the equal sign, and the complement is on the right side. (We have used an equal sign to represent the links between the parts of this sentence pattern.)

This sentence pattern may include other words that give more information about the subject or the complement. Words other than the subject, linking verb, and complement are *modifiers.* (Modifiers can occur in other sentence patterns, as well.) In the next two examples, you can see how the **S = LV = C** pattern looks with various types of modifiers.

> Example 2. The appellant in this case is Sammie Lynn Puett, a commissioner of the Tennessee Department of Human Services.

      S   LV   C
The appellant is *Sammie Lynn Puett.*

Example 3. The court was correct in granting plaintiff Clark's motion for a preliminary injunction.

        S   LV   C
The court was *correct.*

From these examples, you can see that the following characterize an S = LV = C pattern.

1. The subject (S) tells *who* or *what* the sentence is about.
2. The complement (C) describes the subject by answering the questions *who?* or *what?*

The cases are *what?*	distinguishable
The appellant is *who?*	Sammie Lynn Puett
The court was *what?*	correct

3. The verb only connects or links the subject to the complement. It does not tell about any action.

The modifiers — the words or word groups that are *not* part of the basic pattern — usually answer other questions such as:

where?	which one?
why?	in what way?
how?	to what extent?

If the first example reads

> The cases are thus distinguishable

it would have a modifier (*thus*) between the verb and the complement. This sentence could be represented as

S = LV-mod = C

In the third example ("The court was correct in granting . . . ") the modifier, which happens to be a word group, appears at the end of the sentence. So, "in granting plaintiff Clark's motion for a preliminary injunction" gives details about the complement, "correct," by telling what the subject did that was correct. Example 3 could be represented like this:

$$S = LV = C\text{-mod}$$

Finally, in Example 2 ("The appellant in this case is Sammie Lynn Puett . . . ") both the subject and the complement have modifiers— "in this case" and "a commissioner of the Tennessee Department of Human Services." This sentence could thus be represented as follows:

$$S\text{-mod} = LV = C\text{-mod}$$

Modifiers can also appear in other positions, but no matter where they appear, they do not change the basic sentence pattern.

EXERCISE

In each of these sentences, circle the subject ⬭, underline the verb once _____, and underline the complement twice _____.

Example:

(The private interest) to be protected in this case <u>is</u> the <u>lifestyle</u> of the appellee, Jessie Clark.

or

The private (interest) to be protected in this case <u>is</u> the <u>lifestyle</u> of the appellee, Jessie Clark.

   a. The effect of this statute is the same on Reverend Farewell.
   b. Farewell's interest in his driver's license is more vital than the average person's interest.
   c. The procedural safeguards were sufficient to protect the recipient's interests.
   d. In *Mathews*, the third factor considered by the court was the governmental interest involved, including any fiscal and administrative burdens resulting from additional requirements.
   e. Therefore, the notice requirements in *Benton* are not applicable in the case of Ms. Clark.
   f. Because of the language of the lease, our client would probably be unsuccessful in getting a second renewal.
   g. With only a 30 percent reduction in funding, the agency was still able to offer these services to some recipients.
   h. According to the *Procedures* manual, staff members in county and local offices are responsible for providing assistance to recipients wishing to make an appeal.

b. *There = Linking Verb = Subject (Th = LV = S)*

There is another type of sentence pattern that uses the linking verb: It begins with the word *there*, followed by a linking verb and a subject. In this type of sentence, the word *there* has no meaning. It does not indicate a particular place or area as it does, for example, when it is used to distinguish *there* from *here*. It simply fills the place the subject usually occupies in the sentence so that you can put the subject after the linking verb. Normally, the subject comes before the verb, but you might want to put the subject after the verb if you want to add modifiers to it. (You may have noticed that the first sentence in this paragraph follows this pattern.) We will represent this pattern this way:

$$Th = LV = S$$

The following examples show how the word *there* serves as a filler in what is normally the subject's position in the sentence.

There must, however, be an opportunity for a fair hearing before suspension of a driver's license.

<u>There</u> must be <u>an opportunity</u>.
　Th　　LV　　　　S

In fact, there seems to be no way for Farewell to ever get his property back.

<u>There</u> seems to be <u>no way</u>.
　Th　　　　LV　　　S

In this case, however, there is no compelling state or public interest.

<u>There</u> is <u>no compelling state or public interest</u>.
　Th LV　　　　　　　S

There was not any attempt by the Department to determine the severity of the injuries or the amount of the damages allegedly caused by Reverend Farewell.

<u>There</u> was not <u>any attempt</u>.
　Th　　LV　　　S

Only a few verbs are linking verbs, but they can be combined in many ways. Table A-1 shows how basic linking verbs can be combined to form multiple-word linking verbs. The past tense (and subjective) forms appear in parentheses.

In addition to the basic linking verbs in Table A-1, a few other verbs can serve as linking verbs. These verbs sometimes serve as linking verbs and sometimes as action verbs, as shown in Table A-2.

TABLE A-1

Basic Linking Verbs	*Examples of Combined Forms*
to be	should have been
am (was)	was to have been
is (was)	could have become
are (were)	will become
to become (became)	ought to have become
to seem (seemed)	seemed to be
to have to be (been)	seems to have been
has to have been (had to have been)	may have seemed
have to have been (had to have been)	had to be
other verb + be	will have to be
can be (could be)	
will be (would be)	
shall be (should be)	
may be (might be)	
must be	
ought to be	
is going to be	

TABLE A-2

Verb	*as Linking Verb*	*as Action Verb*
appear (appeared)	when it means *is, was, or seem(ed) to be*: She appeared anxious.	when it means *was present*: She appeared as a witness. when it means *enter(ed)* or *walk(ed)* into: She appeared on the stage.
look (looked)	when it means *is, was*, or *seem(ed) to be*: The chances of winning looked bleak.	when it means *positioning the eyes* to *see*: He looked at the jury. when it means *examine(d)*: He carefully looked through the records.
feel (felt)	when it means *is, was*, or *seem(ed)*: He feels optimistic about the outcome.	when it means *touch(ed)*: She felt the child's forehead. when it means *sense(d)* or *recognize(d)*: I feel the breeze.
sound (sounded)	when it means *is, was*, or *seem(ed)*: Her argument sounded logical.	when it means *made a noise*: The alarm sounded when the window broke.

TABLE A-2 (*cont.*)

Verb	as Linking Verb	as Action Verb
		when it means *attempt to discover another's opinion* or position (always occurs with the word out): She had *sounded out* the plaintiff's attorney before drawing up the settlement.
smell (smelled)	when it means *is, was,* or *seem(ed)*: The room smells musty.	when it means *recognize an odor*: He smelled the smoke.
taste (tasted)	when it means *is, was,* or *seem(ed) to be*: The bread tasted fresh.	when it means *recognize a* flavor. She tasted the curry in the rice. when it means *test by placing in the mouth*: I'll taste the sauce.

EXERCISES

1. In each of the following **Th = LV = S** sentences, underline the complete linking verb once _____ and circle the subject ⬭.

   Example:

   Furthermore, there is ⬭conflicting evidence⬭ regarding the status of homemaker services as mandatory or optional.

   or

   Furthermore, there is conflicting ⬭evidence⬭ regarding the status of homemaker services as mandatory or optional.

   a. In summation, there would be very little chance of convincing a judge to allow our client to renew the lease a second time.
   b. This way there will be no direct conflict with public policy.
   c. There seems to be no need to discuss the element of consideration.
   d. Clearly, then, there are many policy arguments both for and against enforcement of the contract.
   e. In jurisdictions adopting an invasion of privacy tort, there has been a clouding of the distinctions of existing tort laws.

2. Review of the first two patterns. Some of these sentences fit the **S = LV = C** pattern and some the **Th = LV = S** pattern. Underline the verb and complement or verb and subject. Indicate which pattern the sentence fits.

Example:

> In this case, however, <u>there is</u> no compelling state or public <u>interest</u> indicated by the facts. **Th = LV = S**

or

> In this case, however, <u>there is no compelling state or public interest</u> indicated by the facts. **Th = LV = S**

    a. With *in personam* jurisdiction readily available, there is no need for the state to suspend Reverend Farewell's driver's license.

    b. In this case, the timeliness of the hearing was merely coincidental.

    c. Under Georgia law, this unverified report is sufficient to trigger the process for suspending Reverend Farewell's driver's license.

    d. There is no evidence within the report to substantiate this claim.

    e. Suspension of an individual's driver's license is a provisional remedy depriving the person of important property.

    f. Any evidence of an oral statement contradicting the terms of the lease would probably not be admissible as evidence.

    g. There is little or no indication of the intent of the parties to create a perpetual right to renewal in the lease.

    h. In that case, as here, there was no stipulation regarding the amount of rent to be paid for renewal.

    i. For these reasons, the *Andrews* decision is applicable in this case.

3. The Passive Voice

a. *Subject ← Verb (S ← V)*

This pattern, Subject ← Verb, is a variation of the first two patterns, Subject → Verb and Subject → Verb → Object. The difference, symbolized by the direction of the arrow, is that in the first two patterns the subject is the actor, the *"doer" of the action*, whereas in this pattern, the subject is the *person or thing being acted upon*. In fact, in the S ← V sentence, the subject of the sentence is the same person or thing that would have been the object in the S → V → O sentence. If you think about what the sentence is saying, you can see what is going on.

S → V	S → V → O
Lawyers litigate.	Lawyers litigate cases.

but,

S ← V

Cases are litigated.

In such sentences, the actor, if present, must be tacked onto the end of the sentence with the introductory word "by."

$$S \leftarrow V$$

Cases are litigated by lawyers.

In such sentences, the actor — the "doer" of the action — **is not the subject of the sentence.**

This type of sentence (S ← V) is called a *passive sentence*. This is precisely because the subject is **not** doing the action but rather is being acted upon; the subject is the passive recipient of the action. The verb is said to be in the "passive voice."

Try identifying the subjects and verbs in the following sentences (the actor may or may not be present):

Ms. Clark is represented by Ms. Burns, acting as court-appointed counsel for Appellee.

In November 1979, a statewide review of the Tennessee Social Service program was conducted.

The notice requirements of *Goldberg* were further defined in *Vargas v. Trainor*, 508 F.2d 485 (1974).

You may have noticed that in a passive sentence the verb must consist of **at least two words.** One word is the root verb with the *past-participle* ending (usually "-ed" or "-en"); for example, "represented," "eaten." The other word is some form of the verb *to be*, which is there to direct the action back to the subject; for example, "*is* represented," "*was* conducted," "*is being* eaten."

TABLE A-3

Forms of the Verb *to Be*

am	was	be	(*be, being,* and *been* occur only when
is	were	being	the entire verb includes 3 words or
are		been	more, e.g., are *being* eaten, ought to
			be eaten, will have *been* eaten)

TABLE A-4

	Present	Past	Past Participle
REGULAR VERBS			
add-d	determine	determined	determined
	recognize	recognized	recognized
add-ed	act	acted	acted
	interpret	interpreted	interpreted

IRREGULAR VERBS (verbs that do not take -d or -ed in their *past* forms)

	Present	Past	Past Participle
past and past participle the same	hold	held	held
	find	found	found
	has *or* have	had	had
all 3 forms the same	put	put	put
	hit	hit	hit
all 3 forms different	begin	began	begun
	do	did	done
	drink	drank	drunk
	drive	drove	driven
	speak	spoke	spoken
	show	showed	shown

EXERCISES

1. For each of these sentences, circle the subject. Indicate whether the pattern is S → V (subject as actor, active voice) or S ← V (subject as receiver, passive voice). The complete verbs appear in capital letters.

   a. Under the standards of *Vargas*, these reasons MUST BE PLACED on the notice in order to satisfy the due process requirements.
   b. The homemaker services of appellee Jesse Clark ARE PROVIDED by the State under Title XX of the Social Security Act.
   c. The Georgia suspension procedures FAIL TO REFLECT a balance of Reverend Farewell's interests with the interests of the state and the private party.
   d. Again the Louisiana system HAS SOUGHT to minimize the risk of error.
   e. To meet the standards of *Vargas*, the recipients of benefits MUST BE fully and adequately NOTIFIED of the reasons for the termination or reduction of their benefits.
   f. Within ten days of receiving the notice, Mrs. Clark COMPLIED by having Ms. Burns contact the local agencies.

2. In these sentences, circle the subject and underline the complete verb once. Indicate whether the sentence is S → V or S ← V.

   a. The fundamental rights of due process were set forth by the Supreme Court in *Fuentes v. Shevin*, 407 U.S. 67 (1972).
   b. The appellant has been seriously harmed by the suspension of his license.
   c. The Georgia Department of Public Safety further erred in acting as a trial court, a violation of the Supreme Court's ruling in *Mitchell*.
   d. Outright seizure of property by a state has only been allowed under special circumstances.
   e. Because of the nature of the fixtures, damage to the realty and to the plumbing and heating equipment might result if they are removed.
   f. In *Warrington*, great weight is placed on the intention of the party to permanently affix the articles to the property.
   g. In order to convert the first floor to a men's clothing shop and the second floor to an apartment, several alterations were made to the premises by Brooks.
   h. In all probability, our client will not prevail on the issue of renewal of the lease.
   i. This liberal treatment of trade fixtures has not been confined to Maryland.

b. *Subject ← Passive Verb → Object (S ← V → O)*

Although the verb may be in the passive voice, if it is a transitive verb (that is, a verb that normally can have an object), it can still take an object. The object still answers the question *what?*

In this case, the recipients were paid *monthly benefits* under the Federal Aid to Families with Dependent Children program.

         S   V   O
The recipients were paid monthly benefits

Recipients were paid *what?* Monthly benefits.

Here are other examples of passive voice sentences that have an object.

Recipients of optional benefits are not given a constitutional right to the perpetual continuation of their benefits.

         S   V   O
Recipients are not given a constitutional right

In the instant case, Reverend Farewell was not granted a fair hearing by the Georgia Department of Public Safety.

S   V   O

Reverend Farewell was not granted a fair hearing

As a quick review, identify the sentence pattern in the following two sentences. In which sentence is the subject the doer and in which sentence is the subject the receiver?

In the January 15 letter, Honeywell demonstrates its acceptance of the offer.

The court will be shown the primary evidence of an accord and satisfaction.

S   →   V   →   O

Honeywell demonstrates its acceptance

S   ←   V   →   O

The court will be shown the primary evidence

EXERCISES

All of these sentences have action verbs and objects. For each, circle the subject, underline the complete verb once, and underline the object twice. Indicate the pattern as S → V → O or S ← V → O. Only use the S ← V → O representation when the form of the verb (*to be* plus the past participle) directs the action toward the subject (passive structure).

a. With an action for breach of contract, our client might be awarded damages under the doctrine of reliance.
b. When applying for insurance from All-Risk, the appellant did not authorize an investigation into his past medical history.
c. The leading Supreme Court case on point, *Winslow v. Baltimore*, follows the same reasoning as *Lewis*.
d. Brandon was denied insurance from All-Risk because of his hospitalization over 18 years ago.
e. The Court should not usurp the legislature's power by creating a tort action for invasion of privacy.
f. The removal of these articles would, no doubt, seriously damage the realty.
g. The Michigan Supreme Court, in the more recent *Beaumont* proceeding, modified its earlier publicity requirements.
h. In *Warrington*, the Delaware court followed this doctrine of maintaining the original condition of the lessor's property.
i. Unlike the recipient in *Mathews*, Mrs. Clark was not given a meaningful chance to respond to the termination of her benefits.

4. More Complex Constructions

a. *Active Sentences with Direct and Indirect Objects*

Basic sentences can get even more complicated than the patterns shown above. A simple active sentence can have more than one object. So far, we've dealt with sentences that have only one object that answers either *what?* or *whom?* However, some sentences have two objects — a Direct Object (**D.O.**) that answers the question *what?* or *whom?* and an Indirect Object (**I.O.**) that answers the question *to or for whom?* Remember, to have both objects, a sentence must be active, not passive.

PASSIVE   Recipients of optional benefits *are not given* a constitutional right to the perpetual continuance of their benefits.

Recipients are not given [*what?*] a constitutional right
    S   V   O

The U.S. Constitution *does not give* recipients of optional benefits a right to the perpetual continuance of their benefits.

The U.S. Constitution does not give [*to whom?*] recipients
          S   V   I.O.

[*what?*] a right
       D.O.

PASSIVE   In the instant case, Reverend Farewell *was not granted* a fair hearing by the Georgia Department of Public Safety.

Reverend Farewell was not granted [*what?*] a fair hearing
      S   V   O

ACTIVE   In the instant case, the Georgia Department of Public Safety *did not grant* Reverend Farewell a fair hearing.

The Department did not grant [*to whom?*] Reverend Farewell
      S   V   I.O.

[*what?*] a fair hearing
       D.O.

From these examples you can see how an active sentence, which by definition has the actor in the subject position (that is, *before* the main verb), can end up having two objects, one answering *what?* and the other answering *to whom?* or *for whom?* When the two objects appear without any prepositions (to, for), the first is usually the indirect object — answering *to or for whom?* When the indirect object follows a preposition, it usually appears after the direct object.

The Department did not grant <u>Reverend Farewell</u> a <u>fair hearing</u>.
       I.O.   D.O.

The state paid <u>recipients</u> <u>monthly benefits</u>.
     I.O.   D.O.

The Department did not grant a <u>fair hearing</u> to <u>Reverend Farewell.</u>
         D.O.   I.O.

The state paid <u>monthly benefits</u> to <u>recipients.</u>
     D.O.   I.O.

b. *Active Sentences with Object and Complement*

In some cases, when you rewrite a passive sentence as an active sentence you do not end up with a direct object and an indirect object. Instead, you get a direct object (answering *what?* or *whom?*) and a complement. You may recall, from earlier in this section, that a complement is a noun or adjective that describes the subject in a sentence with a linking verb (such as the verbs *to be, to become, to seem, to appear*). In the sentences presented here, the complement answers the question *to be what?*

PASSIVE In *Snaidach*, default on a loan was not considered an extraordinary situation requiring special protection.

     Default was not considered an extraordinary situation
      S   V   C

     Default was not considered *to be what?* an extraordinary situation

ACTIVE In *Snaidach*, the court did not consider default on a loan an extraordinary situation requiring special protection.

     The court did not consider default an extraordinary situation
      S   V   O   C

     The court did not consider *what?* default
     The court did not consider default *to be what?* an extraordinary situation

PASSIVE   In *Sullivan*, the physician was held liable for breach of contract.

The physician was held liable
    S   V   C

The physician was held *to be what?*   liable

ACTIVE   In *Sullivan*, the court held the physician liable for breach of contract.

The court held the physician liable
    S   V   O   C

The court held *whom?*   the physician
The court held the physician *to be what?*   liable

In the passive form, the *Sullivan* and *Snaidach* examples appear to be like the earlier examples of $S \leftarrow V \rightarrow O$. However, when they are translated into the active voice and the actor is in the subject position, you can see that they were really $S \leftarrow V \leftarrow C$ sentences. What may have appeared to be an object is actually a *description* of the receiver of the action.

EXERCISES

Each of these sentences has an action verb. Some have objects and some do not. For each, circle the subject and underline the verb once. Then, if the sentence includes objects, underline the objects twice. You do not need to distinguish between direct and indirect objects. If an object has a complement, underline the complement with a dotted line.

Examples:

In *Goldberg*, the (state) paid recipients monthly benefits under the Federal Aid to Families with Dependent Children Program.

In *Sullivan*, the (court) held the physician liable for breach of contract.

a. In the hearing, Farewell could not introduce evidence on the issue of his liability for the accident.
b. Given the language of the lease, the court will probably not grant Brooks another renewal.
c. As a result, a Maryland court would probably consider the relationship between Pat and Tracy adulterous.
d. On appeal, the *Miller* court, in light of the uncertain construction of the lease, did not grant the lessee a right to perpetual renewals.

e. In *Hartberg*, a provision in the lease gave the landlord the right to all temporary and permanent improvements by the lessee.

f. The need for a tort protecting privacy interests was first espoused in 1890, in an article by Samuel Warren and Louis Brandeis.

g. In *Della Corp. v. Diamond*, the Delaware Supreme Court denied a tenant restaurant operator the right to remove a custom-cut carpet.

h. The Restatement (Second) of Torts, §652B, does not make this physical aspect of intrusion a requirement.

i. A similar line of reasoning has been used in numerous cases, including *Tureen v. Equifax, Inc.*

j. The Fair Credit Reporting Act directly addresses the central problem of the case presently before this court.

5. Summary

1. English sentences appear in a number of basic patterns:

- Subject → Verb (**S → V**)
- Subject → Verb → Object (**S → V → O**)
- Subject = Linking Verb = Complement (**S = LV = C**)
- There = Linking Verb = Subject (**Th = LV = S**)
- Subject ← Passive Verb (**S ← V**)
- Subject ← Passive Verb → Object (**S ← V → O**)

2. Modifiers provide additional information and answer questions like:

when?	what kind?
where?	in what way?
why?	to what extent?
how?	under what conditions?

REVIEW EXERCISES

Here are two passages from student papers. For each sentence, circle the subject and underline the verb once. If a sentence contains other necessary parts (the word *there* in **Th = V = S** or any object or complement), underline those parts twice. Indicate whether the pattern is **S = LV = C** or **Th = V = S** or **S-V** or **S-V-O**.

a. First Passage

(1) The Georgia procedures for suspension of an individual's driver's license do not reflect a proper balance of the interests of the licensee, the state, and the

private party initiating the suspension. (2) Further, the Georgia procedures fail to mandate a fair hearing on the issue of suspension in a timely and meaningful manner. (3) The Georgia procedures for driver's license suspension are unconstitutional. (4) The Georgia procedures violate the Fourteenth Amendment's safeguards against deprivation of property by the state without due process of law. (5) The decision of the Georgia Department of Public Safety to suspend Reverend Farewell's license pursuant to state procedures should be reversed.

b. Second Passage

(1) In *Pearson*, the plaintiff's own employees had removed confidential files from the plaintiff's office without authorization. (2) The employees, in turn, gave the defendants the confidential files. (3) The information from the files was used by the defendants to write several newspaper columns about the plaintiff. (4) The court found the conduct of the plaintiff's employees to be an improper intrusion. (5) However, the court did not hold the defendants liable for receiving the information. (6) Here the case is much the same. (7) Metro Data Services, Inc., in providing a necessary service to its client, has made certain inquiries in a reasonable manner — no bullying, no threats, no physical intrusion, no force. (8) The investigators simply received the information by listening. (9) There has been no improper intrusion on the part of Metro Data Services, Inc.

B Word Groups That Function as Units

If you have worked through section A, you should be able to recognize a number of common sentence patterns. However, many of the sentences you produce for legal documents will not be as simple as those you worked with in section A. In fact, the sentences that you are likely to have the most trouble with will probably be relatively complex. To be able to analyze more complex sentences well enough so that you can identify and solve structural problems, you will need to understand three concepts.

1. Groups of words can function as a unit. These units can take the place of the necessary elements of a sentence (for example, the subject, the verb, the object) or the optional parts of a sentence (for example, modifiers — adjectives, adverbs, and so on).
2. A word group that functions as a single unit may have its own subject and verb.
3. A sentence may contain two or more basic patterns. These basic patterns may be alike (for example, $S \rightarrow V \rightarrow O$ and $S \rightarrow V \rightarrow O$) or different (for example, $S \rightarrow V \rightarrow O$ and $S \leftarrow V$).

1. Compound Sentence Elements

The sentences we have looked at so far have contained only one of each of the basic pieces (or elements) that make up that particular sentence pattern — one subject, one verb, one object, and so on. Many of the sentences you write and encounter, however, will contain more than one of each basic piece. Two or more basic pieces joined together and used in place of one such element in a sentence pattern are often referred to as *compound* elements.

> S   V & V   S   V &   V
> Lawyers advise and litigate. Clients hesitate and then remunerate. (compound verbs)

> S   V   O & V   O
> The Washington legislature has followed other states and adopted the Uniform Code. (compound verb and object)

The important point is that the basic sentence pattern remains unchanged even with the addition of compound elements. In the above examples, the sentence patterns are still S → V and S → V → O, respectively; they simply contain compound elements.

Find the sentence elements and identify the patterns of the following sentences. (Remember to start by looking for the verb(s).)

Federal courts have exclusive jurisdiction over some actions and concurrent jurisdiction with state courts in other actions.

Most civil rights actions and some admiralty cases must always be tried in federal courts.

2. Groups of Words Can Function as Units

a. *Compound Structures Serving as Necessary Elements*

The subject, object, or complement of a sentence may consist of more than one word. Here are a few examples. The words that join the compound subject, object, or complement are in capital letters. Compound structures appear in italics.

Compound Subject

> *The heating system* AND *the plumbing fixtures*, being replacements, cannot be removed by our client. (S ← V)

> *The intention* of the parties AND *the ease* of removal of the fixtures are two important factors in determining a tenant's right to fixtures. (S = LV = C)

NEITHER *the carpet* NOR *the air conditioner* poses this problem of altering or injuring Finn's building. (S → V → O)

Compound Object

The tenant can probably remove BOTH *the carpet* AND *the frame*. (S → V → O)

Brooks installed *a window air conditioner* to cool the first floor AND *an electric heat pump* with a forced hot-air duct system to warm the whole building. (S → V → O)

Compound Complement

Reverend Farewell's hearing was NEITHER *fair* NOR *meaningful* in terms of the standards set forth by the court in *Fuentes*. (S = LV = C)

Given recent decisions, your chances of recovering damages in a Massachusetts court are *good* BUT NOT *definite*. (S = LV = C)

Verbs, too, can be compound. Because verbs may have objects or complements, compound verbs can appear in different ways.

Compound Verb

1. The two verbs forming the compound may share an object or complement:

   Our client *purchased* AND *installed* a window *air conditioner*. (S → V + V → O)

   Because of policy issues, many courts *have been* AND *are* still reluctant about upholding implied contracts in family-like relationships. (S = LV + LV = C)

2. Each verb may have its own object or complement:

   The Minnesota courts *should follow* the current *trend* of jurisprudence AND *recognize* an *action* for tortious invasion of privacy. (S → V → O + V → O)

   In *Lynch*, the contract between the parties *was considered independent* of their meretricious relationship AND *was held* to be *enforceable*. (S = LV = C + LV = C)

   A challenge to the lessor's termination of the lease *would be costly* AND *would* probably *yield* an unfavorable *result*. (S = LV = C + LV → O)

3. One of the verbs may have an object or complement and the other may not:

   In *Mathews*, the recipient *was adequately informed* of the reason for the agency's action and *was provided* procedural *safeguards*. (S ← V + V → O)

At the end of the investigation, the defendant's report on the plaintiff *was held to be "confidential"* and *was submitted* only to All-Risk, the defendant's client. (**S = LV = C + ← V**)

4. Both verbs may be action verbs that are not followed by an object or complement:

In *Hartberg*, the carpet *was attached* to wooden strips and *could be removed* with no damage to the floor. (**S ← V + ← V**)

From the examples, you can see

1. That compound structures can appear in any pattern (**S = LV = C, Th = V = S, S-V,** or **S-V-O**) and
2. That compound structures are formed when items are joined by a connector. The connectors *and, or, nor, but, for, so,* and *yet* are often called coordinating conjunctions.

EXERCISES

Some of the necessary elements in these sentences are compound structures. Analyze each sentence by following these steps:

1. Circle the subject. Underline the verb once.
2. If a sentence contains other necessary elements (the word *there* in **Th = V = S** or any object or complement), underline those elements twice.
3. Indicate whether the pattern is **S = LV = C** or **Th = V = S** or **S-V** or **S-V-O**.
4. Circle the symbol in the pattern for the compound element (e.g., if there is a compound subject in an **S-V-O** sentence, circle the **S**: (**S**)-V-O).

   a. To be binding, an offer to enter into a contract in the future must specify all of the material terms and leave nothing to be agreed upon in future negotiations.
   b. Her pregnancy and the subsequent delivery of her third child are clear indications of the operation's failure.
   c. The Minnesota legislature has considered the issue of privacy and has enacted legislation protecting specific classes of people.
   d. As part of the application process for insurance, an investigation of the applicant's background may occur and is often required.
   e. The ex-wife had some knowledge of the appellee's mental illness.
   f. Contrary to the defendant's contention, to be eligible the recipient of homemaker services must show both physical need and financial eligibility.

g. As a result of this invasion of his privacy, the appellant has suffered injury to his reputation and mental and emotional distress.

h. This information was compiled without the appellant's knowledge or consent and was sent to All-Risk on January 7, 1994.

b. *Entire Phrases as Subjects, Objects, or Complements*

The same sentence can be written in many different ways. Look at these versions of the sentence about Reverend Farewell's license (the verb and its object or complement are in italics):

1. The Georgia Department of Public Safety *suspended* Reverend Farewell's *driver's license.* S → V → O

   This *reduced his ability* to pay the damages. S → V → O

2. In effect, the suspension of Reverend Farewell's driver's license *reduced his ability* to pay the damages. S → V → O

3. The effect of the suspension of Reverend Farewell's driver's license *was a reduction* in his ability to pay the damages. S = LV = C

4. In effect, suspending Reverend Farewell's driver's license *reduced his ability* to pay the damages. S → V → O

5. In effect, the suspension of Reverend Farewell's driver's license *meant reducing his ability* to pay the damages. S → V → O

6. In effect, suspending Reverend Farewell's driver's license *meant reducing his ability* to pay the damages. S → V → O

The first three examples look like the sentences you have already worked with. Example 1 has two simple verbs: *suspended, reduced.* The verb of the first sentence in Example 1 has been made into a noun and has become the subject of the sentence in Example 2: *the suspension.* The subject in Example 3 is *the effect.* The idea of the verb in Example 1 (*reduced*) has become part of the modifier (*reduction*) in Example 3. The other word groups before the verb in Examples 2 and 3 (*of Reverend Farewell's driver's license*) are also modifiers. They answer questions like *which? what kind?*

In Example 4, however, the subject is the entire word group *suspending Reverend Farewell's driver's license.* The ideas that were in the modifiers have become part of the subject.

In Example 3, the verb from the second part of Example 2 (*reduced*) has become a noun (*reduction*). It is now the complement of the sentence, *a reduction.* The rest of the sentence after the word *reduction* modifies the complement. It answers the question *what kind of reduction?* In Examples 5 and 6, the entire word group *reducing his ability* is the object of the verb *meant.*

We can make entire word groups into subjects or objects or complements when the key word of the subject, object, or complement can have a verb form using *-ing* (suspending, reducing) or *to* (to suspend, to reduce).

Here you see that

verb	can become	*noun*	or	*-ing* form	or	*to* form (infinitive)
suspend		suspension		suspending		to suspend
reduce		reduction		reducing		to reduce

The important point is that *-ing* word groups and *to* word groups can function as single units within a sentence. The examples above show *-ing* word groups as subject and object.

The *to* form of a verb (like *suspend* or *reduce*) creates the same effect — it can make modifiers into necessary elements.

Original	The effect of the suspension of Reverend Farewell's driver's license *was a reduction in his ability to pay the damages.* (S = LV = C)
With *to* phrase as complement	The effect of the suspension of Reverend Farewell's driver's license *was to reduce his ability to pay the damages.* (S = LV = C)
With *to* phrase as subject and complement	In effect, *to suspend* Reverend Farewell's driver's license *was to reduce his ability to pay the damages.* (S = LV = C)

From these examples you can see

1. That *to* phrases (infinitives), as well as *-ing* phrases, can serve as necessary elements (as subjects, objects, or complements) answering the question *what?*
2. That when a *to* phrase appears as a necessary element, the entire word group functions as a single unit.

A reminder. To be a necessary element, an *-ing* or *to* phrase must answer the question *who?* or *what?* Not all *-ing* and *to* phrases are subjects, objects, or complements. In fact, most are just modifiers or parts of modifiers and answer modifier questions like these:

when?	which one?
where?	what kind?
why?	in what way?
how?	to what extent?

For instance, both the *-ing* phrase and the *to* phrase are modifiers in this sentence:

> The effect of *suspending Reverend Farewell's driver's license* is a reduction in his ability *to pay the damages.* (**S-mod = LV = C-mod**)

The *-ing* phrase is part of the modifier that begins with *of* and answers the question *which effect?* The *to* phrase is a modifier by itself that answers the question *what kind of ability?*

EXERCISES

Some of these sentences have subjects, objects, or complements that are *-ing* phrases or *to* phrases. Analyze each sentence by following these steps:

1. Circle the subject and underline the verb once.
2. If a sentence contains other necessary elements (the word *there* in **Th = V = S**, or any object or complement), underline those elements twice.
3. Indicate whether the pattern is **S = LV = C** or **Th = V = S** or **S-V** or **S-V-O**.
4. If a necessary element is an *-ing* or *to* phrase, circle the symbol for that element.

Examples:

> In effect, (suspending Reverend Farewell's driver's license) reduced his ability to pay the damages. (**S**)-V-O

> In effect, (to suspend Reverend Farewell's driver's license) was to reduce his ability to pay the damages. (**S**) = LV = (**C**)

a. Gathering certain types of information was recognized in *Tureen v. Equifax, Inc.,* 571 F.2d 411 (8th Cir. 1978), as a legitimate business need.

b. *Benton* involved an across-the-board cut in specific types of optional services, including dental services.

c. The purpose of the agency's action may have been to ensure a better quality of services for recipients.

d. Accepting the *Marvin* rule would seem to be going against state policy by encouraging cohabitation and common law marriages.

e. We will attempt to support our contention by supplying the court with evidence from conversations between you and Doctor Cooper.

f. Since the *Warrington* court's decision, determining a tenant's right to fixtures has centered on two important factors — the lessee's intention and the ease of removal.

  g. The notice did not actually require Mrs. Clark or her representative either to go to the local agency or to write a letter.

  h. To convince one medical doctor to testify against another doctor is difficult.

  i. According to the appellant, terminating homemaker services was a matter of state policy.

  j. In *Warrington*, the Delaware Court also promoted this doctrine of maintaining the original condition of the lessor's property.

3. Clauses

a. *Independent Clauses*

We will complete this series on the basic parts of sentences with a discussion of *clauses*. A clause is any group of words containing at least one subject and one verb. That group of words may, of course, contain any of the other parts of a sentence (elements) we have discussed, but to be a clause, it must have a subject and a verb. All of our previous examples, even those with compound elements, have contained one clause.

   S   V
  Lawyers litigate.

   S   V & V
  Lawyers advise and litigate.

       S   V   O & V   O
  The Washington legislature has followed other states and adopted the Uniform Code.

There are two kinds of clauses: independent (main) clauses and dependent (sometimes called subordinate) clauses. An independent clause can stand alone as a sentence; it expresses a complete thought. (An independent clause that is linked to another independent clause in a sentence is called a *coordinate* clause.) **All sentences must contain at least one independent (main) clause.**

  All three examples above are independent clauses; and all of the examples used so far in these lessons have contained one independent clause each.

  Look at this example:

         S   V   O   S   LV
  In *Marker*, one defendant had waived immunity, and two other defendants were
   C
  immune.

Here, there are two independent clauses joined by the word "and." The sentence patterns for the clauses are S → V → O and S = LV = C, respectively. We have identified the independent clauses and sentence patterns in the following sentences. Note that a word group *must* contain both a subject and a verb to be an independent clause.

      S → V → O   S ← V
The defendant mailed the check on January 8, but it was received too late.

         S   →   V   →   O   S
The Minnesota legislature has considered the issue of privacy and it

     V → O
has enacted legislation protecting specific classes of people.

To join together two independent clauses in such a way that each remains an independent clause, you can only use one of the following seven connectors (or connector pairs):

    and   so   but
        for   yet
   (either)/or   (neither)/nor

These connectors are also known as *coordinating conjunctions*.

b. *Dependent Clauses*

Like independent (main) clauses, dependent (subordinate) clauses also contain at least one subject and one verb. The difference is that dependent clauses do not express a complete thought and cannot stand alone as a sentence. Thus, they are always found attached to a main clause. Dependent clauses always begin with words like "because," "if," "since," "when," "although," "why," and "whether." In the following example, the dependent clause is *underlined*.

If the first two requirements are met, the court should not consider the third requirement.

The sentence patterns in the above sentence are S ← V and S → V → O, one pattern for each clause. Notice that the dependent clause, which begins with "if," does not express a complete thought but that the main clause does. The following pairs show the difference between independent and dependent clauses:

Independent Clause	*Dependent Clause*
The termination of a statutory entitlement would be a deprivation of an important right. (S = LV = C)	why the termination of a statutory entitlement would be a deprivation of an important right
There must be an opportunity for a fair hearing before the suspension of a driver's license. (Th = V = S)	whether there must be an opportunity for a fair hearing before the suspension of a driver's license
Our client would not prevail on the issue of renewal of the lease. (S → V)	that our client would not prevail on the issue of renewal of the lease
The courts in Massachusetts have awarded damages in cases similar to yours. (S → V → O)	how the courts in Massachusetts have awarded damages in cases similar to yours

From the examples you can see that in each pair, one word (*why, whether, that, how*) makes the difference between the independent clause in the left column and the dependent clause in the right column.

The word added in the right column transforms what was an independent clause into a dependent one. In each case, the added word functions as a *connector*. When a connector (which is sometimes a *conjunction* and sometimes a *relative pronoun*) transforms an independent clause into a dependent clause, the dependent clause must be connected to an independent clause.

In the following sentences, we have underlined both clauses and have identified the main clause with an **M** and the dependent clause with a **D**:

        M   D

<u>The court will only grant the motion when the appellee has filed three weeks or more before the trial date.</u>

        D   M

<u>Because the office may have erred, the court must notify both parties before it can assign custody.</u>

c. Relative Clauses

Relative clauses are a special kind of dependent clause. They are like other dependent clauses in every way but one — relative clauses do not have regular nouns or noun phrases as subjects. They are called "relative" clauses because instead of beginning with a normal subject, they begin with a relative pronoun — "that," "which," or "who(m)" — which shows the *relationship* of a noun in the main clause to the explanation or description in the relative clause. The relative pronoun, in a sense, serves as a proxy for the noun that would otherwise be the subject of the relative clause. The difference between relative clauses and other dependent clauses is illustrated in the following sentences. The dependent (or relative) clause is italicized and the word that the clause modifies is in bold lettering.

Example 1

Dependent Clause

In the present case, however, the record provides **evidence** *that a determination of eligibility was made on an individual basis* (dependent clause answering the question *what kind?*).

The verb within the dependent clause ("was made") has its own subject ("determination").

Relative Clause

The *Mathews* court considered the fiscal and administrative **burdens** *that would result from additional requirements to protect procedural safeguards* (relative clause answering the question *what kind?*).

The verb within the relative clause ("would result") is a proxy for the word that the clause is modifying ("burdens").

Example 2

Dependent Clause

In addition, the *Marvin* rule gives people incentives to avoid marriage, an **institution** *that the State wants to protect* (dependent clause answering the question *what kind?*).

Relative Clause

In Maryland, adultery is not a criminal offense, perhaps indicating a **public policy** *that would favor the enforcement of the contract between Pat and Mary* (relative clause answering the question *what kind?*).

Note that although other dependent clauses may answer the question "which one?" or "what kind?" a relative clause **only** answers the question "which one?" or "what kind?" Remember also that only three words can create relative clauses:

who (or whom)
which
that

Here are examples of each of these words as connectors for relative clauses.

WHO
Our client, *who lived in an arguably adulterous relationship*, may have some difficulty in enforcing the oral promise.

The State is required to continue providing Title XX benefits to any recipient *who files an appeal within ten days*.

WHICH
The State of Massachusetts recognizes an alternative form of compensation, *which is more appropriate in your case*.

The social service agencies, *which deal directly with recipients*, are in the best position to determine eligibility.

THAT
The only Maryland case *that speaks to this problem* is *Delashmut v. Thomas*, 45 Md. 140 (1876).

Marvin was a highly publicized case that set a precedent for other jurisdictions.

d. *Dependent Clauses as Part of an Independent Clause*

An interesting feature of dependent clauses is that they can serve as either a necessary or an optional part of an independent clause, taking the place of a subject, an object, or a complement. The following examples show how this can work:

Dependent Clauses as Subjects

Why the termination of a statutory entitlement would be a deprivation has been explained in Goldberg. (S ← V)

How the courts in Massachusetts have awarded damages in cases similar to yours has varied from court to court. (S → V)

Whether there must be an opportunity for a fair hearing before the suspension of a driver's license is another due process issue. (S = LV = C)

Dependent Clauses as Complements

Another issue to be resolved is why the termination of a statutory entitlement would be a deprivation of an important right. (S = LV = C)

The most likely outcome is that our client would not prevail on the issue of an additional renewal of the lease. (S = LV = C)

Dependent Clauses as Objects

Counsel must explain why the termination of a statutory entitlement would be a deprivation of an important right. (S → V → O)

You must understand how the courts in Massachusetts have awarded damages in cases similar to yours. (S → V → O)

From these examples, you can see that a dependent clause can function as a unit, as a necessary element in a sentence. Here are the connectors that most often create dependent clauses that function as subjects, objects, or complements in sentences:

what	whatever	why
when	whenever	how
where	wherever	whether

that (the most common connector)

EXERCISES

Some of the subjects, objects, and complements in these sentences are dependent clauses. Analyze each sentence by following these steps:

1. Circle the subject and underline the verb once.
2. If a sentence contains other necessary elements (the word *there* in **Th = V = S** or any object or complement), underline those elements twice.
3. Indicate whether the pattern is **S = LV = C** or **Th = V = S** or **S-V** or **S-V-O**.
4. If a necessary element is a dependent clause, circle the symbol for that element.

Examples:

Whether there must be an opportunity for a fair hearing before the suspension of a driver's license is a due process issue. S = LV = C

You must understand how the courts in Massachusetts have awarded damages in cases similar to yours. S-V-O

a. In the same way, only the aggressive recipients of the notice would learn that their services were terminated on the basis of need.
b. The question to ask is whether the method of gathering data would be objectionable to a reasonable person.
c. A jury should determine if the publicity requirement was met.

    d. The reason for the court's insistence on proof is that patients often transform doctors' statements of opinion into firm promises.

    e. On the basis of these reports, the state agency determined that the recipient was no longer disabled.

    f. The issue at hand is whether the terms of the lease are sufficient to justify a second five-year renewal.

    g. The court found that these procedural safeguards were sufficient to protect the recipient's interests.

    h. That you did give birth to a third child is clear proof of a breach of the doctor's promise.

    i. Appellee does not consider what information would be appropriate for the party requesting the investigation.

    j. What the appellants fail to consider is the impact on existing law of the adoption of this tort.

e. *Clauses Serving as Modifiers*

Dependent clauses can also serve as *modifiers* within independent clauses. Dependent clauses that modify can be formed in the same way as dependent clauses that serve as necessary elements. As these examples illustrate, one word makes the difference between the independent clause in the left column and the dependent clause in the right column.

Independent Clauses	*Dependent Clauses*
Our client moved into Funn's building in January 1980. (S-V)	when our client moved into Funn's building in January 1980
He had the right to have his case reconsidered. (S-V-O)	because he had the right to have his case reconsidered
There is an assessment of need involved in the termination of benefits. (Th = V = SO)	if there is an assessment of need involved in the termination of benefits
A determination of eligibility was made on an individual basis. (S ← V)	that a determination of eligibility was made on an individual basis

To understand how these dependent clauses serve as modifiers, which are optional elements, you must see them within complete sentences. Here are the four dependent clauses functioning as single units within complete sentences.

When our client moved into Funn's building in January 1980, he converted the first floor into a men's clothing store (dependent clause answering the question *when?*).

The recipient in *Mathews* was afforded adequate procedural protection *because he had the right to have his case reconsidered* (dependent clause answering the question *why?* or *in what way?*).

Because of the possibility of error, a more detailed notice is necessary *if there is an assessment of need in the termination of benefits* (dependent clause answering the question *under what circumstances?*).

In the present case, however, the record provides evidence *that a determination of eligibility was made on an individual basis* (dependent clause answering the question *what kind?*).

From these examples, you can see

1. That dependent clauses can serve as modifiers, and
2. That some of the connectors that create dependent clauses (for instance, *when* and *that*) can create either modifiers or necessary elements.

Here is a list of connectors that create dependent clauses that can function as modifiers:

although	even though	that	while
after	if	than	when
as (or as if)	in order that	though	where
because	so that	until	whereas
before	since	unless	

A sentence may have more than one dependent clause serving as a modifier. Here are two examples. The modifiers that are dependent clauses are in italics.

why?   *Since the recipients did not have a property interest in homemaker*
when?   *services,* they were not entitled to due process *before the services were terminated.*

when?   *When the lease ended,* the tenant removed the toilet *that he had*
which?   *installed for his own use* and replaced it with the original, broken toilet.

EXERCISES

Some of these sentences contain modifiers that are dependent clauses, and some do not. Analyze each sentence by following these steps:

1. Underline every necessary element once.
2. Indicate whether the pattern is $S = LV = C$ or $Th = V = S$ or $S-V$ or $S-V-O$.

3. If any modifier is a dependent clause, underline that modifier twice. (Some sentences contain no dependent clauses; some contain one, and some contain two.)

Example:

Because of the possibility of error, <u>a more detailed notice is necessary</u> <u><u>if there is a need assessment involved in the termination of benefits</u></u>. S = LV = C

NOTE: The first word group beginning with the word *because* is a modifier answering *why?* However, it is *not* a dependent clause because it does not have its own subject and verb.

a. Although Maryland courts have never decided this issue, there is substantial authority from other jurisdictions to support the contention that contracts between cohabiting parties are enforceable.
b. Since none of the recipients filed a timely appeal, the state is not required to continue their benefits.
c. The appellant has been employed as a police officer for the City of Wabash since 1980.
d. If the court follows the common law, then Smith would be guilty of adultery unless the adultery statute is declared unconstitutional.
e. Before a provider agency may participate in a Social Security program, it must establish a plan to provide recipients with an opportunity for a fair hearing whenever their benefits are terminated.
f. The notice requirements in *Benton* are not applicable in the case of Mrs. Clark because the termination of her homemaker services involved both an assessment of need and a complete denial of all homemaker services.
g. Without this requirement, recipients would not have any protection against errors in calculating the amount of their grants.
h. An intrusion is "physical" when it is an intrusion into a place where the plaintiff has secluded himself.
i. One of the lessor's contentions is that carpeting is realty if it has been custom cut to fit the building's contours.
j. In *Lewis* the court blocked an attempt to renew a lease a second time even though the lease provided for renewal of all the lease provisions.

Analyze each sentence in this passage by following these steps:

1. Underline every necessary element once (e.g., S, V, O, C). Remember that a necessary element may be a single word, a compound structure, or a word group (a *to* phrase or *-ing* phrase or a dependent clause).
2. Indicate whether the basic sentence pattern is S = LV = C or Th = V = S or S-V or S-V-O.

3. If any modifier is a dependent clause, underline that modifier twice.
4. If any modifier is a relative clause, circle it.

(a) There are several cases that deal with enforcing contracts between nonmarried partners. (b) In *Tyranski v. Piggins*, 44 Mich. App. 570, 205 N.W.2d 595 (1973), Mrs. Tyranski was a married woman who had lived with Piggins for approximately four years. (c) When Piggins died, she brought an action against the ancillary administrator of Piggins's estate. (d) She sought title to the house that they had lived in together. (e) The title was held in Piggins's name. (f) The court of appeals held that their illicit cohabitation did not render all agreements between them illegal.

4. Summary

1. Groups of words can function as units. These units can be either necessary or optional elements of the sentence.

- The subject, verb, object, or complement of a sentence can be a compound structure.
- Compound structures can appear in any sentence pattern.
- Compound structures are connected by coordinating conjunctions (and, but, for, so, yet, (either)/or, (neither)/nor).
- An entire phrase can function as a subject, object, or complement if the verb of the phrase is an *-ing* or *to* form.

2. Two or more sentences (independent clauses) can be joined into one by a coordinating conjunction.
3. A word group can have its own subject and verb (dependent clause) or just its own verb (relative clause).

- A dependent clause can be either a necessary element of the sentence or a modifier.
- Relative clauses serve as modifiers.

REVIEW EXERCISES

Analyze each sentence in the two passages below by following these steps:

1. Underline every necessary element (i.e., the basic parts of the sentence) once. Remember that a sentence may have more than one core pattern.
2. Indicate the basic pattern of each sentence (e.g., **S = LV = C** or **S-V-O** *but* **S-V**).

a. First Passage

(1) This is a case of first impression in Maryland, and as such, it is impossible to give a definite prediction of the outcome. (2) While cases dealing with similar issues seem to point toward the possibility that *this* contract will be enforced, the courts may be reluctant to adopt a general rule permitting recovery in all

cohabitation cases. (3) To the extent that the court relies on the generally applicable rules stated in earlier cases, there is a greater likelihood of recovery. (4) Several recent decisions in other jurisdictions have upheld contracts between cohabiting couples, but there have been two recent decisions denying recovery. (5) The public policy contained within this memorandum suggests a possible justification for the court to enforce contracts between cohabiting couples.

b. Second Passage

(1) In summary, the courts will not enforce a promise when the consideration given is merely cohabitation. (2) The courts are split on the sufficiency of home-making duties, some allowing *quantum meruit* recovery. (3) In our case, Tracy provided lawful consideration in return for a promise, i.e., financial support in the form of payment of rent, food, etc. (4) Since the promise was based on lawful consideration and did not arise expressly from Pat and Tracy's illicit relationship, the promise is enforceable despite the illicit relationship, and recovery should be allowed. (5) As long as the adequate consideration is independent of the illicit nature of the relationship, the courts have not barred the parties from making enforceable promises.

C Correcting Serious Errors

This section focuses on three errors in professional writing.

- Problems with subject-verb agreement
- Incomplete sentences
- Garbled sentences

The information in this section builds on the material that we presented in the previous sections. Specifically, it assumes that you already know:

- What a subject is
- What a verb is
- What a modifier is
- What an independent clause is
- What a dependent clause is

If you do not know these terms, you will need to work through sections A and B.

1. Subject-Verb Agreement

The verb in every sentence must match its subject in number. If the subject is singular, the verb must be singular; if the subject is plural, the verb must be plural.

You know the basic subject-verb agreement rule: Add an -s or -es to present tense verbs whenever

1. The subject of the verb is singular, and
2. That subject is any word other than the words *I* or *you* (I go, he *goes*).

Only the verbs *to be* and *to have* are exceptions. These two verbs have special forms in the present tense (*see* Table A-5). Compare them to the verb *to claim*, which follows the usual pattern: Add an -s (or- es) to the verb when the subject is a singular word other than *I* or *you*. The verb *to have* is different from the usual pattern in one way: Instead of adding an -s, you change the spelling to *has*. The verb *to be* is different from the usual pattern in two ways. First, the correct forms are not based on *be* (they are not *I be, you be, the plaintiff bes, we be,* and so on). Second, there are three present tense forms (am, is, are), not just two, as with other verbs (claim, claims, or have, has).

The verb *to be* is different from the usual pattern in the past tense as well as in the present tense. *To be* is the only English verb that changes between singular and plural in the past tense as well as in the present tense.

TABLE A-5

PRESENT TENSE

Type of Subject	Typical Verb	to have	to be
SINGULAR SUBJECTS:			
I	claim	have	am
you	claim	have	are
he, she, it (or any singular subject other than *I* or *you*)	claims	has	is
ANY PLURAL SUBJECT: (we, you, the plaintiffs)	claim	have	are

PAST TENSE

SINGULAR SUBJECTS:			
I	claimed	had	was
you	claimed	had	were
he, she, it (or any singular subject other than I or you)	claimed	had	was
ANY PLURAL SUBJECTS: (we, you, the plaintiffs)	claimed	had	were

Most errors in subject-verb agreement in legal writing occur in these situations:

a. The subject and its verb are separated. The writer pairs the verb with the wrong noun.
b. The number of the subject is unclear. The writer treats it as a plural when it is actually a singular or as a singular when it is actually a plural.

a. *Problems Created When the Subject and Verb Are Separated*

Normally, subjects and verbs appear next to one another in both complex sentences and simple sentences. The following sentence, for instance, contains four subject-verb pairs—one in the main clause and three in independent clauses. Yet in each pair the subject and verb appear next to one another.

> This *language suggests* first that *it is* well recognized that *abuses do occur* within the consumer reporting industry and second that the appellant's *claim is not based* upon an isolated incident.

However, the word just before a verb may not always be its subject. Instead, the nearest word may be part of a modifier that separates the subject and verb. Here are two examples.

> The *language* of various state statutes *suggests* first . . .
> The *provisions* of the Fair Credit Reporting Act *suggest* . . .

In sentences like these, you must ignore the words in the modifier and make your verb agree with the subject of the sentence, not with the nearest word.

The agreement errors that arise when subjects and verbs are separated are easy to make and difficult to detect. Cognitive psychologists have demonstrated that our short-term memory span is limited to seven items, plus or minus two. So people can hold only five to nine items in short-term memory at one time. Then they either recode the items ("chunk" them into fewer items) or forget them. If many words separate the subject and verb, you are likely to "lose" the subject before you get to the verb. The real subject may be dropped from short-term memory or it may be transformed in the recoding process.

Try to keep verbs near their subjects, and check each verb to be sure it agrees with its subject.

EXERCISES

Some of these sentences contain incorrect verb forms and some do not. If there is an incorrect verb form, correct the form of that verb. Then circle the subject you have made the verb agree with. If every verb in a sentence is correct, place a C (for *correct*) in front of the sentence.

a. The trend of recent decisions in other jurisdictions has been to enforce agreements when the agreements are not based solely on sexual services.
b. If the relationship between two contracting parties include illegal behavior, courts are inclined to declare the promises between the parties unenforceable.
c. In *Winslow*, a new lease containing the same terms and covenants were executed every five years from 1872 through 1892.
d. Most of the cases involving this tort action have required the physical invasion to be somewhat analogous to what is required for trespass.
e. Our second claim is that the contract interest of persons are not subordinate to an unenforced policy consideration.
f. The rules governing fixtures in a vendor-vendee relationship is stricter than those governing landlord-tenant relationships.
g. When the terms of renewal in a lease is ambiguous, the lease will be construed as granting the lessee the right to one renewal.
h. Fixtures annexed to realty are generally held to have become part of the realty and as such are inseverable from it.

b. *Problems Created When the Number of the Subject Is Unclear*

Most of the time it is easy to tell whether a subject is singular or plural. There are two ways to judge. You can judge by the meaning (*she* is singular because it means "one female"; the word *several* is plural because it means "more than one"). Another way to judge is by the form. Most plural words end in -s or -es (clients, laws, cases, statutes). In some situations, however, neither the meaning nor the form clearly indicates the number of the subject. This happens

1. When the plural form of the subject does not end in -s or -es;
2. When the subject is a collective noun or an indefinite pronoun (we will define these terms in the next few pages); or
3. When the subject is a compound structure.

1. The plural form of the subject does not end in -s or -es. There are some exceptions to the rule that plural subjects end in -s or -es. Some nouns form their plurals by a change in spelling. Most of these exceptions do not create problems because they are common words (men, children). You know the meaning is plural and you immediately recognize the alternate spelling as the plural form. A few are less common in everyday speech, but common in professional writing.

Singular	Plural
criterion	criteria
datum	data
phenomenon	phenomena
alumnus	alumni
alumna	alumnae
formula	formulae or formulas
curriculum	curricula or curriculums

Many of the words that once had unusual plural forms, e.g., formul*ae* as the plural for formula, are becoming "regularized" so that formul*as* is now an acceptable plural. The best advice we can give you is to check a recent dictionary whenever you have doubts about the plural form of a word.

2. The subject is a collective noun or indefinite pronoun. *Collective nouns* are labels that transform a group of individuals into a single unit (jury, legislature, team, staff, committee). In American English we focus on the idea of the single unit and treat these words as singular subjects even though the meaning is, in some sense, plural. Here are several short sentences with collective nouns as subjects. Note that the verb in each case is singular.

> The *jury has* reached a verdict.
> In the past two years, the *legislature has* convened for six special sessions.
> When the judge called the recess, the defense *team was* relieved.
> The editorial *staff is* being sued.
> The *committee believes* that the projections are not realistic.

Indefinite pronouns are a small group of frequently used pronouns. Most of the pronouns in this group are singular; only two are plural.

Indefinite Pronouns that Are Singular

one	anyone	anybody	anything
each	someone	somebody	something
either	everyone	everybody	everything
neither	no one	nobody	nothing

Indefinite Pronouns that Are Plural

few   several

These indefinite pronouns do not cause problems when they appear next to their verbs. Despite a sense of their plural meanings, you would not write "everybody are" or "everything are." Problems arise when indefinite pronouns are separated from their verbs. And, because indefinite pronouns are vague, they are often followed by phrases that clarify their meaning — so they are often separated from their verbs.

	indefinite pronoun	*phrase to clarify the meaning*	*verb*
SINGULAR			
INCORRECT:	Each	of the facts	have been discussed.
CORRECT:	*Each*	of the facts	*has* been discussed.
INCORRECT:	Neither	of these cases	deal with adultery.
CORRECT:	*Neither*	of these cases	*deals* with adultery.
PLURAL			
INCORRECT:	Several	of the facts	needs clarification.
CORRECT:	*Several*	of the facts	*need* clarification.

A few indefinite pronouns can be either singular or plural depending on the meaning of the noun or pronoun they refer to. Only four words belong in this group — *some, none, any,* and *all* (*see* Table A-6).

TABLE A-6

Correct Examples	*Meaning*
Some	
SINGULAR	
Some of the responsibility is ours. Some of the food seems to be spoiled.	a portion of; a noncountable quantity, an amount of
PLURAL	
Some of the courts have decided favorably.	a few, several, a number of, etc.
None	
SINGULAR	
None of the courts has ruled on this. None of the information was available.	not a single one; not a single portion of
PLURAL	
Of all the opinions, none are as clear as this one.	not all of them taken together

TABLE A-6 (*cont.*)

Correct Examples	*Meaning*

Any

SINGULAR

| If any of the elements is missing, the action will be unsuccessful. | any single one; any single portion of |
| If any of the responsibility lies with the corporation, it must accept it. | |

PLURAL

| Submit your recommendations; if any are reasonable, I will consider them. | however many fall into the group |

All

SINGULAR

| All of the tape has been erased. | the whole or total |
| All of the money is in the trust account. | |

PLURAL

| All of the issues have been identified. | each one counted separately |
| All of the depositions are ready. | |

3. The subject is a compound structure. Compound subjects are those connected by *and*, (either)/*or*, or, (neither)/*nor*. When you join two subjects with the word *and*, you create a new plural subject. The idea of the *and* compound is "more than one" or X *plus* Y. When you join two subjects with the word *or* or *nor*, nothing changes because the idea is choice, not addition. So, when you use *or* or *nor* to join two subjects, you do not create a new plural. Instead, you just make it clear that you have two possible subjects. The problem then is to determine which of the two subjects joined by *or* or *nor* should govern the verb. The answer is to make your verb agree with the second subject, the one nearer the verb. Here are several examples of compound subjects followed by correct verbs.

Compound subjects joined by *and* (verb agrees with subject, which is plural):

Homemaking duties and financial support have been widely recognized as valid legal consideration.

Reverend Farewell is charging that *the Director and the State have* violated his constitutional right to due process.

Compound subjects joined by *or* or *nor* (verb agrees with second subject):

Neither the State nor the child's parents have made any showing of the need for financial assistance.

Neither the child's parents nor the State has made any showing of the need for financial assistance.

Even if the court finds that *either the household services or the emotional support is* sufficient, it will probably find that the financial support is adequate consideration.

Even if the court finds that *either the emotional support or the household services are* sufficient, it will probably find that the financial support is adequate consideration.

Sometimes modifiers follow one or both elements of a compound subject. These modifiers do not affect the compound structure — *and* compounds still convey the idea of addition and take plural verbs; *or* or *nor* compounds still convey the idea of choice, and the verb agrees with the second element of the compound structure. Here are some examples with modifiers added.

Compound subjects that are modified and joined by *and* (plural verb):

The risk of erroneous deprivation through miscalculations *and the probable value* of additional procedures *are* slight in this case.

Reverend Farewell is charging that *the Director* of the Department of Public Safety *and the State* of Georgia *have* violated his constitutional right to due process.

Compound subjects that are modified and joined by (either)/*or* or (neither)/*nor* (verb agrees with the second subject):

Neither the State of Georgia nor the *parents* of the injured child *have* made any showing of the need for financial assistance.

Neither the parents of the injured child nor the *State* of Georgia *has* made any showing of the need for financial assistance.

Be careful not to confuse a compound modifier with a compound subject.

Simple subject followed by compound modifier	A *deprivation* of any length and severity *is* subject to close scrutiny.
Compound subject followed by modifier	The *length and severity* of the deprivation *were* not considered excessive.

EXERCISES

One verb in each of these sentences is incorrect. Write the correct form of the verb and circle the subject that you have made the verb agree with. Some of the errors occur because the subject and verb are separated and some because the number of the subject is unclear (unusual plural form, collective noun, indefinite pronoun, or compound subject).

a. There is no question that the parents of the minor has a valid cause of action if it can be shown that the doctrine of attractive nuisance applies.

b. Each of the cases cited above have held that the touching must be objectionable to the reasonable person.

c. A jury of the plaintiff's peers need to decide whether the method used by Metro Data Services was objectionable and whether the disclosure violated his right to privacy.

d. In addition, neither the Maryland Court of Appeals nor the Maryland Court of Special Appeals have ever construed the statute.

e. Thus, the appreciation of the value of privacy and the public excitement over the issue has dulled the senses of legislators who have made invasion of privacy a tort action in their states.

f. In Maryland, neither of these activities are considered criminal, perhaps indicating a public policy that would favor enforcement of the contract between Pat and Tracy.

g. The requirements for and the definition of "public disclosure" has been given extensive treatment by authors of legal treatises and by the courts.

h. From case law, Prosser, and the Restatement (Second) of Torts, criteria has been developed to use in determining whether or not there has been a public disclosure of private facts.

c. More Complex Problems with Separated Subjects and Verbs

Now that we have discussed special subjects (collective nouns, indefinite pronouns, and compound subjects) and subjects and verbs separated by rather short phrases, we will look at two more complex variations of separated subjects and verbs.

The verb is in a dependent clause but the word it must agree with is not. Many dependent clauses contain their own subject-verb pairs. Within those clauses, the subject and verb may appear next to one another or they may be separated by modifiers.

S-V in independent (main) clause	This *language suggests* first
S-V pair in dependent clause	that *it is* well recognized that
separated S-V pair in dependent clause	*abuses* within the consumer
	reporting industry *do occur*
S-V pair in dependent clause	and second, that the Appellant's
	claim is not based upon an
	isolated incident.

One kind of dependent clause—the relative clause—is different. It may contain a verb but no subject. The verb in the relative clause must agree with the word that the clause modifies. Here are a few examples with the entire relative clause italicized. The verb in the clause and the word it must agree with are in boldface type.

Who clauses:

SINGULAR   The appellant is not the only **one** *who* **has had** *his privacy invaded.*

PLURAL   The exact number of **people** *who* **have already seen** *the report* is unknown, and the potential number of people receiving copies is unlimited.

Which clauses:

PLURAL   In addition to these two **cases,** *which clearly* **state** *the rule of*
SINGULAR   *replacements,* there is a binding **case** in Maryland *that* **bars** *removal of the forced air system and the upstairs plumbing fixtures.*

That clauses:

SINGULAR   Georgia is the only other **jurisdiction** *that* **has preferred** *to follow the majority in enforcing express agreements between cohabitants.*

PLURAL   Michigan is one of the **jurisdictions** *that* **recognize** *a tort action for invasion of privacy.*

The verb in these examples is separated from its subject by several short phrases or by a long clause. We have looked at subjects and verbs separated by no more than six words. In some sentences, however, the subject and verb may be more than six words apart. Look at these examples of incorrect sentences. The subjects and verbs are italicized.

A *change* in policy to prevent hardship and injuries caused by the enforcement of statutes against "meretricious and illicit" relationships *have been upheld* in several jurisdictions where the conflict has arisen.

The *fact* that the legislature has begun to regulate these various businesses *establish* the concern over the possible misuse of private information gathered for "legitimate" business purposes.

However, the *rules* that govern fixtures for a mortgagor-mortgagee relationship or a vendor-vendee relationship *is* stricter than those that govern landlord-tenant relationships.

Changing the verb form will make sentences like these grammatically correct, but it will not make them effective sentences. (To produce better sentences *and* avoid the errors that can be caused by separated subjects and verbs, you need to follow the guidelines presented in Chapter 10). Here are sample revisions of these sentences. Revision of sentence 1 avoids the separated subject-verb problem by using the active voice, revision of sentence 2 by eliminating unnecessary words, and revision of sentence 3 by putting the parts of the sentence into logical order.

REVISION OF 1   Several jurisdictions have upheld a change in policy to prevent hardship and injustice that is caused by enforcing statutes against "meretricious and illicit" relationships.

REVISION OF 2   The legislature has begun to regulate various businesses because of its concern over the possible misuse of private information gathered for "legitimate" business purposes.

REVISION OF 3   The rules that govern fixtures are stricter for mortgagor-mortgagee and vendor-vendee relationships than for landlord-tenant relationships.

EXERCISES

1. Identifying and Correcting Errors

    Each sentence contains at least one error in subject-verb agreement. Find and correct the incorrect verb forms. For each incorrect verb, circle the subject (either a word or compound structure) it is supposed to agree with and draw a line from that circled word to your corrected verb. Some of the errors appear because the subject and verb are separated and some because the number of the subject is unclear (unusual plural form, collective noun, indefinite pronoun, or compound subject).

    a. Furthermore, the regulations for implementing the program also imposes a duty on the state to provide adequate and timely notice and to provide an opportunity for a fair hearing in accordance with the standards of due process set forth in *Goldberg v. Kelly.*

    b. Appellee Clark contends that because her friend who telephoned the various agencies was not told how to perfect an appeal, Clark's opportunity for a fair hearing and her chance to have her services continued pending that hearing was not adequate.

    c. If the court interprets the adultery statute in terms of changing social attitudes toward cohabitation, as have other jurisdictions, and show more interest in prevention of hardship and injustice, then Tracy's chances of recovery becomes better.

d. Any damage incurred by plaintiffs in such a suit are seen to be offset by the benefits one receives from the companionship and potential of the child.

e. The doctor is liable to you for any consequences that has arisen or will arise from his breach of contract.

f. In 1937, the Maryland Court of Appeals established that it would not enforce contracts that are based on the consideration of past or future intercourse or that in any manner promotes or furnishes an opportunity for unlawful cohabitation.

g. The legislature recognized the need of society and business for the gathering of information and have expressed that recognition in Minn. Stat. §65B.20 (1980).

h. The Minnesota legislature, by enacting the Minnesota Data Privacy Act, Minn. Stat. Ann. §15.162.169 (West 1976), and the Privacy of Communications Act, Minn. Stat. Ann. §625A.01-23 (West 1976), have established Minnesota as a leader on the issue of privacy.

2. Rewriting Sentences
Now rewrite sentences a, c, f, g, and h. Your goal should be to improve the sentences. As you rewrite, try to reduce the distance between the subjects and their verbs.

2. Incomplete Sentences

Incomplete sentences are often called sentence fragments. The most common causes of fragments are:

- Leaving a necessary element out of the main (independent) clause
- Putting only part of a verb in the main (independent) clause
- Letting a dependent clause stand alone

a. *Leaving Out Necessary Parts of the Clause*

The simplest fragments are incomplete because they are missing necessary elements, that is, they are missing a verb or missing both the subject and verb. Here are two examples, followed by correct versions of each of them. The fragments are italicized. If you need to review necessary elements, see section A.

Missing subject and verb

INCORRECT   The procedures established by the state for perfecting an appeal for a fair hearing were in compliance with federal regulations. *Providing Ms. Clark with a practical and reasonable opportunity to communicate her desire to obtain a fair hearing and to have her services continued pending the outcome of that hearing.*

CORRECT   The procedures established by the state for perfecting an appeal for a fair hearing were in compliance with federal regulations. The *procedures provided* Ms. Clark with a practical and reasonable opportunity to communicate her desire to obtain a fair hearing and to have her services continued pending the outcome of that hearing.

Missing subject and part of a verb

INCORRECT   The facts and details of his illness and hospitalization were not well known. *Until recently, not even known by his employer, co-workers, or friends.*

CORRECT   The facts and details of his illness and hospitalization were not well known. Until recently, the *details were* not even known by his employer, coworkers, or friends.

or

The facts and details of his illness and hospitalization were not well known — until recently, not even known by his employer, co-workers, or friends.

Notice the two possible ways to correct fragments. We've used each in one of the two correct versions of the second example. *To correct some fragments, you must add words*, that is, add the missing necessary part or parts of the clause. In the first example, both a subject and a verb had to be added because the original fragment contained neither. In the first correction of the second example, a subject and part of a verb (*were*) had to be added for the sentence to make sense.

To correct other fragments, you only need to change the punctuation. This method of correcting fragments works only when the fragment (or sentence piece) is short and really belongs with another sentence — either the already complete sentence that precedes the fragment or the one that immediately follows it.

Because these simple fragments will make sense and seem complete in context, they are not always easy to identify. To identify them, read "bottom up" — i.e., read the last sentence of a paragraph, then the second-to-last sentence, and so on. As suggested in the proofreading section of Chapter 12, reading from the bottom to the top slows you down and makes you judge sentences as individual units. You will be less likely to supply the missing noun or verb mentally if you read from bottom to top.

EXERCISES

If there is a fragment in the groups of sentences below, underline it and then correct it either by changing the punctuation or by rewriting it as a complete sentence. If every sentence in the group is a complete sentence, place a C (for *correct*) in front of the sentence.

a. Recent case law has established that doctors can never guarantee a particular result of an operation. They can only inform the patient of the expected result of the operation. Therefore, we do not have sufficient evidence to support a cause of action in negligence.

b. Thus we will sue for the difference between your promised condition (sterility) and your present condition. The damages will include the cost of your child's care until he reaches an age of self support. The out-of-pocket expenses for the operation by Dr. Cooper and the cost for another tubal ligation. We will also sue for any physical pain and mental anguish you have suffered as a result of Dr. Cooper's breach of contract.

b. *Letting a Dependent Clause Stand Alone*

The following examples should remind you of the common and correct uses of dependent clauses. In these examples, each dependent clause is italicized. (If you need more information on dependent clauses, see pages 414-415.)

Examples of dependent clauses as necessary elements

as subject	*What Mel said to Bill about options to renew* is insignificant because Bill subsequently signed a lease.
as object	Dr. Cooper told his patient *that the operation would result in sterility.*
as complement	The precise question is *whether the lease creates a right to perpetual renewal.*

Examples of dependent clauses as modifiers

explaining *when?*	The State acted within its discretion *when it reduced the amount of Title XX funds allocated to homemaker services.*
explaining *under what conditions?*	A notice is timely *if it is mailed at least ten days before the date of the intended action.*

explaining
why?

Since homemaker services are an optional Title XX benefit, the recipients are not statutorily entitled to these services.

When dependent clauses are used correctly, they are attached to independent clauses. If a dependent clause is not connected to an independent clause, the dependent clause is considered a sentence fragment. Here are passages with incorrectly used dependent clauses followed by correct versions of the same passages.

Fragment that is one dependent clause

INCORRECT

The *Moore* court based its decision on contractual theories. *Although the underlying principle condemning misappropriation of a person's name or picture has been recognized by other jurisdictions as being within the realm of privacy interests.*

CORRECT

The *Moore* court based its decision on contractual theories, although the underlying principle condemning misappropriation of a person's name or picture has been recognized by other jurisdictions as being within the realm of privacy interests.

or

The *Moore* court based its decision on contractual theories. However, the underlying principle condemning misappropriation of a person's name or picture has been recognized by other jurisdictions as being within the realm of privacy interests.

Fragment that is two dependent clauses

INCORRECT

There is no need to discuss the element of consideration or even special consideration. *Because, in this state, words of reassurance are not recognized as promises, which are required to complete the bargained-for exchange.*

CORRECT

There is no need to discuss the element of consideration or even special consideration because, in this state, words of reassurance are not recognized as promises, which are required to complete the bargained-for exchange.

Changing the punctuation is the most common way to correct fragments that are dependent clauses. By changing the punctuation, you attach the dependent clause to the sentence it belongs with. Another way to correct a dependent clause fragment is to delete the word that makes the clause dependent. If you use this method, be certain that the relationships among your ideas remain clear (see the second correction of the *Moore* example, where the word *however* is added to keep the idea of contrast when the word *although* is deleted).

EXERCISES

Some of the groups of sentences below include sentence fragments, and some do not. Some of the fragments are simple fragments and some are dependent clauses. If there is a fragment, underline it and then correct it.

a. The statute itself can be attacked as archaic and nonfunctional. No person has ever been charged with adultery for the 285 years that the statute has been in effect. Even though ample opportunity has existed for the state to prosecute admitted adulterers after divorce proceedings. In addition, the fact that the legislature has allowed the $10 fine to remain as the prescribed punishment indicates that the state does not take the statute seriously.

b. Courts are, in fact, going beyond enforcing only express contracts. Many states are finding that a party may recover in other ways. For example, by implied-in-fact contracts, which look at the intent of the parties, or by implied-in-law contracts, which courts sometimes rely on to prevent unjust enrichment. There is no reason to believe that Maryland, in 1990, will not follow the trend.

c. If the court declares Reston's promise unenforceable due to the nature of his relationship with Miller, Reston will retain all the possessions that he accumulated during their cohabitation. A house in Roland Park, two Mercedes Benz automobiles, a 60-foot yacht, a condominium at Hilton Head and one at Aspen, and 10 percent of Roberto Duran, all in his name only. Even though Miller provided the financial and domestic support that allowed Reston to pursue the medical career that enabled him to acquire these possessions. This would create an injustice far outweighing the court's interest in protecting the sanctity of marriage.

d. However, most courts are willing to enforce express agreements if part of the consideration is some kind of financial contribution. For example, in *Tyranski,* the court was persuaded by evidence that the plaintiff had contributed $10,000 toward the house that they agreed the defendant would convey to her. Similarly, the plaintiff in *McHenry* contributed her income, personal property, savings, and unemployment benefits.

e. If the courts in Maryland follow the majority of the states that so far have been faced with this issue, Tracy should be able to recover her share of the jointly accumulated property. Maryland cases have established grounds for such recovery. By espousing the doctrine of recovery as long as the contract is not based solely on the grounds of the meretricious relationship. The courts may separate the sexual agreement from the property agreement, and there is no legislation that would bar recovery.

c. *Putting Only Part of a Verb in the Main Clause*

Sentences with partial verbs are also fragments. Here are two examples.

Example 1

INCORRECT   The invasion of the appellant's right to privacy *based* upon the theory that the appellee's acts were an unreasonable intrusion into the appellant's private affairs and that the dissemination of this information to All-Risk Insurance Company constituted public disclosure of private facts.

CORRECT   The invasion of the appellant's right to privacy *is based* upon the theory that the appellee's acts were an unreasonable intrusion into the appellant's private affairs and that the dissemination of this information to All-Risk Insurance Company constituted public disclosure of private facts.

Example 2

INCORRECT   The *Kalicki* court *adhering* to the doctrine of disfavoring perpetuities when it held that the tenant would be allowed only one renewal because the language in the lease did not clearly indicate an intention to create a perpetuity.

CORRECT   The *Kalicki* court *was adhering* to the doctrine of disfavoring perpetuities when it held that the tenant would be allowed only one renewal because the language in the lease did not clearly indicate an intention to create a perpetuity.

or

The *Kalicki* court *adhered* to the doctrine of disfavoring perpetuities when it held that the tenant would be allowed only one renewal because the language in the lease did not clearly indicate an intention to create a perpetuity.

Both of these examples contain dependent clauses, but the dependent clauses are not problems because they are not standing alone. The problem in both examples is that the verb of the independent clause is incomplete.

In the first example, the verb is passive but the word that directs the action back to the subject is missing. You must add the word (*is*) that directs the action back to the subject. (For additional information on passives, see pages 397-399.)

The second example involves an *-ing* verb form instead of an incomplete passive verb, but the principle is the same. An *-ing* verb form cannot stand alone as the verb in an independent clause. You must also have a form of the verb *to be* (is, are, was, were). This sentence is incomplete:

A woman trying to recover unpaid wages from her deceased employer's estate.

This sentence is complete:

A woman was trying to recover unpaid wages from her deceased employer's estate.

Fragments caused by partial verbs are likely to appear in legal writing because it is complex writing that often uses the passive voice and other multi-word verb forms such as the *-ing* verb form (called the progressive). The most common way to correct these fragments is either to add the words that are missing from the verb (*is, was*) or to change the form of the verb (*adhering* to *adhered* or *being* to *is* or *was*).

A second way to correct fragments caused by partial verbs is to add information onto the sentence.

FRAGMENT:	The woman locked in the closet.
CORRECTED:	The woman locked in the closet *was a judge.*

You can only use this method, however, when the fragment is short and you have new information to add.

EXERCISES

Some of the groups of sentences below include sentence fragments, and some do not. When you see a fragment, underline it and then correct it either by changing the punctuation or by rewriting it as a complete sentence. If every sentence in the group is a complete sentence, place a C (for *correct*) in front of the group.

a. The doctor was negligent in that he subjected you to an unreasonable risk of harm. The doctor assured you that the operation would work, but it did not. Therefore, subjecting you to the unreasonable risk of having a third child that you had specifically told the doctor you did not want.

b. Your conversation with Dr. Cooper did not create an enforceable agreement. There is no need to discuss the element of consideration or even special consideration. Because, in this state, words of reassurance are not recognized as promises, which are required to complete the bargained-for exchange.

c. It could be argued that the attractive nuisance doctrine does not apply because the homeowner was in compliance with the local building code requirements for maintaining an artificial structure in his backyard. That the homeowner is released from liability for injuries caused to trespassing minors because he had taken all necessary precautionary measures by erecting a six-foot fence.

d. The general rule is in our favor. While the parents of the child appear to have a valid cause of action. It is important to take into consideration the fact that their case depends on the application of the doctrine of attractive nuisance. This doctrine reflects the traditional social interest in the safety and welfare of children.

e. In *Vargas*, the recipients were at least notified that their case workers would explain the reasons for the reduction or termination of benefits. In the present case, those receiving notice believed that they knew the reason that their benefits had been terminated when, in fact, they knew only part of the reason. The "reduction of funding" reason may indeed have misled many recipients.

f. The argument against this interpretation based on the Equal Rights Amendment, Md. Const. Declar. of Rights Art. 46 (1972) (hereafter ERA), which states that "Equality of rights under the law shall not be abridged or denied because of sex." Because of this law, both parents are responsible for child support.

g. The contract in *McCall*, though, can be distinguished from the contract between Pat and Tracy. In the *McCall* case, Frampton requested that McCall leave her husband and her employment and live with him. In *McCall*, then, part of the actual consideration was to commit adultery.

3. Garbled Sentences

When the meaning of a sentence is unclear because the structure of the sentence is unclear, the sentence is garbled. We distinguish garbled sentences from sentence fragments in this way: A sentence fragment is missing a necessary element; it is incomplete. In a garbled sentence, all the parts are there, but they do not form a coherent whole. We distinguish garbled sentences from problems with subject-verb agreement in this way: To correct a problem in subject-verb agreement, you usually only need to adjust the verb. To correct a garbled sentence, you probably need to rewrite, or rethink, the entire sentence.

Sentences can become garbled in many ways, but this section will deal with two of the most common:

1. When there are tangled lists and misplaced modifiers (sentences that become garbled or contain certain illogical structures because the writer tries to put too much into the sentence and to compact it too tightly).

2. When there are mismatched beginnings and endings (sentences that become garbled because the writer begins the sentence with one kind of structure and ends it with another).

a. *Problems with Tangled Lists and Misplaced Modifiers*

The writer of the following sentence has lost control of it in the process of adding items to the list.

His conviction that he can successfully perform the operation, his understanding of what you wanted, and your understanding of his understanding, its implications and results are very clear.

The result is a garbled sentence that makes little sense. What, for example, is supposed to be "very clear"? His conviction? His understanding? Its implications? Implications of what?

Here, using a little more information, are two rewrites of the garbled sentence.

REWRITE A	It is clear that the doctor believed he could successfully perform the operation, that he understood you wanted to be sterile, and that you knew he understood what you wanted. The implications and results of this situation are also clear.

REWRITE B	Three facts are clear: (1) the doctor was convinced that he could successfully perform the operation, (2) he understood that you wanted to be sterile, and (3) you knew that he understood what you wanted.

In both rewrites, the original main verb and complement (*is clear*) have been moved to the front of the sentence. Each sentence now begins with the basic pattern (S = LV = C). Beginning with the basic pattern has two advantages:

1. It provides the reader with a context for the details that follow, and
2. It keeps the subject and verb together.

Both rewrites also signal the beginning of each item in the list. Rewrite A uses the word *that* to signal a new item and Rewrite B uses numbers. In Rewrite A we have made the confusing last part of the original sentence into a separate sentence. Doing so shows it to be an empty sentence. What does it mean? In Rewrite B we have dropped this part of the original sentence entirely.

Here is another example of a garbled sentence. In this case, however, only part of the sentence is garbled (the dependent *if* clause):

> If the birth of this child aggravated your back condition substantially and the pregnancy was the direct result of the breach coupled with the ability to document and measure either in days lost from work or a new injury, the court may grant you compensation.

The writer of this sentence has also lost control in the process of adding items to a list. The items in this case are conditions. Here are three possible rewrites of this sentence. The first two are longer than the original and the last one is slightly shorter than the original.

REWRITE A	The court may grant you compensation *if you can prove that* the pregnancy was the direct result of the breach, *that* the birth of this child substantially aggravated your back condition, *and that* you either lost days from work or developed a new injury as a result of the pregnancy and birth.

REWRITE B   The court may grant you compensation for your back injury *if* the pregnancy was the direct result of the breach *and if* the birth of this child substantially aggravated your back condition. *However,* you must be able to document and measure your losses either in terms of days you lost from work or in terms of the new injury you developed.

REWRITE C   *If* the pregnancy was the direct result of the breach *and if* the birth of this child substantially aggravated your back condition, *then* the court may grant you compensation, *but* you must be able to document and measure your losses.

Because the meaning was unclear in the original, each rewrite is based on a slightly different interpretation of the original. Although the meaning varies from rewrite to rewrite, each version has a clear, untangled structure. In Rewrite A, we provided structure by

1. Putting the main clause first
2. Putting the basic parts of the dependent (if) clause at the beginning of the clause
3. Making the three conditions modifiers to the dependent (*if*) clause
4. Giving the three conditions parallel structures, introduced by *that.*

In Rewrite B, we provided structure by

1. Putting the main clause first
2. Giving even more context (modifying the main clause with the phrase "for your back injury")
3. Putting the two main conditions in parallel clauses, introduced by *if*
4. Breaking the long sentence into two sentences
5. Signaling the relationships between the sentences by using *however.*

In Rewrite C, we provided structure by

1. Making the sentence an *if, then* sentence
2. Putting the two main conditions in parallel clauses introduced by *if*
3. Signaling the relationships among the ideas in the sentence by using *then, but*

Any one of these rewrites is better than the original. Reading the original, you cannot immediately tell that the clause beginning *the pregnancy* is a second *if* clause, because the *if* is not stated. The phrase beginning *coupled with* is unclear because you don't immediately know what it modifies. The word *either* is ambiguous because the two choices are not written with parallel structures. Because the main idea comes at the very end of the sentence, you don't have any context to help you understand the *if* clauses. You may have asked yourself, "What is this all about?" And then, after reading the end of the sentence, you may have had to go back to the beginning to reread the first part.

Here is a third example of a garbled sentence. In this sentence, the problem is that the last phrase is in the wrong place.

> I have rejected the idea of bringing a third cause of action in negligence since this must be established by showing departure from a recognized standard practice *by medical testimony.*

The reader tries to link *by medical testimony* to *a recognized standard practice.* But that's not where the phrase fits, so the reader gets confused. The easiest way to correct this problem is to move the phrase.

REWRITE A   I have rejected the idea of bringing a third cause of action in negligence since this must be established *by medical testimony* showing departure from a recognized standard practice.

Moving the phrase so that it is next to the word it modifies (*established*) does correct the problem of ending the sentence illogically. However, the sentence can be improved if other changes are made.

REWRITE B   I have rejected the idea of bringing a third cause of action in negligence since *negligence* must be established by medical testimony *that shows the doctor departed* from a recognized standard of practice.

This version is longer than version A because this improved version includes words that make the relationship among the pieces clearer.

EXERCISES

Each of these sentences is difficult to understand because the writer lost control while adding information. Rewrite each sentence so that your interpretation of its meaning is clear. You may move parts of a sentence around, add words, repeat words to mark the beginning of each item in a series, change nouns to verbs, divide the sentence into two or more sentences, or make other changes.

a. In the past judges have dismissed such "past conversations" as evidence on the ground of hearsay.

b. In light of this factor, we must pursue your case by establishing that an express contract was made between you and Doctor Cooper in that Doctor Cooper promised you the desired result of infertility to the effect that, without such a promise, you would never have consented to the operation in the first place in return for any consideration (or payment) to him therefor.

c. Also the plaintiff should recover a substantial amount of money for the support of the child based on the doctrine of reliance.

d. This standard of care is higher than that of the reasonable, prudent person and it requires doctors to use the presumed skill and knowledge that is possessed by the profession and a standard of good practice in the community.

e. The harm caused was not limited to physical and mental suffering but also the incurring of financial responsibilities that you were unable to afford, and the doctor knew of when he promised certain results.

f. The doctrine of reliance applies in this instance which states that the courts can award damages to the plaintiff for the purpose of undoing the harm which his reliance on the defendants caused him.

g. One who engages in a business, occupation, or profession must exercise the requisite degree of learning, skill, and ability of that calling with reasonable and ordinary care.

h. As a result of our conversation of November 5, 1992, concerning the feasibility of commencing a lawsuit against Dr. Cooper for your recovery of damages sustained from his failure to perform a successful sterilization operation as requested and expected by you on January 30, 1988, which resulted in the unanticipated birth of your third child, I have compiled and incorporated in this letter both background information related to decisions of cases similar to your situation and have charted a basis for action to recover as a result of Dr. Cooper's failure to successfully perform your requested surgical operation.

b. *Problems with Mismatched Beginnings and Endings*

The second common way that a sentence becomes garbled is when a writer begins a sentence with one structure and ends it with another. Here is one example.

> Also considering your fear of another pregnancy because of back problems aggravated by the delivery of your second child, puts the statements by the doctor firmly into the category of a warranty of the successful performance of a tubal ligation.

The front half of the sentence is a participial phrase (*considering* . . .). When you begin a sentence with a participial phrase (a phrase that acts like a dependent clause), you must make the subject of the independent clause the same as the subject of the participial phrase. The last half of the sentence (*puts the statements* . . .) assumes a subject that is not present. The independent clause is incomplete or nonexistent. One way to rewrite this garbled sentence is to complete each half.

REWRITE A   Also considering your fear of another pregnancy because of back problems aggravated by the delivery of your second child, *you would have insisted on assurances that the operation would be successful. Your insistence and the doctor's responses* put his statements firmly into the category of a warranty of the successful performance of a tubal ligation.

Although this rewrite solves the problem of the mismatched parts, it is not as clear as it could be. A better solution would be to rewrite the sentence as the story it, in fact, tells.

REWRITE B   Because of back problems aggravated by the delivery of your second child, *you feared another pregnancy*. Given this fear, *you insisted on assurances* that the tubal ligation would be successful. The doctor's *responses,* which led you to agree to surgery, *constituted a warranty* of his successful performance of a tubal ligation.

Dividing a garbled sentence into two or more sentences is often an effective solution.

Sometimes, the only indication of a problem in a sentence is that the writer has repeated the subject unnecessarily. In this example, the italicized *it* is incorrect.

As in *Adams* and in *Benton*, this broad reason, while it may not allow Mrs. Clark to decide conclusively whether she should appeal for a fair hearing, *it* does serve its limited constitutional purpose by providing her with notice of the advance claim against her and by affording her an opportunity to present her objections at an evidentiary hearing.

This sentence has the structure of the sentence

My sister *she* came yesterday.

This sentence could be corrected just by dropping the second subject (*it*):

REWRITE A   As in *Adams* and in *Benton*, this *broad reason*, while it may not allow Mrs. Clark to decide conclusively whether she should appeal for a fair hearing, *does serve its* limited constitutional *purpose* by providing her with notice of the advance claim against her and by affording her an opportunity to present her objections at an evidentiary hearing.

However, this change still leaves one very long sentence. Dividing the information into two sentences would make the point clearer.

REWRITE B   The *broad reason* given in this case, as in *Adams* and in *Benton, may not allow Mrs. Clark* to decide conclusively whether she should appeal for a fair hearing. The *broad reason does,* however, *serve its* limited constitutional *purpose* by providing her with notice of the advance claim against her and by affording her an opportunity to present her objections at an evidentiary hearing.

In this rewrite, the second half of the sentence is almost unchanged, but it is a separate sentence. The only changes are (1) the added word *however* to signal the relationship between the two sentences, and (2) the use of the noun (*broad reason*) in place of the pronoun *it.*

The sentence can also be improved even if you want to keep it as one sentence. Rewrite C illustrates the positive effect of keeping the necessary elements of the independent clause together, choosing an appropriate word (*although*) to introduce the modifier, and dropping the reference to other cases.

REWRITE C   Although the broad reason may not allow Mrs. Clark to decide conclusively whether she should appeal for a fair hearing, the *broad reason does serve its* limited constitutional *purpose* by providing her with notice of the advance claim against her and by affording her an opportunity to present her objections at an evidentiary hearing.

From these sample rewrites, you can see that garbled sentences with mismatched halves can be rewritten in many ways. Some methods simply correct the error (Rewrite A), and some make the sentences more comprehensible (Rewrites B and C).

Here is a shorter sentence that has mismatched halves.

> If given the appropriate information you might have chosen another avenue to solve your problem, but you were denied this choice by Dr. Cooper.

Because of errors in punctuation in the first half of the sentence, the reader expects all of the *if* clause to modify the second part. In fact, the second half is a second independent clause. The sentence should read

REWRITE A   If given the appropriate information, you might have chosen another avenue to solve your problem; but you were denied this choice by Dr. Cooper.

The mismatched second half is really a second sentence.

REWRITE B   If given the appropriate information, you might have chosen another avenue to solve your problem. However, you were denied this choice by Dr. Cooper.

The first sentence in Rewrite B is still difficult to understand. The combination of words, *if given,* is unclear. The reader does not know who the subject of *given* is.

REWRITE C   If you had been given the appropriate information, you might have chosen another avenue to solve your problem. However, you were denied this choice by Dr. Cooper.

You could make the sentences even clearer (as either one or two sentences) by using the active voice.

REWRITE D   If Dr. Cooper had given you the appropriate information, *you might have chosen* another *method* of solving your problem, but *he denied you this choice.*

Rewrite D improves the sentence by using the active voice (*Dr. Cooper had given* and *he denied you*) to emphasize the doctor's responsibility. Substituting the word *method* for *avenue* also improves the sentence. (*Avenue* is a metaphor for *method* and therefore harder to understand.)

Just as the halves of an entire sentence can be mismatched, the halves of a dependent clause can be mismatched. Here is an example.

The *Steffes* court evaluated the equities involved and determined that in allowing the defendant to prevail would be allowing him to be unjustly enriched.

The overall structure of this sentence is sound.

court	evaluated	*equities*	and	determined	*that*
S	V	O		V	O

The problem is that the halves within the dependent clause (the *that* clause) are mismatched.

in allowing . . . would be allowing . . .

This mismatch can be corrected either by changing the first half of the clause or by changing the last half.

REWRITE A   The *Steffes* court evaluated the equities involved and determined that *allowing* the defendant to prevail *would be allowing* him to be unjustly enriched.

REWRITE B   The *Steffes* court evaluated the equities involved and determined that *in allowing* the defendant to prevail, *it would be allowing him* to be unjustly enriched.

EXERCISES

Each of these passages contains at least one garbled sentence. Some sentences have only one kind of problem and some have several. The problems include mismatched beginnings and illogical structures. Rewrite each garbled sentence so that your interpretation of its meaning is clear. You may move parts of the sentence around, add words, delete words, repeat words, change nouns to verbs, divide the sentence into two or more sentences, or make other changes.

a. If our client should care to raise a contention that the "option to renew" which he was granted in the pre-1990 telephone conversation can be offered as parol evidence to allow him to renew once more would almost definitely be ineffective.

b. Remembering that fixture law is interpreted in favor of the tenant in landlord-tenant situations, this should help our argument of the carpet remaining the personal property of Brooks.

c. Maryland law provides no precedent to guide the courts in deciding this issue. But in other jurisdictions, cases presenting the question of determining what renewals will be allowed when a lease presents options or covenants for renewal, and no specific number of renewals is expressed, as in the Brooks lease, it has been held that provisions or covenants of renewal will allow only one renewal in addition to the original term.

d. In the 1978 case under discussion, that no matter how firmly attached to the realty an object is, if it was placed on the property by the tenant for the purpose of his business, it is a trade fixture and remains the property of the tenant.

e. The notice requirements of *Goldberg* were further defined in *Vargas v. Trainor*, 508 F.2d 485 (7th Cir. 1974). Where the court held that the reasons for termination must be placed in the notice itself and the notice, which required a recipient to meet with a case worker in order to discover the reasons for termination and to decide whether to appeal, was not adequate.

f. Whether homemaker services were terminated solely due to a reduction in funding or whether it was also determined that some recipients were less needy than others, the social service agencies that deal with these recipients directly are in the best position to make these decisions.

g. Furthermore, based on your telephone conversation with Dr. Cooper in July, during which he further assured you that you could not be pregnant gives rise to an action of malpractice because if he had properly treated and cared for you, a duty which he owed you, your unwanted pregnancy could have been terminated by alternative means in sufficient time.

h. This letter is intended to give you some information about how the courts in Massachusetts generally decide on cases similar to yours and that your chances of recovering damages to this extent are good but not definite.

i. As far as any information obtained by Metro from neighbors and Brandon's ex-wife, it would seem that as a matter of general knowledge by the public, although the facts regarding Brandon's illness are not something common to everyday conversation, they were not matters that were considered private and under the exclusive control of Brandon so as to be protected from reasonable inquiry and disclosure in the manner in which they were disclosed.

4. Summary

1. The verb must match the subject in number. Problems are created by:

- Subject and verb being separated
- The number of the subject being unclear

2. Sentences must be complete:

- Include all necessary elements of the sentence
- Don't let a dependent clause stand alone
- Be sure the verb is complete

3. Be sure sentences are clear. Garbled sentences are caused by:

- Problems with tangled lists and misplaced modifiers
- Problems with mismatched beginnings and endings

Appendix B

Formatting Legal Documents

A | The Importance of Format in Legal Documents

As an attorney, your writing efforts may be concentrated on clarifying substantive legal issues and on creatingg appropriate, strong, persuasive legal documents. However, the way a document appears on the page can actually have a great bearing on its success. When you practice in a particular area of the law, you must not only master the content of the documents you are called upon to create, you must also master the forms they are required to take. This often involves complying with formal formatting rules imposed by such intended recipients as various courts, legislative bodies, or federal or state agencies. An incorrectly formatted document could render the best legal analysis invalid, negating countless hours of careful, substantive legal work. We address some of these formatting rules below.

In addition to learning formal formatting requirements, you should also consider document format and appearance in a more general sense. Clear, consistent formatting can enhance the effectiveness of any document you write for anyone, at any time, for any purpose. Like the rules for clear writing in the chapters above, the elements of formatting that we discuss here apply in any context. Personally and professionally, you have likely encountered problems trying to understand poorly formatted documents. Compare, for example, the two insurance policies in Chapter 8. You can see the effect that formatting techniques — type size, typeface, and layout — can have on a document. How eager would you be to pick up and read a document (particularly one outside your area of expertise or study) composed of long, unbroken blocks of densely packed text in tiny print? Attorneys are often responsible for composing insurance policies and similar documents, but they do not routinely focus on — or even seem to consider — those documents' appearance. Attorneys do not often consider whether a document visually notifies a reader that the document's contents are important, or, in fact, whether the document's appearance conveys anything at all to the reader.

If you seek to maximize the impact of what you write, you should not overlook the importance of its physical appearance: The way a document looks can help determine whether the reader forms a positive or negative impression of its content. The content of a poorly formatted document may be perfectly understandable, even polished, but it will still fail to present information in the most easily accessible way. A reader who views a document as daunting may never read it at all, may skim it, or may misread it. On the other hand, a well formatted document is inviting, easier to read, easier to absorb, and easier to use. Proper use of formatting techniques can help ensure that a document carries its message to the reader simply and effectively.

B The Components of Graphic Design

The main components of graphic design are:

1. *Structure:* the headings that divide the document into manageable topics.
2. *Type:* the size of the type, the type face (font), and the type style — roman, **boldface**, or *italic*
3. *White space:* the margins and the space surrounding text, quotes, footnotes, etc.
4. *Special treatments:* the various ways of highlighting particular points or sections of a document (lists, block indention, etc.).

Another, less important, component is the paper used for the text and cover: its color, finish, and weight.

Before you can begin using these graphic elements, you need to know what your constraints are.

- Are there preexisting format restrictions?
- Is your document intended for a particular audience (such as a law school professor, a partner in your firm, an elderly client, the general public, the Supreme Court)?
- Is there a limit on the total number of pages?
- Are there other limits or specifications (such as type size, typeface, margins), mandated, for example, by court rules?

If there is a predetermined formula for presenting the material to your audience (such as the restrictions on Supreme Court documents), you may have very few decisions to make. For example, the United States Courts of Appeals require that briefs be written in 14-point type when using Times New Roman. Some circuits permit you to use 12-point type in the footnotes, but some require 14-point type even there. If, however, there are no preexisting specifications, you will need to think carefully about your formatting options. By considering your audience and your constraints, you will be better able to use the appropriate format and graphic techniques in the final product.

The first aspect of format you may have to deal with is length. If length is a constraint, you should monitor your document's length through each draft, using the word counter and the page counter in your word processing software.[1] Knowing how long your document will be in its final form will help you decide on the best way of presenting it.

For example, if your document is a product warranty that will be included on an enclosure card in the packaging of a small product, you will not be able to fit ten pages of typed copy on it. However, if you have written three pages of copy rather than the ideal two pages, you may be able to change the typeface (the term for an individually designed alphabet that has an identifiable look, such as Arial, **Souvenir**, `Courier`, or Times New Roman) and type size to accommodate the full three pages in two. You may, of course, be sacrificing legibility to some extent, but it may be worth the trade-off. Know your priorities, and once you have satisfied your top priorities, compromise for the best overall effect.

C Meeting Length Requirements

If your final document has a length requirement, you must first determine the length of your draft. This is easily done using the length tool included in your word processing program. Such tools also include the total character count, with and without the spaces between the words. (You can get an idea of what your document will look like by using the "print preview" feature.) Your program will also tell you the total number of lines in the document and the total number of pages. Note, however, that these last two totals, unlike the word and character counts, are highly dependent on the typeface and type size you are using, as well as on the space between the lines (known in printing as "leading").

If the final page count is more (or less) than your length requirement, there are a number of adjustments you can make. (But remember that any of these can affect the legibility of your document—and the goodwill of your professor, client, or judge.)

1. Change your margins to increase (or decrease) the number of characters per line.
2. Use "ragged" (unjustified) right margins and hyphenation. This will maximize the number of words per line. Conversely, if your document is

---

1. The federal appeals courts use word limits rather than page limits and require that you certify that your document is less than the upper word limit. *See* Fed. R. App. P. 32(a)(7). Under Fed. R. App. P. 32(a)(7)(B)(iii), footnotes count toward this limit, but the "corporate disclosure statement, table of contents, table of citations, statement with regard to oral argument, any addendum containing statutes, rules or regulations, and any certificates of counsel do not account toward the limitation." You should therefore make sure that your word processing program is set to count all of the words in the substantive portions of your document, including the footnotes. In *DeSilva v. DiLeonardi*, 185 F.3d 815 (7th Cir. 1999), the court required counsel to show cause why he should not be sanctioned for certifying that his brief was within the word limit set by the rules when in fact his software had failed to count the words in the footnotes.

too short, use justified right margins and no hyphenation to increase the spacing between words.

3. Switch type fonts from a wider font, such as Courier New, to a narrower font, such as Times New Roman or Garamond (or vice-versa, if you wish to lengthen the document).

4. If permitted, change the type size. Be careful, however. The most comfortable type sizes to read — depending on the typeface (font) — range from 9 to 14 points; however, 10-point Times New Roman is far more difficult to read than 10-point Courier New.

5. Change the leading (spacing) between the lines.

Any one of these adjustments, or a combination of them, may help you meet your length requirements. Each will have a measurable effect on the final appearance and legibility of the document, so you should carefully weigh the decision before making any adjustments final. Single-spaced copy with narrow margins in a small, narrow typeface will give you the maximum amount of text per page — but it will also cause the maximum amount of eyestrain (and annoyance) for your reader.

If the more mechanical ways of modifying your document to fit space requirements are not sufficient, or if they result in an unreadable document, you will need to edit down the amount of copy. Once you have finished editing the draft, you can recount the number of words and lines and choose the best format for your document.

D Structure

Once the copy is complete, the first step you must take in formatting the final document is to quickly review the structure and organization of the draft. Focus on the document's signposts — the headings.

If you have organized your document well during your pre-writing and writing stages, you should have a visible structure that will provide a good roadmap for your reader. Carrying the roadmap metaphor further, your document should use headings as signposts that signal changes in subject matter and that clearly lay out the progression of your thoughts from introduction to conclusion.

1. Headings

Before determining what each heading should look like, double-check your document to ensure that the headings are working the way you want them to:

• Are there enough headings? Can the reader move about in the document quickly and easily? Is the structure clear?

- Are the headings informative? Are they too long? Do they use parallel grammatical structures?
- Are lower-level headings introducing material that belongs under a main or primary heading?

After you are satisfied with the content of your headings, you must then decide how they should appear. To work most efficiently, the more important headings should have more visual impact than the less important ones. The physical appearance of each heading should reflect its position in the hierarchy of headings. As you go through this section, notice the various techniques—capitalization, italics, boldface, spacing, and position—that can help establish this hierarchy.

The headings in your document—their precision, clarity, and capacity to inform—will convey the structure and logic of your document's content. In any word processing program (e.g., Word or WordPerfect), the options for headings are almost limitless. In addition, word processing programs can format headings for you, based on the number of levels of headings you use and the heading style you choose.

Be wary, however, of including too many levels of headings. Anything beyond four levels can make a document harder, rather than easier, to follow. Also, for anything you produce in final form on a computer, all of the headings should be in the same typeface (e.g., Times New Roman), and should vary only with regard to type size, type style (**boldface** or *italics*), and type case (ALL CAPITALS, SMALL CAPITALS, or Initial Caps).

A document's headings could be structured as follows:

MAJOR (PRIMARY) HEADING
(14-point, all caps, bold, centered)

First Level Heading
14-point, initial caps, bold, centered

Second Level Heading
(12-point, initial caps, bold, left-justified)

Third Level Heading
(12-point, initial caps, italic, left-justified)

Run-in heading. (12-point, sentence case, bold, indented, followed by a period, a dash, or several spaces, with the text immediately following)

There are many other variations on levels of headings. Remember, however, not to let your document's headings get too complicated.

2. Capitals

Using solid capital letters ("caps") is a common way to add weight to a heading. For short, primary headings, you can use all caps. However, solid capital letters are more difficult to read than lowercase letters, and they should therefore be used sparingly. In fact, anything more than four or five words in all caps slows down reading speed significantly. This is because it is far more difficult to distinguish among capital letters, which are all the same height, than it is to distinguish among lowercase letters, which have very different shapes and heights. Don't put large blocks of text into capital letters unless you are required to.

Boldface also adds visual weight to primary headings.

FACTS OF THE CASE

SUMMARY

For longer primary headings or for any secondary headings you can use initial caps, capitalizing the first letter of all words except prepositions of fewer than four letters and articles (a, the). Exceptions: in a heading, you should use an initial capital for the first *and last* word, even if it is a preposition, e.g., "What Are We Afraid Of?", "In the Land of the Blind" and after any form of punctuation, e.g., "Disability Law: In the Land of the Blind.")

If you have many levels of headings, you can use boldface with secondary headings, along with initial caps, to provide another level of distinction from lower-level headings.

DEFENSES IN DEFAMATION CASES

Privileges in the Public Sphere

For lower-level headings, you can use either non-bold initial caps or an initial capital and followed by all lowercase letters; that is, you would capitalize the first letter of the first word only.

DEFENSES IN DEFAMATION CASES

Privileges in the Public Sphere

Legal proceedings and reports

You can also move lower-level headings to the left margin, with or without boldface or initial caps:

DEFENSES IN DEFAMATION CASES

Privileges in the Public Sphere

Legal proceedings and reports

At even lower levels, you can use italic or italic + bold headings, and, finally, "run-in" headings. For run-in headings, start with a paragraph indent. Use any variation of capitalization, with or without boldface. End the heading with a period. Continue with the text immediately, i.e., run the heading into the text. For extra impact, you can italicize the heading.

... otherwise lawful private activities, and otherwise permissible uses of private property, on whatever grounds such private bodies deem appropriate — including grounds that would be clearly forbidden to the state itself.

Summary of Argument. Conferring on church leaders the uncontrolled power, within a 500-foot radius, to decide who may serve or sell liquor to whom invests ecclesiastical officials with governmental ...

or

... otherwise lawful private activities, and otherwise permissible uses of private property, on whatever grounds such private bodies deem appropriate — including grounds that would be clearly forbidden to the state itself.

Summary of Argument. Conferring on church leaders the uncontrolled power, within a 500-foot radius, to decide who may serve or sell liquor to whom invests ecclesiastical officials with governmental ...

Because word processing programs provide the option of italics, there is no need to underline any headings other than, perhaps, the primary heading — and even that is not usually necessary.

3. Spacing

The importance of a heading can also be changed by varying the space around it.

To set off any dominant heading, you can make it "freestanding," i.e., give it a line of its own with space above and below. A primary heading might have two lines of space above and one line of space below.

. . . otherwise lawful private activities, and otherwise permissible uses of private property, on whatever grounds such private bodies deem appropriate — including grounds that would be clearly forbidden to the state itself.

Summary of Argument

Conferring on church leaders the uncontrolled power, within a 500-foot radius, to decide who may serve or sell liquor to whom invests ecclesiastical officials with governmental . . .

To set off a secondary heading, you can leave one line of space above and below *or* one line of space above and no space below.

. . . otherwise lawful private activities, and otherwise permissible uses of private property, on whatever grounds such private bodies deem appropriate — including grounds that would be clearly forbidden to the state itself.

Summary of Argument

Conferring on church leaders the uncontrolled power, within a 500-foot radius, to decide who may serve or sell liquor to whom invests ecclesiastical officials with governmental . . .

or

. . . otherwise lawful private activities, and otherwise permissible uses of private property, on whatever grounds such private bodies deem appropriate — including grounds that would be clearly forbidden to the state itself.

Summary of Argument

Conferring on church leaders the uncontrolled power, within a 500-foot radius, to decide who may serve or sell liquor to whom invests ecclesiastical officials with governmental . . .

To set off a lower level heading, you can use a run-in heading, as described above.

4. Position

As the examples above indicate, another choice you may have to make is where to position the headings. Some options include the following:

1. Center all headings between the margins.
2. Place all headings at the left-hand margin.
3. Center primary headings and put lower level headings at the left-hand margin, as shown on page 00, above.
4. "Hang" lower level headings in the margins, outside the text area, as illustrated below.

BLANK INSURANCE COMPANY
A . . . . insurance company herein called the company

In consideration of the payment of the premium, in reliance upon the statements in the declarations made a part hereof and subject to all of the terms of this policy, agrees with the insured named in the declarations as follows.

(For policy issued by two companies)

In consideration of the payment of the premium, in reliance upon the statements in the declarations made a part hereof and subject to all of the terms of this policy, severally agree with the insured named in the declarations as follows, provided the Blank Casualty Company shall be the insurer with respect to coverages . . . . and no other and the Blank Fire Insurance Company shall be the insurer with respect to coverages . . . .

PART I—LIABILITY, PERSONAL INJURY PROTECTION,

PROPERTY PROTECTION, MEDICAL PAYMENTS AND PHYSICAL DAMAGE

INSURING AGREEMENTS

1 Coverage A
Division 1—Bodily Injury Liability—Statutory—The Commonwealth of Massachusetts—(This Coverage is Compulsory)

The company will pay on behalf of the insured, in accordance with the "Massachusetts Compulsory Automobile Liability Security Act," Chapter 346 of the Acts of 1925 of the Commonwealth of Massachusetts and all Acts amendatory thereof or supplementary thereto, all sums which the insured shall become obligated to pay by reason of the liability imposed upon him by law for damages to others for bodily injury, including death at any time resulting therefrom, or for consequential damages consisting of expenses incurred by a husband, wife, parent or guardian for medical, nursing, hospital or surgical services in connection with or on account of such bodily injury or death, sustained by any person or persons during the policy period as defined in Item [3][2] of the declarations and caused by the ownership, operation, maintenance, control or use of the insured motor vehicle upon the ways of the Commonwealth of Massachusetts or in any place therein to which the public has a right of access.

This division of coverage A is subject to the following provisions:

(1) No statement made by the insured or on his behalf, either in securing this policy or in securing registration of the insured motor vehicle, no violation of the terms of this policy and no act or default of the insured, either prior to or subsequent to the issuance of this policy, shall operate to defeat or avoid this coverage so as to bar recovery by a judgment creditor proceeding in accordance with the Laws of the Commonwealth of Massachusetts. The terms of this policy shall remain in full force and effect, however, as binding between the insured and the company, and the insured agrees to reimburse the company for any payment made by the company under this policy on account of any accident, claim or suit involving a breach of the terms of this policy.

(2) Notwithstanding the provisions of the Cancelation Condition of this policy, if this policy is canceled by the company and subsequently the effective date of cancelation is changed by an order of the Board of Appeal or by a decree of the Superior Court or Municipal Court of the City of Boston or a Justice of either, under the provisions of the Massachusetts Compulsory Automobile Liability Security Act, the insurance provided in this coverage shall be canceled as of the date of cancelation effective by such order or decree and premium adjustment shall be made accordingly; if after the issuance of notice of cancelation by the company, a finding that such cancelation is not proper and reasonable or is invalid is made under the provisions of said Act either by

the Board of Appeal from which finding the company takes no appeal, or by a decree of the Superior Court or Municipal Court of the City of Boston or a Justice of either, the company will continue the insurance provided in this coverage in full force and effect if such order or decree is based upon a complaint made prior to the effective date of cancelation stated in the company's notice, and will reinstate the insurance provided in this coverage in full force and effect as of the date specified in such order or decree if such order or decree is based upon a complaint made within the ten days after the effective date of cancelation stated in the company's notice. If the company shall cease to be authorized to transact business in the Commonwealth of Massachusetts, this policy shall be canceled and premium adjustment shall be made on a pro rata basis as of the effective date of the new certificate of insurance filed by the named insured with the Registrar of Motor Vehicles in Massachusetts, or if no certificate is filed, then as of the effective date of the revocation of registration of the insured motor vehicle.

(3) This policy, the written application therefor, if any, and any endorsement, which shall not conflict with the provisions of said Massachusetts Compulsory Automobile Liability Security Act and all Acts amendatory thereof or supplementary thereto, shall constitute the entire contract between the parties.

(4) The Other Insurance Condition of this policy shall be applicable to this coverage only in the event that other insurance referred to therein is carried in a company authorized to transact insurance in the Commonwealth of Massachusetts.

(5) This agreement is made in accordance with Sections 112 and 113 of Chapter 175 of the General Laws of Massachusetts.

Division 2—Personal Injury Protection—Statutory—(This Coverage is Compulsory)

The company will pay, in accordance with Chapter 670 of the Acts of 1970 of the Commonwealth of Massachusetts and all Acts amendatory thereof or supplementary thereto, subject to any applicable deductible, all reasonable expenses incurred within two years from the date of accident for necessary medical, surgical, X-ray and dental services, including prosthetic devices, and necessary ambulance, hospital, professional nursing and funeral services, and, in the case of persons employed or self-employed at the time of an accident, any amounts actually lost by reason of inability to work and earn wages or salary or their equivalent, but not other income, that would otherwise have been earned in the normal course of an injured person's employment, and for payments in fact made to others, not members of the injured person's household, and reasonably incurred in obtaining from those others ordinary and necessary services in lieu of those that, had he not been injured, the injured person would have performed not for income but for the benefit of himself or members of his household, and, in the case of persons neither employed nor

5. Type Styles

As you no doubt know, word processing programs can produce italic and boldface type in any of a number of typefaces (fonts). In your hierarchy of headings, you should use boldface for higher level headings because it tends to dominate a page. Italic type, with or without boldface, works well for lower, freestanding headings or for run-in headings (although run-in headings can be bold roman, if necessary). Type styles can be graded, as follows, from most to least visible.

Boldface

Boldface Italic

Italic

Roman

If your document has only one or two heading levels, you may prefer the more subtle effect of italic type. Remember, however, that your headings are signposts and should be easy to spot on the page. The reader may never notice roman run-in headings that are not bold, for instance.

6. Type Size

In any word processing program, you will have a wide range of type sizes from which to choose. Type size is measured in *points*. Here are some examples.

6-point type

8-point type

9-point type

10-point type

12-point type

Any point size from 9 to 14 points will usually be comfortable to read (although the optimal range for readability varies from typeface to typeface). Whether producing a document by word processing or having one professionally typeset, try to keep the type size within these bounds. The "fine print" that you may have seen in some legal documents is usually 6 points or less.

E White Space

White space makes an important contribution to the final appearance of your document. Small changes in the white space surrounding the text, headings, quoted items, and footnotes can totally transform the readability, as well as the look, of your document. If you fill your pages to the edges with type and squeeze headings into the text, your document will look impenetrable. Your document will have made a bad impression even before your reader has started reading it; in fact, your reader may not want to read it and may *not* read it,

Adequate margins open up the page and give it a less formidable appearance. Having ample space around headings, and using special treatments such as indented quotations and bulleted lists, will set these items off from the text and allow them to be identified quickly. The page is broken up visually into smaller, more manageable units, which improves reading speed and comprehension.

Wide margins, however, mean shorter lines of type and fewer characters per page, and this means more pages. Your use of white space and wide margins must obviously be tempered by length constraints. Balance your decisions against your goals and constraints for the best overall effect. If you have many headings, for example, you can use their surrounding white space to compensate for smaller margins and more characters per line. The same is true if your document contains numerous text items that call for special treatment. If you open up space around these items, you can draw attention away from relatively narrow margins.

F Special Treatments

Your document may consist of continuous text with headings and footnotes as the only variations. Many documents, however, contain elements that could benefit from special treatment: quotations, lists, tabular material, charts, figures, etc. Using special treatments for these elements adds to the visual interest of your document. A special treatment should stand out from the text, but not so much as to disrupt the flow of the text and the reader's concentration. Overusing these highlighting tricks can result in choppy text that distracts the reader.

1. Quotations

Excerpts from outside sources are frequently candidates for special treatment. According to the Blue Book, a quotation of 49 or fewer words should be enclosed in quotation marks but not otherwise set off from the rest of the text. Quotations that run fifty or more words must be indented on the left and right without quotation marks. This is called a block indent. Quotation marks within a block quotation should appear as they do in the original.

> We are, of course aware that, if possible, statutes are to be construed to avoid constitutional defects. But no reasonable reading by us of "church" when expressly defined as "a church or synagogue building dedicated to divine worship," can transform section 16C into a religiously neutral law . . .

It is not necessary to use quotation marks for excerpts set up as block indents, because the format signals that the material is quoted.

Remember that more than half a page of indented copy becomes ineffective because the reader loses the contrast between the longer and shorter lines and begins to consider the shorter lines normal. A large chunk of block quotation can be put in an appendix.

If you are not held to Blue Book standards for a particular document, you might wish to indent a short quotation that is particularly important or if it is the shortest of a series of excerpts of equal importance. To maintain its status within the series, the shortest should also be set off from the text.

2. Key Points

If you want to highlight a key point in your argument, you can use a different type style (italic or boldface) to make it stand out from the text. For even greater impact, you could use the block indention described above to physically separate your point from the text and focus attention on it. If you combine these options, using indention and italic or boldface type, you will further emphasize the key point. As with block indention of quotations, however, do not overdo it, or you will lose the effect you were trying to achieve.

3. Lists

Lists are an excellent way to make collections of thoughts or questions more manageable and more visible. They work best if the items are similar in nature and importance and if they can be expressed in a parallel structure. Lists are the perfect way to synthesize information into the most readily usable format. They focus the reader's attention and add some visual interest to the page.

Lists can be set up in any number of ways, using numbers, letters, or bullets, to name a few. Double-check your draft to be sure there are no lists embedded in the body of the text which would be more effective if broken out and given special treatment. The main options for distinguishing a list from the surrounding text are:

1. *Space:* Use a line of space above and below your list, or even between the items of the list, to make it a visually identifiable unit.
2. *Indention:* As with quotations, you can indent your list to set it off; lists can be indented only at the left or at both the left and right.
3. *Special characters:* Numbers and letters are most commonly used to label items in a list. However, if the quantity of items is unimportant and the items are not mentioned later, you can lead off with
   - *Bullets.* Bullets (included in the "symbols" section of your word processor's toolbar) are useful for short lists, especially those consisting of items expressed in single words or short phrases.
   - or – *Dashes.* These are useful for introducing longer lists composed of sentences or paragraphs.
   - ☐ *Boxes.* These work best for checklists or when literally or figuratively ticking off items would be useful to the reader.
4. *Double-column format:* When you have a long list of short items, consider breaking it into two columns.

Index